The "Twelfth" Has Good Prospects

Prospects are good for the "twelfth" shoots on Dalhousie estate.

Birds were helped by the dry earlier in the year.

Intermark, which was partly retained by the late Earl of Dalhousie for private ing, has been taken by Mrs Dorothy Hartman, London. The Duke of borough and Mr Barbara Dalrymple

4.30—CLYST HANDICAP HURDLE
Two miles.

Mrs. D. Hartman's Sir Melville	6 12	2
Maj. R. A. Byass's Black Magnet	6 11	8
Mr. L. F. Redfern's Tacitus	8 11	8
Mr. R. J. Clark's Nobby's Pet	6 11	5
Mrs. K. Marsh's Michael Collins	6 11	0
Mr. C. L. Lloyd's Red Sheik	6 10 11
Mr. G. R. Morgan's Latus	8 10	2
Mr. P. M. Evans's Posthumous	a 10	1
Mr. R. C. May's Walison	a 10	0

Another woman in the motoring news is Mrs. Dorothy Hartman, head of a firm which distributes some leading American cars in Britain, who will be the only woman exhibitor at the Motor Show To-night she gives a party to introduce a "Golden Anniversary" Cadillac, which, being nearly 20ft. long, is too large to go on her Court stand.

Woman imports cars

BEAUFORT ALL

Revi ton

all over 700 guests Duke and supplied by Geoffre

committee was co hess of Beaufort ce Spicer, Mrs G Pope and Mrs W R. J. Tuckett (T retary.

hose taking par and Duchess of tess of Westmor er, Mrs Guy Gib y Apsley, Mrs L ndry, Major H. T L. Tremayne, Sir Pitman, Sir C. C Thompson, Co ugh, Mrs D.

MRS. HARTMAN
James Gunn's portrait.

MAN director on the America to-day artman.

CUN LI

SHIP
CLASS
FROM
ADDRESS IN
USA OR
CANADA

NOT W

Mrs. Hartman runs then

FOUR

TWO

Mrs. DOROTHY HARTMAN, this year's hostess with the mostest (she has Charlie Chaplin for her Christmas charity party), talked about her Aberdeens "bred for beef" . . . there was GREER GARSON cooing ab her shorthorns . . . and CE DESMOND, swears ne

The British Colonial HOTEL NASSAU

The official opening branch was performed D C M Hartman, of Lond Reigate, who paid tribute tribut of the governor Mr and Mrs

60 men will take a blonde boss out

And when summer outing they asked her lunch with us." man accepted— their hospitality Christmas party. Now, lunch wil a yearly "mus

A marriage has been arranged shortly take place between Ca W. Hartman and Lady Dalrymple. Lady Dalrymple daughter of the late Captain Abbott, R.N., and the late

Maud Coleno's Daughter

The Life of Dorothy Hartman
1898–1957

Dorothy Cynthia Mirabelle Hartman

John Dann

Front cover image:
James Gunn's portrait of Dorothy Hartman
by kind permission of Dodo's granddaughter Norma Salmon de Rauville
of whom it is said 'looks most like her'

Matador
9 Priory Business Park,
Wistow Road, Kibworth Beauchamp,
Leicestershire. LE8 0RX
Tel: 0116 279 2299
Email: books@troubador.co.uk
Web: www.troubador.co.uk/matador
Twitter: @matadorbooks

ISBN 978 1785899 713

British Library Cataloguing in Publication Data.
A catalogue record for this book is available from the British Library.

Printed and bound by CPI Group (UK) Ltd, Croydon, CR0 4YY
Typeset in 11pt Aldine by Troubador Publishing Ltd, Leicester, UK

Matador is an imprint of Troubador Publishing Ltd

For
Ethel, Veronica, Erika and Norma

"Rather a nice painting, that one of Gunn's.
It is a portrait of a fish wife!"

Contents

Act IV Captain Hartman's Business   149
(1933–1942)

Act V Nicky Vansittart – 'at last'   233
(1938–57)

After the Curtain   333

Acknowledgements

The biographical material of Dodo's life has been compiled from open sources, with the exception of some private papers and personal recollections of a small group who actually knew her. However the interpretations of events and characterisation surrounding her life, together with any mistakes are mine alone.

A special thanks to Val and Terry Pothecary, who generously shared their research on the Lewis family connections, and provided an introduction which became inspirational for this story.

A particular thanks to Veronica Lavoipierre (née Salmon), Dodo Hartman's granddaughter who acted as 'family liaison' and her mother's spokesperson, who unstintingly gave of her time in answering many questions and together with the wider family, wholeheartedly encouraged the book research, giving introductions and access to family letters, documents and photographs (Salmon papers).

Generous thanks to Prudie Mennell (née Vansittart) who kindly responded to my request for information about her father and Dodo, providing painstaking replies, a personal interview, and helpful comments. Her son Jonathan Mennell also added some interesting vignettes.

Rosemary Fitch, a cousin of Clive Gwinner (who married Betty Hartman, Dodo's stepdaughter), kindly responded to my request and gave helpful insight to the Gwinner-Hartman family.

Tim Rice, great grandson of Georg Hartmann (Bobbie Hartman's uncle) and family historian, kindly shared research, particularly on the family business Suter, Hartmann & Rahtjen's Composition Company.

David Hayward, General Motors historian, whose published research of the Vansittart connection stimulated the original interest and offered additional material on Lendrum & Hartman Ltd.

Pat Woor (née Abbott) Dorothy Hartman's niece, who kindly answered correspondence, providing photos, a personal interview, and contributed childhood memories about her family. A personal thanks to former children of the Stumblehole estate, Jean Pelham (née Summerfield), who supplied a newspaper cutting, photos and shared memories, likewise, Audrey Cook (née Cooper), who provided many additional anecdotes of Hartman's household guests and staff, photos and memorabilia as well as providing a 'lost' personal ivory bound *Book of Common Prayer* from Dodo's marriage to Bobbie Hartman.

There are nameless individuals who have helped by publishing material such as the Griffin family, and others who kindly made contact including Cynthia Jones Heesaker in Canada, (Gwinner family), Sally Davis (biographer of Gabrielle Borthwick), Lynne Scofield (Farr family), and Alison Segarty (Manchester family) who also provided family photos. Geoffrey Carverhill, automotive historian and author of "The Lendrum & Hartman Story" in *Classic American Magazine*, published in three parts June–August 2006. The late Russell Johns, whose article "Buick By-Gones" featured in *Motor Sport* magazine, October 1980 about his life with Lendrum & Hartman provided a first-hand account. Jim Keeble, writer, "Gibraltar: Hands off the Rock", a reference to Philby and Burgess, *Daily Telegraph*, travel article, October 2002; Michael Thornton, journalist, "The Siren who Disappeared" about Frances Day, published *Mail Online* March 2008; Keith Morfett, *Daily Express* journalist who wrote Dodo's obituary in November 1957. Finally, thanks to the publishing team at Troubador and copy editor Imogen Palmer.

Attributions for song lyrics quoted: "The Boy I Love" written by George Ware (1885); "Hold your Hand Out, Naughty boy!" lyrics by C. W. Murphy, music by Worton David (1914); "Won't You Come and Play With Me?" sung by Shirley Kellogg in the revue *Push and Go!*, words by G. P. Hawtrey, music by Alfred Plumpton; "Hello! Hello! Who's your Lady Friend?", lyrics by Worton David, Bert Lee, music by Harry Fragson, (1915); "We're in the Money", music by Harry Warren, lyrics by Al Dubin, from the film *Gold Diggers of 1933*; "At Last" written by Mack Gordon and Harry Warren in 1941 for the musical film *Orchestra Wives;* "Wish me luck (as you wave me goodbye)", music by Harry Parr-Davies, lyrics Phil Park (1939).

Extracts from poems and books: *"… like the distant roll of thunder at a picnic"*, *Marginalia (1965–68)* courtesy of the estate of W. H. Auden, *"Oh, what a tangled web we weave"*, Walter Scott, *Marmion: A Tale of Flodden Field,*

Canto VI, XVII, (1808); J. B. Priestley's *The Edwardians*, courtesy estate of J. B. Priestley (1970); *History of the First World War*, B. H. Liddell Hart (1930), courtesy Liddell Hart Military Archives, King's College London; *"The handsome woman in the hansom cab…"*, *Augustus John*, courtesy Michael Holroyd (1996); *"… I can live on tick at this pub in Saint-Jean"*, *Fiesta: The Sun Also Rises,* courtesy Hemmingway Foreign Rights Trust (1954).

Image credits

Images featured in this book are from various private and public sources. They include the Salmon family, Prudie Mennell, Pat Woor, Alison Segarty and the author. Permissions have been sought where possible and others are acknowledged. Whilst every effort has been taken to contact copyright owners, I apologise in advance for any omissions and would be pleased to insert the appropriate acknowledgement in any subsequent edition.

The following images are gratefully acknowledged: [1] Augusta Manchester, kind permission of Alison Segarty; [2] Maud Coleno (aka Maud Abbott), kind permission of Pat Woor; [3] 'Captain' William Abbott; kind permission Pat Woor; [4] T. S. Warspite; kind permission of Gary Vaughan's postcard collection; [5] Brown's Dairy, 176 Camden High Road c.1900; [6] Officers of 2nd Bat. *Kings Shropshire Light Infantry* in France, Dec. 1914, kind permission of the Shropshire Archives; [6a] *Hippodrome Theatre,* London (postcard); [6b] cover *Push & Go* programme; courtesy of Goldsmiths University, WW1 popular musical theatre research; [7] and [8] Dodo's child Ethel, kind permission of Salmon family; [9] Sir David Charles Herbert Dalrymple c.1918, courtesy of the curator of Newhailes House, National Trust for Scotland; [10] *The Royal Albion Hotel,* Brighton c.1900, courtesy of Timothy Carder, Ed. *The Encyclopaedia of Brighton 1990*; [11] Newhailes House, Musselburgh, and [12] Newhailes House, library c.1959, courtesy of *Scotlandsplaces.gov.uk*; [13] Newhailes library chairs, courtesy of Sotheby's New York auction (Lot 9) catalogue Jan. 2012; [14] Lady Ermine Elibank (Nov. 1939); [15] Gideon Murray, 2nd Viscount Elibank, kind permission of the National Portrait Gallery (license: 10388/21017); [16] The Honourable Gabrielle Borthwick, kind permission of the National Portrait Gallery (license: 10395/21018); [17] Harry Ennisdale at Baynards Park, Surrey; [18] Helen Ennisdale, RMS *Queen Elizabeth* cocktail party, courtesy *Life* magazine

1948; [19] *Plaza hotel*, New York; [20] *British Colonial Hotel*, Nassau (postcard); [21] *Palácio Hotel*, Estoril, courtesy of the hotel's archive collection; [22] Suter Hartmann advertising displays, courtesy of *Grace's Guide to British Industrial History*, and Beamish Museum, Co. Durham; [23] Lendrum & Hartman Motor Show catalogue October 1951, courtesy of *Grace's Guide to British Industrial History*; [24] Alfred P. Sloan, Wikipedia commons; [25] James D. Mooney, courtesy of his grandson David Hale Mooney, *www.geni.com*; [26] Edward VII and Mrs Simpson's Buicks, Lendrum & Hartman showroom 1936, (The Mellier) courtesy of Glebe Asset Management; [27] and [28] Northease Manor, c.1939 courtesy of Carmen Harvey-Browne, head teacher of Northease Manor School; [29] Luckington Manor; courtesy of *www.rightmove.co.uk*; [30] Dodo Hartman on her hunter *Precentor,* kind permission of the Salmon family; [31] Dodo and Bobbie at Luckington Manor c.1942 courtesy of the estate of Albert Swaebe, and *Tatler & Bystander* magazine; [32] Berkeley House Hay Hill, courtesy of *www.zoopla.co.uk*; [33] Dodo and Lord Lyle c.1952, unknown magazine – Salmon collection; [34] Stumblehole Farm, croquet lawn c.1956, © author; [35] Dodo's Pekinese dogs, Stumblehole c.1956, © author; [36] Frank Gear, Dodo's butler c.1956, © author; [37] Valerie Hobson & 'Jack' Profumo c.1950s; [38a] Frances Day c.1930s; [38b] Frances Day c.1952, courtesy of Hans J. Wollstein *www.hjwollstein.blogspot. co.uk;* [39] Charlie & Oona Chaplin, courtesy of *chaplinfortheages.tumblr. com;* [40] Dodo, *Café de Paris*, Dec. 1953, unknown newspaper – Salmon collection; [41] Baron studio portrait of Nicky Vansittart, kind permission of Prudie Mennell; [42] Dodo Hartman (portrait) kind permission of the Salmon family; [43] A lock of Dodo's hair, kind permission of the Salmon family; [44] Dodo with horse, Luckington c.1942, courtesy of the estate of Albert Swaebe and *Tatler & Bystander* magazine.

Sources

The Internet; how did we live without it? It served as a window into the digital libraries and records now available. *Ancestry.com* provided access to a wide collection: the registers of births, marriages and deaths, census and electoral rolls, military and medal records, passenger ship manifests – together with US port arrivals documents – providing a wealth of personal details, airline passenger records, telephone, trade, city, and school directories, probate and divorce records, not to mention the many family researchers who generously publish their material. Other sources included the author's own papers; *Bradshaw's Railway Guide*; *The British Newspaper Archive* – a wonderful source of social history, as are *Flightglobal* and *Motor Sport* magazine archives, The National Archives and the Met Office historical climate data.

Abebooks.co.uk provided a reliable source for out-of-print books.

Website originators that have been helpful include Matthew Lloyd who created *arthurlloyd.co.uk*, a valuable resource about music halls and their many artistes. Darryl Lundy of Lundy Consulting Ltd., *thepeerage. com* provided genealogical details of the peerage in Britain. Martin Robb's family history blog *mprobb.wordpress.com* provided useful research on the Aldridge-Holiday (Abbott) families. Jos Leiper's blog added helpful information and images of Baynard's Park and the Ennisdale's *locatepeoplepp.blogspot.co.uk*. To compare the change in the value of British money over time, the UK Inflation Calculator has been used from *www. moneysorter.co.uk*.

Before the Curtain

The former Lady Dalrymple, and now the widow Dorothy Hartman, known to her intimates as Dodo, had been a glamorous society hostess and successful business woman. Her life spanned five decades, three marriages from the music halls to the jazz age, through two world wars to the birth of rock and roll. But it was not how it had begun.

Dodo really didn't want her early life recalled, she had gone to some lengths to reinvent herself (and parentage too), and the past truths could have jeopardised her present fiction.

This is her story, because it falls short of a detailed biography, as there are no diaries, papers or photographs for the first half of her life to refer to, and if they had existed, they would have been airbrushed out of the picture long ago. As if the certain past had never existed.

There are of course official records and some newspaper cuttings – they could not be edited out, although some of these too have been recorded with a touch of the family obfuscation, sending the researcher in a different direction.

However, we get a glimpse of the pert young showgirl, and the parts played by her family. In charting her progress it was necessary for the writer to occasionally speculate with these small factual jigsaw pieces to form a mostly true story narrative.

Dodo had been suffering from a heart complaint for some time for which there was no cure. Her fate had been sealed as inevitably 1957 drew to a close. No amount of wealth could prevent it – *"like the distant roll of thunder at a picnic"*. [1]

A past secret had surfaced in the last few years, so she had made a new will. The contents of which, once revealed, would cause surprise after her death, and continue to cause family acrimony.

In the last few weeks she had taken to bed, attended only by her servants, private secretary and the occasional visitor. The time usually spent in her Mayfair apartment at Berkeley House during the week would now continue, the weekend entertaining at Stumblehole Farm in Surrey put on hold. Despite her illness she still insisted on the high standards expected of staff.

In fact, in her remaining weeks she had dismissed her London cook Ivy Hinton over an incident concerning some inappropriate menus. She had sent for her dependable Stumblehole cook, whose maternal nature instinctively coaxed 'the patient' to eat simple and nourishing dishes to encourage her failing appetite.

Dorothy Hartman was widely acknowledged for her generosity with household and business staff, not to mention the beneficiaries of her various charities and children's home. The farm and estate children had been collecting firewood for weeks, and unusually Dorothy had given permission to use any remaining straw in the barn, with the effect that the bonfire burnt for four days like a funeral pyre, [2] although the weather was not promising as it had been stormy and wet since the beginning of November. It wasn't surprising that she had provided £25 worth of fireworks for their annual 'Guy Fawkes' bonfire night celebration at her farm. Then on the same evening of 5th November 1957 at around eight o'clock, she died quietly with only Henry Rowan, her physician, Helene Dupont, her lady's maid and loyal butler Frank Gear in attendance.

Keeping a vigil, her close confidant and executor Nicky Vansittart was devastated. The following day, whilst household staffs were coming to terms with events, Gear had the unenviable task of officially registering her death with the Westminster Registrar. Dorothy's personal secretary Marjorie Jordan, had telephoned Mrs Farr with the news, one of many on her contact list; she was the wife of the Rector of St Mary and St Ethelbert church in the Wiltshire village of Luckington; Dorothy's country home during the war years.

She knew what to do. Making her way to the nearby village of Sherston, she entered the High Street post office, and took a telegram blank from the rack; away from prying eyes and local gossip she composed a brief message to send to South Africa.

=MOTHER DIED 5TH CREMATION MONDAY = FARR + [3]

But to observers, Dorothy Hartman didn't have any children –did she? There was Mark, a distant stepson from her marriage to Sir David Dalrymple, and a married stepdaughter Betty Gwinner, from her late husband Frederick Hartman's first marriage – but no other children. The press had always reported she was childless.

This was a complete mystery to everyone including her business partners, household staff and particularly the executor of her will, a close friend.

Her life had been one long performance – but in death it now began to unravel.

Act I

A Child of the *Fin de Siècle*
(1898–1915)

"The boy I love is up in the gallery,
The boy I love is looking now at me,
There he is, can't you see, waving his handkerchief,
As merry as a robin that sings on a tree."

Chorus of a music hall song, made famous by Marie Lloyd
– not to mention Maud Coleno

-1-

New woman

Maud Coleno's daughter was born into late Victorian London at the beginning of 1898. This was the *fin de siècle* – an explosive cocktail of endings, beginnings and transitions, a remarkably dynamic time. The naughty nineties was a period of fun-loving laxity, especially in sexual morals. It was an age of tremendous change, not only in morals but art, politics, science and society, all revolutionised by the emergence of new theories and challenges to tradition. It was a time of heightened uncertainty and the questioning of old values as the century was coming to its end.

In Britain, by 1891 nearly half the women were in the paid workforce, with the overwhelming number in domestic service, textiles and clothing factories – the working class occupations. But for those with any talent, the stage offered an independent life for many of them through the burgeoning demand in the music halls – and stardom for a few.

★

In London a few years earlier, the women and teenage girls working at the Bryant and May Factory in Bow took part in what became known as the Match Girls' Strike. Over a thousand had refused to work – sparked by an unfair dismissal combined with poor working conditions. Their factory day lasted fourteen hours; their meagre pay was often fined excessively on some minor pretext, and the conditions produced severe health complications as a result of working with white phosphorus. The strike publicity caused a public outcry, and within a month they had won concessions and their strike ended.

It was an emerging form of emancipated womanhood. The figure of the 'new woman' threatened conventional ideas – both social and sexual – about ideal Victorian womanhood. In 1867 the London Society for Women's Suffrage had been formed; and three years later the Married Women's Property Act was passed by Parliament, which allowed married women to own their own property. Previously, when women married, their property transferred to their husbands. Divorce heavily favoured men, allowing property to remain in their possession. This act allowed women to keep their property, married, divorced, single or widowed.

Around the mid-1890s the term 'new woman' had drifted into circulation with the foundation of the National Union of Women's Suffrage. A rebellion that was free-spirited and independent, educated and uninterested in marriage and children. Women's rights were promoted in literature by sympathetic authors like Grant Allen, who published a novel *The Woman Who Did* in 1895, creating controversy right from the start with conservative readers. However, the social mood was changing, and Allen's title could have served as a template for the child of this story.

★

The new industrialisation was making England the richest country and London the greatest city the world had seen in size, wealth and grandeur. Yet it was also a city where poverty and disease were rife. It had seen its population rise six-fold in a century and together with its outer villages and suburbs, it reached six million in 1900.

It became a magnet absorbing over half of all migrants from within Britain itself, as well as immigrants, created by the revolutions and political struggles of late nineteenth-century Europe, bringing many from Russia, Poland, France, Italy and Germany. This cosmopolitan mix filled its neighbourhoods, occupying the bright streets and dingy courts of the capital with their trades, languages and customs.

The influx of people fuelled a need for social entertainment, more than just the old meeting places, taverns and coffee houses of the eighteenth century, where men met to drink and do business.

A new type of entertainment developed out of these pubs – the music halls, introducing performers who sang songs whilst the audience now ate drank and joined in the singing. These became so popular that entertainment was put on two or three times a week. By the 1870s over three hundred music halls had been built in London alone, such as the *Alhambra* in Leicester Square, the *Oxford Music Hall*, famous for its lively barmaids, and hundreds more scattered across the British Isles.

★

New performers were needed to fill the stages at all these brash new *Empires* and *Palaces* that soon sprang up to meet the emerging middle-class demand, so young women – often the daughters of supper club and tavern veterans – stepped into the spotlight for the first time.

A typical music hall bill would feature a chairman keeping order with a gavel; a comedian or two; dancers in daring costumes; novelty acts like jugglers, contortionists, trapeze artists or trick cyclists; a drag act, and a magician.

However, singing and the comic song remained at the heart of music hall – and the star was always the singer. Men like Albert Chevalier and then George Robey were adored, but it was the women and their signature songs that topped the bill.

-2-

Cow's Cathedral

London at the turn of the twentieth century was a city full of crowded streets with the pervading smells of chipped potatoes, horse dung (1,000 tons deposited daily – by something like 300,000 horses) and old leather. Whilst at night the city was characterised by leaping naphtha flames along the main roads, the glittering multi-coloured shop windows, the sound of street barrel organs, brightly lit music halls with their enticing posters and the highly decorated pubs with their ornate mirrors and plate glass windows.

The streets littered with cigar and cigarette ends, mud and straw created a wave of specialist trades such as 'sweepers' – to clear your path across the road, 'uniformed shoe-blacks' –to clean muck off footwear, and 'link-boys' brandishing flaming torches, who would appear as if by magic in thick fog to guide you.

In the winter months, when dusk gathers in the mid-afternoon, the looming buildings would merge into a dark labyrinth of shadows beyond, created by a 'London particular' – a nick-name often used to describe the fog –taken they say from the special brown Madeira wine produced for the London market from around the reign of Queen Anne. In 1871 a *New York Times* article referred to *"London, particularly, where the population are periodically submerged in a fog of the consistency of pea soup…"* because of its similarity to that colour and consistency – very thick and often yellowish green.

You could smell and taste the fog, smoky sulphur, which produced a choking sensation. The product of a million coal fires burning cheap bituminous coal in open grates, polluting the atmosphere with clouds of filthy black smoke, which could not easily disperse, carrying noxious fumes, infections and lung diseases.

The city resounded with a symphony of foghorns on the river and thousands of people coughing in the street. This image of London became fixed in the imagination of the world – a place where caped policemen flitted in pairs between gas-lamps through the sulphurous haze, and men worked all day at counters and ledgers by artificial light and in the winter, never saw the sun.

★

London has always been a city of villages, each becoming absorbed by the steady expansion from the old city limits, but even today they retain much of their individuality.

The district of Camden lies just three miles north of the City of London, on the road through Kentish Town towards Hampstead and Highgate. It was a rural setting in the early nineteenth century, which had been slowly developed because of its location, canals and then later the railways enabling it to become a thriving economy.

Most of Camden's early houses had been designed for middle-class families. These houses, built in yellow stock brick, were typically of three storeys, with a basement service area and often an attic containing the servants' quarters. Some smaller two-storey cottages had also been erected for the less affluent.

No one in the middle of the nineteenth century depicted the rural suburbs of London better than Charles Dickens, and Camden in particular, in which he sets many of his fictional characters – where as a boy, he lived with his impoverished family. His memories of that time were vividly brought to life in his later novels. His home, a four-roomed house in Bayham Street – then a rural area, backing on to meadows – became the setting for the Cratchit family in *A Christmas Carol* (1843). Bob Cratchit used to run from his home in Camden to the City each day thus saving bus fares, a round trip distance of six miles. Other fictional residents were Polly Toodles family who featured in *Dombey and Son* (1846), his novel in which he describes the coming of the railways to Camden. His old house yet again becomes the setting of his impecunious Micawber family in *David Copperfield* (1849). Camden was also the location where Dickens installed his teenage mistress, the young actress and meuse Ellen Ternan after he left his wife.

By the end of the nineteenth century most of the housing stock was now soot-stained and run-down. Multiple-occupancy had become the norm: large houses originally built for the middle classes and their servants had been divided into apartments, and few premises were without boarders or lodgers.

At the heart of Camden's community the *Bedford Music Hall* had reigned supreme for over thirty years. It was demolished in 1898 and a new theatre, The *Bedford Palace of Varieties*, was built on the site a year later. It would feature performers like Marie Lloyd, Little Tich and later both the actor Charlie Chaplin and singer Gracie Fields appeared there.

Near the junction of Camden High Street was another much older institution, the *Mother Red Cap* pub, so-called after Jinny Bingham otherwise known as 'The Shrew of Kentish Town', whose chequered love life included sheltering highwaymen. She lived up to her legend as a witch in a cottage with her black cat, where the pub now stands. It was rebuilt in its present form in 1875 and by 1898 it was run by landlord Walter Holden. It still stands today, although renamed the *World's End*.

★

On the other side of the same road at the junction of Camden High Street and Kentish Town Road, where the workhouse stood until 1817, Thomas Brown, a farmer since 1790 had opened his dairy in 1822. Brown's Dairy in its early days was a no-nonsense utility place, but in its later years had developed all the *'folie de grandeur'* of a late Victorian public house. The interior of the shop was handsomely fitted up and contained some elegantly carved oak frame work, with costly embossed and engraved plate glass, the work of an eminent West End firm and manufactured expressly for the premises it included large glass cases of gaily feathered stuffed birds. The whole edifice was known locally as the 'Cows' Cathedral'. [1]

By the 1890s this family-run dairy at 176 Camden High Street had sub-divided their property and created a number of additional low rent shops with lodging rooms above.

The shop front at number 176a was taken by Arthur Robert Miles for the St Pancras (West) Conservative Association; 176b was occupied by John Pfund, a provision dealer; 176c was a fried fish shop run by a Swiss national Antonio Monico, and from 176d, Robert Fairbairn operated his tailor's shop.

★

The weather in London during December 1897 had been mild and changeable, with frost and fog; there had also been some rain with thunderstorms. After the rain, the roofs of London would glisten when the winter sun shone through. This effect came from the unique building material used in Victorian London – almost universally provided by the mountains of Wales, shipped from Lord Penrhyn's quarries near Snowdonia. The dark blue-grey Welsh slate, the most durable in the world with a life expectancy of over 150 years had become the roofing of choice for Victorian buildings.

There had been a typical 'London particular' on the 18th December, so dense was it, that amongst other events a rugby match between *Cardiff FC* and *Blackheath FC* had to be cancelled. As the incredulous Welsh Club secretary later recorded:

> *"… but that conveyed little of what a London fog was like… On this particular occasion we set off from Charring Cross about 11.30 a.m. and in the ordinary course should have arrived at Blackheath Station about 35 minutes later, but on this occasion we proceeded by such easy stages that we arrived at Blackheath about 4 p.m. It was as black as night there, so we immediately got into a train to go back to Charring Cross, which station we ultimately reached at 7 p.m., having practically been on the train for six hours."* [2]

As December moved into the New Year of 1898, the weather was generally dull, dry and abnormally mild for January.

The crowded rooms above Robert Fairbairn's tailor's shop in Camden High Street were rented to two families with children, and a couple of single lodgers, altogether around a dozen or so inhabitants occupying this small terraced building. Here we find the Yarmouth family; a bus conductor, his wife and one-year-old son. The other family were William Hurley, a tailor's porter, his wife Julia and their four sons George aged eight, Edward six, William three, and Joseph just nine months old.

Other lodgers included an Egyptian, Mohamed Abdow who was a Turkish bath attendant and Edward Griffiths, a Welsh railwayman.

It was amongst this medley cast that on Tuesday 4th January 1898, in a cramped room and in reduced circumstances the attractive twenty-four-year-old music hall artiste Maud Coleno, who could not write her name, gave birth to a daughter in secret. She was named Dorothy Maud Abbott.

A month later on 12th February Maud Coleno – whose married name was Maud Wainwright – falsely registered the birth under the name of Alice Edith Abbott.

Alice of course was unaware that her husband had fathered a child – but all this would emerge in due course. In the meantime William Abbott and Maud Wainwright had to think of what to do with their love child, little Dorothy.

The winter of 1897–98 had been generally snow-free up to this point, when a low pressure tracked southwards across England and by February gave London its first big snowfall of the year. The Christmas pantomime at the *Drury Lane Theatre* was appropriately *Babes in the Wood*, with Dan Leno and Herbert Campbell, and by March the fog had returned.

★

In a few short years all trace of these rooms and buildings would have disappeared. The occupants dispersed. The shops and dwelling houses on the corner site of Camden High Street and Kentish Town Road, including Brown's Dairy, were sold for demolition in December 1903, and the dairy moved across the road to Park Street.

This was to make room for the new Camden Town Underground station, to the Charing Cross, Euston & Hampstead Railway (now the Northern Line). The station was finally opened in 1907 by then Prime Minister, David Lloyd George, and the location of the former 'Cows' Cathedral' dairy was redeveloped by the Midland Bank (now HSBC).

-3-

Maud Manchester

"the only and original"

Two years earlier in 1896, a twenty-one-year-old versatile and attractive music hall artiste Maud Manchester, now calling herself Coleno on stage, had enjoyed a reasonably successful but exhausting provincial theatrical tour from February to October. She was very much in the mould of the 'new woman', from a young age used to theatrical life on the stage, managing men and chauvinism, fending for herself whilst travelling the country on tours, performing twice nightly.

Born three days before Christmas in 1873 at number 2, Little Newport Street, Soho Emily Augusta Maud Mary Manchester was the youngest daughter of John Richard Manchester. He was a shoemaker, who also described himself as a bootmaker and cordwainer – essentially a shoemaker who made fine soft leather shoes and other luxury articles of footwear.

He was born in Portsmouth in 1836. His father James had been a brickmaker but died when he was around five years old, so his widowed mother Sophia Golding brought up her three children; the older twins, Ann and James born in 1826, and John the youngest. Both the boys became shoemakers, a trade they had learnt from their mother Sophia, who was earning a living as a shoe-binder.

In 1857 John Manchester married Augusta Franklin in the twelfth-century parish church of St Mary's, Portsea, which had been rebuilt fourteen years earlier; the same church where Charles Dickens was baptised in 1812. They were both twenty-one and illiterate, making their mark with a cross on the parish marriage register.

Augusta's father had died around the time she was born, and like her husband John she was brought up by a widowed mother, Jemima Sarah Rogers, who in the same church twenty-seven years earlier had married a shipwright's apprentice, John Franklin.

After John and Augusta's marriage, they lived first at Jury Row and later 19 Hay Street. They had seven children, four boys and three girls. Augusta the eldest was born in 1861 but died four years later. Jemima (known as Minnie) followed in 1864, then John in 1866 and Robert in 1869, all born in Portsea.

By the late 1860s they had moved along the Sussex coast to Church Lane, Littlehampton. Eventually John took his family to London to seek work, settling initially at 38 Great Windmill Street, Soho, next door to the *Ham & Windmill* pub (now the *Lyric*), where they had another son named Edward who died shortly after birth. They soon moved to 2 Little Newport Street, where Maud their youngest daughter was born, followed by Augusta's last child Henry, born five years later – but he too was a sickly boy and died aged two.

The family was forced to move with the demolition of large numbers of old houses, including some in Little Newport Street, for the formation of Shaftesbury Avenue and Charing Cross Road. In the 1880s, Soho was ceasing to be primarily residential, and was becoming an area to which people came to work in shops, eating houses, warehouses and small factories, or to seek entertainment. The site of their old house is now the side-facing part of the *Hippodrome Theatre*, which opened in January 1900. The exterior was built in the typically ornate fashion of the period, designed in the so-called 'free-classical' style, using red sandstone, red brick and terracotta. It opened with a music hall revue featuring Little Tich and (in one of his first roles) Charlie Chaplin.

Maud was a natural cockney performer; she could sing and dance and it became clear she was born to entertain. By the time she left school (unable to write) the family had moved to Margaret's Place, in Lambeth. With family encouragement and a pair of her father's dancing shoes she embarked on a tentative life in music halls. In February 1886, she set out for her first performance to Sheerness, home to a Royal Naval dockyard, appearing at the *Wellington Palace of Varieties* in the high street. The proprietress Mrs Brisley had agreed to engage Maud for a week, a month short of her twelfth birthday. It was an amazing start – the beginning of a promising stage career that in the next few years would take her all over the country from Sheerness to Leeds.

1886, February: "That clever little song and dance artist Miss Maud Manchester heads the bill."

Sheerness, *Wellington Palace of Varieties.*

Harry Manchester, a family friend who was six years older, but no relation, was also appearing on the stage and by December that year Maud and Harry had joined together to form a theatrical duo. They were appearing in London at Islington's *Deacons Music Hall* in March 1887, as the theatrical newspaper *The Era* reported, *"Mr Harry and Miss Maud Manchester are satisfactory song and dance artists…"*

The hall was demolished four years later to make way for yet another new road, Rosebery Avenue, close to another much older theatre *Sadler's Wells* (where Maud would later perform). Established in the seventeenth century, it too became a music hall in 1879 and featured performers such as Marie Lloyd and Harry Champion.

The Manchester double-act was to earn good press reviews over the next few years and with them, new bookings.

1888 February: "Harry and Maud win hearty applause…"

Sheerness, *Criterion.*

1889, July: "… and among the new comers are the Manchesters, who sing and dance cleverly."

Alhambra Music Hall, Manchester.

1889, August: "The Manchesters, duettists and dancers, fully deserved the enthusiasm evoked by the way in which they rendered their duets. Their dancing won them numerous recalls."

Northampton *Palace of Varieties.*

It was during a provincial tour in 1889 whilst in Sheffield that she came to the notice of another couple of Harrys. These young men were Harry Wainwright and Harry Marr, both five years older, local friends with a love of music and theatre.

The Manchesters first performed in Sheffield at Edward Norburn's *Milton Music Hall* in late August. The local press commented, *"The Manchesters eccentric duettists and dancers made their first appearances here on Monday."*

When Maud sang the song "The Boy I Love", popularised by Marie Lloyd, one of the leading music hall artistes of the time, the two Harrys, watching from the gallery were infatuated.

"… The boy I love is up in the gallery,
The boy I love is looking now at me,
There he is, can't you see, waving his handkerchief…"

They were captivated by this young, attractive and amusing artiste, who seemed to only sing to them; they contrived to meet her, waiting at the stage door.

Wainwright was born into a Yorkshire steelmaking family in Hermitage Street; later they moved to Lansdowne Road in Ecclesall Bierlow, one of the parishes that made up Sheffield. It was a time when the town was developing fast and it would be granted a city charter a few years later. It was renowned internationally for its steelmaking, fine silverware and cutlery. Harry, although musical, had inevitably followed his father, Henry, a silver finisher, into the steel industry, becoming a steel roller. This was hard manual work. He had left his overcrowded home and taken lodgings at South Street, Moor where he could practice his music – and secured an evening position as a jobbing musician. Sheffield had at least seven or eight theatres and musical halls at the time.

Harry Marr lived with his widowed mother in the Langsett Road and was working backstage at the *Grand Theatre of Varieties*. A few years earlier the same theatre had been leased by the Leno family – whose son Dan would become a leading music hall comedian and musical theatre actor. Marr was nursing the ambition to become an actor manager, with his own touring company. The two Harrys were both in their early twenties and in their different ways yearning for a theatrical break. Glimpsing the magical world of the stage and catching the eye of one young amusing actress in particular, the footlights beckoned.

Maud was still only fifteen, and as Wainwright and Marr discovered despite the Manchesters sharing the same surname they were not related

– just stage partners. Maud enjoyed the attention of her two 'extra' Harrys, and by the time they left for their next engagement they all had become friends.

They returned later in November, engaged by Miss Garrod to perform at the *Bijou Music Hall* in West Barr, and as the press announced: *"The Manchesters head the Bill."*

Maud and her three Harrys enjoyed each other's company and whilst in Sheffield, the theatrical pair would share the same 'digs' at 26 South Street, Moor, arranged by Wainwright, whilst still working in his day job in the steel industry.

At the end of the Manchesters' performances in Sheffield, they had agreed to keep in touch, returning to London in time for the traditional Christmas pantomime season.

The following year in 1890, Harry and Maud were on tour again, appearing in Warrington at the *Hop Pole* in Horsemarket Street as 'character vocalists' (the pub still exists today) and in November appearing at *Lewis's Music Hall* in Barnsley, where the press declared: *"… good turns are filled by Harry & Maud Manchester vocalists and dancers."*

In the spring census of 1891, we learn that Maud Manchester is now seventeen, describing herself as a theatrical professional – who indeed she was, living with her widowed mother in Lambeth; her father John had died in 1883. The visitors at that time were Harry Marr – now calling himself *de* Marr – and Maud's theatrical friend Dorothy Newell with her eight-month-old son Brian, her husband James (away on tour) was an actor too.

Harry Wainwright had also left Sheffield, and had travelled to London, still eager to become a full-time musician or perhaps an actor, and particularly to be with the enchanting Maud again.

He enjoyed her stories and easy laughter, mixing with her theatrical friends – all of whom it seemed called Harry.

At home Maud would lapse into her cockney dialect spoken since childhood; after a long spell on the boards she would declare *"Blimey, I wasn't half glad to put me feet up"*, and on meeting a friend the greeting would usually be *"Wotcher"*, jokingly asking *"Up to yer old tricks?"* or *"What's the game?"*, perhaps enquiring, *"'Ower yer feelin'?"* or if she hadn't heard the answer, *"Come again?"*, only to be told she had *"clorf ears"*. On leaving, a goodbye would be *"S'long"*.

After performing in the London halls, they would sometimes congregate for a 'knees-up' (cockney impromptu singing, dancing, and drinking) at the Lambeth home of Maud's mother Augusta in Cornwall Road, which leads into the junction known as The Cut dominated by the *Old Vic Theatre*, as it is universally known today.

It was here that Harry Wainwright secured his first London booking as a musician. *The Old Vic* – the popular nickname of the *Royal Victoria*, originally known as the *Royal Coburg* – had been renamed and recognised for bringing theatre to the 'common people'.

Charles Dickens wrote, *"Whatever changes of fashion the drama knows elsewhere, it is always fashionable in the New Cut."* In 1871, the theatre was rebranded and reopened as *The New Victoria Palace* in an attempt to shed earlier misfortunes, but financial troubles persisted and it was twice put up for sale during that decade. At the time Augusta Manchester was living locally, the theatre had become the *Royal Victoria Coffee Music Hall* run on strict temperance lines, where the young Lilian Baylis had become the theatrical manager. By her efforts the Shakespeare Company would be formed by the beginning of the First World War, making the *Old Vic* its home.

★

Wainwright was serious about his new career and who he wanted to marry. Maud would eventually fall in love with this 'northern' Harry who had given up his job, travelled to London and proposed. She had been on tour with Harry Manchester since she was twelve, some five years ago – time for a change and some romance.

They found a place together in Lambeth and after what would be a final performance with Harry Manchester, in the summer of 1891 they returned from tour with good press reviews. They had performed at *Barnard's Palace of Varieties* in Chatham late August/early September as duettists and dancers with a press review exclaiming *"…and the Manchesters, duettists and dancers also appear with marked success."*

★

Maud Manchester married her 'boy in the gallery' Harry Wainwright during an exceptionally warm, late September Sunday in 1891, at the parish church of St John the Evangelist in Larcom Street, Walworth – one of the new wave of Victorian churches built only thirty years earlier. They had little money, but as the song continues,

> *"... Now, If I were a Duchess and had a lot of money,*
> *I'd give it to the boy that's going to marry me.*
> *But I haven't got a penny, so we'll live on love and kisses,*
> *And be just as happy as the birds on the tree."*

Maud made her mark in the register as she too was illiterate, like her parents. The church was a short walk from the Elephant & Castle, and it was witnessed by Maud's older sister Minnie (Jemima) and her husband, George Huthwaite, a house decorator – they had married in the same church eight years earlier.

After his stage separation from Maud, Harry Manchester ended up marrying Maria, another actress, six years later – a music hall artiste from Warrington, who he had met on tour. They would settle in Leicester and raise two children, Daisy and Harry.

By the summer of 1890, Harry Marr's fifty-seven-year-old mother Sarah had died in Sheffield and left the family £2,000. With this inheritance, it was time for Harry to implement his theatrical dream. A few years later Harry de Marr had married Edith St Claire, a London-born actress, some twelve years younger and they appeared in pantomime together. He would eventually become an actor-manager of theatres in Warwickshire and Northamptonshire, and later ran a travelling concert party in the West Country with mixed fortunes.

After Maud and Harry Wainwright married, quite soon she discovered they were not *"as happy as the birds on the tree"*, because Wainwright had a jealous streak and it had led to the break-up of the Manchester double act. The booking Maud and Harry had made as duettists with the *Phoenix Theatre*, Dover in October had to be undertaken by Harry alone, revising his act – resulting in a humiliating apology to the theatre management. He was forced to place an advertisement in *The Era* on 17 October stating:

> *"MR HARRY MANCHESTER*
> *Character Vocalist and Artistic Dancer, thanks to Gus*
> *Leach Esq, for Paying me as Much, within a few shillings,*
> *as we should have had jointly, thus proving which was the*
> *Artiste. Success of programme, PHOENIX, DOVER, Nightly."*

In the following years Maud also performed solo in London, often at the *Theatre Royal* – the one in Church Street, Marylebone, still as Maud Manchester, now billed as a comedienne and expert dancer. By the summer of 1895, she was once again touring the provinces. In June she performed at the *Grand Theatre*, Gravesend as a serio-comedienne and dancer, and in August at the *Empire*, Northampton. By the late summer she had enlisted the support of the theatrical agent Ernest de Vere in York Road, Lambeth who described himself in advertisements as:

> *"DRAMATIC, MUSICAL AND VARIETY AGENCY.*
> *ALWAYS VACANCIES FOR FIRST CLASS TALENT.*
> *Office Hours – 10 till 6.*
> *Consultations in 'all Languages'."*

De Vere, a former music hall singer from Bohemia now in his forties, had built a career for himself promoting and representing many artistes including his wife, the well-known music hall comedienne Miss Stella De Vere, who had died two years earlier (she had been popular enough to appear on Ogden's cigarette cards).

He was a contributor to benevolent funds, a Freemason and made a speciality of pantomime engagements for his clients at Christmas. His advertisements in *The Era* announced Maud thus:

> *"The Only and Original*
> *MAUD MANCHESTER, Comedienne and*
> *Expert Dancer, Brilliant Success of London Season.*
> *MARYLEBONE Nightly. Bradford, Leeds, Portsmouth, and*
> *Every Town of Note to follow. Agent E De Vere"*

In contrast in the September 7 issue of *The Era*, Maud's announcement featured on the same page as Marie Lloyd, who was in big demand –

managing to appear in three London halls nightly – the *Pavilion* in Piccadilly Circus, *Metropolitan* in Paddington and the *Tivoli* in the Strand.

On Maud's provincial visit to the *Leeds City of Varieties*, the press were a little muted in their praise: *"Maud Manchester was successful in her songs."* In October she was in the West Country appearing at the *New Tivoli Theatre of Varieties* in Bristol.

★

The Wainwrights' infatuation with each other soon diminished; there is a difference between the 'girl on the stage' and real life perhaps. The 'boy in the gallery' had lost his appeal too. Maud and Harry drifted apart with their different theatrical careers, Maud used to her independence earning her living (such as it was), travelling around the music halls.

By 1895 Maud had embarked on a nine-month tour of the provinces. Harry Wainwright had decided against his musical ambitions and instead found success on the stage, as well as some new amusement in the form of Edith Kilner, a Manchester-born actress.

Harry Wainwright's possessive jealousy had caused Maud to break up with her stage partner, and she continued gamely with a solo career, under the same name. It became increasingly confusing, as well as distracting to explain, so it was time for a change – both in name and agent.

She became 'Maud Coleno' and her new 1896 tour was launched by theatrical agents Lofthouse and Leon, who placed an advertisement in *The Era* in February:

> *"Miss MAUD COLENO*
> *Vocalist and Dancer.*
> *Finishes To-night, Empire, Newcastle.*
> *Monday next, South Shields.*
> *Sole Agents, Lofthouse and Leon."*

With Leon the silent partner, Lofthouse had been the proprietor of the *Oxford Music Hall* in Liverpool, and a similar hall in Dublin, but failed to make these businesses succeed. He moved to London and started an agency of his own in the York Road, and after he died his daughter carried on the agency.

In February, Maud Coleno was 'launched' at the *Newcastle Empire* as a vocalist and dancer with an up-and-coming comedian Harry Tate (whose catchphrase *'Good-bye-ee'* was later to become the inspiration for the popular song in the First World War, written in 1917). He was a year older, born Ronald Macdonald Hutchinson, in Scotland, and before going on the stage had worked for Henry Tate & Sons, the sugar refiners from whom he took his stage name. It was a friendship that would continue throughout her career.

Moving on to South Shields Maud played at *Thornton's Theatre of Varieties* as a burlesque actress and dancer, then in March appeared at the newly opened *Empire Palace Theatre* in Sheffield, where the local press describe her as *"an attractive burlesque artiste and dancer."*

The tour took her to Sussex in April performing at the *Brighton Empire Theatre of Varieties*; Maud appeared as a vocalist and dancer with Harry Ford the comedian (they were the same age), in front of an audience of over a thousand. The same month, travelling up north again, she played at the *Leeds City of Varieties* where she topped the bill.

Travelling south again to the *Portsmouth Empire Palace*, she is billed as a comedienne and in October appears at the *Southampton Empire* as a vocalist, taking second billing.

Even six years after the Manchesters had ended their partnership; Maud was still remembered and in demand as the advertisement in *The Era* on September 11, 1897 shows:

> *"WANTED, to Thank all those who answered*
> *My last week's Advertisement, Pleased to hear from*
> *Artistes who previously Played in my Pantomime, Will*
> *Harry Demarr and Maud Manchester write; also Arthur*
> *Picardo. Dodson's Varieties, Batley, Yorkshire."*

This was the glorious high noon of music hall; from the 1870s through to the beginning of the First World War it was a unique mix of social comment, sexual innuendo, musical brilliance, physical poetry and visual spectacle. It celebrated the grotesque, the defiant, and the carnival; above all it was about personality and the give-and-take between stage and stalls.

It was frequented by all classes, chronicled by great writers, admired by creative geniuses like the painter Walter Sickert who loved the music halls. He would immerse himself in the theatrical world in his desire to capture modern life. For Sickert the music halls were a serious subject for art – a spectacle of light, colour, movement and sound, with female performers who he found a never-ending source of artistic inspiration.

The life of a music hall artiste, one of the many hopefuls, was hard and demanding. They earned at best around two pounds a week – and that included evening and matinee performances. Then their accommodation on tour, 'diggings' or 'digs' as they were known, would be about sixteen shillings for full board, which came out of their pay – not to mention agent's fees. At that time there was no union to fight for better conditions, not until the music hall strike of 1907 and it was after *Variety* and Equity became involved that the problem of pay was resolved, after a fashion, but this came too late for Maud's career.

Like many other members of her profession, especially those in touring companies, they had a particularly hard time of it, often not knowing when one engagement would end or the next would begin. They worked long hours, six days a week for low wages, and typically eight shows per week – six evening performances and two matinees, with Sunday the rest or travelling day. There was little opportunity to build up savings against hard times, and when forced to stop working through illness or maternity, they could quickly find themselves in dire circumstances.

Even when work was plentiful stage artistes were commonly subjected to many privations, because whilst rehearsing for a show, no payments were made until its opening night. In London with its many theatres and music halls, the problem was exasperated with the so-called dead hours they would have to endure between daytime rehearsals.

The stage manager would generally post on a noticeboard each morning the scenes being rehearsed and the times at which each session was to begin. It was then incumbent upon the players involved in each of those scenes to present themselves at the proper time. For those not involved in any given scene, however, not only was their presence not required, it was even unwelcome, since they would only get in the way.

A player arriving at the theatre at eleven each day might find their presence was not required until later or perhaps they would finish early and have to wait around until reporting for the evening performance at eight.

These dead hours meant that for most they could not return home, as often their digs would be miles away, and the additional cost of travelling was too prohibitive. So they walked the streets, sometimes drawing out a cup of tea in a cheap café.

Aware of these deprivations, a group of philanthropists with the support of royalty in the form of Prince Christian, later Aide-de-Camp to Queen Victoria, led by Lady Louisa Magenis, daughter of the third Earl of Belmore, opened the *Rehearsal Club* in 1892 managed by the Reverend John Fenwick Kitto, vicar of St Martin in the Fields. It would be open to cover those so-called 'dead hours' from eleven till eight, providing a haven in the heart of London's 'Theatreland' as a space to rest, read, eat and drink at modest prices and socialise between morning and evening performances.

-4-

William Abbott

"Hold your hand out naughty boy"

B y the spring of 1897 Maud had met and fallen for an older married man, the so-called publisher William Abbott. As the lyrics of a contemporary musical hall song explained:

> *"(Abbott) got down to breakfast, and his wife said to him*
> *'What kept you late last night?' He answered, 'That's all right,*
> *I stayed down at the office, dear, just for an hour or two*
> *I'd some pressing work to do.'*
> *Just then the saucy servant standing near*
> *Bent down and whispered in his ear,*
> *Chorus:*
> *Hold your hand out naughty boy*
> *Hold your hand out naughty boy*
> *Last night in the pale moonlight*
> *I saw you, I saw you*
> *With a nice girl in the Park*
> *You were strolling full of joy*
> *And you told her you'd never kissed a girl before*
> *Hold your hand out naughty boy."*

William Vernon Abbott was born in Islington in March 1857 at the same house and baptised in the same church of St Mary's, Islington as his older sister Charlotte Elizabeth a year earlier. It was the church where the young

Charles Wesley, one of the leaders of the Methodist movement, began his preaching in the eighteenth century.

William's twenty-year-old mother Elizabeth – with both parents dead – had chosen to give birth amongst her maternal grandparents the Aldridge family in Vernon House, at 6 Barnsbury Square. By the time he was four, his parents had returned to Devon, his father John James now the manager of a savings bank in Plymouth, adding two more sisters Jesse and Esther, all living comfortably at 4 Albany Place with two local girls Sarah Hollet, a general servant and a fifteen-year-old child's maid, Emma Churchward.

The Abbotts were Devon wool merchants. William's father John James Abbott like his father before him had lived and traded in Bradiford and Pilton villages, close to Barnstaple in North Devon since the eighteenth century. By the 1850s William's grandfather was employing over thirty people in his business.

William's father John met Elizabeth Holliday as a young girl, when she was a scholar at Miss Faulkner's Girls' Seminary in Instow, some six miles away.

Elizabeth was the only child of John Holliday, a ship-owner, who had married Esther, the daughter of Richard Aldridge, a Thames lighterman and Old Trinity House Custom House agent in the City of London. They lived in Islington and their daughter Elizabeth, named after her grandmother, was born in the summer of 1837. By the time Elizabeth was ten, her paternal grandfather Richard Aldridge had died. Little is known of her father John Holliday after this time, described as a master mariner. It is assumed he had died – possibly at sea.

With the help of family connections, Esther Holliday (now an annuitant widow) and her daughter travelled to Instow. The village is situated in North Devon on the estuary where the rivers Taw and Torridge meet, on the opposite bank the shipbuilding village of Appledore.

Her mother initially lodged at 2 Torrington Lane with John Baller and his wife Mary, a retired customs house comptroller in his seventies.

Elizabeth attended Miss Falkner's Seminary for Girls, a small school of around ten pupils located at 5 Bath Terrace, facing the estuary. Bath Terrace had been built in the 1830s as a series of grand Georgian houses, the home of retired military and naval families with a sprinkling of successful local business people. The seminary was run by a young Yorkshire woman, Mary Faulkner, with the help of Adelido Bertin, a Flemish governess.

Esther Holliday had been suffering from cancer for around fifteen months, and had moved to Bideford. She died of a carcinoma whilst in lodgings at Bull Gardens on 19 June 1853 at the young age of thirty-nine, attended by a Mary Ann Mock, a local widow and laundress of Honestone Lane.

It left Elizabeth a fourteen-year-old orphan. There must have been some legal issues with her will perhaps, as the probate relating to Esther's personal estate, which amounted to less than £900, was only granted to Elizabeth in March 1880; by that time she had been married for twenty-seven years!

A few months later in November, Elizabeth married John James Abbott in Exeter in the parish church of St David's. They probably ran away together because both exaggerated their ages and the witnesses were possibly friends, not family. However they declared they were living at St David in Bideford, which might have been true. John described himself as a 'gentleman' but must have been still with his father's wool business. Elizabeth strangely states her father's profession as a lieutenant in the *Royal Navy*, and possibly still alive – although her mother Esther had long described herself as a widow and was in fact an annuitant.

John left the family wool business in Pilton after he married Elizabeth and established himself first as a savings bank manager in Plymouth then as an insurance agent, first in Devon then later London. Their marriage it seems was happy, as over the following twelve years they went on to have eight children – six girls and two boys.

Charlotte, the eldest child, named after her paternal grandmother, was born three years later in 1856, followed a year later by William. Another girl, Jesse, was born in Ilford, Esther in Plymouth, Hannah in Barnstaple, then Lilian, Edith and the youngest John all born in London.

Around 1880, William's father returned to London to continue his insurance business, whilst living at 5 Barnsbury Square, Islington, where his wife Elizabeth Holliday had spent her early childhood.

Initially the Abbott family had split themselves between Islington and Barnstaple. Charlotte, Jesse and the youngest John travelled with their father to London, whilst their mother Elizabeth and William, together with the younger children Esther, Hannah and Edith remained in Bradiford Cottage, Pilton. By this time their eldest son William Abbott had become a house and estate agent. Within a few years he –together with his mother, sisters and younger brother – had all reunited and moved to Islington.

After moving to London the restless William secured a position as a milk contractor, which is how he met the attractive twenty-one-year-old Alice. She was the eldest daughter of a seemingly well-to-do Lancashire merchant George Griffin. Alice was living away from home in St James, Holloway, and William on the Lambeth Road.

They were married in June 1884 in the twelfth-century church St Mary-at-Lambeth. Where, sixty odd years earlier, Captain William Bligh, of the mutiny on the *Bounty* fame, had been buried. William exaggerated his father's profession describing him as a ship broker – he was in fact an insurance broker, but Alice correctly declared her father a provisions merchant.

Originally, Alice's father George Griffin had been a chemist in Bolton, living comfortably with his wife Sarah Morley, two daughters Alice and Florence, the younger girl known as 'Florrie', together with a house servant. George, a kindly looking man, bearded with piercing eyes, above average height at five foot nine with dark hair, was considering ways of improving his income. He believed that he could make even more money through business, and sometime in the early 1860s went into partnership with two others, as cotton waste dealers in Bolton-le-Moors. One of these was his father-in-law, John Morley. [3]

However, by 1866 Morley withdrew from the business and George and fellow partner John Seldon Scowcroft continued without him. Clearly the business was not a success as a year later, George and Scowcroft dissolved their partnership by mutual consent, and George reverted to being a chemist and druggist, running a shop at 60 Deansgate in Bolton.

Sarah Morley died in 1868, and two years later George left Lancashire with his two daughters and moved to London.

Within a year he had met Amy Naylor; they were married that summer. George and his second wife lived in some style at number 1, The Crescent, a fashionable part of Clapham, close to the Common. Within ten years they had produced five children, two girls and three boys, and maintained three servants.

In October 1880 events revealed George's businesses had started to unravel. First, he was a witness at the Old Bailey in a trial for forgery by his brother-in-law Hugh Murray alias John Watson, then in February

1882 he was cited in 'Petitions for Liquidation'. He had been involved variously as a mining agent and later trading as Clive & Co., a steam-packing manufacturer.

Worse was to come: by the summer of 1888 he found himself with two others on trial for deception and fraud at the Old Bailey. [4] George was found guilty and sentenced to fifteen months' hard labour. As he was unfit for the usual hard labour occupations, he was given the job of distributing library books. When he left Wandsworth Prison essentially a ruined man, the family had moved into 32 Somerleyton Road, Brixton in much-reduced circumstances.

★

By 1891 Alice and William Abbott had been married seven years, with William describing himself as a managing director, of no specific company, and they were now living at 121 Alderney Street, Pimlico. By coincidence his younger sister Jesse was established as a companion to an elderly widow living further along the same street.

In November 1893, Alice heard that her father George Griffin, now in his fifties with greying hair, had again been convicted of fraud. It was his second offence; this time he was given two sentences of five months to run consecutively and sent to Wandsworth Prison. His wife Amy visited him that Christmas, where he complained of the cold and lack of adequate blankets in his cell. He fell ill and died the following year of pneumonia in April 1894, aged fifty-three. There was an inquiry but the prison was absolved of any blame.

The news was devastating to Alice; the combined humiliation of his imprisonment, downfall of her family and finally the death of her father had a profound effect. William's private hopes for any financial help with his many business ideas were unfulfilled.

William and Alice's marriage was childless so far, and in the ten years or so of marriage they hadn't settled anywhere for very long. They started married life in Plough Road, Clapham Common, and then moved to Cambridge Street near Hyde Park, and back south of the river to Brixton. A few years later they set off for the naval town of Gravesend in Kent, followed by Southampton before returning again to London settling eventually in Pimlico near Victoria, at 150 Warwick Street.

By 1898 William was describing himself as a book publisher. He had inherited a family trait of occasional obfuscation and would often exaggerate his professional status – which continued throughout his life. However he did have strong and continuous links with the wider print industry. Although he was not trained as compositor, a skilled job requiring a long apprenticeship, and usually membership of the trade union – of which of course there is no record.

William's father had become a reasonably successful insurance broker and his eldest and still unmarried daughter Charlotte continued in the same business when he retired, and moved to her own house in Northumberland Park, Tottenham.

Charlotte referred to herself first as an annuitant, then as an authoress around the turn of the century, whilst continuing as an insurance broker with an office in Bishopsgate. It seems she did write novels [5] – how successfully isn't known and she could also have contributed items to the many new journals appearing on the book-stands.

Publishing was going through some dramatic changes at this time. Serialisation of stories as Dickens pioneered in the cheap, popular press allowed him to reach a far wider audience than many of his literary contemporaries, but had now had its day. A new magazine culture emerged during the last two decades of the nineteenth century, which saw the appearance of over forty new journals and by 1910, something like 150 quarterlies and nearly 800 monthlies in London.

This was the age of the short story; a few years earlier when Conan Doyle's Sherlock Holmes stories began to appear, they were an immediate and extraordinary success, and ushered in the 'detective story'.

William and Charlotte were close, born within a year of each other in Islington, and together with Charlotte's interest in writing and William in 'publishing' they had interests in common and despite all, their sibling relationship endured.

William's younger sister Jesse had been a companion to a Mrs Elizabeth Griffiths in Pimlico for a short while, and after her death, went to live with Charlotte in Tottenham, north London.

Esther had become a governess to the Cox family in Falmouth but due to ill health returned to London, where she died in 1891 at the age of thirty.

Hannah, or Anna as she was known in the family, became a district nurse in Camden, remained a spinster, inherited some money from Charlotte and died in Bournemouth in the winter of 1929, leaving her estate of £649 to an Abbott relative.

Edith became a house matron, moved to Gloucester in the West Country and remained a spinster all her life.

Lilian, the Abbotts' youngest daughter – and the only one to marry – wedded a bank clerk William Dalton Smith fifteen years her senior, in 1892 and they had a daughter who they named Lilian Catherine. When William died in 1909, Lilian ran a boarding house in Elms Avenue near the pier in Eastbourne for many years. She never remarried and died aged eighty-seven, leaving £2,177 to her daughter.

John James junior, the youngest Abbott child, left home and became a town-traveller (credit draper). He married Amelia Lawrence around 1890 and they had a son, Edmund. Ten years later, John James in his early thirties together with his nine-year-old son Edmund both died during the spring of 1900 at Grove Lane, Camberwell. He left £531 to Amelia.

–5–

The Jubilee party

By the summer of 1897, Maud and William knew they were having a child, and the whole country was celebrating, as it was also Queen Victoria's Jubilee. It was to be a party to end all parties.

The country came together to celebrate not just in London, but throughout Britain and across the empire. The spirit of Victorian philanthropy was kept alive and well with street feasts laid on for 400,000 of London's poorest residents. Tea magnate Sir Thomas Lipton sponsored the event, which included free bottles of ale and pipe tobacco. The parties went on into the evening, with a chain of beacons lit across Britain; a series of civic festivities in the newly-created Jubilee cities of Nottingham, Bradford and Hull; fireworks displays; and the 'son et lumière' illumination of St Paul's Cathedral for the first time. By order of the government, and to much disgust from the Temperance Movement, pubs remained open all night until two-thirty in the morning.

★

The same summer, Florrie Forde left her native Australia, and on August Bank Holiday, she made her first appearances in London performing at three music halls – the *South London Palace,* the *Pavilion* and the *Oxford* – in the course of one evening. She became an overnight star. This was much to the envy of the existing music hall stalwarts who had given their early lives to the stage and the rigours of touring. Talent is important, but being in the right place at the right time is how stars are born.

★

The dilemma of Maud's baby daughter Dorothy was resolved inevitably by Augusta. For the immediate future she would enjoy a loving grandmother's attention, allowing Maud to work. Since the death of her husband she had often looked after the children of Maud's theatrical friends as well as family grandchildren from time to time. Augusta had brought up six children of her own – two had died in infancy, and she was now in her early sixties, living in Blackfriars at 15 Great Charlotte Street.

William Abbott's sisters were not enamoured with his behaviour towards his wife Alice and even more so on discovering he had fathered a child with a music hall actress. Their sympathy lay with poor Alice – she had not only suffered the humiliation and the loss of her father, their brother had turned out to be a selfish and violent husband too.

However, Maud and William's affair continued – and it seemed to endure. They met whenever they could, often at Great Charlotte Street.

The need to earn a living was pressing and the footlights beckoned. When Maud was on the London stage, she lived at home with her mother Augusta and baby Dorothy. But on 'the touring circuit' it was as usual in theatrical digs. She was now performing as Maud Abbott, leaving her old music hall acts for new roles in dramas and comedy farces. Maud was used to the life of a touring artiste – a typical daily hand-to-mouth struggle simply to get by – food and lodging, maintaining a wardrobe (since you must dress well in order to find work), and now the addition of a child to maintain.

★

With hundreds of performers travelling all over Britain, the Music Hall Artistes' Railway Association was set up in 1897 by music hall artist Dan Leno, the editor of *The Encore*, the music hall journal and another performer, Eugene Stratton. It had a definite purpose in mind – to secure cut-price fares from the railway companies. It rapidly signed up over 5,000 members and proved so successful that *The Stage* suggested that it ought to extend its scope *"to cover all matters appertaining to music-hall artistes"*. This eventually happened in 1907 with the formation of the Variety Artists' Federation.

★

In January 1899, Maud joined the cast of *The Intruders*, a new comedy in four parts, with Fanny Brough in the lead role, and Maud playing Lady Diana Moepham, a society lady. The play opened at the *Theatre Royal* in Worcester on the 14th, and was cautiously welcomed with a *"cordial reception"*.

Fanny Brough, born in Paris, came from a theatrical family and is remembered for her comedy roles. In 1891 Brough had become the first president of the Theatrical Ladies' Guild, an organisation created by another actress Kittie Carson to help destitute actresses who were about to become mothers. It may have been through her influence that Maud secured the role, having recently given birth.

By the time the play had arrived in the London suburbs of Brixton in February, it received a poor press review: *"… but the piece in its present form at least, is hardly strong enough to flourish in the London air."* However, Maud's performance seemed to be acceptable: *"… and Miss Maud Abbott and Miss Edith Milton being efficient as two local Society ladies."*

The review went on to declare: *"… we fear the piece would have small chance of success at a West-end theatre."*

The played closed soon afterwards. Two years later, Fanny Brough went on to appear in the first opening of George Bernard Shaw's controversial play *Mrs Warren's Profession* at the *New Lyric Club*, in London.

★

Maud found herself in another comedy farce, *My Soldier Boy*, this time with more success. Joining Alfred Maltby's touring company fresh from their West End success at the *Criterion Theatre* Maud was to play the role of Lydia Mendle, the smart wife of the protagonist stepson.

The tour opened in March at the *Grand* in Croydon where *The Era*'s own correspondent wrote: *"Miss Maud Abbott acts with spirit and ability as Lydia Mendle."* Followed by the Elephant & Castle, then on Monday bank holiday 3rd April at the *Queen's Opera House*, Crouch End where the press exclaimed:

> *"The play represented here this week, does credit to the company responsible for the production. On a Bank Holiday evening what better could be wished than a thoroughly amusing farce such as the comedy under review is? As Lydia Mendle Miss Maud Abbott plays with graceful ease and effect."*

The same month the play toured at the *Sheffield Lyceum* and at the month's end in Dublin at the *Gaiety Theatre*, in South King Street where Maud received another good review: *"My Soldier Boy occupies the boards here this week, and is cleverly performed by Messrs Alfred Maltby and Roper Sypers Company... Miss Maud Abbott does well in the part of Lydia Mendle."* Another reviewer described, *"Miss Maud Abbott as Lydia displayed exceptional ability and gained golden opinions."*

In May the play toured Liverpool at the *Prince of Wales Theatre*, on to Bradford at the *Theatre Royal*, where the press review announced, *"... as Lydia Miss Maud Abbott is praiseworthy,"* and *Newcastle Theatre Royal*, where Maud's review declared, *"Miss Maud Abbott is bright and piquant as Lydia Mendle."*

The tour ended and Maud returned to London to be reunited with her daughter and William again after a break of four months.

During the summer months she resorted to her old music hall repertoire as Maud Coleno, comedienne and played for the summer season at the *Royal Aquarium*, where it advertised, *"A great holiday programme... 13 hours continuous entertainment for one shilling."* The *Royal Aquarium and Winter Garden* was a place of amusement in Westminster, popular with members of Parliament, and located opposite the Abbey. By the time Maud was treading the boards it was acquiring a risqué reputation, with unaccompanied ladies promenading through the hall in search of male companionship. The all-day variety entertainments turned less respectable too, including billiard matches, novelty acts and side-shows of all kinds, and commercial stalls offering perfumery and gloves. It was demolished in 1903.

★

With the summer season over Maud went on tour from October to December, this time joining Leonard Boyne's touring company in a drama by Cecil Raleigh and Seymour Hicks called *Sporting Life*. Maud played a leading role as Norah Cavanaugh, daughter of Lord Woodstock (the hero) and horse trainer. The plot has many twists and turns, centering around the Derby, and a boxing match when the hero was supposed to knock out the champion of England, and in doing so retrieve his fortune and estates.

They opened on Broadway – the *Deptford Broadway Theatre* – and

Maud received a good review: *"Norah is excellently enacted by Miss Maud Abbot."* In November they played at the London *Alexandra Theatre North* and in December at the *Brighton Eden Theatre* in Sussex where the press declared: *"The acting is uniformly excellent… Miss Maud Abbott made a charming Norah."* The tour finally returned to London before Christmas 1899 with the closing performance at *The Grand,* Islington. The play was later made into a film in the 1920s.

★

Augusta Manchester's health had been failing and after a week or so of very cold, dull days she died of pulmonary tuberculosis and exhaustion on Friday 9 March, 1900 at her home at 15 Great Charlotte Street, Blackfriars with Maud by her bedside. It was a sad time for the Manchester children, with both parents now deceased. Maud's married sister Minnie living in Kennington had her hands full with four daughters ranging from fifteen to three, and her older brother Robert in Walworth with four young children under the age of ten and one on the way – which meant she had to find someone else to look after two-year-old Dorothy.

-6-

Country girl

The death of her mother presented Maud and William with a dilemma. Augusta had been looking after Dorothy whilst Maud earned a living on the stage. Harry Wainwright had long since disappeared from Maud's life whilst William was still hesitating. He had yet to make the break from Alice; despite their disintegrating marriage, he had not created a permanent home for his 'secret family'.

The solution came from one of William's friends, Mark Twaites – much the same age – a compositor in the print industry. Mark and his wife Harriet lived in Islington with their children, one of whom, Clarence, was also in the printing business.

Harriet's parents, the Gittus family, lived in Worcester and were already looking after their grandchild James and would be willing to look after Dorothy. Their nineteen-year-old daughter Maud Twaites also boarded there. She was a teacher in the local school, which would be helpful, and any extra income would be welcome. The arrangement would help William and Maud get on their feet to sort out their respective marriages.

During Easter in the middle of April 1900 Dorothy was introduced to Maud Twaites, who was visiting her parents in London, and would as agreed accompany her on the return train journey to her grandparents' in Worcester. Thomas and Maria Gittus, now in their seventies, lived with their single daughter Clara, a dressmaker, and looked after a grandchild James Mulligan, the son of their youngest married daughter Agnes.

Thomas Gittus was a retired bricklayer, and the family lived in Swineherd, a hamlet just outside the city, about two miles south-east on the road to Spetchley.

By coincidence, a year earlier Maud had spent a week in Worcester making her début in the opening of a stage play called *Intruders*, playing the part of a society lady at the *Theatre Royal* in Angel Street at the start of a short-lived tour. It was the same theatre that Sarah Siddons, the famous eighteenth-century actress also made her acting début.

Worcester is dominated by its twelfth-century medieval cathedral, on the banks of the River Severn, and became an industrial town in the nineteenth century. Iron foundries were opened and engineering flourished. The now famous Lea & Perrins Worcester sauce was first sold by its creators in 1838, at their dispensing chemists in Broad Street. The city was also renowned for its glove industry. By the time Dorothy was boarding with the Gittus family, large companies such as Fownes, one of the world's leading glove makers were employing hundreds of people, outsourcing much work to local villages. Other industries such as vinegar-making and pottery, as well as brickmaking – the trade of Thomas Gittus, continued to thrive.

What was a temporary solution for two-year-old Dorothy had lasted over three years. It was in many ways an idyllic and quiet rural setting, largely unchanged for centuries with its clean air and starlit nights in total contrast to the winter fog, city sounds and dirt of London. Dorothy would benefit from having the young teacher in the same house. Although Maud taught in the local school she would have found time for the children, James her seven-year-old nephew and two-year-old boarder Dorothy.

After her grandparents died, Maud would continue living in Swineherd with the kindly Clara Gittus. Maud remained a spinster all her life, eventually on her death in 1942 leaving a small legacy to James Mulligan, her nephew.

★

In the meantime Miss Coleno returned to the stage in the summer of 1900, and we glimpse the newspaper cuttings to see her on tour with her valise again, appearing at the *Bijou Theatre*, Teddington.

William Abbott, although still nominally residing with Alice in Warwick Street, South Belgravia, was becoming increasingly restless. After sessions at the *Marquis of Westminster* public house with his friends he would return home full of drink, use threatening language and was occasionally violent. In the summer of 1900 whilst under the influence of drink, he attacked Alice and permanently damaged her eye.

Eventually William was forced into confession about his affair with Maud Coleno, and worse still Alice learnt the child she longed for with William had been born to a music hall actress instead. This was the last straw, following the humiliation of her father's imprisonment and death.

Events came to a head by February 1902 when William eventually walked out of the house telling Alice he was going down the road to buy cigarettes – he did not return. [6]

She managed to trace his new address, at the same time started divorce proceedings, a brave move for a woman at that time but she had no choice. After the 1884 Matrimonial Act, women who left their husbands could no longer be imprisoned, and power was given to the courts regarding the custody of any children. However, men could divorce for adultery but women had to prove cruelty as well. With the support of her sister Florrie, she moved to Kensington.

When William did a 'bit of a runner' as the cockneys say, and left Alice, he had actually moved in with Maud Coleno and they had settled at 3 Great James Street, north of Bedford Row, spending most of 1902 living together.

Maud had assumed the name of Abbott as easily as a new stage part. It was the first time they had spent more than a night together.

Around the same time we find Harry Wainwright, Maud's estranged husband, still with Edith Kilner but she too was now calling herself Wainwright. They were living together with Edith's sister Violet in the market town of Atherstone, in a modest house in the Tamworth Road. The town was well known for its hat industry, situated on the old Roman road of Watling Street between Nuneaton and Tamworth.

Maud and Harry with their individual theatrical careers had been apart for some years; the drift continued and they lost contact. Harry eventually married Edith in 1913 in her home town of Chorlton, Lancashire. Although the marriage was bigamous, he described himself as a widower – which in a way he was.

★

In the meantime Maud continued to find work in London and to tour the provinces. In February 1903 Maud appeared in Robert Stelling's company at St Leonard's Pier in Sussex, in an Anglo-American production called *The Shadows of a Great City*, playing a minor part in a drama about lives in New York. It would later be made into a film in 1915.

In March, Maud appeared in the *Night of the Party*, at the *Theatre Royal* in Sheffield. It was a Weedon Grossmith farcical comedy in three acts. Maud again played a minor role of 'Baby Hastings', and as the local lady correspondent simply wrote noncommittally: *"Baby Hastings (Miss Maud Abbott) wears pale blue satin."*

By October 1903 Alice had filed her petition, instructing her solicitor Ernest Van Tromp of 16 Essex Street to pursue the case for adultery and cruelty in the High Court of Justice. By the end of the year William had sworn an affidavit admitting his adultery with Maud Coleno on 'divers' occasions.

It was during the divorce evidence that Alice discovered her name had been used as the mother of William's daughter with Maud. In January 1904, Alice and Maud then had to make a 'statutory declaration' before the St Pancras Superintendent Registrar declaring Emily Augusta Maud Mary Wainwright as the rightful mother of William's child Dorothy.

The case was not contested and a decree nisi was granted in March 1904, with the final decree six months later.

As part of the divorce settlement William was instructed to pay maintenance to Alice at a rate of one pound per week for the rest of his life and also to pay her legal costs.

Alice had started a new life after moving to the West Cromwell Road, running a boarding house. She managed it alone for several years until 1930, when her younger sister Florrie came to live and help with the house. She described herself as a widow, understandably, as divorcee carried such a stigma at that time. Her venture must have been modestly successful because she had retired to St John's Wood, and when she died in St Mary Abbot's hospital in Kensington during 1941 she left £847 to her solicitor. Florrie had died a year earlier, leaving much the same amount.

★

In November 1903, whilst William's divorce was proceeding they had news from Worcester that Maria Gittus had died, followed six months later by her husband Thomas. They had both been in their seventies and were buried in the local parish church of All Saints in Spetchley.

Maud Twaites and Clara Gittus offered to continue boarding the six-year-old Dorothy at Swineherd as she was considered one of the family. With Maud's patient help she was able to read and write her name (unlike her mother and grandmother) and they reported she was a quick learner.

★

In the philosophy of Aristotle, there is a saying: *"Give me a child till he is seven and I will show you the man."* It is a Jesuit maxim too and true for all children in the formative years where adults influence values and cultural beliefs. For the first six or so years, Dorothy had been in the company of and influenced by older women. Her independent mother and loving grandmother Augusta, then the kindly women of the Gittus family, Maria the grandmother, Clara the dressmaker and Maud the teacher. Men like old Mr Gittus appearing only in the background, who she could wrap around her little finger in a jiffy, and her distant father William yet unknown. This maternal environment, combined with the extra attention all pretty girls receive from older men, would shape her later life and Dorothy liked nothing better than being admired.

Despite the stage performances and nomadic life, Maud missed her only daughter (an emotional gene it seems she was unable to pass on) and with William's divorce now settled felt it was time to bring their 'love-child' back to London to begin a new family life together.

-7-

Ingénue in the chorus

Maud Twaites had agreed to accompany Dorothy to London on her next visit to Harriett and Mark, her parents, now in their fifties living in Islington at 17 St Peters Street. Maud Abbott would meet her at Paddington station at the allotted time.

This would have been a great adventure for the six-year-old – travelling on a Great Western steam train with their green engines and chocolate and cream painted carriages. They travelled from Worcester Shrub Hill station passing through the apple blossoms of the Vale of Evesham, into the Cotswolds to Oxford and through the Thames Valley countryside to the smoking chimneys of London, a journey taking just over three hours, arriving with a hiss of steam at Paddington.

The Abbotts had now rented a house off the Essex Road at 66 Halton Road, Islington and they settled into family life, finding a local Church of England primary school for Dorothy. St Mary's was a natural choice, nearby in Little Cross Street (now Shillingford Street) and it was the church where her father William and her aunt Charlotte, the two eldest of the Abbott family, had been baptised in Upper Street.

This must have been a strange new world for the six-year-old, transported from the quiet regular seasonal life of the countryside in Worcester, to the new irregular noisy world of suburban London, and, with a new man in the house – her father, she was told.

★

By the summer of 1906 Maud was once again on the stage, touring in Jessie Millward's company. She appeared at the *Theatre Royal*, Manchester in *School for Husbands*. It was a comedy in four acts, set in the eighteenth century at the home of Lady Belinda Manners. The plot is based on a neglected wife determined to pay her husband back in kind, all of course ending happily. It was written by Stanislaus Stange, a Liverpool-born playwright and lyricist who had made his name and career in America. Jessie Millward, an established actress, came from a theatrical family and had played many times with the great actor-manager Henry Irving and also appeared in New York on Broadway. Although Maud Abbott's character Betty appears first in the billing, the role was a minor one as she was not getting the bigger parts anymore. In any case, she was six months pregnant with another child.

In October she gave birth to a boy, named William John (they called him Jack), a young brother for the eight-year-old Dorothy.

★

The following year, a music hall strike commenced at the *Holborn Empire* in London and lasted for two weeks. It all related to poor pay; some members of the profession earned less than thirty shillings to three pounds a week, on top of which they were forced into matinee performances with no extra pay, and often had fees deducted for agents – whether they actually had one or not. Many of the music hall 'stars' like Marie Lloyd identified with their plight and went on picket lines outside theatres in London and the provinces. The music hall and theatre impresarios capitulated and the result was an improvement in the terms for the performers.

All this came too late for Maud who now had a child to look after – but she saw in her daughter Dorothy the looks and artistic temperament that could just create a future stage career.

★

William continued in the 'publishing' business and now called himself a journalist. His mother Elizabeth had died a few years earlier and his father John James had retired, living with his daughters Charlotte and Jessie at 10 Beresford Road, Highbury, north London.

In the spring of 1911 William and Maud took their children for a little family holiday to Southend-on-Sea, a seaside resort on the Essex coast in the Thames estuary, just before Easter, visiting their friends the Fulcher family. William had first met George and his wife Grace when George was a 'life-assurance' agent, working for his father in London.

George had now taken up a position with the local Municipal Electricity Company, and their eldest son Harold was a compositor in the print business. William was describing himself as a 'journalist – working from home'.

By the summer they had decided to marry. So, quietly and without fanfare in the middle of the working week on 17 August, William now fifty-four and Maud thirty-seven tied the knot (albeit bigamously) at the Holborn registry office, witnessed by their friends Fred and Rita Rutter. William's friendship with Fred, an insurance clerk, dated back to the boozy days of his previous marriage to Alice. Both had been habitués of the *Marquis of Westminster* pub in Pimlico.

Maud was now officially Mrs Abbott – although she had auditioned and been playing that role for many years.

In the meantime they had moved from Islington, and were now living in Roseberry Square, Holborn, one of the new model mansion flats built on the clearance ground left over from a public improvement scheme. Dorothy was thirteen and her younger brother Jack just five.

★

Dorothy grew up to be blonde, beautiful and artistically talented. The boom in musical comedy had begun in the early 1890s, which led to a great increase in demand for pretty girls to fill up the chorus lines. The impresario George Edwardes established the *Gaiety Theatre* in the Strand; it quickly became the home of musical comedy and his troop of 'Gaiety Girls' soon earned international renown, the crème-de-la-crème of chorus lines, setting the pattern that all others would follow.

For a time, the demand was so much greater than the supply that almost any girl with an attractive figure could find profitable work whenever she wanted it. The shortage of supply of suitable applicants did not last long however. Stories circulated in the press telling of glamorous lifestyles and favourable marriages to members of the aristocracy brought hopeful young aspirants flocking to London from all over the country.

The pay for chorus girls fell as the competition for places increased, since managers could then pick and choose and could get all the girls they needed on the meagrest of wages. Soon, only the prettiest and most talented could find regular work at all, and then it was a life of hard work and plenty of it. Besides being pretty, the chorus girl had to be able to dance, sing, and act, as well as having unlimited energy. One girl might commonly make five or six changes of costume in an evening, and figure in ten or a dozen numbers in which she did more work than the man or woman who had the song, and all the time she must look happy. And when it came to costumes, she had to provide all her own tights and dancing shoes (Dorothy had inherited a pair made for her mother by her grandfather John Manchester) – unlike the high-priced principals, whose costumes were furnished to the last detail by the management.

Despite these hardships, the fascination of stage life, in contrast to factory work or domestic service, made it difficult to consider settling down into a regular situation after appearing before the footlights with all its adrenalin, excitement and audience attention. This is perhaps why any girl who had once been in the chorus was reluctant to try any other occupation.

There was a glamorous side to the profession – meeting wealthy audience members. And there were instances where chorus girls did indeed become famous, either because they succeeded in their dream of becoming a brilliant actress (like Gertie Millar), or perhaps snared a rich and influential husband with marriage into the aristocracy like Rosie Boote, the 'Gaiety Girl' who became the Marchioness of Headfort, or at the very least secure a wealthy middle-class businessman.

Since the 1880s the press had been full of stories of showgirls marrying into the aristocracy, and the English courts were far more sympathetic to the girls' point of view in any 'Breach of Promise' case, a golden age that ran well into the 1920s. The court awards made to jilted actresses were astonishing. In 1897 Viscount Dangan was ordered to pay £10,000 to the young actress Phyllis Broughton after he reneged on his promise to marry her. And the same year Dorothy was playing on the West End stage, the actress Daisy Markham sued the Earl of Compton, heir to the Marquis of Northampton, who withdrew his proposal – he was made to pay £50,000 plus all the costs of the court case.

★

In July 1912, the first Royal Command Performance was held at the *Palace Theatre* in London's West End in front of King George V and Queen Mary. The show was to raise funds for the Entertainment Artistes' Benevolent Fund, which had been created a few years earlier. It was a great success and became an annual event, eventually changing its name to the Royal Variety Performance, which continues to this day.

Many of the artists performing were from the music hall tradition – the first show included Vesta Tilley, Harry Lauder, Maud's friend Harry Tate doing his 'motoring sketch' and the great Russian ballerina Anna Pavlova. Notably absent was Marie Lloyd because the organisers considered her act to be too risqué for royalty. Instead she staged a rival show on the same night at a nearby theatre, billed as 'By Command of the British Public'.

★

Maud had secured a place for Dorothy at a dancing academy in Brixton run by Sydney Russell, who had a production troupe of six to eight girls engaged in various reviews and shows throughout the country. He had promised to secure an engagement for Dorothy in Paris. It had not materialised and the Abbotts were forced to sue him to recover £50 damages for breach of contract. Their case came before Judge Parry [7] at Lambeth County Court in December 1913.

At the time, they were living at 4 Princeton Street, off Bedford Row. The judge ruled that the defendant, who had paid £10 into the court, thought it a generous way of meeting the claim; he therefore awarded that amount to the Abbott family – but no order for costs. All reported in *The Era* the week before Christmas.

★

The friendships of the stage can be long lasting; Maud had toured with the young and now famous comedian Harry Tate – they were much the same age, and had both appeared together many times. He always made her laugh he could give remarkable imitations of many 'stars' of the time, both male and female performers like Dan Leno and Marie Lloyd.

Harry was a member of the *Vaudeville Club* in the Charing Cross Road, where a certain homeopath Doctor Crippen, the husband of music hall performer Belle Elmore, had frequently played cards with artists in the afternoons. It was also the headquarters of the 'Grand Order of Water Rats', a theatrical charity which Harry had presided over a year earlier as 'King Rat'. He was well connected, happy to help a friend and influenced a role in the chorus for Maud's young daughter. It was a new musical *Hullo Tango*, which was opening at the *Hippodrome* in December 1913. It replaced *Hullo Ragtime* and was considered even more lascivious.

Harry would appear with a 'beauty chorus' of forty dancing girls, including Dorothy. The other stars included Shirley Kellogg (the wife of the producer and scriptwriter Albert de Courville) the American singer who had popularised ragtime and now the Argentine tango in Britain.

Years later, in his book *The Edwardians*, J. B. Priestley reflected:

"It was denounced… as an immodest dance of low south American origin, a kind of going to the dogs in a very elaborate fashion… the men, not all of them young, were trying to look like the riffraff of Rio… girls of decent parentage were swaying and slinking in to perdition. What was the country coming to?"

The country thought different it seemed; the show was a great success and it ran for 485 performances, continuing through 1914 to the beginning of 1915.

★

During the summer of 1914 Archduke Franz Ferdinand was assassinated in a faraway Balkan city, Sarajevo, sparking a political touch-paper in Europe. A month later on the 4th August Britain declared war on Germany; allied with France, the country began to mobilise, and eight days later also declared war on Austria-Hungary – coincidently and prophetically the traditional start of the 'shooting season'.

The British Expeditionary Force landed in Flanders and within weeks was engaged in their first confrontation on European soil since Waterloo in 1815 at the Battle of Mons.

Four divisions of the BEF, commanded by Sir John French, struggling and heavily outnumbered against the German First Army had no option but to retreat – but did so in good order over two weeks to new defensive positions.

Britain's 'contemptible little army' then withstood the onslaught of the Kaiser's army – three times its size – and fought it to a standstill. The massed rifle fire of the professional British soldiers inflicted heavy casualties on the Germans. The later success in September at the first Battle of the Marne followed by the First Battle of Ypres ended the German sweep into France and marked the beginning of the trench warfare that was to characterise World War One.

As war historian Liddell Hart would later write:

> "... their defence had length without depth. Its shallowness was the measure of their numerical weakness, but also the supreme tribute to their moral strength. The 'thin red line' of the past was never so thin as the line at Ypres – and never so hardly tried. The 'thin khaki line' withstood a strain that lasted for weeks compared with the hours of the past... Ypres saw the supreme vindication and the final sacrifice of the old Regular Army. After the battle was over, little survived, save the memory of its spirit." [8]

More soldiers were needed. Regiments were called back from the empire and a recruitment campaign began. The mood of the country had changed – what was once billed to be 'all over by Christmas' was now apparently likely to last longer. In January 1915, Britain suffered its first civilian casualties from air attacks when two German Zeppelins dropped bombs on Great Yarmouth and King's Lynn on the eastern coast of England. Although only a few people were killed and a dozen or so injured it created widespread panic, and alarmist stories about German agents provoked anti-German feeling. This would later lead to infrequent rioting, assaults on suspected Germans and the looting of stores owned by people with German-sounding names.

★

Maud had secured her daughter's stage career but her health was failing. Her son Jack had often been sent to relatives in Barnstaple, when she or more probably his father couldn't cope.

Years later Jack's daughter Pat would recall her father's stories from childhood, describing watching his mother dance from the wings many times at *Sadler's Wells*. By that time the *Daily Chronicle*'s theatre critic, S. R. Littlewood, was describing the theatre as *"a poor, wounded old playhouse"* and by 1915, it had closed its doors.

Maud had been on the stage over twenty years since that first tentative performance at the age of twelve. She had essentially lived out of a valise for most of her life, touring England and Ireland many times, enjoying the adulation of audiences, and whilst she hadn't found stardom, she had enjoyed some successes and good reviews. Although still only in her late thirties, she was worn out, and the greatest stage enemy was aging. It was a young woman's profession and as Maud grew older, work became increasingly more difficult to come by as younger girls came along. No doubt the family's precarious income had forced them to move lodgings every few years – it was an itinerant sort of life.

★

Hullo Tango had been a great success and Dorothy was engaged to appear in another *Hippodrome* musical called *Push and Go*, again with Harry Tate. Rehearsals would start soon and the show would open in late spring 1915.

It was shortly after Dorothy's appearance in the West End run of *Hullo Tango* that Maud, now slowly dying, had been found a place in Battersea General Hospital, known locally as the 'Anti-viv'. It had been established by the secretary of the Anti-Vivisection Society – strongly against animal experiments and research. This small charitable hospital had mixed fortunes and on the outbreak of war in 1914, had dutifully allocated twenty beds for the military.

Maud had been diagnosed with tuberculosis, a major cause of death in Britain at that time, typically caused by poor living conditions, such as overcrowding and malnourishment. There was no known cure.

Some weeks later on Saturday March 6 1915, Emily Augusta Maud Mary Abbott died of heart failure brought on by the tuberculosis. She was just forty-one.

The news was predictable but nevertheless a great loss to William, Dorothy and her younger brother, eight-year-old Jack. William had been with Maud at her death and was inconsolable – until that is, he met someone else.

William had spent the first twenty years of his life in Devon and never fully lost that soft country brogue, which may account perhaps for the misspelling in the records of his third marriage – his surname was recorded as 'Abbett'. Within eighteen months or so of Maud's death he had met a middle-aged French woman from Brittany, and converted to Catholicism.

A month after his father John James died in Islington at the age of eighty-three, William, now sixty, had married the thirty-six-year-old Marie Louise Gély, a single lady living at 50 Wymering Mansions, a respectable redbrick mansion block in Maida Vale. She was a Catholic and they married on 14 April 1917, at the French church of Notre Dame de France in Leicester Place, a little side street off Leicester Square. It had been built in the 1860s by the Marist Fathers for the French community in London.

Marie declared her father, of independent means, was deceased and William registered his address as 97 Petherton Road, Islington, temporarily living with his sister Charlotte. She also acted as a witness to their wedding. William announced his occupation as that of purser on the TS *Warspite*, [9] a training ship for boys, whose appointment required them to be of good character and go to sea at the end of their training. It was run by the Marine Society, and the ship was moored on the Thames, off Charles Street at Greenhithe. Less than a year later the ship was destroyed by fire – apparently started deliberately by three boys, the remaining 200 or so on board had to transfer to the nearby TS *Worcester*. By this time William, Marie and Jack were living at 71 St George's Road in Lambeth.

Quite how William and Marie met or what brought on a change of occupation and religion, or in fact what became of Marie, is not clear.

However, her arrival in the Abbott household was fortuitous for eleven-year-old Jack. It was the beginning of a happier childhood; he would spend time in France with his stepmother, where he learnt to speak the language fluently. [10]

William's ambivalent connection with the Navy in his role as training ship purser would metamorphose into 'Captain Abbott RN' on all Dorothy's official records.

A few weeks after Maud's death, *Push and Go*, the new revue by Albert de Courville opened on 10 May 1915. The principals were Violet Loraine

– herself once a chorus girl – together with Harry Tate. Joining them was a number of American artists including Shirley Kellogg (from *Hullo Tango*), Arthur Swanston, Anna Wheaton, and of course Maud Coleno's daughter Dorothy Abbott in the chorus.

Act II
Captain Lewis Takes Leave
(1915–1923)

"I wish you'd come and play with me,
For I have such a way with me,
A way with me, a way with me.
I have such a nice little way with me,
Do not think it wrong."

Sung in the West End revue Push & Go, Hippodrome 1915

-8-

The gas cloud at Ypres

"On the 22nd of April 1915 the sun was sinking behind Ypres. Its spring radiance had breathed life that day into the dead town and mouldering trench lines which guarded it… momentarily relieved by the fragrance of a spring day's sunshine. As that fragrance faded with the waning sun… an evening hush spread over the scene… the hush was false… at five o'clock a fearful din of guns broke out… and to the nostrils of men nearer the front came the smell of devilish incense… those nearer still to the trenches north of Ypres saw two curious wraiths of greenish-yellow fog creep forward, spread until they became one and then, moving forward, change to blue and white mist." [1]

It was the first German gas attack on allied lines, and when the fighting had finally died down by the end of May the British loss was 59,000; nearly double that suffered by the Germans who attacked them. The Second Battalion *Kings Shropshire Light Infantry* had been part of the defence at the Second Battle of Ypres and the battalion were badly mauled, taking many casualties. After six months of fighting they were relieved and moved to a (then) relatively quiet part of the front.

May was a bad month for the war in England. On the 7th a German submarine sank the liner *Lusitania*. In the same week, a Zeppelin raid struck the east coast, and people read about Germany's first use of poison gas reported from the trenches of the Western Front.

When Captain Edwin Lewis, the KSLI battalion's quartermaster, arrived on leave in London he found himself a stranger in his own country. He had been based in India for over twenty years, serving Queen and empire. Since that time both his father and later his mother had died in their native Wales. The remaining family of his younger brothers and sisters were now scattered – he had lost touch.

Lewis had been serving in Secunderabad, in the Andhra Pradesh region of central India, when the order came to mobilise for war. The battalion sailed from Bombay on the SS *Neuralia*, a troopship chartered from the British India Steam Navigation Company, arriving in Plymouth in November. After some re-equipment in Salisbury, they landed in France as part of the 27th Division at Le Havre on 21 December.

Since January 1915, the battalion had taken part in some of the hardest fighting in the Ypres Salient at St Eloi, St Julien and faced the chlorine gas attack. The effect was devastating as 60 per cent of the casualties had to be repatriated and half of these were still unfit by the end of the war, over three years later.

★

Edwin Lewis was born in January 1869 in the small market town of Knighton in mid Wales, near the English border. His father William Lewis was an itinerant farm labourer and his mother Jane Miles had been a servant at Selly Hall at Llanfair Waterdine. He was initially brought up by his maternal grandparents (the Miles family) as his mother was now in service to the family of farmer Richard Bright at his 260-acre Upper Hall Farm at Heyope in Radnorshire, farming dairy cattle and sheep. Edwin's parents eventually married in 1876, at the Methodist Chapel in Knighton. With an eight-year gap they went on to have five more children – three boys and two girls. Two of Jane's earlier babies died at birth, then followed William born in 1877, Hugh (known as Harry) in 1879, Eliza in 1882, Albert in 1883 and Alice Jane in 1884.

After elementary schooling Edwin became an agricultural labourer like his father, then at eighteen a groom to a Mr Turner of Wem, Shropshire, and entered the local militia. He later joined the *King's Shropshire Light Infantry* working his way up through the ranks. He left Wales as a Non Commissioned Officer when the regiment was sent to India just before the turn of the century. After arriving he was commissioned as a lieutenant in March 1901. Anticipating his new status and extra money – he was now thirty-one – he had married the eighteen-year-old Scottish-born Elizabeth Elliot, daughter of a regular artillery soldier, a few months earlier in Poona.

It was a journey some ten hours away by train, around 1,800 feet above sea level in the cooler Deccan plateau, on the banks of the Mula-Mutha River, away from the heat of the regiment's base in Secunderabad.

Later the same year Elizabeth gave birth to a daughter, Agnes, named after her grandmother, who died at birth on 23 November and was buried (as is traditional in India) the following day.

Promotion, particularly for officers from the peace-time ranks in the Indian army was very slow, and eventually Edwin gained his captaincy in 1911 at the age of forty-one.

Shortly before Edwin's battalion had been recalled to England at the outbreak of war, his personal life imploded. His wife had found a new admirer. Their personal relations had withered away; perhaps lack of prospects, the death of their only child, all added to the deterioration of their marriage in the heat and monotony of Imperial India.

Elizabeth's admirer was Frank Jerome Maitland King –known as Peter. His father was the grandson of the sixth Baron Peter King, and a descendant of the first Baron Ockham – Lord Chancellor in the early eighteenth century. A family descendant, William King (1805–1893) had married Ada, the only daughter of Lord Byron, later becoming Earl of Lovelace.

'Peter' King had entered the *Royal Engineers*, gaining the rank of colonel, as a family biography reveals:

"By this same circumstance the escapades of Nunk's cousin Peter King, a soldier in India, and Nunk's (Alick Hamilton) generosity had brought Ethel and Gore-Browne tangibly close in a way that at last gave more hope of permanence. Peter had fallen in love with a married woman (Mrs Lewis) and made known his plans to marry. He promptly plummeted from family grace, (Stewart) Gore-Browne replaced him as heir and, virtually, adopted son." [2]

Clearly, Elizabeth Agnes Lewis – known as 'Cissie' – reciprocated Peter King's affections; he seemed a better catch. After her divorce they married in Bengal in October 1914, just weeks before Edwin Lewis sailed for England.

They remained in India enjoying their silver wedding anniversary in Mandalay, Burma, which was duly announced in *The Times* in October 1939. Two years later, Peter King died followed by Cissie in Shillong, North East India in 1945.

-9-

Love at the Cavendish

The newspapers had been full of the outrageous attack by a German submarine which torpedoed the Cunard liner, RMS *Lusitania*, off the Irish coast in early May. It sank in eighteen minutes killing 1,198 men, women and children. In the same week, a Zeppelin raid dropped over hundred bombs on Southend, killing one woman. The reported events, made a horse panic and bolt through the window of Boots the Chemist, and provoked an outpouring of anti-German sentiment.

On his journey from a French port to London, Edwin had fallen in with other officers hell-bent on enjoying themselves in London. The newspapers were now describing (albeit in guarded terms) the first Zeppelin attack on London the previous Monday, and the anti-German riots that broke out the following days.

On arrival there was a rush to leave the train as fellow travelling companions shouted their farewells and dispersed into the night. Edwin and two other officers were amongst the last to leave and sauntered together towards the station entrance. They had no firm plans, but thought they would spend some time in London seeing the shows before leaving to visit their respective families in the country – but first, where to stay?

Pausing in their uniforms outside Victoria station, assaulted by the sounds and smells of London, they were approached by the coachman of the *Cavendish* hotel who indicating to the lady waiting, invited them all to stay at the hotel. Mrs Lewis, the proprietor, often met incoming soldiers from the Flanders front and 'adopted' them for the duration of their stay.

Rosa Lewis was at the height of her social fame, a little older than Edwin. She had a flawless complexion, a good figure and dressed carefully.

But it was her personality that made her really attractive to men. She had begun life as a scullery maid at twelve – the same age Maud Manchester took to the stage – and became one of the greatest cooks in England, a friend of King Edward VII and Kaiser Wilhelm II too. (One of Rosa's first actions on the declaration of war was to take down the signed photograph of the Kaiser and hang it in the lavatory.)

Rosa Ovenden, as she was born, embarked on her career as a freelance society cook and caterer, going out to cook in some of the greatest houses in the country. Lady Randolph Churchill was the first to employ her, followed by the Savilles and the Asquiths.

Her reputation and her society contacts, many of whom became personal friends, grew until by 1897 at the age of thirty she was 'the most unusual, successful, socially acceptable caterer' in England. In 1893 Rosa had married the exotically named butler, Excelsior Tyrel Chiney Lewis. It was a marriage of convenience. A married woman would appear more respectable whilst acting as concierge of apartments in a house in Eaton Terrace, where His Royal Highness could entertain in private and discreetly. Excelsior became jealous of her many clients and admirers and eventually took to drink; the marriage was not a success.

In 1902 she purchased the lease on the fashionable *Cavendish* hotel in Jermyn and Duke Street. She said she hoped it would be something for Lewis to do for himself while she continued catering. Under his management the hotel lost money – she suspected fraud – and his drunkenness drove away custom. Rosa in her own mind at least 'separated' from Lewis, but never officially divorced. She also had him declared bankrupt owing debts of £5,000.

With customary energy, Rosa developed the *Cavendish* into a replica Edwardian country house and acted the role of perfect hostess, so that guests felt they were invited to a (slightly raffish) house party. Later some of her regular clients, such as Lord Ribblesdale and Sir William Eden took permanent rooms there and became regular clients. Eden died in his suite at the hotel in February 1915, a few months after his eldest son was killed at Ypres.

The Edwardian whirl of grand scale entertaining came to a sudden end with the outbreak of the Great War. She threw herself into the war effort by turning the hotel into 'a social first aid centre' for servicemen, rich or poor. Typical of the very singular Rosa was to invite them to stay as guests and then omit to charge them, or to provide food and drink and find the wealthiest officer to foot the bill. Thousands of 'her boys' as she called them, would later testify to her generosity. But her 'boys' were not the only guests at that time – the politicians, particularly the energetic Lloyd George still came. The generals, Kitchener, Roberts and Cowans, discussed policy there.

The young Diana Cooper, the glamorous socialite, was forbidden by her mother to enter Rosa's notorious establishment, which made it all the more enjoyable, and would visit two or three evenings a week. [3]

This was a new world for Edwin and his companions –enchanted like many others at the prospect of Rosa's exciting house party. From the moment they arrived at the Duke Street entrance and were welcomed by the hotel's ever-faithful porter Scott – followed not far behind by his faithful dog Freddy – their leave had truly begun. Through the hallway full of luggage, the large central table bearing its load of neatly folded newspapers, a Bradshaw rail guide of course and the rest of the space littered with abandoned tennis rackets and the like, and a long clock in the corner. The furniture was as dark as perhaps their future – but with the lingering smell of beeswax. Champagne and entertainment were the order of the day.

★

Amongst Edwin's fellow officers was Lieutenant James Stock, some twenty-two years younger and attached to the eighth Battalion *East Lancashire Regiment*. It had been formed in September 1914 as part of Kitchener's Third New Army and had spent the winter training in billets near Bournemouth. There was a rumour they were to proceed to France later that summer, so it was the last opportunity for leave.

Edwin and James hit it off; they swapped stories and Edwin was able to talk at least in part about the realities of the front. They both found they had links with Wales. During the first night's party it was realised Edwin and Rosa were not related (as he first thought) and there was much laughter at the confusion. However, during the party conversation Rosa revealed she knew the Welsh borders and Shropshire well. She told her enchanted audience of her employment as cook to Frank Bibby, heir to the Bibby shipping fortune, during her stay at his estate at Sansaw Hall near Shrewsbury with its extensive Victorian greenhouses. As Rosa enthused, he was a keen racing man and two of his horses had won the Grand National.

During the following day, after cashing a cheque at the Charing Cross branch of the army bankers Cox & Co., Edwin together with James strolled amongst the sandwich board men, the flower girls around Eros, messenger boys running breathlessly by, and black taxis darting through the streets, as they relaxed for a moment into the normality of civilian life.

Later they and a few others took in some West End shows, all within walking distance of the *Cavendish*. A musical comedy *Tonight's the Night* at the *Gaiety* and *Watch Your Step* at the *Empire* with music and lyrics by the American Irving Berlin. In good spirits, they returned to their hotel where Rosa, the 'cheeky, raucous cockney sparrow' was again holding court.

James Stock had promised to visit family in Wales and invited Edwin to come along, as he had lost touch with his younger brothers and sisters. He would be his guest at Brynllwydwyn House near Machynlleth – home to his grandmother Maria Campbell. In her earlier life as Maria Walmsley, she had married William Yeeles who died young leaving her with two young daughters to bring up. The daughters had married in turn, and James was her grandson by the younger daughter Caroline.

Then somewhat late in life Maria had married Francis Maule Campbell, a retired wine merchant in 1902. Campbell in his youth had been one of the eight men who formed The Football Association in 1863 and later helped codify the first Laws of the Game. He had played for *Blackheath FC* but soon withdrew the club after a disagreement about the exclusion of 'hacking' in the laws. Blackheath went its own way and followed the rugby code instead.

James' father had been an army surgeon who died in 1908; his mother now lived in Malvern. Both he (as an exhibitioner) and his older brother John were at *Keble College* Oxford before joining the army. John was now serving with the *Devonshire Regiment*.

The journey to Wales was uneventful, as they departed Paddington through the back streets of west London into the rolling green countryside which swept past the carriage windows. The train had a luncheon car and as they dined, they reminisced about the army. The train stopped at Shrewsbury, Edwin recalling it was where he left for India some twenty years earlier. The train moved onwards through Welshpool into the mountains and on to the market town of Machynlleth in the Dyfi Valley.

The house was some four miles from the station, where the pony and trap had transported them at a steady pace along a winding road, to a great welcome and an unexpected surprise. The Campbells, now in their seventies, were very hospitable and keen to learn the news, as they now lived alone with just a few servants in attendance, curiously one with the same surname as Captain Lewis.

That evening at dinner, to Edwin's surprised embarrassment he discovered that his younger sister Eliza who he hadn't seen since she was a ten-year-old – she was now thirty-three – had been employed by the Campbells as a house parlour maid.

Whilst James and the Campbell family were kind and understanding about Edwin's connection with their servant, he felt uncomfortable and embarrassed about staying longer. The following day he found some time to talk with Eliza – catching up on twenty years of family news. He had of course heard about his parents' deaths whilst in India, but little of his younger siblings.

He learnt that his brother William had married Clara Williams in 1902; they now had three children, and lived in Shrewsbury. Hugh had married Lillian Jeffreys and moved to Salisbury. Albert was a groom with the *Kings Shropshire Light Infantry* at their military stables in Coleham, he too had married – a local girl, Mary Vernon, in 1907 and was also living in Shrewsbury. They had three children, two girls and a boy, and his youngest sister Alice was still unmarried.

He spoke little of India, of his divorce or the loss of his daughter, as his family seemed strangers now. Just names he found difficult to place – he simply wanted to cut short his stay and return to London. It would be the last time Eliza or any family would hear from him.

Arriving alone at the *Cavendish*, his forlorn face was enough for Rosa's maternal instinct to take charge and do what she did best – arrange for some entertainment to cheer him up.

Tickets were obtained for the new show *Push and Go* at the Hippodrome, which had received some excellent reviews.

Together with some other 'house guests', he strolled along Jermyn Street, towards Piccadilly and to the theatre the other side of Leicester Square – they were not disappointed.

Push and Go was an extravagant revue produced by Albert De

Courville, which had opened in May. The principals were Violet Loraine and Harry Tate, together with a number of American artists including Shirley Kellogg, Arthur Swanston and Anna Wheaton.

The revue comprised of sketches rather than one single narrative, which was becoming increasingly popular in the West End during the war. It was a jingoistic show adapted to the times with an anti-German scene where a German man and his two sons sang a song entitled *"We Hate the English"*. A patriotic 'battleship scene' and a rousing rendition of *"Don't Forget the Navy"*, where British sailors are *"the true blue boys… keeping you safe and sound"* and 'the Zeppelin scene' where these airships were depicted like giant sausages, and the German sausage becomes *"ze greatest product of German genius und German Kultur."* Admiral Von Tirpitz and Field Marshall Von Hindenburg later appear in this sketch – the latter as a dachshund.

The revue had taken its name from a Lloyd George speech made as Chancellor of the Exchequer a few months before the show opened. When he described how he needed a network of able, young businessmen, known as 'push and go' men who were able to encourage greater production efficiency in factories, in response to the shortage of artillery shells available at the front. Lewis the quartermaster understood all that.

It was the American Shirley Kellogg who had started a new craze, as she sang *"Won't You Come and Play With Me?"* It had been included as an additional number in the show, originally made popular on Broadway by Anna Held, a Ziegfeld singer and actress.

From a gangplank that had been placed out towards the stalls, she would hurl dozens of rubber balls into the audience – this activity quickly caught on in other West End shows.

The audience loved the participation and on one occasion a party of officers began a bombardment of their own – Kellogg responded with such energy that the officers held out a white flag. These missiles were often carried off as trophies. Back in Flanders, one officer held the ball on the end of a bayonet and it was shot through from the German trenches whilst he sang the words from the show;

> *"Won't you come and play with me*
> *I wish you'd come and play with me,*
> *For I have such a way with me,*

A way with me, a way with me.
I have such a nice little way with me,
Do not think it wrong."

To his surprise and delight, on returning to the *Cavendish*, Rosa had invited some chorus girls from the same show to join a supper party in the Elinor Glyn room, apparently named after the romantic writer whose novel *Three Weeks* sold millions when published in 1907, a torrid story centred around a Balkan queen who was in the habit of receiving her lovers lying on a tiger skin. Glyn is credited with popularising the concept of the 'It Girl', a term for a beautiful, stylish young woman who possesses sex appeal without flaunting her sexuality.

The young girls arrived famished, and surrounded by dazzling uniforms of all descriptions, they tucked in to the sandwiches and devilled chicken Rosa's kitchen had provided, and were warmly welcomed to the room's impressively ample purple couch. Rosa had chosen well, the three prettiest 'It' girls to enchant 'her boys', as she called the soldiers.

Mary German and Maggie Matthews – Dorothy's closest friends – had been in the show from the beginning and had been instrumental in persuading her to come to the party, as it was her first time to venture out since her mother died in March.

The champagne flowed and Edwin and Dorothy found themselves talking about the show and how much fun it had been. Someone in the supper party produced a ball – a souvenir of the show, and the girls were encouraged to throw it in the air in turns amongst the soldiers in the room. Edwin caught Dorothy's throw, and for the first time since leaving India he was enjoying himself and enchanted by the attention of this bubbly, petit young dancer.

-10-

A marriage of convenience

The *Push and Go* revue did very nicely, and some weeks later attracted the visiting Belgian King Albert and his wife Queen Elizabeth of Bavaria, guests of King George V and Queen Mary. By the late summer, to her dismay, Dorothy realised she was pregnant.

Lewis had returned to France and slipped into the quartermaster's routine of following up on equipment, learning that the recent shortages should now improve with the promised Lloyd George reforms. The battalion had moved to another sector of the Somme, giving them time to consolidate the trench lines.

As September came to a close there was a combined British and French offensive around Artois-Loos using gas for the first time – some of it drifting back on the British lines. The aim was to break through the German Front, but it did not succeed in making any headway and they suffered heavy casualties. In early October bad weather closed in.

Some months after his return, Lewis received a parcel from the *Cavendish* hotel in London. Intrigued, he opened it to find a selection of Fortnum's biscuits, jam, and of course tea together with a letter written by Rosa on blue hotel notepaper, emblazoned with the hotel's motto *"In Deo Confido"*. She explained about the approach by Dorothy seeking his contact details, and also explaining why.

She reminded him of his stay, and suggested replying using the *Cavendish* as an address where Dorothy could be contacted. The *Cavendish* had long been used as a 'Poste Restante' by the *habitués*. She also ventured to say in forthright Rosa fashion that on his next leave she would be happy to host a wedding breakfast. Lewis was stunned and then equally thrilled, as his thoughts returned to those happy moments during his leave. His response was immediate.

There was a regimental rumour they would be returning to England – and transferred elsewhere. Since the Second Battalion had landed in France nine months earlier, only six of the original eighteen officers remained alive – in addition they had also lost 287 of their men. The old battalion had changed irrevocably. Lewis was now forty-six and feeling his age, and with the strain of warfare his health was affected. A few days later the rumour became a reality with the news that the battalion was to return to England by the end of October.

In the meantime, after her visit to Rosa at the *Cavendish,* whose practical maternal advice had been to *"get as much out of men as you can",* Dorothy was still appearing nightly at the *Hippodrome.*

She had eventually confided in her Aunt Charlotte – her father's older sister in Highbury. Her father had been drinking heavily since the death of his beloved Maud, and who knew how he would react without her calming influence. It was fortunate she did. Dorothy showed Charlotte Lewis's reply letter addressed to Miss D. Abbott c/o *The Cavendish*, Duke Street, London, as Rosa was acting as the go-between. It was clear he would agree to marry her.

Charlotte was aware that Parliament had passed a malevolent piece of legislation two years earlier known as the 'Mental Deficiency Act', that allowed women to be classified as moral imbeciles as well as mental ones; this included unmarried mothers who could not support themselves, and Dorothy would fall into that category. Some of these women didn't even have to be medically diagnosed to be classified as an 'imbecile' and could be committed, if under twenty-one, merely on the word of a parent or even guardian – never to emerge from the institutions in which they were incarcerated. The Act was only repealed in 1959. [5]

Charlotte, now in her forties, had never married, was naturally independent and keen on the suffrage movement. Since the retirement of her father John James Abbott, she had taken over the family insurance business in Bishopsgate, although she still continued with her writing. She had always been the sensible one in the Abbott family and would arrange to meet Lewis on his next leave.

That was sooner than expected as the *Shropshires* had now landed in England. The battalion had been regrouped and now formed part of the twenty-seventh division, ordered to Salonika in the Balkans in November. Their embarkation began on the 17th but Lewis would remain in England;

due to his age and health he had been seconded to a staff job, where his knowledge and skills could be used effectively in the rapidly expanding War Office.

He would be attached to the Quartermaster General's directorate under the very able Major General Sir John Cowans. Edwin had known of him since his appointment as Director-General of Military Education for the Indian Army under Lord Kitchener. This directorate quickly outgrew the War Office in Whitehall and spilled into various locations around London, where the expanded team would support the fighting men at the front. The government had requisitioned the *Metropole Hotel* in Northumberland Avenue, to provide accommodation for government staff. Described when it opened in 1885: "... *the hotel's location particularly recommends it to ladies and families visiting the West End during the Season; to travellers from Paris and the Continent, arriving from Dover and Folkestone at the Charing Cross Terminus;...*" After the war the hotel would be the location of the famous 'Midnight Follies', London's first cabaret-style evening entertainment.

Although still under military command, for the first time since leaving India Lewis had found himself a desk job, and whilst often long hours it offered greater flexibility and some weekends free.

★

The Abbott family had generations of connections in Devon, and in many cases Charlotte was still handling the insurance policies of many people in Barnstaple and the surrounding villages. Charlotte had found a couple who would be happy to adopt an Abbott family child – the youngest son in William Goaman's family. The Goamans had farmed for generations at Woolfardisworthy (pronounced Woolsery), about ten miles westward towards Hartland. Titus was the seventh child of Elizabeth Tucker, his Cornish mother, who had died when he was four.

Old William had remarried Jane Rodgers with whom he had another child. His forty-one acre farm could not provide for all and Titus had left home to seek work in industrialised south Wales as a carpenter and joiner, returning home from time to time. In Wales, he had met and married Frances Cook in 1908 and they were now living in Treforest, a village on the River Taff, south-east of Pontypridd. After eight years of marriage, they were so far childless.

Although Dorothy had been compelled to marry Edwin, she was adamant she didn't want the baby and despite being pregnant was devoid of any maternal feelings, and determined to finish the show. *Push and Go* was due to close in late December, and her closest friends Mary and Maggie were already in rehearsals for a new Albert de Courville revue *Joyland*, again with Harry Tate and the effervescent Shirley Kellogg, due to open on 23 December.

Dorothy Maud, now seventeen years old and six months pregnant, had moved into Edwin's lodgings at 61 Cartwright Gardens, a boarding house in Camden, today known as the *Harlingford Hotel*. In one of its earlier incarnations it had been the home of the famous publisher Andrew Chatto, the founder of Chatto & Windus.

During the day, from her second floor window overlooking the square, she would watch soldiers drilling and training in the gardens opposite. Unknown to her at the time, amongst those young soldiers was the twenty-two-year-old Shropshire-born poet Wilfred Owen, who had just joined the *Second Artists Rifles*. As he wrote to his mother:

> "… *We do all this in shirt sleeves in Cartwright Gardens, a 'crescent-garden' bounded by the usual boarding houses. I have scarcely seen an officer. … we had to practice salutes (on trees) this very morning… it is really no great strain to strut around a West End square for six or seven hours a day, walking abroad one is admiration of all little boys and meets an approving glance from everyone…*"

Three years later, he was killed a week before the armistice in 1918. Most of his poems were published posthumously, which include – perhaps prophetically – "Anthem for Doomed Youth".

★

In contrast, whilst the pregnant Dorothy was preparing to marry Edwin, the newspapers were full of another 'peer and the showgirl' story, this time concerning the actress Evie Carew and her so-called scandalous marriage with a serving officer, Rowland Winn. The Winn family knew nothing of the wedding until the *Daily Mirror* reported the story in December 1915. The newspaper claimed that the couple had married eight weeks earlier, by special licence at St Saviour's Church, Paddington and that *"not even the bridegroom's nearest relatives had been aware of the romance"*. Evie Carew was described by the paper as *"one of the most beautiful and charming chorus girls on the London stage"* whilst Rowland's bravery was commended with the newspaper reporting that *"he had gone to the front almost at the beginning of the war"* and had *"more than once been severely wounded"*. Despite all that, Evie and Rowland's marriage was to be a success.

On a very wet, but rather mild December day, the 23rd, a simple marriage ceremony took place at St Pancras registry office at the top of Judd Street, a short walk from Cartwright Gardens. The seventeen-year-old Dorothy married Captain Edwin Lewis, automatically, carelessly and without love. He was forty-seven. Unlike her mother and grandmother she was able to write her name. Mary German and Margaret Matthews, her friends from the show, were the only witnesses.

Despite the standing invitation they did not hold a wedding breakfast at the *Cavendish*.

On signing their marriage certificate, Edwin and Dorothy were both 'economical with the truth'. Although Dorothy declared her real birth name, she wrote her age as nineteen and created a fictitious naval title (captain) for her father; he might have been amused by that had he been there. Edwin too lowered his age a little saying he was forty-five, and gave his deceased father a fictional first name and elevated his status, declaring him James 'of independent means' – he was in fact William, a farm bailiff when he died fifteen years earlier.

Edwin, for the sake of Victorian propriety, had given his address as *Beacon House*, Torquay, although in truth he had actually stayed there earlier. It was a small private hotel, run by Lucy and her elderly husband John Crossley, located close to the sea front taking up numbers 8 and 9 Beacon Terrace. It was his base whilst arranging a nursing home for Dorothy's confinement – away from the feared Zeppelin raids of London.

Lewis had found a suitable place for the childbirth at the Kent House nursing home in the Falkland Road. He had booked it for three weeks. Nothing it seemed was too good for his wife and forthcoming baby. It was a splendid late Georgian town house that had been built in the 1830s on a rise, with rear gardens overlooking Torre Abbey and the bay beyond.

However, when Dorothy arrived and unpacked, the matron noticed she had not brought any baby clothes, [6] an indication of her intention.

Ellen Hollis was an experienced nurse manager, in her fifties, who with her French nursing partner Maria Camus and her younger sister managed the nursing home. They had several servants and a cook and were looking after a variable group of five or six patients. She had on call if needed the Irish-born doctor Walter Halpin, an experienced surgeon and physician in his late fifties who resided with his wife and daughter next door in Falkland Lodge.

On Friday 3rd March 1916, Dorothy was safely delivered of a healthy baby girl. Edwin was elated by the news but Dorothy was simply relieved.

They had put a personal advertisement under 'girl for adoption' in the *Western Mail,* a newspaper circulating in south Wales, in order to provide Titus and Frances (and any neighbour who read it) with some evidence of the propriety of the arrangement.

Edwin eventually registered the birth on the 24th and reluctantly recorded the baby's name as agreed. He used the proposed adopted mother's chosen name, Ethel Florence Goaman – but recorded Edwin Lewis and Dorothy Maud Lewis, formerly Abbott, as the parents. Any last hope that his newly married wife just might change her mind and keep their daughter was dashed. Devoid of any maternal instincts, she was adamant about giving the child away.

The nursing staff at Kent House as instructed took the baby girl to Torquay railway station and there met and handed her to Titus and Frances Goaman. Everything had been arranged. The Goamans returned to south Wales with their baby daughter and the start of a new family life.

At that time child adoption had no legal status in Britain. It was an informal and generally secretive procedure, which gave the adoptive parents no rights whatsoever. A biological parent could (and in some cases, did) appear at any time and demand custody of a child they had neither seen nor contributed to the care of for years at a time. This continued until 1926, when the first Parliamentary Act was passed which regulated this in England and Wales. However the Goamans were assured this would not happen, and it didn't.

During Dorothy's confinement, Lewis had been invited to stay with Charlotte Abbott and her elderly father in Highbury. On returning to London from Torquay he had hoped they just might perhaps begin their marriage again. Dorothy had other ideas. She was a strongly independent girl – with something of her mother's confidence – now particularly aware of her manipulative charm on older men. For Dorothy, the transition from ingénue chorus girl to shrewd actress had begun.

★

Later that summer, Dorothy received the news that Aunt Minnie, her mother's older sister, had died at the age of fifty-two, and with her death all close ties with the Manchester family had gone. Although unknown to her, she had a younger cousin with aspirations for the stage too. Rene was Robert Manchester's youngest daughter (her mother's older brother) –she would become a dancer performing under the stage name of 'Renee Chester'. Renee would receive modest reviews as she danced and sang through the twenties and thirties in various touring musicals like *Seaside Frolics* and *Sea Dogs*, and a pantomime *Little Jack Horner* at the *Alhambra*.

Since the marriage to Lewis and the birth of her daughter, Dorothy had grown apart from her father – they were never close anyway, she had lived away for much of her early childhood he was in many ways a stranger. Her younger brother Jack was now ten and still at school. William – never very good at families – had been unable to cope with events given to bouts of drinking and Jack had often been sent to relatives in Barnstaple, as his daughter later recalls: *"I always felt that he had not had an easy life and did not enjoy a normal happy childhood."* [7]. William now had his French wife Marie Louise, who fortunately had taken a shine to young Jack.

Dorothy had already created a fictitious persona for her father and was beginning to leave her past behind.

Edwin had wished that their marriage could perhaps survive but deep down probably knew it was a forlorn hope. Dorothy did not want the domesticity of marriage, and she simply didn't want children. She wanted the opportunity to use her talents and the freedom life on the stage offered. She had persuaded Lewis she would be unhappy playing the seventeen-year-old housewife, and perhaps deep down in herunspoken knowledge, feared she would end up being his nursemaid too.

By the autumn Dorothy was back on the stage under her maiden name, as if nothing had happened.

The years that followed their relationship – such as it was – reflected in many ways that of her mother Maud Manchester and first husband Harry. It was doomed by separation.

Edwin had given her a small allowance, opening an account with Cox & Co., and alone again, moved from one residential hotel to another as his health deteriorated.

The solitude was only interrupted with occasional visits from Dorothy – when she was in town or needed extra money. Their relationship had metamorphosed from brief lovers to one of daughter and surrogate father.

-11-

In praise of older men

With this freedom, Dorothy had secured a part in W. Buchanan Taylor's roaring farce ironically titled *Snookums' being the Adventures of the Newlyweds and their Baby*. It had earlier successfully toured Scotland, and due to cast changes, gave Dorothy an opportunity. One of the touring actors Eric Melbourne was arrested at the *Sheffield Hippodrome* for failing to present himself under the Military Service Act –to which he pleaded guilty, and was promptly arrested. Dorothy was now able to show off her talents twice nightly, as the farce continued its provincial tour. The tour moved to Hull in September followed by the *Hippodrome* in Manchester's Oxford Street, and the week after at the *Royal Hippodrome* in Liverpool where the local paper the *Post & Mercury* wrote a favourable review:

> *"… Buchanan Taylor's farce has laughter writ large across every page of the book, introduces the newlyweds and their baby. The farce entitled 'Snookums' is fashioned upon the ideas embodied in the cartoons of Mr George McManus. Last evening's audiences found much enjoyment in the following adventures of Mr and Mrs and Baby Newlywed. There is some pleasing music… and the dresses and scenery are big factors in the spectacular features. A capable cast includes Miss Rhoda Gordon, Miss Dorothy Abbott…"*

The concert party ended with a performance at the *Palace Theatre*, Bath in early December. It had been a reasonably successful tour and more importantly Dorothy was back on the stage, in the theatrical thick of it and making new friends.

★

For Edwin it was a routine desk job at the Quartermasters Directorate in Whitehall, and a lifetime of army discipline had stood him in good stead. He would avidly scan the newspapers looking for familiar names. The casualty lists published regularly would feature those killed on the Western Front and elsewhere, a constant reminder the country was at war and paying a heavy price. That November he was saddened to read about the death of Captain James Stock with whom he had shared his brief leave at the *Cavendish* and later in Wales; he had been killed in action on the 15th in the Somme offensive. He was twenty-five.

Whilst he was ruminating on the loss of most of his fellow officers in the old battalion, he received a letter from the War Office just before Christmas, December 1916. He was to be promoted to Major, a satisfying acknowledgment of his twenty-five years' service in the army with the *Kings Shropshire Light Infantry* – in peace and war, and comforting to know he'd receive a welcome increase in pay.

★

Dorothy no doubt shared Edwin's exciting promotion and graciously decided to use her married name in future shows. She had secured a London chorus role in the Ugar and Langley musical revue *Crackers*, described as a 'bon-bon of delight in two pulls and a bang', before it went on tour to the provinces.

The revue opened to good reviews at the *New Empire*, Burnley in February 1917, *"The stage settings are the prettiest imaginable as are also the dresses. Mr Ugar is the funny man, with a whirlwind of quips and jokes. Set in a Cracker factory where the girls are prepared to go on strike… The chorus of girls deport themselves charmingly."*

The travelling concert party continued to the *Theatre Royal* at Exeter in April, *Empire Theatre*, Sunderland in May, *Empire Theatre*, Bristol in June, *Empire*, Middlesbrough and *Rotunda*, Liverpool both in July. After the tour, on returning to London, Dorothy learnt her last surviving grandparent – her grandfather John Abbott – had died in Islington during March. He was eighty-two.

★

That summer Edwin received notice that because of his failing health he would be invalided out of the army in September at the age of forty-eight, receiving a life-time pension at the rank of major. He would receive about fifty-six shillings per week. It was just enough to live on.

The pre-war average weekly wage varied from twenty-six to thirty-four shillings, but at the same time, half the women employed were only receiving around ten to fifteen shillings. As the war demands progressed, London bus drivers in 1917 were earning sixty shillings per week; cleaners, never the best paid, were getting forty shillings.

By 1918 even agricultural labourers, the lowest paid manual workers were earning sixty to seventy shillings a week. Munitions workers earned considerably more, anything from 120 shillings to an astonishing 200 or even 400 shillings per week.

By January 1918, Edwin's health was not getting any better, after a relapse – the first since retirement – he took to the south coast for the sea air to convalesce, taking a room at the *Haslemere Private Hotel* in Montpelier Road which runs directly down to the Brighton sea front. Whilst staying at the hotel he received notice that he was eligible for the newly authorised Silver War Badge, awarded to all military personnel who were discharged as a result of sickness or wounds contracted or received during the war, either at home or overseas.

During and after the war, tens of thousands suffered mental disorder, palpitations, dizziness, insomnia, headaches –and for want of a better diagnosis they were all lumped together as victims of shell shock or 'gas neurosis'.

The badge had been issued after numerous assaults by members of the women's suffrage movement who had asked their members to give white feathers (the sign of the coward) in the streets to men who appeared to be of military age to shame them into service.

★

The Ugar and Langley revue *Crackers* had been a great success and was due to go on tour yet again, with Harry Ugar and Ella Langley and a new cast. By the time the revue had reached the *Grand Theatre*, Derby in May Dorothy had managed to get herself out of the chorus and was now enjoying second billing.

The revue returned again in July by popular demand, and as the *Derby Daily Telegraph* conceded:

"... and the other characters are all capably sustained... including Miss Dorothy Lewis as Memie... The singing of both the solos and concert party was above average, and there is a very capable orchestra. Altogether 'Crackers' provide a pleasant twice nightly show."

The tour included other major cities; Manchester *Metropole*, Salford *Royal Hippodrome*, Birmingham *Theatre Royal*, Aston and *Bordesley Palace Theatre*. The week of the New Year was spent in Scotland with Dorothy on stage at the *Alhambra Theatre*, Stirling, with a demanding week's schedule which included special holiday matinees over four days at 2.30, followed by twice nightly, 6.50 and 8.50pm.

★

The war of opposing armies had been reduced to a stalemate with its series of ebb and flow attrition. The battles on the Western Front, gradually absorbing and then killing thousands of young men in a series of battles with names that still reverberate in the country's collective consciousness, Ypres, Loos, the mud at Passchendaele and Somme and by the end over a million – the flower of a generation – had been lost.

The Americans had joined the Allies in 1917, but were not effectively deployed on the Western Front until May 1918.

Then in that summer the collapse of the Central Powers came swiftly. Bulgaria was the first to sign an armistice, on 29 September; on 30 October, the Ottoman Empire capitulated, signing the Armistice of Mudros, then on 4 November the Austro-Hungarian Empire agreed to an armistice, and finally Germany, which had its own trouble with revolutionaries, agreed to an armistice on 11 November 1918 – the eleventh hour of the eleventh day of the eleventh month, ending the war in victory for the Allies. A formal state of war between the two sides persisted for another seven months, until the signing of the Treaty of Versailles with Germany on 28 June 1919.

With the end of hostilities, the big government war machine started to dismantle. The army Quartermaster General John Cowan's work was finished and he was awarded the Grand Cross of the Order of the Bath (GCB). He then abruptly left the War Office in March 1919 to accept a lucrative job invitation from Shell Transport and Trading Company. Leaving the army gave him the freedom to express his disgust at the absence of any reference to the work of the administrative services of the army in Parliament's expression of thanks to the armed forces in July 1919. His letter of protest to Lloyd George was followed by a speech accepting the freedom of his home city, Carlisle, in September 1919. The press reported that he told the audience: *"… the war was essentially a contest of administration, rather than strategy, and asserted that the Quartermasters department had succeeded in meeting all demands placed upon it."* The report went on to say, *"In his opinion the omission (in the parliamentary expression of thanks to the armed services) was lamentable. He mentioned the matter in fairness to his administrative subordinates and co-workers of all grades who did so magnificently, and ensured the success of our fighting men (applause)".* [8]

Reading the newspaper report, Edwin felt proud his war service had been vindicated. In October he applied for his war medals, receiving the '1914–15 Star', 'British War Medal' and the 'Victory Medal'.

Edwin was now living in Surbiton at the *Mountcombe Private Hotel* (Kingston 12651) run by a young couple Timothy and Suzette Ratcliffe. The hotel in Oak Hill Grove was conveniently close to the railway station – just a short walk away. The service to London Waterloo took about thirty minutes, now the newly electrified line had been installed a few years earlier.

★

Shortly after the New Year of 1919 the *Cracker* revue had ended at the *Tivoli Theatre*, Aberdeen in January, with a moderate review from the local newspaper *The Daily Journal* exclaiming that Dorothy Lewis as Memie, a 'flapper', was *"charming in her role"*. The flapper description – particularly in northern England at that time was slang for any lively teenage girl. In the 1920s after the big social changes that followed the end of the First World War, it was used for any young woman, especially one who behaved and dressed in a boldly unconventional manner. They were seen as brash for wearing excessive make-up, drinking, treating sex in a casual manner, smoking, driving automobiles, and otherwise flouting social and sexual norms.

Dorothy returned to London by train in February a few weeks after her twentieth birthday. She had telephoned Edwin at the *Mountcombe* in Surbiton, and he agreed to meet her for lunch at *Monico's* in Piccadilly. It was a sumptuous restaurant in Shaftesbury Avenue which had been opened in the 1880s by two Italian brothers, becoming very popular with well-heeled diners and theatre-goers as their supper restaurant was open till late.

There were dining rooms on several floors marble was lavishly used inside, for the staircase, and for the columns and arches framing the walnut screens that separated the vestibule from the grill-room and bar. Their reflective mirrored walls surrounding the high ceiling would also enhance Dorothy's natural beauty.

She was already waiting for him, sitting at the table alone as he arrived in full uniform. The lunch was attentively served but uneventful, and Edwin briefly basked in the attention his attractive young wife drew. The subject of money came up and he agreed to increase her allowance.

They left together but departed separately; Dorothy headed for the *Rehearsal Club* a short distance away in Leicester Square to catch up on theatrical gossip and news. She was about to audition for her biggest part yet.

Later at one of the many post-show parties, she was introduced to a convivial and wealthy Scottish aristocrat who was a little older – well, nineteen years older – the second Baronet of Newhailes, a large estate near Edinburgh, which he had inherited from his father two years earlier. He lived mostly in London, and had served as a lieutenant commander in the navy during the war.

He had resigned his commission the previous summer, and explained he was conveniently estranged from his wife. His name was Sir David Charles Herbert Dalrymple. He had seen the revue *Crackers* several times, and to him she appeared as his 'bon-bon of delight in two pulls and a bang' – they hit it off immediately, and it led to an affair.

★

The mood of Britain after the Great War had speeded up change dramatically and with it acceptance of cultural changes once unthinkable. It made for a general feeling that life was short and should be enjoyed.

The war also broke down long-standing class barriers. The break was subtle, but the erosion had begun.

Enjoyment was to be the new currency; amongst other things the war had introduced the American influence in music and drinking cocktails. This was the dawn of the jazz age and for the affluent, *Martinis* were the drink of choice.

It would become the era of the 'bright young things', which was how the tabloid press described the young party-loving aristocrats and socialites hell-bent on enjoying themselves – often to excess. Their exploits were to inspire a number of writers, including Nancy Mitford, Anthony Powell, and Evelyn Waugh.

The winsome young actress Dorothy Lewis was eager to become part of the social fun, and David Dalrymple delighted in being her new partner. She was everything that his wife Margaret wasn't – half her age for a start, but there were two things that stood in their way.

Act III
Lord Dalrymple Entertains
(1919–1932)

"Hello, Hello, Who's yer lady friend?
Who's the little lady by your side?"

The opening lines to a popular music hall song of the time, to which the acting
Lady 'Dorothy' introduces Cynthia and Mirabelle … and emerges as Dodo

-12-

The Albion affair

Brighton, originally a fishing village on the Sussex coast, had earned its raffish reputation since the Regency period, and later a more insalubrious reputation as a 'dirty-weekend' destination.

The Prince Regent, later George IV, had commissioned architect John Nash to build a wildly extravagant summer palace, the Royal Pavilion, in the late eighteenth century where he would entertain his mistresses. The Prince's subsequent patronage led to the increase of court followers and by 1780 the building of Georgian terraces that characterise the classic streetscape had started, and the town quickly became the fashionable resort of Brighton.

Hotels followed trade and the *Royal York Hotel* opened in 1819 at Steine Place, followed by the *Albion* built to four floor levels in the classical style a short distance away in 1826. The *Albion* was subject of a sketch by painter J. M. W. Turner in 1834, during one of his coastal expeditions. By 1847 due to its frequent patronage by a number of distinguished visitors, it had changed its name to the *Royal Albion* and the royal coat of arms was duly placed over the entrance.

Queen Victoria disliked Brighton and the lack of privacy the Pavilion afforded her on visits there, especially once Brighton became accessible to Londoners by rail in 1841. She moved to Osborne House on the Isle of Wight.

The renowned philanthropist Angela Burdett-Coutts was widely known as 'the richest heiress in England'; a friend of Charles Dickens and the Duke of Wellington, she would regularly spend part of the year in the *Royal Albion Hotel* with her long-term companion, Hannah.

In February 1894 Oscar Wilde stayed in a room overlooking the sea whilst working on his *Poems in Prose*, the collective title of six prose poems published in July that year in *The Fortnightly Review*.

But by the early 1900s, the popularity of Britain's seaside resorts was once again in decline. Rich and fashionable visitors had departed for more exotic climes, the middle classes were moving further afield, and trade mostly consisted of day-trippers. Around this time, the *Daily Mail* newspaper described it as an *"unenterprising, unattractive and outdated holiday resort"*.

In 1906, Harry Preston, a fifty-year-old charismatic and well-liked local figure in Brighton had bought the hotel and four years later he carried out large-scale alterations, creating a roof garden which overlooked the Palace Pier.

In the newly refurbished hotel, Arnold Bennett began writing part of his *Clayhanger* trilogy while staying in 1910. The same year as Frenchman Andre Beaumont in his Blériot monoplane flew around the skies of Brighton, taking Preston as a passenger. Afterwards he hosted a banquet at the *Royal Albion Hotel* to celebrate the event. Harry, a former publican, had entered the hotel business around the turn of the century. Preston had a wonderful feel for publicity, and he wined and dined the editors of the London newspapers, encouraging them to promote the town and his new hotel to visitors, especially motorists. It started to be referred to as 'London-by-Sea'.

Harry's wife Ellen died in 1913 and a year later he married Edith Collings, the *Royal Albion*'s manageress.

Soon the hotel's fortunes improved and notable guests started to flock again, with many authors, artists, actors and sportsmen residing there throughout the 1920s and 30s.

Over two weekends in March and again after Easter in April 1919, the hotel entertained two guests who signed the hotel's register as Sir David and Lady Dorothy Dalrymple. Away from the prying eyes of friends in London, the party-loving pair was enjoying an affair, but it hadn't been un-noticed.

As the lyrics of a popular music hall song of the time declared;
> *"Hello, Hello, Who's yer lady friend?*
> *Who's the little lady by your side?*

I've seen you, with a girl or two –
Oh! oh! oh! I am surprised at you."

Hello, Hello, stop your little games,
Don't you think your ways you ought to mend?
It isn't the girl I saw you with at Brighton,
Who, who, who's yer lady friend?"

Margaret Dalrymple, the thirty-nine-year-old long-suffering wife of Sir David, believed she had good reason to suspect his fidelity, and unknown to them both, they were followed by her enquiry agent.

-13-

Marriage amongst the clans

The Dalrymples had produced generations of advocates and politicians and embedded themselves within Scottish aristocracy and the establishment. Through marriages they are closely linked with the clans Stewart, Fergusson and Kennedy. All can trace their heritage back to the time of Robert the Bruce and earlier, and through the Stewarts have links to the monarchy.

★

Margaret Anna Dalrymple (née McTaggart-Stewart) had been born in Marylebone in 1880, the middle of three daughters; Susanna born 1878, Frances in 1887 and a younger brother Edward Orde born in 1883. These were the children of Sir Mark McTaggart-Stewart, and Marianne Susanna, heiress to Sir John McTaggart, a Liberal Member of Parliament who became the first Baronet in 1841. After Sir John's death he inherited through his wife the Ardwell estate, overlooking Luce Bay in Galloway some ten miles south of Stranraer, and they became known as the McTaggart-Stewarts. He was a Scottish Tory Member of Parliament for Wigtown Burghs and later Kirkcudbright, created the first Baronet of Southwick in 1892; his country house was twelve miles south of Dumfries, between the rugged foothills of the Boreland Range and the shores of the Solway Firth.

Susanna at twenty-three was the first to marry and became a baroness, having married the thirty-four-year-old Archie Borthwick the twentieth baronet in 1901 at Ardwell, the church of the McTaggart-Stewarts. His grandfather Patrick, the fifteenth baron, had been appointed the first manager of the National Bank of Scotland, when it was founded in Edinburgh 1825. Their Scottish estate was Ravenstone Castle in Wigtownshire, but they spent their time largely in London. Archie followed his father as a partner in the London stockbroker's Borthwick, Wark & Co. in Capthall Court, E.C. They had one daughter, Isolde.

Archie was the only son amongst a family of four sisters. The eldest, Gabrielle was the more outspoken and eccentric who Dorothy would meet by coincidence later in the story.

After a long illness, Archie died in 1910 and Susanna married again in 1916, this time to the sixty-six-year-old Alfred William Maitland FitzRoy, becoming the Duchess of Grafton. They had two daughters.

Her eldest sister Frances had married Archibald Kennedy, Earl of Cassillis (pronounced 'Cassels') in 1903. They had no children and in 1938 he became the fourth Marquess of Ailsa. The title was taken from the Island of Ailsa Craig in the Firth of Clyde, owned by the family. Like Frances, Archie was born in London, a Scottish peer and advocate, and as Marquess of Ailsa, the hereditary Clan Chief of Clan Kennedy. The family's seats included the 300-acre estate Cassillis House and the cliff top Culzean Castle, near Maybole, Ayrshire.

Margaret divided her time between the Dalrymple estate Newhailes in Scotland, and London, living in an apartment at 3 Egerton Mansions in Kensington a short walk from *Harrods*, with her young son Mark who was now four.

She had met David in London at a party whilst he was on leave from the navy, serving as a lieutenant on HMS *Falcon*, a destroyer, part of the channel flotilla. Both parents were prominent Scottish politicians, and the engagement was announced in *The Times* in October; in December Sir Charles Dalrymple was sworn in as a member of His Majesty King Edward VII's Privy Council at Buckingham Palace.

David and Margaret were married six months later in April 1906. It was a society wedding held at St George's, Hanover Square. Margaret was twenty-six and David twenty-seven. The press embellished his rank, no doubt due to family informers announcing him as lieutenant commander, although he was still just a lieutenant.

A few years after his marriage, David's naval career sailed into difficulties. On Trafalgar Day 1908 he was held to blame for fouling his ship HMS *Moy*, a river class destroyer, due to faulty navigation. The

Admiralty were beginning to ask questions about his ability to keep discipline and suspected he was drinking.

In 1910 he was appointed to serve on HMS *Monmouth*, an armoured cruiser on the China Station in the Far East. Margaret had joined him later in Singapore. The Royal Navy's duties in peacetime would consist of patrols and exercises as well as a regular round of entertaining and cocktail parties. The 'Cockers-P' parties as they are known in the navy have been hosted on board *navy* ships since the time of Admiral Nelson.

Officers would entertain guests with the customary cocktails like *Pink Gins*, created by adding a dash of Angostura bitters, usually to Plymouth gin as it is sweeter that the traditional London Dry. Later the navy would add brandy to a non-alcoholic mixture of ginger ale, ice and lemon peel, to create the *Horse's Neck* cocktail – garnished with a touch of Angostura bitters, with a long curl of lemon peel from which it gets its name. It would be prepared in jugs served in industrial quantities alongside gin and tonic.

Entertaining on board has traditionally played an important role in British unofficial foreign policy. Arriving at an overseas port, His Majesty's ships were inevitably welcomed by foreign dignitaries and ministers' officials who would talk more freely on board than they might in more formal settings. There was also the morale-boosting aspect to the parties for some of the ship's company, as unattached local women were often invited.

This social activity took its toll on David – already a bibulous party man – when in February 1911 things came to a head. Captain Duff wrote in his record: *"Whether temperate, I am not prepared to say that this officer is of temperate habit."*

Admiral Winsloe, Commander in Chief (C in C) China Station expressed: *"… his severe displeasure with regard to the disobedience of Lieutenant Dalrymple and general un-officer like conduct, improper absence and untruthfulness. Lt. Dalrymple to be sent home by the first government opportunity."*

David requested permission to retire instead but permission was refused. In March it was announced that: *"Lt. Dalrymple has been dismissed ship by sentence of Court Martial. He intends going home at own expense."* [1]

In April, Dalrymple formally resigned his commission; he was now a civilian after eighteen years in the navy.

That summer, David and Margaret returned to Scotland taking a leisurely and longer route across the Pacific and North America. Having taken passage to Japan, they sailed from Yokohama aboard the Oriental Steamship SS *Chiyo Maru*, which had been built for the first-class trade to North America. Their journey took them via Honolulu, arriving in San Francisco in July 1911.

During the long journey home they conceived their first child and David had decided on his return to England to use his knowledge by applying for a Merchant Navy Master's Ticket.

Back in England, on 17 January 1912, the Board of Trade duly granted him a 'Certificate of Service as Master of a Foreign-going Ship'. Their first child, a daughter named Dorothea Mary, was born in London in March.

Their apartment in Egerton Mansions in Kensington, not far from the Dalrymple family home in Onslow Gardens, would be their London family home for the next ten years or so. The summer and Christmas holidays were spent at Newhailes in Scotland with the Dalrymples or MacTaggart-Stewarts.

In the spring of 1914, Margaret heard her mother, Marianne Susanna Ommaney, Lady MacTaggart-Stewart had died at Ardwell House. She was seventy-four.

The outbreak of war in August 1914 brought the summery idyll of the Edwardian age to a cataclysmic end, and spoiled a perfectly beautiful bank holiday.

At the Oval, Jack Hobbs batting for Surrey against Nottinghamshire in front of a 17,000-strong crowd steadily scored 226. Families who had spent their holiday at the seaside found trains packed with regular soldiers and reservists rushing back to headquarters.

As the British Foreign Secretary, Sir Edward Grey stood at a window in his room at the Foreign Office on the evening of Monday, August 3, watching the lamps being lit as dusk approached, he famously remarked to his old friend John Spender, editor of the *Westminster Gazette*: "*The lamps are going out all over Europe. We shall not see them lit again in our time.*"

The coming war was the sole topic of conversation in shops and offices on Tuesday 4 August, as no announcement came during the day. Then as Big Ben struck eleven o'clock in London, and the government had received no reply from Berlin to the British ultimatum, Churchill, First Lord of the Admiralty, sends a telegram to the Fleet: *"COMMENCE HOSTILITIES AGAINST GERMANY."*

King George V wrote in his diary:

"I held a Council at 10.45 to declare war with Germany. It is a terrible catastrophe but it is not our fault. An enormous crowd collected outside the Palace; we went on to the balcony both before and after dinner. When they heard that war had been declared, the excitement increased and May and I with David (the Prince of Wales) *went on to the balcony; the cheering was terrific. Please God it may soon be over and that he will protect dear Bertie's life* (serving with the Royal Navy – later George VI). *Bed at 12.00."*

★

In November 1914, Margaret now three months pregnant with her second child suffered the devastating death of her young daughter Dorothea Mary – she was just two and a half. They had been staying at Ardwell House, the Scottish estate of her maternal grandfather.

Just after the turn of the century, the MacTaggart- Stewarts had funded the building of a new church within the grounds of their estate which was gifted to the Church of Scotland in 1902. A little further away is the small Kirkmadrine Memorial Chapel, devoted to the memory of the MacTaggart-Stewarts of Ardwell, and their little granddaughter Dorothea is remembered in an inscribed floor tablet:

"In Memory of Dorothea Mary Dalrymple Born March 12th 1912 Died at Ardwell November 21st 1914 Daughter of David and Margaret Dalrymple of Newhailes and Granddaughter of Sir Mark and Lady MacTaggart-Stewart."

★

In August 1914 the British Expeditionary Force embarked for France – and amongst the many vessels leaving, on board the SS *Gloucester Castle* were twenty-five civilian motorists and their cars, all members of the *Royal Automobile Club*. They had placed their services at the disposal of the B.E.F and were now destined to drive officers of the General Staff and Cavalry Division as required. Then in September the Club again offered cars and drivers to the Red Cross and a small unit of motor ambulances and motor cars with their drivers was sent to Boulogne to search for wounded in the neighbourhood of Cambrai and Peronne.

On 2 October, an appeal was made in *The Times* on behalf of the British Red Cross Society for funds to provide further motor ambulances. The response was overwhelming and enough money was raised to run hundreds more vehicles. Another convoy of ambulance cars with drivers and orderlies arrived in Boulogne just seven days later. The work of the Joint War Committee motor ambulance department expanded quickly and soon included hospital trains as well. In 1915 a transport unit was established at Calais.

David, now thirty-six, volunteered as a driver in February attached to the British Committee of the French Red Cross. Many of these drivers like David were gentlemen –volunteers and mostly over military age. Many donated their cars as well as driving them.

In May, Margaret Dalrymple gave birth to her second child, a boy named Charles Mark after his respective grandfathers. He became known as Mark.

David continued as a driver for six months, completing his tour of duty in September. The same month a young man Henry Allingham, who was eighteen at the outbreak of war, put his name down with the *Royal Automobile Club* in Pall Mall where they were asking for volunteers to be dispatch riders. As they were slow in responding, he joined the *Royal Naval Air Service* as an air mechanic instead and within a year his path would cross with Lieutenant-Commander Dalrymple.

The following year in May 1916 David was summoned by the Admiralty to report to C in C Lowestoft, to rejoin the Royal Navy where he was appointed to serve on an Admiralty type trawler, HMT *Kingfisher*. The Admiralty in its wisdom offered a second chance to the wayward lieutenant who 'resigned' in 1911, and he was given the temporary rank of lieutenant commander. It may of course have been 'recall every available officer' regardless of history after two years of losses at sea, which had built to the rate of around 10,000 sailors a year. The navy started badly by losing 1,500 killed in in 1914 at the Battle of Coronel during the early stages of war – where Dalrymple's old ship HMS *Monmouth* had been lost with all hands.

His new ship was one of a number auxiliary patrol vessels based at Great Yarmouth on the Norfolk coast. It was HMT *Kingfisher*, one of four trawlers purchased by the Admiralty and equipped for carrying a seaplane, by fitting a platform aft. The aircraft had to be lowered and raised from the sea using a crane. Its only armament was one six-pounder gun. The other ships were the *Cantatrice, Jerico* and *Sir John French*.

Then at short notice on 29 May, a young air mechanic Harry Alllingham was ordered to join the armed trawler HMT *Kingfisher*, carrying a Sopwith Schneider seaplane. *Kingfisher* was at sea during the Battle of Jutland, shadowing the British Battle Fleet. They subsequently followed the High Seas Fleet taking care to avoid the mines laid by the retreating battleships. As Allingham was to remember later:

> *"On Monday night we were waiting around when along came the whole Grand Fleet all in battle line astern, with a big bow wave, going like hell's bells. It was a wonderful sight. The dreadnoughts came first – three of them. Then came the cruisers and everything else right down to the littlest boats, and we joined up with them and followed. The shells from the Germans came straight for the ship we saw these ricocheting across the sea."* [2]

The battle commenced on Wednesday afternoon, and continued through dusk and much of the night, so it was not possible for the aircraft to act as a spotter. The ship's company were completely unaware of the enormity of the battle in which over 6,000 British seamen lost their lives, until returning to hear the church bells in Great Yarmouth ringing to celebrate the victory, albeit a Pyrrhic one.

David's brother-in-law, Commander John Saumarez Dumaresq, was also at Jutland serving on HMS *Shannon*, an armoured cruiser, part of the second cruiser squadron –although his ship did not see action, she spent many days searching for survivors of the battle, with her sister ship HMS *Defence*.

On June 20 David's father, Sir Charles Dalrymple, died suddenly in his seventy-seventh year at his London home at 97 Onslow Square and he was granted leave for the funeral.

He was buried in Scotland at the local parish church of St Michael's after a private ceremony at Newhailes House and a public service at Inveresk, the village nearby. Sir David, now the second baronet, was one of the funeral pallbearers, alongside Colonel John Adam Fergusson (Charles's brother), Colonel the Honourable R. E. Boyle (his cousin), The Reverend Julius Robertson, vicar of Stourbridge (nephew), Colonel James A. Hope, V.D. (cousin), Mr J. G. A. Baird of Coulston, Mr J. Fergusson of Balgarth (cousin) and Colonel George Fergusson Buchanan of Auchentorlie (cousin).

All the names were dutifully reported in *The Scotsman* on 24 June 1916.

Sir Charles' will was carefully drawn up under Scottish law by the old established firm of Messrs Hope, Todd & Kirk W. S. from their offices in Charlotte Square, Edinburgh. (In Scottish law, W. S. stands for Writer to the Signet, the old name for solicitors, originally having special privileges in relation to the drawing up of documents for the Court of Session which required to be signeted.) The will was published testate later that year on December 19 1916.

It began:

"I, the Right Honourable Sir Charles Dalrymple of Newhailes Baronet, Privy Councillor, being desirous of settling the succession to my means and estate after my death, and of securing as far as I can that my said lands and estate of Newhailes shall not be sold, it being my desire that they be retained in the family…" [3]

Clearly aware of his only son's character, his will was very specific in its terms. The estate was to be held in trust by four trustees, Major-General Charles Fergusson, (his nephew), Forbes Hunter Blair (brother-in-law), Honourable George John Gordon Bruce (seventh Lord Balfour of Burleigh, a cousin), and his son David.

On his father's death Sir David became a relatively wealthy man. Sir Charles had left around £90,000 (£5 million today) in cash and stocks plus Newhailes House and its estate, together with his house in London.

However, the will stated that the four trustees would manage the estate on behalf of his son. David would be unable to act without at least two other trustees.

He however would have sole use of Newhailes House, shooting, forestry during his lifetime, passing it on to his male heir. He received an immediate payment of £2,000 (£121,600 today) and was able to live in

Newhailes rent free, using all its facilities. He would also receive royalties and dividends from the stocks and shares plus earnings from estate mineral rights, but administered by the trustees. On no account could the house or lands be disposed of. The total income of around £4,250 in 1916 would fund the upkeep of the estate. David's sisters Christian and Alice both received £10,000, and an income of £600 per annum, plus all the contents of Sir Charles's London house to be shared equally.

Sir Charles also remembered his servants giving Alice Watkins, his sixty-six-year-old housekeeper £100 and his coachman George Yeates £50.

The will concluded: *"… And I hereby give to my Trustees the fullest powers of administration and management of the whole lands and estates property funds and effects falling under this Trust…"* [4]

★

In the summer of August 1917 another Admiralty-requisitioned net drifter the *Oceans Gift II* was destroyed in an accidental fire off Happisburgh, along the coast from Great Yarmouth towards Cromer. HMT *Kingfisher* went to her rescue and saved all the crew except their captain Clement Minster, who was drowned.

In 1918 at the end of May, Margaret ran an advertisement in *The Scotsman* for a nurse. *"Can any lady recommend experienced, trustworthy nurse for a boy of 3? Suitable to be left in charge, needlewoman, over 30 (Apply) Lady Dalrymple, Newhailes."*

It shows the concern Margaret must have had for her marriage – perhaps an attempt to move closer to him in Yarmouth?

In the summer David returned to Newhailes on leave lasting some two weeks; despite any reconciliation attempt it seemed David had returned to his ship, estranged from his wife.

Then on 15 July *The Scotsman* reported a visit to Newhailes by a hundred members of the 'Old Edinburgh Club', a local history society, founded in 1908 concerned with all aspects of the city's history.

As the paper announced, *"… and by permission of Fleet Commander Sir David Dalrymple Bt. they were received by Lady Dalrymple and Sir Mark McTaggart-Stewart."*

Margaret and her father had to host the event, and a sense of déjà vu must have descended on Margaret when a few days later she learnt of the news.

The Navy reports David is absent from HMT *Kingfisher*. His old behaviour once again let him and the Navy down and he faced a court martial, charged with being absent without leave. It was a serious offence at any time but particularly in wartime. Sir David pleaded guilty as charged and sentenced *"adjudged to be severely reprimanded and dismissed from HM service."*

He made an unsuccessful appeal against the decision. However, the sentence was confirmed by the First Sea lord Admiral of the Fleet, the Lord Wester Wemyss.

Wemyss could have made no other decision. Like Dalrymple a naval cadet at HMS *Britannia*, but an entirely different personality. A leader and fighting sailor in the Nelsonian tradition, he had an illustrious and highly decorated naval career. Six months earlier he had replaced Sir John Jellicoe as First Sea Lord and encouraged the Commander of the Dover Patrol to undertake more vigorous operations in the Channel, ultimately leading to the launch of the Zeebrugge Raid in April. The sentence was confirmed on 27 July and Lieutenant Commander Dalrymple duly dismissed from the service.

⋆

On tour at the time was the popular Ungar and Langley musical revue *Crackers* with full London cast, the 'bon-bon of delight in two pulls and a bang'. Amongst the cast was the captivating Miss Dorothy Lewis.

David was a civilian in London when the war ended on 11 November 1918. As the crowds converge on Downing Street to hear the Prime Minister announce that the war will end at eleven o'clock, and more crowds gather in London's Trafalgar Square to celebrate the victorious end of the Great War, David celebrated too. He would finally be awarded the British War and Victory medals in 1925.

To cap it all in that autumn of 1918 the world was swept by Spanish flu, a disease far more virulent than its name suggests. In Britain over a 150,000 died, many of them young people who for some reason were especially susceptible.

After the war society changed dramatically, it was now undoubtedly more democratic. Previously under-represented groups such as women and, in particular, the working class became better organised and more powerful during the war. This, in turn, encouraged the growth of less deferential attitudes, as did the cross-class experiences of the trenches. There had been a disproportionately high percentage of casualties among the landed classes, and the strict class hierarchy of Edwardian Britain disappeared for good in the immediate post-war years.

-14-

A very public divorce

'Après la guerre'

In March 1919 the press was full of an aristocratic divorce, that of Lady Idina Wallace – now temporarily staying at the *Royal Albion* hotel in Brighton.

She was the daughter of the eighth Earl De La Warr, who had earned the nickname 'Naughty Gilbert' after running away with a French can-can dancer. She inherited her father's hedonistic spirit and would scandalise a generation. Over the coming decades she would marry five times and became immortalised as 'The Bolter' by novelist Nancy Mitford. She married her first husband, Captain David Euan Wallace of the *Life Guards* in 1913. Wallace divorced after her affair with a Captain Charles Gordon in December 1918 at the *Metropole* in Brighton. Soon after her divorce from Wallace, she married Gordon but divorced him in 1923, marrying Josslyn Hay the twenty-second Earl of Erroll – eight years her junior, and promptly moved to Kenya.

The same month the *Royal Albion* entertained another furtive aristocrat, Sir David Dalrymple and 'Lady Dorothy' Dalrymple. By coincidence, some twenty years later Dorothy would host a fashionable Sussex Hunt party where the guest list would include the Earl of Erroll – but not 'The Bolter'. She had by that time divorced him as he had been cheating her financially.

In May 1919 David was again on top form and arrested for drunkenness, after stopping off at a pub in Putney. It was dutifully recorded in the press as:

"BARONET FINED FOR DRUNKENNESS
At the South-Western Police Court on Thursday, before Mr Banks K.C.,

Sir David Dalrymple was fined for having been drunk while in charge of a motor-car.

It was stated that he pulled up outside a public house at Putney on Tuesday, and as he alighted from the car a constable noticed that he was the worse for drink."

In anticipation of Margaret's impending divorce and perhaps of David's overspending, creditors were demanding payment. The terms of the trust his father had instigated really only provided income based on the interest accrued from investments payable twice a year. Since there was no additional income from the navy, his expenditure since his father had died some two years earlier had exceeded his ability to pay off creditors in the short term. He was advised to declare himself bankrupt. This might have been a legal necessity to counteract any future claim by his wife.

As his estate was in Scotland and family trust was under Scottish law, the sequestration of Sir David took place in Edinburgh. In the Scots law of bankruptcy the term 'sequestration' is used, that of taking the bankrupt's estate by order of the court for the benefit of the creditors.

Charles John Munro, a chartered accountant and partner in one of Edinburgh's most experienced firms specialising in bankruptcy Messrs Romanes & Munro, with chambers at 50 Frederick Street, were appointed to handle Sir David's sequestration. It took place at the Sheriff's Court House on 30 July 1919. Sir David's creditors were asked to attend their chambers later on 12 August 1919.

Munro had been appointed a Trustee and Ballantyne Lewis a commissioner. The details of his bankruptcy were never published, but it is clear that David Dalrymple continued to receive an income from the estate trust.

Regardless David still partied on; he had become a social dipsomaniac enjoying the feverish hedonism of the Jazz Age, which was taking hold at the dawn of the twenties and he had a new young interest – a blonde actress that enjoyed partying as much as he did.

For ten years the moneyed classes in Britain and America partied without heed for the reckoning. It was an era of excess, when money seemed limitless and they believed the boom would never end.

Midway through this decade Noël Coward sang: *"Cocktails and laughter – but what comes after?"* in C. B. Cochran's 1925 revue *On with the Dance*, which opened at the *Palace Theatre,* Manchester, later transferring to the *London Pavilion.* It was also the decade that led up to the devastating economic collapse of the thirties.

★

In London, no establishment was considered complete without an American bar and at hotels like the *Ritz Carlton,* Piccadilly and other well-known West End restaurants diners arrived early to spend a preliminary half hour chatting over an aperitif. This was also the golden age of the cocktail. At the *American Club* in Piccadilly, 'Collins' was declared to be the London champion shaker. 'Nick' was highly regarded at the *Royal Automobile Club* in Pall Mall and 'Harry' was now the presiding genius at *Ciro's Club.* Indeed, Harry published one of the first cocktail books *Harry's ABC of Mixing Cocktails* in 1919, a book that is still in publication today. According to Noël Coward, *"A perfect martini should be made by filling a glass with gin, then waving it in the general direction of Italy,"* a reference to the origin of the other ingredient, vermouth.

In late 1919, *Ciro's* re-opened its London restaurant and swiftly re-established itself as a leading society rendezvous and destination of choice of Dorothy and David. Among European high society, the restaurant club had become an institution and perhaps the first quality restaurant chain in Europe; it started in Monte Carlo, with branches in Paris, London and Biarritz. Each venue was regarded as far more than a restaurant but the very centre of fashionable life.

In London, *Ciro's* had originally opened in Orange Street at the back of the National Gallery in May 1915 as a private club. The building had once been the Westminster public baths but was converted into a handsome venue of beautiful proportions with a sliding roof that could be opened in the summer. There was a main large square room with a gallery flanked by imposing pillars to the ceiling with a delicate décor of lettuce green and old gold in Louis XVI style. On the ground floor there was a thicket of tables, chairs and a platoon of waiters and a more decent dance floor than the Parisian establishment. There was also an American bar and grillroom decorated with chintz curtains and framed caricatures of French artist Georges Goursat, famous during the belle époque, under his pen name 'Sem'. In the early 1920s he had also produced the first depiction of a Chanel No 5 bottle in a sketch.

The bar was presided over by Harry MacElhone, a Scot from Dundee who had worked in Nice and Enghien-les-Bains, a spa resort in northern Paris and later became famous in Paris running *Harry's Bar* in the Rue Daunou.

★

Inevitably the news of David's divorce broke in London and was repeated in various edited forms in the provincial press and Scotland. *The Times* reported on Saturday morning 8th November 1919:

"BARONET DIVORCED.
LADY DALRYMPLE'S SUCCESSFUL SUIT

An undefended petition for divorce was heard by Lord Sands in the Court of Session, Edinburgh, yesterday at the instance of Dame Margaret Anna Stewart, or Dalrymple, against Sir David Charles Herbert Dalrymple, Bt., of Newhailes, Mid Lothian. The petitioner, who is 39, stated in her evidence that the marriage took place in April, 1906, and that there was one child surviving. They lived happily together for some time, but after about three years the respondent ceased to live with her. She had not seen him nor received any letters from him for a considerable time. Having reason to suspect the respondent's fidelity, she, in April last, instructed her agents, and it was ascertained that the respondent had lived with a woman in a Brighton hotel. She identified two hotel registration forms as being the handwriting of her husband. Two other forms of the same dates were signed 'Dorothy Dalrymple'. They were not the handwriting of the petitioner she had not been in Brighton on those dates.

In answer to his Lordship the petitioner stated that there were intervals of happiness up till 1917, but her husband was given to intemperance. She last lived with him in June, 1918. There was no rupture. The defender just went away after having come to Newhailes and having stayed there for two weeks. Witnesses from the Albion Hotel, Brighton, a porter and book-keeper stated that the respondent and a woman, who was not the petitioner, was addressed as 'her Ladyship', had resided in the hotel in March and April. Lord Sands granted a divorce, giving the custody of the child to the petitioner. The Court also decided the question of aliment for the child, who is 4½ years old. The petitioner asked for £500 a year, but that amount was opposed by counsel for the respondent. The petitioner's counsel said that Lady Dalrymple had just sufficient means for her own needs, but she was prepared to restrict the claim for the child to £400, though his Lordship should keep in mind the position that the boy would one day occupy, and the education he would require to fit him for the position as heir to the baronetcy. Lord Sands, in fixing the child's aliment at £300, said that it could be subject to reconsideration in the event of its being found that the respondent's alimentary income had increased beyond what he would be allowed to enjoy, notwithstanding his bankruptcy."

The aliment (Scots law – maintenance, alimony) fixed for their child was well above even the most expensive public school – *Harrow* for example had fees of around £207 per annum in 1920. In awarding aliment for their son, Lord Sands – an arch Conservative – despite Margaret's excessive demands still erred generously on her side. He was a leading layman in the Church of Scotland, an establishment man, Conservative Member of Parliament and knighted two years earlier.

In the aftermath Margaret Dalrymple left Newhailes and declared: *"in future her permanent address will be Croy, Maybole, Ayrshire."* She had taken her son Mark and decided to live close to her sister Susanna, the Countess of Cassillis.

Newhailes was to be let furnished and an advertisement appeared in *The Times* on 12 November:

"THE MANSION-HOUSE OF NEWHAILES TO BE LET FURNISHED, FOR SUCH A PERIOD AS MAY BE AGREED ON, WITH IMMEDIATE ENTRY

Situation – The Mansion-House of Newhailes is situated about 5 miles from the Post Office, Edinburgh; 16 minutes by rail from Waverley Station or 45 minutes by tramcar from Edinburgh and 5 minutes from Musselburgh.

The house is 18th century with a fine front and circular flight of steps to front door, and a courtyard in front with pillared entrance. The interior is very hansome and ornate, with richly-panelled walls and pictures inset. At the back there is a grass park of 2½ acres surrounded by terraces. There is a private entrance from Newhailes station to the grounds."

The advertisement went on to describe the number of bedrooms, reception rooms and facilities, saying the drainage was in good order and the house connected to the Edinburgh telephone exhange (Musselburgh 132), asking interested parties to contact Messrs Hope Todd and Kirk W. S. of 19 Charlotte Street, Edinburgh.

The house it seems was difficult to rent, and it was again advertised in February 1920 and repeated in May and again in August. By December 1921 it was again advertised to let in *The Times* and *The Scotsman*, hoping to attract a family by adding:

"This house has been THOROUGHLY MODERNISED, and has been fitted throughout with ELECTRIC LIGHT."

-15-

The Dalrymple's of Newhailes

D avid Charles Herbert Dalrymple was born in Kensington, London on 29 March 1879 and baptised two months later. He was descended from a long line of Scottish lawyers. His father, Sir Charles Dalrymple, was called to the bar at Lincoln's Inn in 1865. He entered Parliament in 1868, and later represented Ipswich from 1886 to 1906.

He was created Baronet of Newhailes in 1887, and sworn of the Privy Council in 1905.

The 120-acre family estate was Newhailes House, Musselburgh about six miles eastward along the coast from Portobello and Edinburgh. It had originally been built in 1686 by the architect James Smith, who designed it as his family home.

It came into the family possession in 1709 when purchased by Sir David Dalrymple of Hailes (1665–1721). The first baronet, he served at different times as Solicitor General for Scotland, Lord Advocate, and Auditor General of the Exchequer. His older brother, Sir John Dalrymple, the first Earl of Stair (1648–1707), also an advocate and politician became one of the darkest figures in Scottish history when he organised and authorised the 1692 Glencoe Massacre, killing some of the Clan MacDonald, concerning an oath of allegiance in the aftermath of the Jacobite uprising.

A new library wing was added to hold his vast collection of books and the house became known as an intellectual hub. Philosopher David Hume was among those who borrowed from its collection. Each succeeding generation added to the estate. Dalrymple's son, Sir James, commissioned the Great Apartment. His son David Dalrymple (1726–1792), a Scottish lawyer, historian and antiquarian, was a friend of author and biographer James Boswell. In a letter to him of December 2, 1763, Dalrymple described his own state of mind as follows:

> *"I am happy; I go my way in peace; I apply myself to the duties of society, and in filling the empty places of my brain with useful studies, I close it to metaphysical chimeras. Do thou likewise, my dear friend, and be happy; as happy as your very humble and most affectionate Dav: Dalrymple."*

Later Christian Dalrymple unexpectedly inherited the house in 1792, and it was she who designed the landscape of the surrounding estate, including the creation of the flower garden. Christian also began to use the library as a ballroom, famously hosting glittering dances and soirées there.

But it was the library that was the most renowned feature, described by Dr Johnson as *"the most learned room in Europe"*. It was considered to be the most important contemporary collection to survive from the period of the Scottish Enlightenment. It was composed of approximately 7,000 volumes, containing British and foreign works from the sixteenth to the eighteenth century, plus numerous pamphlets and prints, maps and music. They included the manuscript of Lord Hailes' *Annals of Scotland*, annotated by Samuel Johnson, and letters of his contemporaries, including philosopher David Hume, the historian William Robertson, James Beattie and Edmund Burke.

In the late 1890s the guests reported to have visited Newhailes apart from the wider family were largely political, such as the Speaker of the House of Commons Arthur Wellesley Peel, later the first Viscount Peel. Joseph Chamberlain was a frequent visitor, best known as the leading imperialist of the day in Britain, as a Liberal Unionist before he joined the Colonial Office.

The exception was a visit by the third Marquess of Bute himself, a landed aristocrat, industrial magnate and philanthropist. He was related to the Royal House of Stuart and the Coutts banking family. His visit coincided with his involvement with a notable company law case, relating to the insolvency of the Cardiff Savings Bank (1892) concerning a duty of care to which he was acquitted.

The Times would typically report the arrivals and departures of prominent people, as they did on 25 October 1901:

"Mr. and Mrs. Chamberlain arrived in Edinburgh yesterday evening, the right hon. gentleman having engaged to address a meeting there today. The Colonial Secretary was received by Sir Charles Dalrymple, M.P., whose guest he will be at Newhailes, Musselburgh, during his visit, and after being introduced to several prominent members of the local Unionist party he drove away with his host amid cheers."

Much later in 1926 and again in 1935, the house hosted Princess Victoria Louise Sophia Augusta Amelia Helena of Schleswig-Holstein – known simply as Princess Helena Victoria, Queen Victoria's granddaughter on her way to Balmoral. She was a guest of Archibald Kennedy Earl Cassillis (later fourth Marquess of Ailsa) and David Dalrymple's sister-in-law, Frances Countess Cassillis (née McTaggart-Stewart) who were renting the house at the time.

★

David's mother, Alice Hunter Blair, was the second of four daughters of the large family of thirteen children of Sir Edward Hunter Blair, the fourth baronet and Elizabeth Wauchope. The Hunter Blair's ancestral home was Blairquhan Castle, rebuilt in the 1820s in Tudor style, situated near Maybole in South Ayrshire. Hunter Blair was from an old and influential banking family. Sir William Forbes, James Hunter & Company went on to become one of the most successful of the Edinburgh private banks. He became a Justice of the Peace and Deputy Lieutenant of Ayrshire.

Alice had married Sir Charles Dalrymple in 1884 and David was the second of three children. His mother died of complications when he was five, two days after giving birth to his younger sister Alice.

As a result Sir Charles sent his children away. Perhaps he thought it best they were brought up in a family environment – something he felt unable to offer in his bereavement. David and his older sister Christian were sent to live with their Aunt Dorothea – his mother's sister in Scotland, and young Alice sent to Aunt Eleanor (Dalrymple-Fergusson), her father's youngest sister in Worcestershire.

Dorothea had married David Boyle and they lived at Shewalton House, a 2,000-acre estate backing onto the River Irvine. Six years later, after the death of George, the sixth Earl of Glasgow, David Boyle his cousin inherited the title becoming the seventh. He decided to sell the Shewalton estate and instead buy back Kelburn Castle near Fairlie, north Ayrshire as it had been in the Boyle family since the twelfth century. Before he died, George had made it bankrupt because of his over-generous endowments to various church buildings.

The Boyle's large family moved to Kelburn in 1890 with their five sons and three daughters, together with David and Christian Dalrymple.

Captain David Boyle had a long career in the navy serving during the Crimean War (1854–55), and the Second Opium War (1856–60), and no doubt his stories probably influenced young David to choose the navy rather than follow the family tradition into the law.

One such story, later included in his memoirs, was about when HMS *Birkenhead* a troopship went ashore and sank near Cape Agulhas (South Africa), in 1852; *"… that the horses and dogs contrived to swim to land through the surf, thick with kelp-weed, and that one officer was saved by clinging to his horse's mane, though most of the men who tried to swim were entangled in the weed and drowned."*

Another ancestor, David Boyle (1772–1853), who as Lord Boyle, a member of the Privy Council of George IV, and Lord President of the Court of Session had been the presiding judge sentencing the infamous Edinburgh murderers and body-snatchers Burke and Hare in 1828. [5]

Boyle joined the Royal Navy at twelve, spending ten years in sailing ships, and later served as commander of HMS *Niobe*, a four-gun sloop that was wrecked on the rocks on Miquelon Island off Newfoundland during fog in May 1874, although he was later exonerated.

He was appointed Governor of New Zealand in 1892 for a period of five years. His cousin Sir James Fergusson had also served in that capacity twenty years earlier.

The same year, David Dalrymple was enrolled at the *Royal Naval College Britannia* as a thirteen-year-old, graduating as a midshipman in 1895. He was an average cadet, failing some exams but eventually promoted to sub-lieutenant in 1900 and whilst serving on HMS *Boxer*, a destroyer, was described as *"a hard working zealous officer"*. [6]

On his coming of age the children of Newcraighall and district – the village close to Newhailes estate – presented him with an illuminated address featuring the crest of HMS *Boxer* together with that of the Dalrymple family. He later served with the battleship HMS *Ocean*, which was transferred to the China Station in response to the Boxer Rebellion. Whilst serving in the Far East in 1902, together with a few fellow officers he became a Freemason – attached to the *Lodge of Perseverance* in Hong Kong and later *King Edward VII Lodge* in Lui Kung Tao, a leased territory in northern China.

His elder sister, Christian Elizabeth Louisa, at the age of thirty-two married a Royal Naval officer Commander John Saumarez Dumaresq, in 1907. The wedding was held at St Peter's Episcopal Church, Musselburgh. John had been born in Australia but moved to England as a young child. Like David Dalrymple he had joined *Britannia* as a cadet and by 1910 was promoted to captain. He was recognised as one of the navy's most innovative officers and he devoted much of his time to the science of naval warfare. He invented a calculating instrument by which the rate of movement of enemy warships could be determined within seconds; this range-finder, named the 'Dumaresq' by a grateful Admiralty, gave naval gunnery an unprecedented accuracy.

As captain of HMS *Shannon* he took part in the Battle of Jutland, was widely respected and later promoted to rear-admiral. After a posting to Australia on his return journey to England, he was taken ill and died in the Philippines in 1922. They had five children, two girls and three boys.

★

David's younger sister Alice Mary (named after her mother) was sent to her Aunt Eleanor, wife of the Rector of Hartlebury in Worcestershire, a village between Worcester and Kidderminster. The rector was the Reverend David Robertson, son of Lord Benkoline, a Scottish judge. He had graduated from *Trinity College* Cambridge and they had been living in the seventeenth-century rectory since 1880. He was also the rural dean of Kidderminster, Chaplain in Ordinary to the Queen (Victoria), and chaplain to the Bishop of Bath and Wells.

David and Eleanor had three children, two girls and a son some ten years older, so Alice grew up the youngest within the larger family. The rector was a renowned historian, edited and wrote numerous articles for the *Worcestershire Historical Society* as well as publishing a Christmas carol.

Alice remained with the Robertson family until she was sixteen, when she together with her older sister Christian returned once again to live with their father in London at Onslow Gardens. Their father Charles had brought the Newhailes housekeeper Mrs Watkins to London to manage the household, and employed Emily Tuskins, a woman in her fifties, as governess to Alice. Alice never married, later moved to Scotland and died at Halkerston Lodge, close to Newhailes in the village of Inveresk, Musselburgh in 1959.

Eventually, as the male heir, Sir Mark Dalrymple the third Baronet inherited Newhailes. After the death of his father, he was taken on a world tour by his widowed mother (then Lady Blake). They left England for New York on the Cunard SS *Berengaria* in November 1935, across the USA to San Francisco and on to Honolulu in December. Their arrival was reported in the *Sydney Morning Herald* as passengers on board the TSS *Maunganui* from Honolulu in February 1936. They returned to England via Ceylon (Sri Lanka) by P&O SS *Strathaird* in May. Apart from Churchmead House, their country home in Datchet (which was requisitioned in 1939 by the army), they kept a London house at 26 Chelsea Square.

★

After the Second World War, Mark married Antonia Marian Amy Isabel Stewart in 1946, the only daughter of the twelfth Earl of Galloway – a military man, once a member of the anti-Semitic *Right Club*. His American wife was Philippa Wendell, whose sister was married to Henry Herbert, the sixth Earl of Carnarvon, whose father had funded archaeologist Howard Carter when he discovered the tomb of Tutankhamun.

They had no children and when Mark died in 1971, the barony became extinct. In lieu of death duties, the government accepted around 7,000 volumes from the Newhailes Library, which were removed to the National Library of Scotland in Edinburgh.

In 1997 Newhailes House was given to the National Trust for Scotland by his wife Lady Antonia Dalrymple, because the cost of upkeep had become impossible and the house was in danger of falling into disrepair. It was to allow it to grow old gracefully through a pioneering conservation policy which does 'as much as is necessary, but as little as possible' to keep the house in good order without disturbing its 'untouched' atmosphere.

Finally in 2011 at the age of seventy-one, Lady Antonia left her apartment in the house and went to live in a cottage on the estate.

-16-

The actress and the peer

After David's very public divorce, Dorothy must have felt she knew everything about him, whilst he probably knew very little about her, or her previous life other than she had been on the stage. That was how she would keep it.

'Mrs Lewis' had not been mentioned in the press as she had signed her hotel account 'Dorothy' Dalrymple. However that mistake led indirectly to provide the adultery evidence and subsequent divorce.

With her mother Maud dead and father – although still alive – kept in the shadows (she heard he had remarried), and promoted unofficially to the role of naval captain, she was now reinventing her family persona. She would soon create some new names for herself – Maud was such a dull name after all.

★

David duly received his divorce from Margaret, and was free to marry again. Dorothy in the meantime had found it more difficult with Major Lewis.

Edwin, tired of her avarice and being used, had for once become stubborn. No, he wouldn't give her a divorce, it was the only power he had. Dorothy the actress was now 'resting' and her expenses had already put a heavy demand on his fixed pension income prompting a move from the leafy enclave of the *Mountcombe* in Surbiton with his comfortable room with the Ratcliffes, to more modest lodgings in Shepherd's Bush at Minford Gardens.

In the meantime Dorothy and David had taken a flat together at 41 Baker Street. David was still wrangling with his estate trustees about his income and this drifted on for the next year or two. In the meantime they would party and visit shows.

Dorothy the chorus girl had secured her Scottish aristocrat, so far so good – he was fun to be with and surely the trustees would release his fortune – after all it was his inheritance, wasn't it? Dorothy would soon learn about the intricacies of the trust and the fact that to the old Scottish families, she would always be the 'outsider'.

The pre-war Edwardian society magazines often posed the question, why were actresses the most unsuitable of women to marry men of high position? Despite the fact that these marriages were generally frowned upon in high society they eventually became commonplace. Actresses were still considered to be more than a little vulgar in polite society, despite the fact that these same people counted amongst theatre's best patrons. Secondly, most of these girls came from lowly backgrounds – because of the former reason, few women of good standing took to the stage – and so would be marrying far above their station. The press had more to say about the offspring of such unions:

> *"If there is anything in heredity at all, what are those children likely to turn out? For one thing, the sense of responsibility to traditions can hardly be developed in them to a very full or satisfactory degree. For their father has shown himself to care little for the dignity of his class, and their mother has been unduly elevated from hers."* [7]

Whilst Dorothy was appearing in the revue *Crackers*, the press featured another 'Peer and the Showgirl' article, this time on the front page of *Daily Mirror* with photos; it featured the nineteen-year-old Gaiety actress Irene Richards who had married Lieutenant Viscount Drumlanrig, heir to the Marquess of Queensbury. It didn't last though; they divorced some eight years later due to her affair with (future husband) Sir James Dunn, a millionaire financier.

In October 1920 Jose Collins, a musical comedy actress playing *The Southern Maid* at *Daly's Theatre* married Lord Robert Innes Kerr, third son Duke of Roxburghe, but continued on the stage after marriage. Her mother was the music hall star Lottie Collins, an icon of the naughty nineties whose risqué style popularised the song "Ta-ra-ra Boom-de-ay". (A century later, her garters were sold by auction at Sotheby's.)

In June 1922 another successful 'Gaiety Girl' Olive May appeared in the press – now Lady Victor Paget, when she married into the aristocracy for the second time – this time to the tenth Earl of Drogheda, Henry Charles Ponsonby Moore, becoming the Countess of Drogheda. After Olive's first marriage to Victor Paget in 1913, it was reported in the *New York Times* she was the American daughter of a Civil War hero and Chicago industrialist. A myth built up to accentuate her stage appearance in America. She was in fact born Olive May Meatyard, the daughter of a London jeweller. Reading about these events, it is entirely consistent for the theatrically trained Dorothy to consider building her own legend.

★

By her twenty-fifth birthday in January 1923, Dorothy had been living with David Dalrymple for five years and still no sign of marriage. Then news reached her that Edwin Lewis had fallen seriously ill – he'd had a stroke and had been admitted to the London County Mental Hospital in Hanwell. He had been living alone at 26 Minford Gardens, Shepherd's Bush.

Two months later Dorothy learnt of her father's death from her young brother Jack. He had died at home on 24 March at 71 St Georges Road, Southwark, at the age of sixty-six, after suffering from an enlarged prostate and cystitis. There was no mention of his wife Maria – perhaps she had returned to France?

Edwin remained in hospital and died a month later on 23 April. The post-mortem revealed he had cerebral softening of the brain (encephalomalacia) due to a haemorrhage.

He was fifty-four and died alone – no one mourned his passing. In recording his details on the death certificate, the resident medical officer introduced for some reason another name, that of Edwin 'Merton' Lewis – possibly an error as his birth certificate only records 'Edwin', as does his army records. The press would later pick up on the second initial.

Dorothy was informed as his next of kin through his bank Cox & Kings. She later approached the War Office for his widow's pension. His younger Welsh siblings were to remain oblivious of his death until many years later.

Dorothy was now free to marry and at the end of the summer on Friday August 31, she and David Dalrymple were wed at Marylebone registry office, the newly built imposing classical style town hall in the Marylebone Road with its stylish marble entrance hall, staircase and lavishly panelled corridors. This imposing building was to become the registry office of choice for future celebrities. Their marriage was announced in *The Times* the next day, repeated in the *Portsmouth Evening News*:

"*NAVAL WEDDING*

LIEUTENANT-COMMANDER SIR DAVID DALRYMPLE, R.N., AND MRS. DOROTHY LEWIS

The marriage took place yesterday at the Marylebone Register Office of Lieutenant-Commander Sir David Charles Herbert Dalrymple, Bt., R.N., of Newhailes, Musselburgh, Mid Lothian, and Mrs. Dorothy Lewis, widow of Major E. M. Lewis, Shropshire Light Infantry, and daughter of the late Captain Abbot, R.N. The bride, who was given away by Mr. John Craig, wore a draped gown of pearl-grey charmeuse, her cloche hat being of ivory georgette. She carried a bouquet of pink and white carnations, and was unattended. The register was attested by Major John Hodgson (late East African Service Corps) and Mr. Philip Page, these being the only other people present at the ceremony. The honeymoon is being spent on the South Coast."

Dorothy had distanced herself from former stage friends and what remained of her family – they knew too much gossip, and the small wedding ceremony was made up entirely of David's friends.

For sake of convention Sir David recorded his address as the *Charing Cross Hotel* in the Strand whilst Dorothy details (their apartment) 41 Baker Street. In completing the register she introduced two new fictional names 'Cynthia' and 'Mirabelle'; she dropped Maud altogether – and with it her past? This time her father becomes Captain William Vernon RN (Deceased) – possibly an incomplete record, or perhaps another way of 'disappearing' her past?

In doing so she set a society trend as three years later Maud Lady Cunard, the wealthy American society hostess, also dropped the name 'Maud' after her husband's death and became 'Emerald'. She believed that Maud with its music hall connotations was rather a 'common' name, and thus needed to change.

Dorothy was now legally Lady Dalrymple, and it would seem as Sir David's wife entitled to an income from the trust estate.

★

The following week a new André Charlot revue opened at the *Duke of York's Theatre* with Noël Coward and Gertrude Lawrence called *London Calling!* The revue's song *Parisian Pierrot*, sung by Lawrence, was Coward's first big hit. Gertie was the same age as Dorothy and both were brought up in Southwark. They had been on the stage as teenagers, her father had a drink problem too but Gertie had the breaks, succeeding in joining the Italia Conti who taught dance, elocution and the rudiments of acting. Earlier she had been sacked by Charlot over time off from a show, and had secured a job singing at *Murray's Club* in Beak Street in early 1919, where Dorothy had been a dancer in between stage engagements, whilst seeing David Dalrymple. It was *Murray's Club* where many crowned heads of Europe let their hair down and later in the early sixties where the 'Profumo Scandal' girls Christine Keeler and Mandy Rice Davies entertained.

★

The 1918 election saw the Conservative government in power, but prices had soared after the war – this was not matched by wages, creating unrest which led to the fall of the Lloyd George coalition government in 1922. The Conservatives returned to power under Bonar Law, but he died shortly afterwards and was replaced by Stanley Baldwin. In seeking a fresh mandate, the election resulted in a hung parliament making way for the first Labour government, which took office under Ramsey MacDonald in 1924.

All this of course was the remote stuff of newspapers. However, the Dalrymples' expenses lived up to more than their income; there was an ongoing demand for extra cash. They kept no servants, their apartments were usually serviced and they dined out on most days. The Trustees finally agreed in November to sell some household items and put them to auction in London as reported in *The Times*:

"Sale of prints at Sothebys including French line portraits the property of the late, Rt. Hon. Sir Charles Dalrymple of Newhailes.

Sold by order of the Trustees

… comprising numerous Impressions by the XVII Century French Engravers, G. Edelinck, A. Masson, R. Nanteuil, F. Poilly, etc., and including Guillaume de Brisacier, after Mignard; Philippe,

Duc d'Orleans; H. De Péréfixe; Henri de la Tour d'Auvergne, Vicomte de Turenne, etc."

★

After years searching for a tenant, it was announced in December that the Earl and Countess of Cassillis would take a lease on Newhailes, Musselburgh, from the trustees of the late Sir Charles Dalrymple, and would take up residence on return from their world tour. Why isn't clear, as they already had several properties, Culzean Castle and Cassillis House in Ayrshire as well as a London house at 22 Charles Street in Mayfair.

Perhaps it was a way of preventing Dorothy from ever taking up residence. From what she understood of Newhailes – they were welcome to it. Despite being leased to the Cassills throughout much of the 1920s Sir David still appeared in the local telephone book.

Margaret, David Dalrymple's first wife, now forty-five married Sir Patrick Graham Blake, the sixty-four-year-old fifth Baronet of Langham in Chelsea, in the autumn of 1925. Mark her son was now ten and still at school. There may have be an opportunity for David now to challenge the ongoing payments for maintenance.

Patrick been previously married but his wife had died the year before. He had a son, Cuthbert, a Lieutenant-Commander in the Royal Navy who fought at Jutland on the destroyer HMS *Termagant* and was awarded the DSO, and a daughter Veronica who married the Rector of Leckhampton in Wiltshire in 1914. She and Patrick had no children. Patrick had difficulty in managing his money and died in debt five years later at Churchmead, their house in Datchet. His family's Bardwell estates in Suffolk were sold, although he did manage to leave Margaret £16,296 in his will, which provided nicely for her and son Mark.

★

As with all generations wanting to declare themselves different, a new set of expressions evolved defining the time – good things were always *"divine"* and bad things *"bogus"*.

They would say *"too perfectly amazing"* when they liked something, and likewise *"too grisly for words"* if disliked. When not feeling or looking their best would declare *"I look a fright"*. On becoming bored it was described as *"too tired making"*, or if disagreeable *"too sick making"* and when amused exclaimed *"just the thing"*. They would often repeat *"Don't I know it darling!"* as confirmation to nearly any remark; when unable to grasp what was being hinted at in social conversation they would be *"slow on the uptake"*, and without funds would declare they were *"stony-broke"*.

The 'bright young things' – a listless bunch, just too young to have fought in the Great War, rich, directionless, obsessed with parties, or perhaps 'pogoing' up the Mall, and any other form of showing off they could dream up. They went on partying, planning activities to amuse like 'treasure hunts' all over London, or organising elaborate hoaxes, perhaps gate-crashing private parties, and thinking up places to hold parties like Tube trains, or ABC teashops, organising events that were *"too perfectly amazing"*!

The twenties saw the opening of many nightclubs and cabaret shows, with London's first cabaret show at the *Metropole Hotel* in October 1921, now back in private ownership after being requisitioned during the war (Edwin Lewis had earlier been posted there as part of the expanded Quartermaster General's Directorate).

'The Midnight Follies' was a huge success, running through till the late 1920s. It had one of the most elegant ballrooms, a big lofty room lit by Chinese lanterns with a cluster of small supper tables arranged in a horseshoe fashion around a good-sized dance floor in the centre. There were also discreet corner alcoves and a few even more discreet boxes, but most sat on larger tables on the edge of the dance floor as 'the wishers-to-be-seen'. Sylvia Ashley made her show debut in 1924, the actress who became famous largely for her marriages to British aristocrats and American movie stars –Douglas Fairbanks being the first.

The same year the *Café de Paris* opened, becoming one of the most fashionable dining haunts in London during the 1920s. Intimate and elegant, it was described by *Vogue* magazine as *"delightfully comfortable"* and by *Dancing Times* as *"the smartest dance restaurant in London"*. It took over the premises of the old *Elysee Restaurant*, at 3 Coventry Street.

The new management team began alterations and redecoration to open as a cabaret-restaurant providing lunches, dances, teas, dinners and a dance supper until two in the morning. They also recruited Martin Poulson, the headwaiter from the *Embassy Club* to ensure success.

To enter, one descended a flight of stairs into a little lounge that led onto the balcony and below the dance floor. The main floor was reached by the famous double staircase that did enable a rather grand entrance. It was not too large or too small, and a perfect size for a café or restaurant of its kind seating 400. The whole place except the dance floor was carpeted in blue-green and the decor was meant to be a replica of the Palm Court of the *Luisitania*.

The grand opening was on Wednesday 28 May, 1924 and every table was occupied, one by Sir David and Lady Dalrymple. The dance, dinner and cabaret cost 15s 6d. Poulson excelled himself with a dance-supper which began with caviars and green turtle and ended with a delicious 'Coeur Flottant'. At 11.45pm a *"frothy, bubbly cabaret"* called *Summer Time Frolics* was staged. It would become a favourite with Dorothy.

Another, the *Kit Cat Club* in the Haymarket opened in the summer of 1925 and immediately became one of the most famous nocturnal haunts in London. Decked out with the last word in restaurant and dance floor equipment, it was regarded as the most sumptuous resort in Europe and was the only club in London that had been built expressly for the purpose of being a club. Such was its popularity that within a short space of time, membership exceeded 6,000 including princes, cabinet ministers, dukes and peers.

This was the time when cocktail barmen and skilful managers could make or break a club's reputation and popularity.

One such man, Luigi, a restaurateur, a small, alert personality who became a business associate of the bandleader Ambrose, took over the *Embassy Club* just after the war and made it extremely fashionable. Situated among the shops in the Piccadilly end of Bond Street, the entrance is through a wide marble passage. The entrance lobby, guarded by some imposing footmen, led to the entrance and to the restaurant-dancing room. It was decorated in violet, jade green and white, luxuriously furnished with sofas and tables along the walls, which held glass mirrors. Each table had a couple of green electric candlesticks with pink shades and amber lights hung from the ceiling. In the centre of the room was the dance floor and at one end of the room, on a balcony – the delightful Ambrose and his orchestra dispensing fabulous sounds.

★

In the West End, the American actress Tallulah Bankhead (four years younger than Dodo) had journeyed to England to appear opposite Gerald DuMaurier in *The Rope Dancers* and thereby launched what was perhaps the most spectacular London stage career of the 1920s. Her calculatedly outrageous public behaviour, her multiple romances and her habit of wearing flimsy lingerie onstage whether the script called for it or not endeared her to fans. After a succession of mediocre dramas that made few demands on her talent, Bankhead confounded her critics with her brilliant performance as a troubled young waitress in the London production of Sidney Howard's *They Knew What They Wanted* in 1925.

The same year, after losing out on the role of Sadie Thompson in *Rain*, Somerset Maugham's new play (he had doubts regarding her acting abilities), she accepted Noël Coward's offer of the leading role of his new play, *Fallen Angels*, at the *Globe Theatre* (now the Gielgud). It was due to open in within four days and practically overnight she committed the dialogue to memory, as Noël later recalled:

> *"She came flying into the theatre with vitality a little short of fantastic… tore off her hat, flipped her furs into a corner and embarked on the first act. On the first night… gave a brilliant and completely assured performance. It was a tour de force of vitality, magnetism and spontaneous combustion."*

The *Sphere* magazine conducted a poll to choose the ten most remarkable women of the day; the Queen, Edith Sitwell, Diana Cooper and Tallulah all made the list.

She was famous not only as an actress but also for her many affairs, compelling personality and witticisms like, *"I'm as pure as the driven slush."* Tallulah inhabited a flat in Mayfair's Farm Street for much of her stay, where infamous parties were held, of which the uninhibited hostess was always the life and soul. Her party pieces included 'knicker-less' cartwheels and naked entrances, which must have created a certain frisson with the conservative set. She returned to the USA in 1931 to star in films; before leaving she had her portrait painted by Augustus John.

Bankhead's first film was *Tarnished Lady*, directed by George Cukor, his solo directorial debut and the pair became firm friends. He had been directing on Broadway and the Astoria Paramount Studios in Queens at the time of Dodo's flirtatious auditioning during the late summer of 1929.

★

On 3 May 1926 the General Strike was called, the result and climax of industrial unrest during the years since the war. Prices and unemployment were high. It was an unsuccessful attempt by the Trades Union to force the British government to act to prevent wage reduction and worsening conditions for hundreds of thousands of 'locked-out' coal miners. A million and a half workers were on strike, especially in transport and heavy industry. The government was prepared and enlisted middle-class volunteers to maintain essential services. Many of the twenties' 'bright young things' found this volunteering a 'bit of a lark' – there was little violence and after a week the Trade Union Congress gave up in defeat.

These events were merely newspaper stories, with little effect on many in London's social life – immune as they were from the deprivation suffered elsewhere. The 'season' was still continuing and duly reported in the glossy journals such as *The Bystander* and *The Tatler*. Meanwhile women's fashions had dropped the frills and fripperies of the early twenties and became much more severe and stark. Bobbed or Eton-cropped hair was inevitably covered in the ubiquitous cloche hat, and by 1925 the skirt shot up to above the knee.

★

The years after Dorothy and David were married were to some extent an anti-climax, as their relationship was based on the excitement of infidelity, now dominated by the boring but constant need for more income, to fund their lifestyle.

Dodo, as she was now being called, soon learnt that just being 'Lady' Dalrymple was insufficient; she needed a purpose, to do something. David had become largely aimless, perhaps without the discipline of the navy, and spending more time with his drinking friends and less with her. The 'party fun' was wearing thin.

Dodo, bored and constantly short of her own money had decided to move back into the theatrical world.

She secured a good part in an Archie Pitt revue touring the provinces, under her old stage name of Dorothy Lewis. The production would be on tour over Christmas. Around the same time the press announced that David's brother and sister-in-law Lord and Lady Cassillis would be returning to Newhailes from Canada and continuing with the lease.

Archie Pitt had been on the stage in a family comedy act in the music halls and met Gracie Fields (born five days after Dodo) in 1915 when they were both in the revue *Yes, I Think So*. Archie was not a successful act but became a successful producer when he persuaded her to perform in one of his own revues, touring the provinces for a couple of years. After appearing in *Mr Tower of London* at the *Alhambra*, Leicester Square in July 1923, Gracie became an 'overnight star' and she married Archie.

Dodo joined his new revue *Orders is Orders*, described as *"an amusing burlesque of the boys in blue, the upholders of law and order."* The tour arrived in Burnley before Christmas, appearing at the *Palace Hippodrome Theatre*. The press particularly liked the dancing of Peggy O'Dare, Fai Robina *"and Dorothy Lewis, the heiress in the case."* The tour continued to Derby and Hull.

Dorothy returned to London, and learnt that the trustees had again agreed to sell some of Newhailes' furniture, releasing some more cash – hurrah, this time some rare antique pieces.

Two library chairs were put up for sale with Frank Partridge & Sons in King Street, who only dealt with the very finest English and French furniture.

Their provenance was impeccable, as described:

"An important pair of George II mahogany armchairs with the original Aubusson tapestry covers by Pierre Mage, circa 1750. From a set of four chairs probably originally commissioned by General the Hon. James Sinclair (1688–1762) or his wife Janet (d. 1766), youngest daughter of Sir David Dalrymple of Hailes, who moved to a house at 60 Greek Street London, after her husband's death. After Janet Sinclair's death the contents of the house in Greek Street were sold by auction, the four chairs being purchased by her nephew David Dalrymple, 1st Lord Hailes (1726–92)

for Newhailes House, Midlothian, Scotland, and thence by descent at Newhailes until sold by Sir David Dalrymple."

The chairs were sold to an American collector, and eventually to other art collectors such as Walter P. Chrysler Jr. They still appear in New York auction rooms from time to time, with a price extremely enhanced.

This sale must have relieved the pressure on their creditors and the days of 'wine and roses' could continue. Most of the socialising revolved around David's friends and sometime his cousins. In the years since their Brighton affair, Dodo had moved in a completely different circle of largely David's social set, drifting apart from her wider family after the deaths of her parents.

One wonders if in moments of reflection Dodo ever gave a thought to her baby daughter – she would be about ten now. What did she look like? Where was she – was she happy? Did she care? There was one exception; when she became particularly lonely, she would make contact with her younger brother Jack, now in his twenties, who was working in the accounts department for a firm in Gresham House, Old Broad Street. They would meet occasionally usually during his lunch hour at a pub in the city – Dodo would pay. Jack and Dorothy's personalities were different as chalk is from cheese, Jack, quiet and thoughtful, whilst Dorothy with her engaging looks, the more assertive. At one of these meetings she learnt he was engaged to Mary Driscoll, a girl a few years younger, living in north London with her father who also happened to be in the print industry – like their own father once, they remembered. Jack and Mary planned to get married soon. During these sibling meetings she learned that her Aunt Charlotte who had helped her when she was pregnant had died suddenly on New Year's Eve, 1927, at Essex Road railway station. She was seventy-two. When probate was announced a few months later, she had left £21 to her younger sister Anna.

★

The Dalrymples now rented a flat at 23 Cork Street in Mayfair and in June, David decided to take Dodo to her first Scottish Ball. It was the annual Royal Caledonian Ball held at the *Cecil* hotel in the Strand in June. The hotel had been built in 1886 in a very spacious and lavish style with over 800 rooms and an enormous entrance courtyard. It was popular with American visitors, as was the large lofty and spacious restaurant with imposing colonnades of rich blue. At one end the vast windows formed part of a hanging terrace, which seemed almost at one with the trees and the gardens of the embankment, overlooking the Victoria Gardens and the river and big windows on the west side giving a glorious view of Westminster. The hotel had the biggest banqueting accommodation in London.

The great and the good would attend and Dorothy could rightly attend as the present Lady Dalrymple.

The event had started sometime in the 1840s as a private gathering given by the Duke and Duchess of Atholl for their Scottish friends who resided in London. It had achieved Royal Patronage under Edward VII and become a major charity ball and one of the events of the London season. The press announced those who intended to be present – a roll call of Scottish aristocracy, including the Duchess of Atholl, Countesses of Cromartie, Countess of Stair, Countess of Rothes, as well as the Duchess of Montrose, Duchess of Buccleuch and Frances Countess of Cassillis – Dalrymple's sister-in-law.

It was a disaster for Dodo – not only did David behave badly but she was also snubbed by the Scottish relations. The new Lady Dalrymple was still the 'actress' and made to feel out of her depth with the old aristocracy; she wasn't accepted. It would have been a total disaster if one Scottish landowner, a certain Lady Ermine Elibank in her late forties, hadn't taken her under her wing.

It was fortunate she did. Ermine was a formidable and kind woman, much the same height as Dodo at five foot three with brown hair and eyes; she had married Gideon Oliphant-Murray, who had inherited the title second Viscount Elibank from his father. He had been a colonial administrator and politician, and was now retired from politics pursuing business interests. Ermine was his second wife and they had no children. They spent their time between estates in Scotland in the Borders and a London apartment. Ermine was a 'lady who lunched' involved in many causes – and not least with women's motoring. This act of kindness blossomed into a new friendship that would last until her death.

As it turned out it was the penultimate ball held at the *Cecil* before it was largely demolished in autumn 1930, and Shell Mex House was built on the site. The event was subsequently moved to the *Grosvenor House* in Park Lane.

David was still behaving badly or as his first wife might have said, 'was given to intemperance'. Dodo moved out of Cork Street and stayed temporarily with Ermine and her husband at St James' Court in Buckingham Gate. It was through this friendship that Dodo was encouraged to learn to drive and take an interest in cars, making new friends.

★

After the war, everyone wanted to be young again; this sense of freedom seemed to apply particularly to the 'new woman'. Dorothy, still in her early twenties, epitomised the change:

> *"The handsome woman in a hansom cab was overtaken by a fast woman in a fast car. Glamour had come to London. There was a whirl of glass beads and pearls, sparkling paste, rouge, plucked eyebrows... sticky scarlet lips, surprised faces. Coloured underclothes broke out in shades of ice-cream: peach, pistachio, coffee...".* [8]

Dancing and motoring were the obsessions of the twenties.

Dodo learnt to drive with one of Ermine's more unusual friends at her driving school in Brick Street, off Piccadilly. It was run by the Honourable Gabrielle Borthwick, a dog lover devoted to her Great Dane and by coincidence, a distant Dalrymple relative by marriage.

Gabrielle had run Borthwick Garage with Lady Gertrude Crawford (daughter of the forth Earl of Sefton); neither it seems were good at managing money, and eventually it ceased trading through a series of bankruptcies. Lady Crawford had briefly been the first chief superintendent of the Women's Royal Air Force in 1918, but resigned when she discovered to her horror she would actually have to work!

Gabrielle was now in her sixties, the eldest daughter of Cunninghame Borthwick, the nineteenth baron, with an estate at Ravenstone Castle in Wigtownshire. He was a partner in the stockbrokers, Borthwick, Wark and Company in London. Her younger brother Archibald had married Dalrymple's first wife's sister, Susanna MacTaggart-Stewart. Archie had died in 1910 and Susanna went on to marry Alfred Fitzroy, becoming the Countess of Grafton.

Gabrielle had been presented at Court and despite 'two seasons', received no marriage offers. Together with her mother Harriet, she spent part of the year in Florence amongst the wealthy English ex-patriot society as guests of Walburga, Lady Paget, a socially effective diplomat's wife at Villa Bellosguardo (a thirteenth-century villa, once owned by poet Guido Cavalcanti, a friend of Dante). Another wealthy arts patron Mabel Dodge Luhan, an American banker's daughter had joined the group and moved into the Villa Curonia – it is said she and Gabrielle had a lesbian affair. [9] Perhaps this could be one reason why she didn't marry.

Lady Paget would later describe Gabrielle (who was staying with her at the time) in a letter to a friend as handsome with black hair.

In the years before the Great War she had been a member of the Gypsy Lore Society, which included amongst its members the artist Augustus John. She had been initiated into the 'Order of the Golden Dawn' in 1891, an organisation devoted to the study and practice of the occult, metaphysics, and the paranormal and within the society followed her own path.

By the time the war began, Gabrielle was taking part in the formation of a trade union for women, the Society of Women Motor Drivers, founded to fight women's corner in the battle to be taken seriously in the motoring trade and have the same rights as its male workers.

The idea of forming what became the Society of Women Motor Drivers had originally come from the London Society for Women's Suffrage, and the society met at its Women's Service Bureau in 58 Victoria Street, London. The idea would later be championed by Lady Elibank.

-17-

Iberian sojourns

Dodo and David had essentially become estranged. Whilst nominally living together, they had moved apart and what started out as an exciting affair with the social round of parties had become boorish with his drinking habit. Dorothy had dropped her family contact since Lewis and to some extent her theatrical friends too, to concentrate on David. This led to isolation culminating in the humiliation at the Caledonian Ball. Ermine Elibank had introduced her to a new and wider set of friends albeit largely female, but all in their own way affirming their independence, away from the influence of men, and in Dodo's case David's drinking partners. David was in many ways continuing the social pattern that led to dismissal from the navy and the divorce from his first wife.

The new Lady Dalrymple was establishing her independence; now able to drive and with time on her hands, she was enjoying a different social life.

In the late autumn of 1928, she was invited to join a party without David travelling to the south of France to the resort of Saint-Jean-de-Luz on the Côte Basque, the northern side of the Nivelle River. The same year, Maurice Ravel had completed his orchestral piece "Bolero" in the village. It was a small sized community, so visitors could easily walk everywhere. Across the bay lay Ciboure (where Ravel was born) with its sardine industry. The British ex-pat community had long established themselves in this little fishing village, a short distance south. It was where the French king Louis XIV married the Spanish infanta Maria Theresa at the thirteenth-century L'Eglise St Jean-Baptiste. Appropriately, the Place Louise XIV was located in the heart of the town behind the Atlantic beach, facing the fishing harbour, which leads into the main shopping street Rue Gambetta as it continues towards the church.

Le Bar Basque in Boulevard Thiers, popular with the Anglo-Americans, was a focal point of ex-pat life. A nod to the English travellers was the *Hotel d'Angleterre* on the sea front; further along the front was the old *Terminus*, now rebuilt and renamed the *Modern Hotel*, which together with the *Golf* were the fashionable hotels of the time. Saint-Jean appears briefly in Hemingway's novel *Fiesta: The Sun also Rises* – Mike, one of the English characters with a perennial liquidity problem explains: *"Oh, something will come through. I've two weeks allowance should be here. I can live on tick at this pub in Saint-Jean."* After the fictional group's visit to the fiesta in Pamplona, another character Lady Ashley could have easily been modelled on Dodo, [10] as her annual allowance had been reduced to half by Scottish creditors.

Saint-Jean was smaller and more intimate that its larger glitzy neighbour Biarritz (where Coco Chanel had opened a boutique on the Rue Gardères) with its casino and fashionable international clientele. Biarritz had become renowned in 1854 when Empress Eugenie (the wife of Napoleon III) built a palace on the beach, which later became the *Hôtel du Palais*. European royalty, including Queen Victoria and King Edward VII and the Spanish King Alfonso XIII, were frequent visitors.

They could stay for months at Saint-Jean, considered culturally more select, at very modest cost; dine, socialise and mingle with ex-pats, particularly the Americans, many of whom would travel down from Paris for the summer. Some moved across the Spanish border to attend the Festival of San Fermín in Pamplona, to watch the running of the bulls and the bullfights in July whilst others wintered on the Basque coast. Saint-Jean-de-Luz was conveniently served by the Paris to Madrid Express and English banks like Lloyds (where Dodo drew her allowance) and National Provincial had established offices in the town. Even an English prep school had been established, that regularly advertised in the English press as having *"a splendid climate for delicate boys"*.

One of those American ex-pats, a foreign correspondent called Ernest Hemingway, whilst living in Paris had recently published his *Fiesta* novel semi-fictionalising his experiences amongst the so-called 'lost generation' of expatriate American and British socialites in the 1920s whose decadent and dissolute lives had been irretrievably damaged by the Great War. This was the good life that Dodo Dalrymple was enjoying, as she was called by her close friends wintering together in Saint-Jean. One could almost hear her say *"Don't I know it darling!"*

It had been in the same resort a few years earlier that English author Ernest Hornung died; his *Raffles* stories, about a gentleman thief in late nineteenth-century London made him very popular. He had fallen ill on the train from Paris, which developed into influenza and pneumonia. The Prince of Wales, later Edward VII had visited the Nivelle Golf Club in 1926, giving it a royal approval. Another resident, Garnett, the American wife of poet Alfred Noyes had also died the same year whilst staying with friends.

Encouraged by her friends – one of whom had introduced her to the scent of Chanel No.5, brought from the *Galeries Lafayette* in Paris – suggested she should re-enter show-business, perhaps the stage again, or possibly a career in films. In the spring of 1929 she travelled the eight miles to Biarritz to visit the American Vice-Consul Roy McWilliams to obtain a visa for the USA.

As plain Dorothy Dalrymple in May she took the Sud-Express, travelling in one of the newly introduced 'Voiture-Salon Pullman' carriages to Paris and taking the boat train from Gare Saint-Lazare to Le Havre, took passage on the SS *De Grasse*, a newly built ocean liner of the Compagnie Generale Transatlantique, commonly known as the French Line.

She travelled cabin class on the sailing via Plymouth, arriving at New York pier 57 on 3 June. She declared she was staying for five months, residing at the *Sanford Hotel*, Flushing, Long Island. Her next of kin was given as Mr Abbott (her brother) of Gresham House, London. She declared she had no occupation, had never travelled to the USA before and had sufficient funds for her stay ($350). Her last address was given as Saint-Jean-de-Luz, to which she was going to return. The immigration officer recorded her personal details – and for the first time we see the thirty-year-old Dodo emerge from the shadows described as being in good health, five foot five inches tall, fair complexion, with blonde hair and grey eyes.

The *Sanford* was a modest, newly opened hotel on Sanford Avenue not far from the Paramount Astoria Studios. During 1929 and 1930, the four Marx Brothers, stars of Broadway and vaudeville, made their first two talking pictures *The Cocoanuts* in May and *Animal Crackers* the following August at the studio. The silent film era was over; with the advent of 'talkies', production at Astoria blossomed. Drawing on the wealth of writing and acting talent of Broadway, the studio profited from its proximity to 'the Great White Way'.

The Letter, released in April 1929 was the first all-talking feature film shot at the studio, earning an Oscar nomination for actress Jeanne Eagels – she was a little older than Dodo and a former Broadway Ziegfeld Follies girl.

During this time she briefly met Gertie Lawrence again, who had travelled from England in early September to film a Cole Porter musical *The Battle of Paris* at the Astoria. Another was the twenty-two-year-old blonde singer and dancer Frankie Schenk, whose stage name was Frances Day. She too had returned from England on the White Star liner RMS *Olympic* in July. She had previously taken dancing lessons at Zelia Raye's dance academy, and had secured an engagement with another dancer John Mills (who went on to become a distinguished actor – knighted in 1976) and they had appeared at the *New Cross Empire* billed as Mills and Day. That had led to a chorus role in the musical *The Five O' Clock Girl* at the *London Hippodrome*, a theatre they both new well. What a coincidence!

Dodo had seen her perform years earlier in London cabaret, and certainly his Lordship enjoyed her performance –dancing with little else other than a feather boa. She had a fund of stories and like Dodo, had become estranged from her husband – the Australian impresario Beaumont Alexander, eighteen years her senior. Frankie and Dodo struck up a friendship that would last on and off for decades.

They were similar in many ways and shared an uncanny resemblance. In later life John Mills would reflect that he thought Frances Day the original *"femme fatale"*. [11]

Dodo had also met George Cukor, son of a Hungarian Jew, one of the up-and-coming young directors at Astoria. His direction of a 1926 Broadway stage adaptation of *The Great Gatsby* had brought him to the attention of the New York critics. However, the promised audition or film part never materialised and looming events were to supersede all that.

★

The 1920s had been a booming time in America for businesses building on post-war optimism and ordinary citizens were borrowing to buy shares in the seemingly never-ending progress upwards of the stock exchange. In the spring of 1929 there had been early signs that the market was over heating, a warning was issued by the Federal Reserve, but buying continued and stocks resumed their advance through June and the gains continued almost unabated until early September. At the end of the month, the London Stock Exchange officially crashed when a top British investor, Clarence Hatry, and his associates were jailed for fraud. This sent shock waves through the city and greatly weakened the optimism of American investment in markets overseas.

Then it happened. The Wall Street Crash was the greatest stock market crash in the history of the United States. It occurred on the New York Stock Exchange on Tuesday October 29 1929, now known as 'Black Tuesday'. The crash started the Great Depression of the 1930s and stock prices did not reach the same level until after the Second World War. It brought the Roaring Twenties to a shuddering halt.

For many in show business there were no smiles. There were no tears either, just the camaraderie of fellow sufferers. The comedian Eddie Cantor lost everything – whilst appearing in the Broadway musical *Whoopee*. Groucho Marx, star of *Duck Soup* and *Animal Crackers*, lost £400,000, while heavyweight boxer Jack Dempsey, one of the first multi-millionaire sportsmen, lost £1.5 million. The Great Depression that followed severely limited Broadway productions; a great number of theatres closed, never again to open.

★

Dodo returned to England. She had kept in touch with David during her winter break in Saint-Jean, but the summer trip to America was a closed door.

The separation had been an opportunity for them both and David in particular to reassess their marriage. In the months she had been away, she learnt that Newhailes was still apparently leased to the Cassillis. David seemed older now and had put on weight; there was of course a twenty-year age gap but his social bonhomie that she had found entertaining all those years ago had dwindled away. His self-neglect and bachelor life had taken a toll. He had moved to Walton House near Regents Park, bought himself a car – still drinking, but now under the medical supervision of Alexander McCall, a consultant in his late forties at the West End Hospital for Nervous Diseases with a private practice in Wimpole Street. He was a fellow Scot, who had qualified at Glasgow University in 1906, now married and living in Ealing.

Dorothy had been publically rejected by the wider Dalrymple family – one could imagine her recounting the tale with a shudder, *"wasn't I though?"* after the humiliation at the Caledonian Ball the year before – she was not about to become his nursemaid too.

With the experiences of France and America fresh in her mind, she knew there could be a different life. New York hadn't worked, but she had a new circle of friends who accepted her for herself and whilst currently dependent on her allowance from the Dalrymple Trust, was not about to divorce him – well not until a suitable replacement emerged.

Determined to improve her circumstances, at the beginning of 1930, she moved to a flat at 12a Chandos Court at the end of Caxton Street near Buckingham Gate. It was an unpretentious yet respectable yellow brick block of some twenty-odd apartments consisting mainly of retired military, some business residents and a number of members of Parliament, the House of Commons being just a short distance away.

On the ground floor there were a few shops, Lewis & Co. tobacconists, Amelia Gibbon Gowns, a café and a florist.

Her immediate neighbour at number twelve was the fifty-year-old Lady Abbas Ali Baig, daughter of Shaikh Ali Abdulla, uncle of the Sultan of Bahrain. She was married to Sir Abbas Ali Baig, some twenty years her senior, a council member of the Secretary of State for India. They had properties in the Indian sub-continent, and when he died in 1932, Lady Abbas returned to India.

Chandos Court was conveniently close to St James' Court [12] in Buckingham Gate, a masterpiece of Victorian-Edwardian mansion blocks built in 1897, with a stone-trim-and-brick-façade style architecture, where Viscountess Elibank lived.

Ermine was heavily involved with 'good causes'. She supported her husband with his colonial and business interests and was a tireless worker on committees and social gatherings, and she drew Dodo into her circle. Ermine was an energetic organiser, correspondent and supported many interests, particularly women's causes. She was a handsome woman around five foot four, with a fresh complexion, brown hair and blue eyes. She was well connected and had many contacts with journalists and provided the press with much social material. This was an ability that Dodo would take note of and later learn to exploit.

Ermine was born in Wales her maternal grandfather was Field Marshal Robert Cornelis, First Baron Napier of Magdala, a career soldier in the Indian Army who had fought in the Anglo-Sikh Wars, and during the Indian Mutiny at the siege of Lucknow. Her first husband Lieutenant Colonel James Aspinwall had died in 1894 and she met and married Gideon some ten years later. He had commissioned her portrait, and she sat for the very fashionable Philip de László in 1925. He was a Hungarian painter known particularly for his portraits of royal and aristocratic personages. He was married to Lucy Guinness, a member of the banking branch of the family. The same year, Laszlo had also painted Lord Louis Mountbatten. A few years later Ermine would again sit for another society portrait, this time at the royal photographers Bassano Ltd. in Old Bond Street.

The Murrays, Earls of Elibank, trace their ancestry back to the seventeenth century and the name is synonymous with a plot to restore Charles Edward Stuart ('Bonnie Prince Charlie') to the British throne five years after his army's defeat at Culloden in 1746. At the time the incumbent earl acted as liaison officer between the exiled 'Young Pretender' and his English supporters in a plot to restore him to the throne – but it ended in failure. They had a property in the Scottish borders at Elibank House, a 200-acre sporting estate on the south bank of the Upper River Tweed.

*

On 24 May 1930, nineteen days out from Croydon, Amy Johnson touched down in Darwin, Australia. She had flown solo the 11,000 miles in her single-engine Gipsy Moth biplane she named 'Jason', becoming the first woman pilot to do so, and she would be awarded 'Commander of the Most Excellent Order of the British Empire' (CBE).

The following August, 1930, the press announced Lady Elibank was amongst those welcoming Amy Johnson home at Croydon airport, civic and government dignitaries including Air Vice-Marshall Sir Sefton

Brancker together with Lord Thomson, the Air Minister. (Both were subsequently killed a few months later when the airship R101 crashed near Beauvais, France during its maiden voyage to India.)

Amy had returned by Imperial Airways, flying in one of their Armstrong Whitworth aircraft named *City of Glasgow*, on the final leg of a journey from Alexandria, Salonika and Vienna where she stayed overnight, arriving at Croydon airport on Monday 4th August.

The same month Ermine was heavily involved with the British Empire Society and was appointed to the women's section, concentrating on hospitality.

In early December 1930, Dodo departed England for a two-week holiday to Portugal with a new travelling companion, James Sanders. He was in his late forties, describing himself as a planter and had lived on and off in Spain, although now in London with a flat in Jermyn Street.

Dodo was moving in influential circles, and had met him at one of Ermine's political social gatherings and they became mutually attracted. He just could be husband replacement material.

Ermine and Gideon would continue to call her Dorothy – as perhaps surrogate parents do – although increasingly she was known now as Dodo and in social circles would be introduced as Dodo Dalrymple.

Ermine's husband Gideon had succeeded his father in 1927; he was an active member of the House of Lords, and an enthusiastic supporter of the United Empire Party established by Lord Beaverbrook. He played golf, and was also a frequent speaker on colonial matters in the house. Ermine's nephew, the son of her sister Grace, Harold Balfour, was an up-and-coming politician who had been elected Conservative Member of Parliament for the Isle of Thanet in 1929.

James found himself talking to Dodo, as both were outsiders on the political scene. He was in business, a merchant like his father, tagging along to the party with his married sisters.

He explained they used to go on family holidays to Switzerland, and 'Cottie' [13] his younger sister had been a fearless Alpine climber and a close friend of Mallory. She had recently returned from a posting to China with her husband Owen St Clair O'Malley, a Foreign Office diplomat. His older sister Grace had married Bertram Okeden Bircham, a solicitor to the Ministry of Labour, who had won the Military Cross in the war serving with the *Hampshire Regiment*.

On the outward shipping manifest they were both registered at 60 Jermyn Street, although James is likely to have made the booking with the Royal Mail line in Cockspur Street without actually knowing Dodo's address – a spur of the moment invitation perhaps, but most certainly he would have known her phone number, Victoria 9511. However, on the return ship's manifest she correctly records Chandos Court.

They sailed on the RMS *Almanzora* first class bound for Lisbon, on the ship's first leg of the Buenos Aires and River Plate service. They left Southampton on the fourth, arriving in Lisbon three days later. James was out to impress.

The new *Palácio* hotel in Estoril on the coast a few miles west of Lisbon had recently opened in the summer of 1930 and quickly become one of 'the' places to stay. It was built in the Art Deco style – an entirely white façade with over a hundred rooms spread over five floors, it was surrounded by newly planted gardens. In November, Prince Takamatsu, brother of Emperor Hirohito of Japan, stayed with his new bride at the hotel during his world tour honeymoon, giving it the seal of royal patronage.

The following month, Lady Dalrymple arrived to give it hers.

James had lived in Spain and spoke the language, understood Portuguese and described himself as a merchant or sometimes a planter. She learnt James's younger brother 'Bobby' had died at the age of twelve – which devastated his mother – and Jack his other brother had been killed in 1915 at Ypres. His eldest sister was married to a schoolmaster and two other sisters had married well, and he was now the only surviving son. Somehow this made him feel guilty.

James Harris Sanders, now in his late forties had been born into a large middle-class family his American mother had died a few years ago and his father died during the war. His father had been a successful international salesman of metal products, until he ran into financial difficulties and finally lost his fortune around 1911.

James seemed restless and hadn't settled into any profession, although Dodo thought he actually might have *"scads of money"*, as he variously described himself as a merchant, a planter, of independent means or simply 'no occupation', living in England or Spain. He rented flats at various addresses in London, St James, Mayfair or Fulham and regularly travelled to Spain and Portugal, usually Vigo or Corunna during the late 1920s and early 1930s.

How he made his money was not clear; Dodo thought he *"talked a lot of rot"* sometimes, but he seemed to have a number of projects on the go, and inferred he was in business with the Marquess of Bute on some Spanish building proposals. Perhaps he was out to impress. We do know he had travelled to Spain and Portugal by ship on many occasions, sometimes with female companions like Kathleen Rudd in 1929 and later Dorothea Stanhope, a twenty-eight-year-old left-wing journalist with *Time & Tide* magazine in March 1931 – a few months before he accompanied Dodo Dalrymple.

He was probably well known to the Royal Mail line stewards.

Their holiday came to a close motoring through Spain to Seville and Cadiz, Algeciras and finally round the bay to Gibraltar.

The preferred old-established *Hotel Reina Cristina* had burnt down a year or so before and was still being rebuilt, so they stayed instead at the *Bristol Hotel*, Gibraltar's oldest and best hotel at the time, located on Cathedral Square. It had been built in 1894 in white colonial style with a small subtropical garden. Since the opening of the Suez Canal, it was a popular stopping point on the shipping route to India and the Far East.

Across the straits a ferry ride away was Tangier, where the old-established *Cecil Hotel* stood for over three decades, the most fashionable hotel in Morocco with its roof terrace overlooking the beach, popular with artists like Henri Matisse, diplomats, dowager duchesses, and writers of international importance.

It was now being challenged by the *El Minza*, a new hotel just opened. Built in the Spanish Moorish style by the fourth Marquess of Bute, John Crichton-Stuart, who had extensive business interests in the area now it was an international zone. He had become the largest foreign landowner in Morocco and was purchasing other properties in Spain, Gibraltar and South America. The *El Minza* offered stunning views over the Bay of Tangier, the Straits of Gibraltar and the Rif Mountains, and it would quickly claim to be the most luxurious hotel in Morocco.

Whilst in Gibraltar, James described one of the latest projects, as they gazed towards the rock summit towering above the La Alameda botanical gardens. He explained it was where they had leased some land off Europa Road and it would be the location of a new 'Crichton-Stuart' hotel. It opened two years later in 1932, named simply the *Rock Hotel*. It too was to become the 'in place' to stay – with guests ranging from Noël Coward to Winston Churchill, and it was where in the hotel's Barbary Bar, which opens out on to the Wisteria Terrace, that spies Guy Burgess and Kim Philby plotted to assassinate Franco, until Burgess got too drunk and Philby decided he was scared of guns. [14]

Dorothy and James returned from Gibraltar first class on the P&O *Mantua*. The 10,000-ton ship had been requisitioned as an armed cruiser during the war, now completely refitted resuming the London-India-Australia mail service. The ship was on the last leg from Bombay and arrived in Tilbury on 19 December.

★

In January of 1931, Ermine launched a new motoring club in London. The club, known as the *Women's Automobile and Sports Association*, had found premises at a house at 17 Buckingham Palace Gardens. The energetic Lady Elibank was president, together with her friends Gabrielle Borthwick as chairman of the executive committee and Lady Iris Capell as vice-chairman.

Gabrielle, now in her mid-sixties, had retired to Surrey, finally moving to Wickhurst House in Broadbridge Heath near Horsham where she died in 1952. The association had been formed to look after the interests of women motorists and sportswomen all over the world as the press announced it was the only club of its kind in the empire. It was affiliated to the *Royal Automobile Club* whose road privileges it also enjoyed. It was a place to stay in London, with simply furnished bedrooms – all decorated by the *Army & Navy* store in Victoria Street. There was also a garage as well as card and billiard rooms. The association already had several hundred members.

Living in London, Dodo became an associate member and attended the launch luncheon party, and was introduced to yet another of Ermine's friends, Lady Iris Capell. Born into an aristocratic family, she was the daughter of George Devereux de Vere Capell, seventh Earl of Essex and his American wife, Adela Beach Grant. Iris was a few years older than Dodo, had studied at Oxford and had served as a nurse at Watford Hospital in the war, and become a keen rally driver. During the Second World War she would work tirelessly with the WVS – Women's Volunteer Service. She never married.

Dodo had been sharing 12a Chandos Court with a certain Mrs May

Wilmot Wilkinson whose son was a contemporary artist and only used it when in town. She had decided to move to her own flat at number 9, giving Dodo her own space. Around this time Dodo reverting to using her title Lady Dalrymple (possibly encouraged by Ermine), and decided to employ a lady's maid.

Rose Brace was duly employed, a woman in her late thirties born into a large family in London who had been in domestic service since her teens. She had recently left the employment of two spinsters, Emily and Ellen Smith in Hampstead, who were supporters of the suffragette movement. They were close friends of feminist novelist Ida Alexa Ross Wylie who wrote under her pen name I. A. R. Wylie. Ida had in effect used their home during the war as a 'safe house' for women who were released from prison where they could recover from hunger strikes without being watched by the police. Rose told of her friendship with an older Welsh woman Rachael Barrett, and how they had sailed to America in 1919 to 'go travelling'. That's something Rose longed to do.

Dodo had now become firm friends with Ermine –living just a few minutes' walk away from each other. In May Lady Elibank had a domestic accident slipping on the floor of her apartment in St James' Court and broke her leg, wrist and hurt her eye. She was laid up for some six weeks. Dodo would become a regular visitor and generally fussed over her. During this enforced inactivity, Dodo learnt Ermine actually wore a monocle to read, although rarely in public and never in press photographs.

Dodo was still seeing James Sanders, and in the summer they embarked on another two-week holiday, this time to northern Spain. They left Southampton on 28 August 1931, again on the Royal Mail line *Almanzora* with its attentive stewards, bound for Vigo. They transferred to shore by the private launch from the *Gran-Hotel Continental*, where they stayed overnight. Years before during the Great War it had been frequented by Dutch spy Mata Hari. [15] The four-storey hotel was conveniently close to the port, and local covered market, only finally closed and demolished in 1966.

The following day they made their way to the fashionable *Gran Hotel Toja*, in Pontevedra situated in the Rías Baixas on the south-western coast of Galicia. It had become a favourite with Spanish nobility with its spa of therapeutic mineral waters, taken from a natural spring discovered on the island in the nineteenth century.

After their relaxing time on the Galician coast they travelled northwards to the ancient town of Santiago de Compostela – still the destination for pilgrims after a thousand years, travelling to the shrine of St James in the cathedral. They continued to the coast at La Corunna – where James explained to Dodo it had been the scene of another 'dramatic' departure 120 years earlier. During the Napoleonic War, a British Army under Sir John Moore, after fighting a successful defensive battle, were eventually evacuated by the Royal Navy.

The couple stayed overnight at the recently opened *Hotel Atlántico* on the sea front in the harbour, before departing on the Royal Mail *Arlanza's* return voyage from South America.

A year earlier the ship had taken King Alfonso XIII of Spain home to Santander after a visit to Britain. The ship had also taken the Prince of Wales and Prince George from Brazil to Lisbon after their tour of South America six months before.

Arlanza anchored off-shore so the embarkation was by the hotel's motor launch at a cost of three pesetas. In addition to passengers the ship was equipped with five holds of refrigerated cargo space for frozen exported meat from Argentina. They arrived in Southampton on 15 September.

After the summer Dodo's involvement with James would lose its appeal; she sensed (correctly) he was really a confirmed bachelor, and his Spanish business ventures seemed to have something of *mañana* about them. Her instinct told her it was time to move on.

★

In December 1931 Lady Elibank received due recognition for her charitable and voluntary work with the League of Mercy. The League had been established by Royal Charter in 1899 by Queen Victoria. It was instigated by the Prince of Wales who became its first Grand President. The object of the League was to establish a large body of voluntary workers who would assist with the maintenance of voluntary hospitals and 'otherwise relieve sickness and suffering'. Central to the annual activities of the League was a notable ceremony at which about fifty people each received a medal known as the Order of Mercy. These were bestowed *"as a reward for personal services gratuitously rendered in connection with the purposes for which the League was established."*

At the annual gathering at Londonderry House in Park Lane, the London home of Charles Vane-Tempest-Stewart, the seventh Marquess of Londonderry and his wife Edith Helen Chaplin, she was conferred with the Order of Mercy, by the Prince of Wales, in her League role as Lady President of Peebleshire, the location of her Scottish estate.

In the New Year of January 1932 Viscountess Elibank, a keen player herself, presented Thelma Carpenter, a twenty-year-old female billiard player with an award cup for winning the women's amateur billiards championship at Burroughes Hall in Soho Square. The old-established firm of Burroughes & Watts were the manufacturers of high quality billiard tables, introducing a number of design innovations over the years, and held a number of royal warrants, as well as supplying the Admiralty and War Office. To encourage the game they supported amateur competitions by providing trophies and the facilities of their match room in Soho Square. They became synonymous with the amateur game.

The same month in the busy social round Lady Elibank attended a reception at the *Ritz* hotel for the Romanian minister Nicolae Titulescu, who was visiting London as Romania's representative at the League of Nations.

As a woman of influence, Ermine was also a member of the *Empress Club* at 35 Dover Street, off Piccadilly. Established in 1897 as a club for women, luxuriously appointed, membership consisted largely of ladies of aristocratic families, including the feminist activist and suffragette Princess Sophia Duleep Singh, daughter of a Maharaja. Her godmother was Queen Victoria. The club had two drawing rooms, a dining room, a lounge, a smoking gallery and a smoking room, a library, a writing room, a tape machine for news, a telephone, and a staircase decorated with stained glass windows depicting Shakespeare's heroines. It also had one of the best orchestras in London.

The following month Ermine's eye inflammation meant she could not attend the annual dinner of the *Lyceum Club* in Piccadilly. Another club for women established in 1904, intended for ladies engaged with literature, journalism, art, science and medicine, where they could meet and discuss matters as men did in their professional clubs. Its first president was Lady Frances Balfour, daughter of the Duke and Duchess of Argyll, and sister-in-law of the British Prime Minister.

In March, Iris Capell invited Dodo as co-driver to join her in her

Talbot entered in the first 1,000 mile *Royal Automobile Club* car rally from London to Torquay, finishing at the *Palace Hotel*. Additionally a *Concourse d'Elegance* was held at the finish. It would be an exciting adventure; over 300 cars had entered including sixty women drivers. The duo managed to finish the race successfully.

Amongst those taking part were the Countess of Drogheda driving a Lyons Swallow SSI Coupe, launched at the 1932 Motor Show, also driving from London, together with Lady Margaret Oldham in a Vauxhall. Countess Igor Ouvaroff in a Bentley and Lady de Clifford driving a Lagonda from Bath, whilst Joan, the Honourable Mrs Chetwynd, a regular on the Brooklands scene and a Le Mans competitor, was driving an MG Midget from Newcastle.

The same month, Lady Elibank received the news that her elderly ninety-year-old mother had died at Old Basing House, her home in Hampshire. She was formerly the honourable Amelia Anne Napier, daughter of Lord Napier. Her children Ermine, her brother Henry and two sisters Grace and Alice all attended the funeral. Grace had married Colonel Nigel Harington Balfour and their son was Harold Balfour, a Conservative Member of Parliament who had served in the *Royal Flying Corps* in the war, winning the Military Cross. He later became the first Baron Balfour of Inchrye – his second marriage in 1947 was to Mary Ainslie Profumo (sister of Jack), daughter of Albert, a barrister and the fourth Baron.

★

Dodo had met another beau, Alex Hill, shortly after his arrival at Chandos Court, and their paths crossed on numerous occasions. He was a tall middle-aged man with a fresh complexion, distinguished greying hair and hazel eyes. Her maid had advised he was living alone, and on a pretext Dodo sent him an invitation to a drinks party at number 12a, to find out more.

She learnt he was estranged from his wife Ruth, and was due to travel to America and Canada on business in April. He was a director of a drugs company and was visiting the subsidiaries in North America. He was about to sail on the Cunard liner *Berengaria* staying at the *Waldorf Astoria* in New York, before travelling to Canada. He should be back in England in June.

When Alex arrived home at Chandos Court on 21 June she invited him again for drinks to learn all about his visit. It had been a successful trip – his first time in North America, and he had returned from Quebec on the *Empress of Britain*. She told him her plans to accompany Lady Elibank to Austria in the summer.

Gideon was attending the British Empire Economic Conference, being held between 21 July and 20 August in Ottawa, with Lord Scarborough and both were sailing to New York. Gideon was travelling in the capacity of chairman of the Federation of Chambers of Commerce of the Empire (now The London Chamber of Commerce & Industry).

The party travelled out a few weeks before, taking their wives. Ermine and Gideon sailed on 25 June with some of the party on the Cunard *Beringaria* staying in New York at the *Barclay Hotel*, built and funded by the Vanderbilt family in 1926 in midtown Manhattan, as a hideaway for the rich and famous.

The conference was a gathering of British colonies and the autonomous dominions, held to discuss the Great Depression.

The eventual outcome would have to admit the failure of the gold standard and abandon attempts to return to it. The meeting also worked to establish a zone of limited tariffs within the British Empire, but high tariffs with the rest of the world. This was called 'Imperial preference', on the principle of 'home producers first, empire producers second, and foreign producers last'. It would also start the adoption of 'Keynesian' ideas such as lowering interest rates, increasing the money supply, and expanding government spending. All this would take weeks of discussions in which wives could take no part. So as agreed, whilst Gideon continued northward to Canada to take part in the conference in Ottawa, Ermine returned to England.

In July, Dodo helped Iris Capell to organise a gala race day at Brooklands in Surrey in aid of Guy's Hospital, a social event which was attended by the Duke and Duchess of York.

After her fall the year before, Ermine was still troubled with her eye and had decided to consult an eminent Austrian ophthalmic surgeon – and then take a holiday afterwards in the Austrian Alps. She asked Dodo to accompany her.

In August they left Croydon for Vienna, flying via Cologne on an Argosy aircraft of *Imperial Airways*. They stayed at the established and unique

Sacher Hotel behind the State Opera House in Philharmonikerstrasse, popular with continental aristocracy as well as King Edward VII.

It had been run by the eccentric Frau Anna Sacher, who built its reputation and success. She had recently died, but her management still upheld the upper-class reputation of the hotel and denied service to guests of non-aristocratic descent, at the same time granting generous credit to impoverished aristocrats. By the time the two ladies arrived it was under some financial strain, but they were still able to indulge themselves with the speciality of the house, Sachertorte, a rich dark chocolate cake with apricot filling.

After a few days' treatment they travelled on to Semmering, a mountain resort south of Vienna taking the little mountain railway, staying at the *Grand Hotel Panhans*. It had been opened in the 1880s by the legendary Viennese chef Vinzenz Panhans; later a new wing was created with 400 rooms, popular with artists and Viennese society – it was where in 1908 Archduke Franz Josef learned to ski on the hotel lawns.

A month later on the first weekend in September, Dodo was with the recovered Ermine Elibank to help organise the social activity of Britain's first flying party – 'A Weekend Arien' as it was announced in the press. Over a hundred invitations were distributed to Continental flyers to attend a weekend of air activity from Thursday to Sunday. Ermine's role was to organise an arrival cocktail party for guests at the *Mayfair Hotel* and a farewell ball on the Saturday before their departure the following day. In the meantime Iris Capell had taken off on a motoring holiday in Scotland, and a week later Dodo was off on holiday too.

On September 10, Lady Dorothy, her thirty-nine-year-old maid Rose (it was her first trip abroad) and Alex Hill departed Southampton for a month's holiday, sailing to Lisbon on the Royal Mail line *Asturias*. The ship had only been recently introduced to their South American trade route to Buenos Aires, with three classes of cabins. The first-class lounge, the reading room and the writing room were all modelled on period examples of architectural work at Houghton House, Norfolk and Harewood in Yorkshire.

Alex had been introduced to Ermine Elibank after their return from Austria and unknowingly past the approval test.

As company chairman, he was taking less of an executive role now, and had more time for himself. It was his holiday invitation, and it was Ermine who privately advised her to take her maid.

Charles Alexander Hill was in his late fifties, born into a middle-class family in Clapham. His father and grandfather were drug manufacturers and Alex (as he liked to be called) followed in the family business of Davy, Hill and Co. He was the youngest of seven children, five daughters and two sons. Educated at private school in Sussex and after taking a Bachelor of Science degree, he became the initiator behind the family firm's plan to amalgamate several smaller companies to create a large and competitive wholesale drug manufacturer, British Drug Houses (BDH), of which he became managing director. They were pioneers in vitamin research, becoming the world's first synthetic producer.

He had married Ruth, daughter of a mining engineer the same year Dodo was born, and they had two boys and a daughter. Ruth Fletcher came from the Lake District and the family lived in Kensington at Courtfield Gardens.

He was now chairman and managing director of BDH and the company had expanded overseas with subsidiaries in Canada and Australia. However, Alex and Ruth's personal life was less successful and they separated around 1930. Alex had moved into flat number 7 at Chandos Court in Caxton Street in 1931, a few apartments away from Dodo Dalrymple.

The couple stayed at the *Palácio* hotel in Estoril that Dodo knew well from an earlier visit with James Sanders, a name she no doubt 'forgot' to mention. The nearby casino had also opened and with the arrival of the *Sud-Express* link, the Compagnie Internationale de Wagons-lits agreeing to extend the service down to Estoril had brought a stream of new continental travellers. The local newspaper *Lisboa-Estoril* publicly acknowledged the electric trains *"granted this area a touch of elegance that steam trains could not."* The hotel now overlooked a verdant garden with a bougainvillea-clad terrace next to the pool. Lisbon was just twenty minutes away. Nearby there were the historic sights of Sintra, and along the coast, now being described as the Portuguese Riviera, the little fishing village of Cascais, popular with writers and artists had turned into an 'in place' after the arrival of the Portuguese royal family some years earlier.

There was time for walking, tennis, and relaxing in the sunshine. Rose had little to do as the hotel staff provided all the services they needed, but she helped dress Dodo for dinner, acted as a confidant, and of course a 'lady's maid' added an air of aristocratic respectably.

It was during this time that Alex told the story of his involvement with the notorious Doctor Hawley Harvey Crippen. It was a year or so after he set up the BDH business [16] when his company was asked to supply a quantity of the drug that was to kill Crippen's wife Cora, the blousy and promiscuous music hall actress Belle Elmore. As a matter of fact Alex would say, *"it was enough to kill twenty people"*. He gave evidence in the Old Bailey trial in October 1910.

Apparently after her death, Crippen had sold Belle's theatrical clothes to Angels [17] in Shaftesbury Avenue, as had Dodo after her mother Maud died.

At the time the music hall star Marie Lloyd (Tilly to her friends) once replied when asked what she thought of Crippen, *"Blimey, I wouldn't trust him as far as I could throw him with my little finger. When he looks at you through them glaa-ses it makes you fink you're going to have an operation."* [18]

Dodo and Alex returned home in mid-October, travelling first class on the RMS *Arlanza* – a ship that was becoming familiar to her, returning from its South American destinations with her welcoming public rooms decorated in English country house style, with ornate columns, fireplaces, drapes, easy chairs and tables, and on the last night before landfall enjoying the traditional 'Dinner D'Adieu'.

-18-

David's dénouement

Dodo had seen little of David in the last few years as they now led separate lives. Through London's social community and his Scottish trustees, David was aware she had a new circle of friends – male and female – and had been travelling abroad.

In November on her return from Portugal she learnt he was now quite ill and likely to die soon. His doctor Alexander McCall had given him only weeks to live, so he had consulted with James Blackburn, his solicitor at Bell, Broderick and Gray of 9 Bow Church-yard to finalise his affairs and wrote a new will.

She was aware that the Newhailes estate was tied up in a complicated trust, and in any case it would pass to her stepson, the seventeen-year-old Mark, along with the title. Clearly there was no love lost with his 'wicked' stepmother, but no doubt there would be some legal provision for her as the current Lady Dalrymple. Although she was not privy to the terms of the will, she assumed that his assets – if not the estate – would come to her.

The same month she accompanied Alex and Ermine Elibank to the annual *'Women's Automobile Club'* dinner at the *Piccadilly Hotel*. The association membership had increased and a large ballroom was needed to host the event. The hotel, with its impressive façade, located close to the Circus, was built at great expense in 1909. At the time it featured Max Jaffa as leader of the two hotel bands, and was renowned worldwide as the best place for music in the late twenties and early thirties, and a favourite with American visitors. It was lavishly decorated with fine oak panelling and a dining room decked with bright crimson carpet with a large and impressive gold pattern, in the general style of Louis XIV decor. Lady Elibank presided together with Lord Wakefield, a significant philanthropist in his seventies, recently raised to the peerage, who had been asked to present trophies. He had founded the Castrol lubricants company, used in the engines of motor cars, aeroplanes, and motorcycles.

★

On a dry and bright London day, Friday December 2, David Dalrymple died of a heart attack at his flat in Walton House, Longford Street. Dodo received a call from his cousin James Fergusson who lived in West Sussex in a country house known as Woodend near Chichester, but had been staying with him in London, and together with Alex McCall his physician, was with him when he died. David had been under medical supervision for months and there would be no post-mortem. Fergusson was making funeral arrangements. There would be a memorial service later.

There was the legal matter concerning the Scottish estate and trust to attend to and she would be contacted later by the estate solicitor Patrick Murray, of Hope, Todd and Kirk, of Charlotte Street, Edinburgh, who had been appointed executor of his will.

It came as no surprise; David had been drinking heavily for some time and their marriage to all intents had ended some years ago. He was gone; there was nothing more to be said.

In the meantime, perhaps a winter's cruise might be 'just the thing' she needed whilst Lady Dalrymple the recently-bereaved widow pondered her inheritance. As the Canadian Pacific's promotional advertisements at the time had encouraged her:

> *"You owe it to yourself,*
> *after a trying year, to take*
> *that well-earned rest far*
> *beyond the reach of*
> *winter's chilly grasp!"*

★

Ermine had been instrumental in organising a banquet for Amy Johnson, the star aviatrix (as the press called her at the time), in the New Year and

Dodo would join her at the event at the *Mayfair* in Stratton Street. The hotel had opened with a fanfare three years earlier with King George V and Queen Mary in attendance. It was just around the corner from the newly opened headquarters of Thos. Cook & Sons, the renowned travel agency in Berkeley Street, describing itself as the 'Temple of Travel' in its promotional posters.

Amy Johnson, now Mrs Mollison having married fellow Scottish aviator Jim Mollison the previous July, had immediately flown off to break her husband's England to South Africa record. They were dubbed 'The Flying Sweethearts' by the press. Amy and her parents would be guests of the Women's Automobile and Sports Association and the invitation list would include some of the most influential and illustrious names in Britain.

On Wednesday 4 January the great and the good came together to honour this admirable woman. A host of aviation and government personalities, many of whom served with distinction in the war, a smattering of aristocracy and royalty and influential businessmen, presided over by the host Viscountess Elibank.

The gathering included Harry Preston, keen amateur aviator and owner of the *Royal Albion Hotel*, Brighton (Dodo had met him – whilst auditioning as 'Lady Dalrymple') – he was a friend of the Prince of Wales, and soon to be knighted for his services to charitable causes; Sir Malcolm Campbell, the racing motorist and motoring journalist, recently knighted by King George V (he was at Uppingham with Bobbie Hartman soon to be a lead player in the Dodo story) and had served in the *Royal Flying Corps*; Lieutenant-Colonel Shelmerdine as Director of Civil Aviation who had also served in the *Royal Flying Corps;* Admiral Mark Kerr who was instrumental in creating the *Royal Air Force* in 1918; Lieutenant-Colonel Moore, a Conservative politician who had become the first man to pilot a powered plane in England, later winning the Military Cross in the *Royal Flying Corps*; Frederick 'Bobbie' Hartman, director and partner of car importer Lendrum & Hartman who had served in the *Royal Naval Air Service* during the war; Winifred Spooner, another female aviator (who had presented Amy with a silver cigarette case at the lunch) and winner of the Harmon Trophy of 1929, would sadly die of pneumonia nine days later. [19]

The aristocracy were out in full force represented by Lady Dorothy

Dalrymple; Lady Iris Capell, a close friend of Lady Elibank; the Countess of Drogheda; the Marchioness of Douro (Duke of Wellington's family); the Marquess of Carisbrooke, Alexander of Battenberg – later Mountbatten, the last surviving grandson of Queen Victoria, now working for the bankers Lazard Brothers.

Viscountess Elibank read a message from the Prince of Wales, in which the Prince said: *"She (Amy) has given proof once again of the reliability of British aeroplanes and of her personal pluck and endurance which has won her universal admiration."* [20]

Three weeks later on 26 January, Dodo with her maid Rose – who was thrilled to be travelling again – embarked on a forty-seven day cruise from Southampton to the West Indies and Panama on board the Canadian Pacific ship *Duchess of Richmond*, with a social friend Lillian Hedley, a married woman in her forties who was a close neighbour of the Elibanks' in St James' Court and her older travelling companion, Sir Ernest Tate, the third Baronet, and director of Tate & Lyle the sugar refiners – he was in his sixties. As a director of Henry Tate & Sons and son of the founder, it was his influence that effected the merger with Abram Lyles & Sons in 1921. For this cruise, they were all travelling without their partners. Tate had recorded his status as single – despite still being married to Mildred.

Other passengers taking the winter sunshine included a high number of wealthy industrialists, but also the parents of the up-and-coming fashion designer, Norman Hartnell; Andrew Murray, Viscount Dunedin, a Scottish politician and judge and friend of Ramsey Macdonald – the then Prime Minister; Lady Ellen Hardwicke who had recently divorced the eighth Earl. Her only daughter Elizabeth had just married Thomas Coke, the fifth Earl of Leicester and would eventually become Lady of the Bedchamber to the Queen in the early 1950s.

The cruise was to take them to Gibraltar, across the Atlantic to Trinidad, Venezuela, Curacao, Panama, Jamaica, Cuba, Bahamas, Porto Rico, Barbados, Grenada, St Lucia and returning via Madeira.

Throughout 1932, Canadian Pacific cruise advertisements ran in the press with offers to the Mediterranean and in the autumn the West Indies:

"Nearly seven weeks cruise to these
enchanting winter sunshine resorts.
Join the Canadian Pacific West Indies

Cruise by the splendid modern 20,000 ton cruising liner
Duchess of Richmond, a ship of Ducal Splendeur.
Beautifully fitted cabins, beds instead of bunks,
fine public rooms, wide decks,
gymnasium, sunbathing pool, etc.
Limited Membership.
From Southampton Jan 28
First Class only.
Minimum rates 80 gns."

After a totally relaxing cruise the ship steamed towards England, passengers learning from the ship's daily wireless bulletin that there had been a great blizzard in February causing widespread disruption throughout the country. However, by the time the ship docked in Southampton on 14 March the weather had improved to a more familiar mild wet climate of an early spring day.

Whilst Dodo had been away, her friend Ermine Elibank had moved out of St James' Court into a new house at 23 Pelham Place, part of a Regency terrace in Kensington. She had it redecorated whilst staying with friends in Alassio on the Italian Riviera. It had become a favourite winter destination for the British who came for the climate, clean air and beach, after the rail line opened up the coast in 1872 to the rest of Europe. Tennis courts, libraries, clubs, tea rooms and a casino were all built and Alassio became one of 'the' spots on the Mediterranean. It inspired the composer Edward Elgar to write a concert-overture whilst staying there – it was a small fishing village then. The fashionable would sit in and outside the popular *Caffè Roma* run by the Berrino family on the palm tree-lined corner of Via Dante and Cavour, an ideal position to watch the world go by.

★

There was a letter waiting for Dodo on arrival at Chandos Court, asking her to make contact with the representative of the Dalrymple estate, James Blackburn, the London solicitor in his office at Ormond House, Queen Victoria Street. What she learnt was devastating. David had made a new will and together with an inventory of his assets, it had been confirmed under Scottish law. She read the contents:

"*This is the last will and Testament of me David Charles Herbert Dalrymple, Baronet, of 2 Walton House Longford Street, …*

I hereby revoke all Wills and Codicils…

I appoint my sister Alice Dalrymple and Patrick Keith Murray of the firm Messrs. Hope Todd and Kirk, Edinburgh to be Executrix and Executor…

Subject to any rights which my wife may have in accordance with the Law of Scotland to claim and receive one third of all my property I give devise appoint and bequeath all my real and personal property of whatever nature or kind and wheresoever situate unto my said sister Alice Dalrymple absolutely…

In witness whereof I have herunto set my hand 17th November 1932, in the presence of

James Blackburn and Alexander McCall." [21]

James Blackburn concluded the meeting by reading the inventory of assets. There followed a list of some furniture, a life assurance, the value of his Buick car, less outstanding payments, and some cash with Lloyds Bank; the total amounted to £1,170-17s-1d, and Dodo's share would be a little under £400. In his final weeks we may see the hidden hand of Dalrymple's first wife influencing the Trustees, although one would expect they would take little persuasion.

The words from the grave still resonating: "*Subject to any rights which my wife* (no endearment – not even mentioned by name) *may have in accordance with the Law of Scotland to claim and receive one third of all my property*".

David had clearly expressed his contempt for their relationship, using Scottish Law to his advantage. Perhaps he knew she could survive and in any case she had helped him spend the available estate money. But he could not deprive her of her title. Guided by the vengeful Margaret, the eighteen-year-old third Baronet Mark Dalrymple had made it abundantly clear that no further funds would be forthcoming.

She was still Lady Dalrymple however; the widow was now without a source of income, no assets to speak of and how long would a few hundred pounds last? She was 'stony' – "*Don't I know it darling!*"

★

As one door closes another opens. As ever the sympathetic Ermine was a source of practical advice; some twenty years older and with a motherly concern, she immediately set about to help her use her title to advantage and find a suitable husband. The relationship with James Sanders hadn't worked out – he was too set in his ways and he never did marry.

Whilst travelling in America three years later he suffered a heart attack at Grand Central Station in Manhattan, and promptly died, leaving just £4 to his married sister Cora.

Alex Hill whilst kind and gentlemanly wasn't for her either – knew too much about poisons for one thing and probably wouldn't divorce his wife anyway. Alex eventually moved from Chandos Court, taking an apartment in Buckingham Palace Road, finally retiring from BDH in 1943 and died in 1948.

Never 'slow on the uptake', what about 'Bobbie' Hartman who she met at the Amy Johnson banquet? He was divorced and his business was apparently thriving; she had enjoyed sharing a table with him, he had amusing conversation, a bit of a charmer really, and was entertaining company. He was certainly a contender and older too.

Act IV
Captain Hartman's Business
(1933–1942)

"We're in the money
We're in the money
We've got a lot of what it takes to get along."

Sung by Ginger Rogers in the musical film Gold Diggers of 1933.

-19-

Third time lucky

"This is Lady Dalrymple's third marriage. She has twice been a widow."
The Edinburgh Evening News, November 1933

Just after the New Year of 1933, and before the traditional Scottish Burn's Night, the Elibanks had a housewarming party at 23 Pelham Place to celebrate their silver wedding anniversary. They had sent invitations out to all their friends printed in the form of a 'wedding invitation' – R.S.V.P. or call on Kensington 7634. It would turn out to be a year of weddings for Ermine and Gideon.

Later in April, Pelham Place hosted a special dinner, arranged for some of Ermine's close friends. The guests included the radiant sun-tanned 'Dodo' Dalrymple and 'Bobbie' Hartman. The newly decorated house interior in parchment yellow situated in a quiet crescent of Regency houses was the perfect setting for an intimate dinner party. The marvellous dining table seating eight was made out of mahogany taken from a complete circular section of a tree. The room's centrepiece was Ermine's portrait by de Laszlo, hung over the dining room mantelpiece, highlighted by a new picture light. The reflection catching the reddish-brown patina of the dining table wood created a very intimate atmosphere. Ermine had taken care with placing guests.

The table setting 'was a divine inspiration' as Dodo and Bobbie found they had much in common. They both loved cars – and of course Bobbie made his money selling them. Not any old cars but big American imports like Buicks and Cadillacs, from his prestigious showrooms in Albemarle Street. He was a good listener and had the ability when in conversation of making one feel they were the only person in the room. He was tall at five foot eleven, with dark hair and blue eyes. He confided that he had also sold a Buick Sports Roadster to her late husband, Lord Dalrymple. The party guests made polite noises about Ermine's de Laszlo portrait, complimenting Ermine on the excellent likeness painted with great skill and dexterity. It had been Gideon's choice of artist. Bobbie not only agreed with the other guests, he was also aware of de Laszlo's Guinness family connections, casually mentioning he'd sold a custom-built Cadillac V16 to Sir Arthur Ernest Guinness a year or so earlier – a salesman is never 'off-duty'. He amused everyone describing some of his advertising stunts in the previous years – one included a couple dancing on the roof of a Buick saloon while it was being driven in London's West End. To prove its hill climbing ability he had another driven up a long flight of stairs in the grounds of the Crystal Palace. [1]

★

Their relationship soon moved up a gear, and they were now seeing each other on a regular basis. He had invited her to stay at newly acquired Northease Manor (Lewes 491), his country house in Sussex, saying he would value her opinion on suggested alterations and decorations. She had mentioned she'd been taught to drive by Gabrielle Borthwick – which amused him as he knew the Brick Street garage off Piccadilly very well. He'd also planned to take part in the RAC rally to Torquay in 1932 but had to pull out for business reasons. He was impressed she had managed to complete the thousand miles with Iris Capell successfully.

He asked if she rode – she didn't – and went on to explain a love of horses; he'd been involved with Arab-bred horses since the late 1920s, and had exhibited one bred by King George V when living in Surrey with his second wife at Ravenswood, on Kingston Hill. He had a keen interest in hunting, now he had a country home he could pursue it. He mentioned that he was a member of the Southdown Hunt, and a few years earlier had been invited to the Badminton Hunt Ball where the Prince of Wales had been guest of honour. He put up at the Grey House in Tetbury a few miles away with a party of fellow guests. (All that was true, but what he failed to mention was he was also entertaining yet another lady during the weekend house party.)

He came around to explain about his marriage – he'd been married twice before, both coincidently named Dorothy. He had married Dorothy Rose in 1912, served in the *Royal Naval Air Service* during the war and later transferred to the *Royal Engineers* – but had to be invalided out. Dorothy Rose was a jealous woman and they divorced at the end of the war.

He then married Dorothy Ailsa, his second wife in June 1923 and despite taking her on a business trip to New York she took no interest in the company he was working to build, finding the socialising tedious. Lendrum & Hartman had recently been made the sole concessionaires of imported Buick and Cadillac cars. He was clearly proud of that achievement after the effort he had put in – actually sailing to New York to pitch for and winning General Motor's concession. They had drifted apart – they had no children – and inevitably he had an affair and naturally Dorothy divorced him.

All this was true, but glossed over in the retelling. His second wife had divorced him over his affair with his pretty twenty-four-year-old secretary Gabrielle Brown, who he had taken to New York on a business trip staying at the *Plaza*.

His daughter Betty from his first marriage had recently married Lieutenant Clive Gwinner of the Royal Navy in July at the medieval parish church of St Mary's in Alverstoke near Portsmouth. It was the same church where by coincidence a hundred years earlier, Dodo's maternal great grandfather James Manchester married Sophia Golding in 1821.

Bobbie didn't attend the wedding – his daughter was given away by her stepfather Horace Soper, as his wife had married again and settled in Hampshire.

Dodo too had practiced her past story explaining she'd been a dancer – with both parents dead, briefly married to an army officer who died of his wounds soon after the war. She married David Dalrymple who she had known since childhood; he'd served in the navy (as did her father) and recently divorced. He became a little aimless as his Scottish estate was largely run by a family trust, but preferred London and loved parties, and this had developed into a drink problem which hastened his recent death.

They were editing their past and both had reinvented themselves for each other. Despite Bobbie's sales ability there was no easier person to 'sell a line' to and Dodo was the better at it.

Apart from the servicing and support staff Bobbie was essentially running the business himself, as his partner Ernest Lendrum had now retired to Maidenhead with the amusing but blousy Ida, his beloved second wife, around nine years older than Dodo. Ida was five foot eight with red hair and hazel eyes, born in a pub in London where her father John Freeman was the licensee, and 'being in the business' naturally progressed to barmaid – indirectly that's how she met Ernest.

Clearly Bobbie needed a wife who could take care of Northease, socialise effectively, whilst taking an interest in his business. Dorothy was ticking all the boxes. She had it seems many political connections through Ermine Elibank, and all these could be useful. He needed a new partner, and Bobbie being a 'lady's man' was out to hunt Dodo.

She of course new just how to respond. She played the grieving widow, but was clearly drawn to his charm. Although she let it be known that 'her fortune' was dependent on her retaining the title Lady Dalrymple – although in truth she was running out of money fast.

A consequence of 'being a woman of slender means' was to cut expenditure. Unfortunately that meant dismissing her lady's maid. Dodo had been a good employer, and given Rose the opportunity to travel with her on holidays to Spain and the Caribbean. However, she knew too much of her past affairs, and any indiscretion would be fatal with a possible marriage in the air. Servants talk; she had to let her go.

Rose found another position through Massey's Agency with the McEwan family at Albert Palace Mansions, near Battersea Park. Dodo was now free to concentrate on Bobbie.

★

As late spring merged into early summer, the promised wedding season started on May 9 with the Elibanks attending the wedding of Lady Mary Crichton-Stuart (eldest daughter of the fourth Marquess and Marchioness of Bute) to Edward Alan Walker (descendant of the Cobbold brewing family) who was in the diplomatic service. The wedding took place at the Brompton Oratory, and later the same month Gideon was playing in the Parliamentary golf handicap at Walton Heath golf course.

Whilst in the USA the same month, the Busby Berkeley musical *Gold Diggers of 1933* was released from Hollywood, although not screened in England till the late autumn. It featured an opening song performed by Ginger Rogers in which the chorus repeats: *"Oh boy, we're in the money, I'll say we're in the money, We've got a lot of what it takes to get along."*

The story turns around four aspiring actresses: Polly the ingénue (played by Ruby Keeler), Carol the torch singer (Joan Blondell), Trixie the comedienne (Aline MacMahon), and Fay the glamour puss (Ginger Rogers). The story begins with a rehearsal for a stage show, which is interrupted by the producer's creditors who close down the show because of unpaid bills. The story continues with ups and downs but all the 'gold diggers' end up married to wealthy men. It would be a good omen for Dodo.

★

The Elibanks' wedding season continued – and it reflects what wide social connections they had. In June they attended the wedding of the Earl of Inchcape's forty-five-year-old son; it was his second marriage, this time to Leonora Brooke, the eldest daughter of the White Rajah of Sarawak at St George's, Hanover Square. She was twenty-two. Her mother Sylvia allowed her daughters to grow up 'wild' with little in the way of boundaries and Sylvia was happy it was said to live vicariously through them. The 'dangerously beautiful' Brooke girls Leonora, Elizabeth and Nancy between them eventually married eight times; Elizabeth, a Royal Academy of Dramatic Art (RADA) trained actress, married the dance band leader and clarinettist Harry Roy.

In August yet another wedding; this time the Elibanks attended the Fairfax-Lucy and Buchan wedding at the Church of Scotland in Pont Street. Alice was the daughter of novelist and politician John Buchan (author of famous spy thrillers *The Thirty-Nine Steps*, *Greenmantle*, etc.). She married Brian Fairfax-Lucy, who was a thirty-four-year-old army officer, who served in the *Cameron Highlanders* and had been an Aide-de-Camp to her father. He also wrote children's books. They later succeeded to Charlecote Park, the Lucy family home, a sixteenth-century country house in Warwickshire, which eventually passed to the National Trust.

As the summer wore on, Bobbie took the plunge for the third time and suggested marriage to Dodo, over an intimate dinner at the recently opened *Dorchester Hotel* on Park Lane which was quickly becoming 'the' place to stay and dine. One can only imagine that sense of relief Dodo must have experienced, perhaps mixed with euphoria, at Bobbie's proposal.

Her agreement to wed must have sent Bobbie into raptures too as he had now secured an aristocratic trophy wife.

Jack Jackson was the *Dorchester*'s new bandleader and on the night Bobbie proposed (25 September 1933), his dance band music was relayed from the hotel over the wireless by the BBC.

As they danced Dodo was reminded of his pleasant scent (she discovered later it was Truefitt & Hill's CAR hair lotion) – his pervading fragrance became indelible. Later the same hairdresser would become a royal warrant holder to the Duke of Edinburgh.

Bobbie assured her he would make her a partner in the company and by marrying him she would not lose out financially, despite losing her title.

Since his divorce, Bobbie had been dividing his time between London and the country. He had a top-floor flat conveniently over his car showroom in the Beaux-Arts building at 26b Albemarle Street known as The Mellier, once the home and showroom of Charles Mellier & Co. Mellier was born in France and became a successful high quality cabinet maker and decorator; one of his most famous commissions had been for the liner, *Mauretania*, built in 1907.

The building now renamed Buick House was the Lendrum & Hartman showrooms. He had also taken a lease on another flat at 73 St James's Street. The entrance was actually in Little James's Street, next to the corner entrance of where Madame Prunier's fish restaurant was located. It has since closed, although its Paris restaurant in the Avenue Victor Hugo still operates, which during the twenties attracted writers such as F. Scott Fitzgerald and Ernest Hemingway.

Bobbie used his St James's pied-à-terre to entertain Gabrielle out of sight of office personnel, and conveniently close to the *Royal Automobile Club* in Pall Mall, one of the best equipped of all the gentlemen's clubs. It possessed an Edwardian Turkish bath, an Italian marble swimming pool, squash courts, a snooker room and of course a restaurant.

Most weekends he would drive down to Northease in Sussex looked after by a local cook/housekeeper. He liked to get away to the countryside and had recently joined the Southdown Hunt near Lewes. The summer before he'd entered the spirit of country life and contributed to the prizes at the Cooksbridge annual Gymkhana Horse and Hound Show.

He had to travel to New York in early December on business and suggested they could combine the trip with a honeymoon – they would stay until the New Year as General Motors were launching a new car event.

In the early autumn there followed a flurry of activity concerning the wedding. Dorothy agreed to leave Chandos Court after she was married and both could use the flat at Albemarle Street whilst in London, and would have Northease Manor as their main country home. As befitting their proposed new status, they should employ a valet for Bobbie and a lady's maid for Dodo to replace Rose – 'who left her unexpectedly some months ago'.

It was usual at the time to advertise for domestic staff in the *Lady* magazine; established in the 1880s it had always been particularly notable for its classified advertisements for domestic service and nannies. However, time was short and Dorothy knew of a domestic agency in Baker Street run by Mrs Ruth Massey. The family firm Massey's had started in the 1840s in the Midlands, and had opened a London office in 1920. As part of their agency process they had introduced the 'Certificates of Character', now known as 'References', which certainly helped with selection. It was through Massey's that Dodo had earlier recruited Rose Brace.

Dodo decided upon a twenty-five-year-old German girl Maria Tebbe who spoke good English and Bobbie acquired a Welsh valet, the thirty-one-year-old Aaron Peters. Unusually for a valet, he also declared he was married and his wife was living in Penarth near Cardiff at the time. With all the documentation needed, change of names and visas, they used the reliable services of Thos. Cook & Son's in Berkeley Street, who with their contacts were able to arrange first-class passage tickets, the necessary new passports and US visas quickly. It was around this time that Bobbie started to refer to his future wife as Dorothea; perhaps subconsciously his third 'Dorothy' should be in some way differentiated.

The pre-wedding party took place at the *Dorchester*, with its sentimental attachments. It had quickly become a leading hotel, from the moment it opened its doors in 1931, hosting a Gala Luncheon with a guest list from the cream of society, including the Foreign Secretary Sir John Simon;

Lord Irwin (later Halifax), recently returned as Viceroy of India; the BBC's Lord Reith; the American-born Grace Marchioness Curzon of Kedleston; the Earl of Rosebery and socialite Margot (Asquith), Countess of Oxford. The colossal, pillar-less ballroom, with its mirrored walls set with sparkling studs, could accommodate a thousand in splendour.

It was immediately adopted for the grandest balls and parties of the Season. The *Dorchester* soon became synonymous with all that was most fashionable in British society. Foyles Literary Luncheons began using the hotel, which brought writers and artists such as novelist Somerset Maugham (a frequent guest up to his death), the poet Cecil Day Lewis and the painter Sir Alfred Munnings.

The success of the new hotel owed much to the trumpeter and dance band leader Jack Jackson. He had originally joined Jack Payne and the BBC Dance Orchestra, but after a disagreement (well, a row actually) left to form his own band at the *Dorchester* in 1933. He was such a success he was put under contract and started a five-year residency. (A few years later they would hire his band to play at a hunt ball at Northease.)

Dodo would change her name from Lady Dalrymple to plain Mrs Hartman, unlike a fellow artiste and a previous Cochran dancer, Sylvia Hawkes. She had married Anthony Ashley-Cooper, son of the ninth Earl of Shaftesbury, titled Lord Ashley, in 1927. However, Sylvia continued to style herself Lady Ashley long after her divorce and even continued to use it through her next four marriages, to amongst others the actors Douglas Fairbanks and Clark Gable.

★

Dodo had learnt well from Ermine Elibank the benefit of the press and in the run-up to the wedding had been speaking to a number of sympathetic journalists, one of whom from the *Western Morning News* announced her wedding in her piece as *"A Bride in Gold"*, a reference to the proposed wedding dress:

> *"Another bride who decided upon a pre-wedding party was Lady Dalrymple, who is engaged to Capt. Frederick Hartman R. E. The last time I spoke to Lady Dalrymple she was suffering from the prevailing chill, ("I look a fright"* she might have said) *hoping that it would not turn out*

to be the dreaded influenza, as she is being married very soon, and almost immediately afterwards sails for America with Capt. Hartman. When the wedding does take place Lady Dalrymple will wear a dress of gold shades in satin and velvet."

Perhaps with the intoxication of the forthcoming marriage and the thrill of having your every word printed in the press, Dorothy advised a local Sussex paper of her pending marriage. It was duly reported in the *Sussex Express*, on Friday November 24 1933;

"A marriage has been arranged and will shortly take place between Captain F W Hartman and Lady Dorothy Dalrymple. Lady Dalrymple is the daughter of the late Captain Abbott R N and the late Countess of Granarni and widow of the late Sir David Dalrymple, Bart. Captain Hartman lives at Northease, Rodmell and is a well-known supporter of the Southdown Hunt."

The Countess of Granarni! Maud Coleno, a cockney to her fingertips would have laughed out loud, *"Cor blimey I wouldn't half love that role,"* you could almost hear her say, and she would have relished the part. William Abbott too would have been getting used to his naval title, but of course they were conveniently dead.

Jack Abbott, her brother, was aware of David Dalrymple's death and her pending new life with Bobbie Hartman. In the meantime he had married Mary Driscoll a few years earlier in the spring of 1930, also at St Pancras registry office – like Dorothy and Edwin Lewis. He was now living in Bethnal Green, and employed at the offices of George R. Cran, a solicitor in King's Bench Walk, EC4.

After her marriage to Bobbie Hartman their relationship would ebb and flow, until her brother had a daughter – the same year Bobbie died, when Dodo started to take interest.

★

On Thursday 23 November, a cold but dry London day, with little sunshine, Lady Dalrymple set out in her gold satin and velvet dress together with her only close friend Ermine Elibank, who had earlier the same day attended the Longland-Gwynne wedding at St Bartholomew's in Smithfield. Priscilla Gwynne was the daughter of an old political friend, Viscount Hailsham, who was providing his house in Portland Place for a reception, presided over by her aunt Viscountess Wolmer. Dodo would later include Hailsham in her social circle, inviting him to Northease.

Ermine with Dodo – clutching her little ivory-bound *Book of Common Prayer,* displaying a silver cross on the cover (later she would write an inscription). [2] She walked the short distance from Buckingham Gate along Caxton Street past the *St Ermine's Hotel* to the red and pink sandstone Victorian building that was the Caxton Hall, corner of Caxton and Palmer Streets. The building had only been established as a registry office the same year, and after the Hartman wedding would in future years become the registry office of choice of the rich and famous, including the following February, Cary Grant and Virginia Cherrill – Charlie Chaplin's leading lady in *City Lights.*

Before it finally closed in 1979 the hall had hosted many celebrity marriages included Donald Campbell (twice), Elizabeth Taylor, Ingrid Bergman, Ringo Starr, Diana Dors (twice) and Peter Sellers.

Only a few friends attended their civil ceremony, Bobbie Hartman's mother Edith and his father Augustus, now in their seventies, solicitor Charles Culross who together with Ermine Elibank acted as the witnesses.

They had arranged a blessing service at Christ Church, Broadway, and a short walk from the registry office. The church had been built in the 1840s in the early Victorian Gothic Revival style, but would be completely destroyed eight years later in the London Blitz.

The press announced their wedding:

> "LADY DALRYMPLE WEDS
> HONEYMOON TO BE SPENT IN AMERICA
> Lady Dalrymple, widow of Sir David Dalrymple, of Newhailes Musselburgh, Midlothian, was married yesterday at Caxton Hall, Westminster, London to Captain Frederick William Hartman of the Royal Engineers. Lady Dalrymple is 35 and Captain Hartman is 49.
>
> Only a few friends were present at the civil ceremony, but a large number of guests attended the religious service which followed immediately at Christ Church, Victoria Street.
>
> The couple came down the register office steps, the bride carrying a Prayer

Book, and walked over to the church, just opposite, together. There they were joined by a number of friends and relatives, including the bridegroom's father and mother, Mr and Mrs A Hartman and Lady Elibank.

No reception was held as a pre-wedding party took place at a hotel on the previous night. The honeymoon is to be spent in America.

This is Lady Dalrymple's third marriage. She has twice been a widow."

The Edinburgh Evening News.

On 2 December, the same day the newly married Hartman's sailed to America, Ermine Elibank attended her final wedding of the year that of her niece Islay Balfour at St Ethedreda's church in Holborn. Islay was the sister of Conservative Member of Parliament, Harold Balfour.

Dodo, Bobbie and their servants Peters and Tebbe together with many cases of luggage arrived at Southampton to board the SS *Bremen*, the 49,000-ton German ocean liner for New York. She was built for the Norddeutsche Lloyd line (NDL) and her sister ship, *Europa,* were the two most advanced, high-speed steam turbine ocean vessels in their day, and both vied in the international competition for the Atlantic 'Blue Riband'. They carried over 2,000 passengers, with 860 of them in first class, which is of course how the Hartmans travelled.

It was sumptuously appointed and a unique feature of both ships was a catapult on the upper deck between the two funnels with a small seaplane, which facilitated a faster mail service. The airplane was launched from the ship several hours before arrival, speeding transatlantic mail delivery by up to a day.

The 1930s saw the golden age of transatlantic ocean liners – each line seeking the lucrative first-class market and attracting the travellers of the day.

Their fellow passengers on that crossing to New York included the socialite 'Chips' Channon, a flashy, wealthy, American-born bisexual, a gifted and flamboyant host. Accompanying him was the equally outrageous and attractive Viscountess Doris Castlerosse, the most notorious courtesan of the 1930s. Born plain Doris Delavigne in the South London suburbs, had slept her way through high society, of whom one observer, the equally forthright Rosa Lewis once remarked, *"You should write a book and call it Around the World in Eighty Beds"* and summed up her opinion of the lady by saying, *"Young Doris may go far on those legs of hers, but mark my words she doesn't know how to make a man comfortable."* [3] Dodo on the other hand made men feel very comfortable. They were all to stay at the *Waldorf Astoria*. The Art Deco hotel is located on Park Avenue, just north of Grand Central Terminal. The building, built over the railway track with its own underground rail platform, opened in 1931. With forty-seven stories, it was at the time the tallest (at 625 feet) and largest hotel in the world. It would host US Presidents, starting with Herbert Hoover, together with societies rich and famous. It would be forever associated with the ubiquitous 'Waldorf salad' – a salad made with apples, walnuts, celery, grapes, and mayonnaise. Cole Porter, a long-time resident of the hotel in the 1930s, even featured it in his 1934 song 'You're the Top'.

It was an exciting time in New York; Prohibition had just ended after fourteen years, and the city was full of activity with the recently-built Rockefeller Center, which had begun a tradition of decorating an enormous Christmas tree in the street level plaza. It was also the opening of Radio City Music Hall, with its first Christmas show being produced in December 1933, along with the RKO musical movie *Flying Down to Rio* and *The Night Before Christmas*, a Walt Disney Silly Symphony, and these ran for two weeks.

★

Captain Hartman had travelled to New York to re-establish his business contacts with General Motors, show off his attractive new wife and to attend the Motor Show – known as the 'Motorama', an automobile show hosted by GM since 1931, showcasing the event in the *Waldorf*'s Grand Ballroom. These automobile extravaganzas were designed to boost automobile sales with displays of prototypes, concept vehicles and other special events including performances and movies. The idea had been developed by Alfred P. Sloan, General Motor's President, whose strong manufacturing and sales organisation skills had projected the company into position as the world's leader in automobile manufacture by the 1930s. In 1934 he also created the foundation that bears his name as a philanthropic non-profit organisation.

He was the man Bobbie Hartman wanted to cultivate and he and his new wife would entertain him any time he was to visit England.

Amongst the General Motors executives they met during the round of meetings and parties were Nick Vansittart, accompanied by his new forty-two-year-old Belgian wife Marguerite and his sixteen-year-old stepson Jean-Louis Geisar, having arrived on the SS *Europa* for the 'Motorama' Motor Show on 4 January.

Nick had joined the General Motors Continental business as sales manager in 1927, and three years later was promoted to regional director for Europe based in Antwerp. The Hartmans returned to Southampton on the same ship's return voyage, arriving on January 12.

With a common affinity with General Motors, their business and private lives would intertwine over the coming years, turning into a friendship that would last for the rest of their lives.

-20-

The Hartmann family

Shortly after returning from America to begin their married life at Northease, in February 1934 they had news that Augustus Hartmann, Bobbie's father, had died at his home in Kensington at the age of seventy-seven. The news was reported in the Kent press: *"The death occurred suddenly on Saturday of Mr Frederick Carl Augustus Hartmann, of 14 Kensington Square, London... for the past six years had used the old Cloth Hall at Cranbrook as his summer residence..."*

He left his fortune of £362,238-11s-1d (£13m today) to his wife Edith and the will had stated: *"Owing to the ever-increasing taxation and having during my life contributed liberally to public as well as private charities, I do not make any bequests to public charities."*

The Hartmanns originally came from the villages of Aumund and Vegesack harbour, part of greater Bremen since the 1800s on the banks of the River Weser in north Germany.

There had been a Captain Augustus Hartmann at Waterloo in 1815, fighting as part of the second line battalion of the *King's German Legion* at La Belle-Alliance. They were some of the finest units in the Duke of Wellington's army during the Waterloo campaign, and by all accounts he survived. [4]

Bobbie's grandfather Hinrich Hartmann was born in 1814, becoming a builder and architect. He married Metta Stricker in 1840 and they had ten children, five sons and five daughters, although some died in infancy.

One of the elder sons, Wilhelm, came to England in 1863 and after his father died, the rest of the family followed.

James Suter, a Swiss silk merchant living in London and Wilhelm Hartmann formed a partnership in 1870, Suter, Hartmann and Rahtjen's

Composition Company, with offices at 18 Billiter Street, London, EC as sole consignees to sell Rahtjen's paint in the United Kingdom.

John Rahtjen had developed a special paint in Germany that was an effective antifouling composition protecting ships' metal hulls, although he had not taken a patent out on the formula.

The Hartmann brothers, Johann, Wilhelm, Georg and later Augustus expanded the business and started to develop the overseas market. In 1878 Augustus, the youngest brother and Bobbie's father, was made a partner in the company on coming of age. The same year Hartmann, La Doux & Maecker had been established with exclusive rights to sell Rahtjen's composition paint in North America. Richard La Doux, a keen art collector had been the Liverpool director of the firm. The business was consolidated in 1888 under Suter, Hartmann & Rahtjen's Composition Company Ltd.

The company became very successful with agencies in Liverpool, Glasgow, Newcastle-on-Tyne and throughout the empire.

By the turn of the century they could boast that their paint composition had been used by more than 430,000 tons of the British Navy, and annually supplied to over 5,436,000 tons of the world's mercantile marine, and most of the torpedo boat destroyers then in service.

They had patented this composition in 1873 and introduced a 'red hand logo' that would feature on future advertisements. At the height of their success they commissioned a painting by the prolific British marine artist Bernard Finegan Gribble of a dreadnought class battleship in a Portsmouth floating dry dock, to promote their product on a series of full-colour enamelled metal advertisement panels displayed around the country. [5]

Friedrich Carl Augustus Hartmann became a naturalised British citizen in 1883 at the age of twenty-six and the same year married Jessie Edith, daughter of William Bellingham, a distiller and wine merchant, of Dalston; she was twenty-one. They set up home with a retinue of servants in a large Georgian mansion house at 54 Lee Park, in the leafy village of Blackheath, which was then in Kent. It would become a prosperous suburb of the expanding London. They had two sons; Friedrich Wilhelm, born a year later in April and three years after that, Carl Herbert.

Friedrich in the immediate family was known as Willie and Carl known as Herbert. Both in turn boarded at *Banstead Hall*, a preparatory school in Surrey run by Edward Jervois Maitland, son of a Devonshire rector, one-time assistant master at *Harrow*. He had recently married and joined the school in 1889 as the new thirty-two-year-old headmaster.

Willie went on to attend *Uppingham* and Herbert was sent to *Charterhouse* in Godalming, boarding at 'Bodeites', one of the new houses – originally Buissonites, named after the Head of Languages at the time, Monsieur Buisson. He apparently ran off with the matron, and so the house was renamed Bodeites in 1881 after his replacement Mr Bode.

Herbert left at the end of Cricket Quarter in 1904. He went on to study at the *Ecole des Beaux-Arts* in Paris between 1906 and 1907. Returning to England, he was articled to the London architect John Belcher. After completing his apprenticeship in 1910 he commenced an independent practice in partnership with Gerald Eckett Dunnage, a fellow architect and surveyor, a few years older.

Dunnage & Hartmann set up offices at 10 Lancaster Place off the Strand, and the same year promoted their practice by advertising in Volume 38 of the *Academy Architecture and Architectural Review*, by Alexander Koch. It featured their entry drawings of a house in South Harrow. Later they were commissioned by Balfour and Esher [6] to submit drawings for a proposed home and department of genetics research station at Storey's Way, Cambridge University in 1912, which was described: *"Even before the official purchase, Esher contacted the architectural firm Dunnage and Hartmann, to draw up designs for the build structures… I think he* (Herbert Hartmann) *has designed an excellent house…"* [7]

★

Herbert was contented to live at the family home at Netherfield House, paying his father ten shillings a week as rent. He never married. After war was declared, knowing his elder brother had joined the *Royal Naval Air Service* in February 1915, he too joined up and six months later, Herbert was commissioned a lieutenant in the *Queen's Own Royal West Kent Regiment*. He served on the Western Front and was killed in action on 2 July 1918 fighting with the Fifth Territorial battalion at the Somme, aged thirty-one. He was buried at Bouzincourt Ridge Cemetery in Flanders.

When probate was announced the following year, he was described as a gentleman of no occupation leaving his father Augustus £2,512.

He is remembered in the *Charterhouse* memorial chapel. It is chilling to imagine that 687 *Charterhouse* boys died in the Great War, about as many as there were boys in the school at any one time at that period. [8] In 1922 Augustus, Edith and Willie attended the unveiling of a memorial at St Thomas à Becket, the thirteenth-century church at Pagham in Sussex where three windows in the north transept are dedicated to their youngest son's memory.

The Suter, Hartmann & Rahtjen's Company made Augustus and his brothers very wealthy. Johann the eldest had established a branch of the business in Cardiff, looking after mercantile shipping out of south Wales from his home at Windsor Esplanade, overlooking the sea. He died in 1899.

Wilhelm had a large house in Blackheath named Bremen Lodge (a reminder of his birthplace), and early in the new century had bought Tangley Mere in Chilworth, in the Surrey hills near Guildford. His brother Georg had married the eldest Bellingham daughter Emily in 1879 and lived nearby in Albury. Emily died ten years later at the age of thirty-five and he got married again two years later, to Bessie Hughes, the twenty-four-year-old daughter of artist William Hughes, a still life painter, who exhibited at the Royal Academy. They lived at Newland in Weston Green, Thames Ditton.

Augustus and his family had also moved to the Surrey countryside to a house known as Chinthurst at Shalford Common near Guildford.

By 1901 Augustus, still in his early forties, had semi-retired and moved the family to Weybridge, buying Netherfield House on the heath, remaining there for the next ten years or so. The house was demolished in the 1960s and the land is now the site of the GSK (GlaxoSmithKline) Laboratories.

Just before the war Augustus and Edith moved back to London to a house at 14 Kensington Square, managed by four servants. It was conveniently close to the high street departmental stores of Derry & Toms, who prided themselves on being the supplier of goods to the upper class of Kensington, together with the stores of Barkers and Pontings.

The square had been laid out in the late seventeenth century, becoming highly fashionable when William III bought Nottingham House and converted it into Kensington Palace. The square was originally called Kings Square and until the 1840s was surrounded by fields. To keep himself occupied in 'retirement', Augustus became a stockbroker with offices at Warnford Court, Throgmorton Street, EC2, where he was joined later by his eldest son, Willie.

Later, in the early 1930s, he became a partner in Medley, Hartmann & Co. Limited, Broad Street Avenue, EC2. They were involved with a number of large share issues in companies ranging from Belle Vue Manchester, to the Lower Ancobra Gold Mine in the Gold Coast (now Ghana).

Around 1910 Augustus commissioned a new holiday home in Sussex, close to the Craigwell estate at Aldwick, between Bognor and Pagham. It was a large house built in the mock Tudor style of the day with extensive gardens, on land between The Grange and Waters Edge, close to the sea shore and beach. The house, named Tyting, was a place where the family could relax.

The south coast climate and rural atmosphere of Aldwick in those late Edwardian pre-war years attracted a number of well-heeled business and political people and soon there was an enclave of numerous individual houses built with names that expressed perhaps the occupants idylls, such as Almora, Pinehurst, Paradise, The Glen, The Thatched House, Summerlands, Meadow Cottage, Kit Kat Cottage, the Wig Wam – all dotted around the estate.

In 1915 Sir Arthur Du Cros bought Craigwell House and the wooded estate of some thirty acres. He was awarded the baronetcy in 1916 in recognition of his war efforts, which included the introduction of the Motor Ambulance Service. He was founder and President of the Dunlop Rubber Company as well as founding director of the Austin Motor Company. He was very much at the centre of politics; he is credited with having been the founder of the modern Conservative Party and it is known that two Prime Ministers, Bonar Law and Asquith, enjoyed his hospitality.

In 1919 he reconstructed Craigwell House in a lavish style, adding a wing to the east and west sides so that every bedroom had a sea view. The very latest technology was introduced. Seawater was pumped to every bathroom; and an electric lift served the three floors, an electric organ was installed (with music piped around the house) and a telephone system run throughout the house – all powered by an electric generator located in the grounds.

The house was put at the disposal of King George V who underwent an operation and prolonged convalescence between December 1928 and May 1929. The house was finally demolished in 1939.

Augustus had landscaped his garden and approached a specialist rose grower, the reputable Messrs. Benjamin R. Cant and Sons of Colchester who had developed a successful rose farm since the 1870s, to stock his garden at Tyting. In his honour the supplier named a new deep-red hybrid-tea variety after him. This cultivation was regularly exhibited at various horticultural shows through southern England, as reported in the *Gardener's Chronicle* in 1913:

> "ELTHAM HORTICULTURAL *(Kent)*
>
> *July 10. – The thirty-fifth annual show in the grounds of Eltham Court proved successful, but a heavy thunderstorm which occurred shortly after the opening hour prevented many from seeing the lovely grounds attached to the Court. In the competitive classes thirteen were provided for Roses. Four competed for the 'North' Cup, valued at 25 guineas and offered for the best collection of 48 blooms, distinct varieties: the 1st prize was awarded to Messrs. B. Cant and Sons, Colchester, who showed handsome flowers, large, clean and highly coloured, including the varieties Captain Hayward, Augustus Hartman, a new variety of a cherry-red colour and faultless shape…"*

> "WOODBRIDGE HORTICULTURAL *(Suffolk)*
>
> *Roses were a strong feature of the exhibition, being represented in eighteen classes. The leading class was for thirty-six blooms, distinct varieties, and the 1st prize was awarded to Messrs. B. Cant and Sons for fine specimens, including the following varieties: – Augustus Hartman, bright cherry-red…"*

In the spring of 1909 the Hartmanns had their first family marriage, Augustus's eldest son Frederick 'Willie' was married to Dorothy Rose Nye, daughter of a well-to-do Sussex solicitor, at the Anglican church of St Georges, Hanover Square. The church became fashionable from its first wedding in 1725 – an ancestor of Queen Elizabeth II, and from its beginning, over a thousand weddings a year were passing through in Regency times. Such as the ill-fated marriage of poet Percy Bysshe Shelley to Harriet Westbrook in 1814, when Shelley abandoned his pregnant wife and ran off to Switzerland with the sixteen-year-old Mary Godwin. The future British Prime Minister Benjamin Disraeli married the ten years older wealthy widow Mary Anne Lewis there in 1839. Handel was a regular worshipper at St George's, during his stay in London. In December 1886, Theodore (Teddy) Roosevelt, the future President of the United States of America, was married to Edith Kermit Carow, apparently only qualifying for marriage by staying for the required period at *Brown's Hotel* in Dover Street.

Augustus and Edith as befitting their social status entertained widely and were involved in many charity events. Typically, one such event, in the summer of 1913, a dinner held at Bathurst House in Belgrave Square, home to the Earl and Countess of Bathurst, was to raise money to secure the Crystal Palace for the nation, a fund promoted by *The Times*.

It was attended by Sir Robert Inglis, chairman of the London Stock Exchange who had contributed £100 towards the £90,000 needed, together with guests Princess Henry of Battenberg (youngest daughter of Queen Victoria), together with Mrs Augustus Hartmann, the Earl of Onslow (a politician who had held various government appointments), and Mr Pandeli Ralli, son of a wealthy Greek family and Liberal politician.

The Ralli brothers traded raw materials and grain in England as well as the USA and India. Originally from the island of Chios in the Aegean Sea, the family left during the turmoil under the Ottoman Empire that resulted in the Chios massacre in the nineteenth century. Through their contacts, which included Lord Byron, they rose to prominence in British business and aristocratic circles.

★

After Herbert's death in the Great War and following the dedication of the memorial windows to him at Pagham's St Thomas à Becket Church in 1922, Augustus and Edith sold Tyting. Perhaps with so many memories, it was time for a change. From around 1928 until his death, he chose to use Old Cloth Hall in Cranbrook Kent as his summer residence –not far from Sissinghurst, home to novelist Vita Sackville-West.

-21-

The Lady Hanson affair

Willie Hartmann was born on 7 April 1884 in Blackheath, growing up within a comfortable Anglo-German Victorian family who through their merchant endeavours had become very wealthy. His father had integrated into English society, becoming a British national the same year he married Edith Bellingham in 1883.

Their children were supervised by a twenty-one-year-old German nurse, Emilie Tiemann from Bremen, and later in the established English tradition, they were sent to the obligatory prep school, *Banstead Hall* in Surrey.

Whether Willie later attended *Charterhouse* isn't clear, but for the last year and a half of his schooling he was a boarder at *Uppingham School* in Rutland. He joined the autumn of 1898, the same term the school played their first rugby match against another school – *Rugby*.

Uppingham was founded by Archdeacon Johnson in 1584 by charter from the first Queen Elizabeth and he was boarded at 'School House', one of the so-called town houses, which had reopened in 1890. In those days, 'School House' was traditionally run by the headmaster, the recently appointed Reverend Selwyn who had arrived from Cambridge a few years earlier as a Doctor of Divinity. Willie Hartmann was one of his pupils.

Edward Carus Selwyn served as the headmaster for nineteen years and during that time, had eight children – six sons and two daughters. His wife Lucy was the granddaughter of Thomas Arnold of *Rugby*. Lucy died in 1895, two weeks after giving birth to a daughter. Selwyn it was said retired under something of a cloud in 1907 [9] and took a lease on Undershaw, a house in the Surrey hills near the village of Hindhead. It had been built by Sir Arthur Conan Doyle in 1897 for his ailing wife Louise, who had died in 1906. It was here he wrote *The Hound of the Baskervilles*. The house, built in the 'Surrey-vernacular' style, was largely composed of red brick and hanging tiles, surrounded by a four-acre woodland garden.

In the years following his retirement Selwyn was to tragically lose four sons; George, Arthur, Geoffrey and Christopher during the Great War. He died in the great influenza epidemic of 1918 – and it is said of 'a broken heart'. [10]

★

At *Uppingham* one of Hartmann's contempories, although a year younger, was Malcolm Campbell who went on to make his name in motor racing and journalism. His father was a Hatton Garden diamond seller, and like Willie didn't attend university. Eighteen years later when the Great War was over, 451 *Uppingham* 'old boys' had been killed, with four winning the Victoria Cross.

He left at the end of the autumn term in December 1899 at the age of fifteen. Out of the fourteen boys leaving *Uppingham* that term, only two went on to university. Some became engineers, or joined the army, others followed their family businesses, and Willie joined Suter, Hartmann & Rahtjen's Company. Although, after a period at the company's head office in Billiter Street, and time spend at the works in Silvertown, at the Royal Albert Docks, East London he decided that the chemical and paint business was not for him. We next hear about Willie as a stockbroker, working with his father at Warnford Court, in Throgmorton Street.

Willie, unlike his more academic brother, clearly preferred the interaction with people. Stockbrokering gave him that control, trust and influence with clients, and he enjoyed the social side and the affect that a positive sales pitch could produce – it was the embryo of a promising sales career, although his personal life was chequered. During 1907–8 he flirted briefly with the armed services, becoming a volunteer in the *Royal Engineers* as a second lieutenant. It was a position he would later embellish and adopt. It was during this time he had met his first Dorothy and a year later married her.

★

In 1909, the weeks leading to Thursday January 21 were mild with sunny periods, and then the weather began to turn colder, as Willie Hartmann with parental blessing married Dorothy Rose, the twenty-two-year-old, youngest daughter of Harry Nye, a successful Brighton solicitor.

Dorothy, one of three children, was born in Albany Villas, Hove – always considered the 'genteel' part of Brighton. The Nyes employed the twenty-four-year-old Lily Napper, Dorothy's cousin, as governess to the children. Harry Nye's practice prospered and by the time of Dorothy's marriage the Nye family had moved to the countryside – an even grander house, the Georgian Broadwater Manor near Worthing (today it houses *Lancing College Prep School*).

After a fashionable wedding at St George's, Hanover Square they settled into a comfortable Edwardian married life. Willie the stockbroker, and Dorothy the housewife in a house Augustus had bought for them called Chinthurst (after their old family home in Shalford Common). It was located on a woodland estate at Worbouys Road, Kingston Hill, bordering on to Richmond Park, and about ten miles away from the Hartmann family at Netherfield House, Weybridge.

They employed two servants, Florence Walter as cook who together with a house-parlour-maid Helen Crawe completed their suburban household.

Life for the newlyweds seemed perfect, when three years later Augustus and Edith were overjoyed to learn Dorothy was pregnant and later gave birth to their first granddaughter, Betty Doreen in January 1912.

However cracks were appearing in Dorothy and Willie's relationship. Like all couples they had rows and these were soon to become public property.

After war was declared on Germany, the initial view was 'it would all be over by Christmas'. However, events predicted it was going to last much longer. Hartmann applied to HMS *President*, the London shore establishment to join the newly formed *Royal Naval Air Service*. On 22 February 1915 he was appointed a temporary sub-lieutenant and gazetted a lieutenant in March. He appears from his service record to have now dropped the additional 'n' in his name.

He joined the *President* the same day as Andrew Aikman Smith, the son of James, a keen 'rugby man' who in the 1920s became the controversial president of Scottish Rugby Union. [11] Like Willie Hartman, Andrew too would be invalided out of the service, spending time at the Royal Naval Hospital Haslar in Portsmouth, after taking part in the Gallipoli campaign.

From his appointment, Hartman was essentially seconded to transport duties in England – far away from the front line. He had a brief period in Ireland in 1916 as Assistant to the Senior Naval Officer at Berehaven in Bantry Bay with the Kite Balloon Station.

During the summer of 1915, one Saturday night whilst returning from Folkestone, he was involved in an accident, knocking down a man as he stepped off the pavement in Sandgate Road, injuring his foot. The local press reported: *"the injured man was attended by the V.A.D. – (Voluntary Aid Detachment), after which he was removed to his home in a taxi-cab."* It didn't say who paid for the cab.

By November he seems to have been recovering from some illness or injury, and found himself in a very fashionable Park Lane hospital. The Astley Hospital for Officers opened in Dorchester House in November 1914 (it was also known as the Dorchester House Hospital for Officers). The building, once the American Embassy and home of the ambassador until his death in 1912, had been lent by its owner, Lieutenant Colonel Sir George Holford.

The hospital had twenty-five beds initially, eighteen of which were in rooms overlooking Hyde Park. The ballroom was made into a sitting room for the convalescents, while other parts of the house were converted into wards and dormitories. It was one of Mayfair's most breathtaking mansions. The most impressive part was the grand staircase. It dominated the centre of the house rising from a great balconied hall, a full three stories. Since 1905 it had been rented by the American Ambassador, Whitelaw Reid, and his lavish entertaining made it the hub of Anglo-American society. It was here Americans rang in the 4th of July, and where Alice Roosevelt Longworth prepared to make her court presentation to the King and Queen.

It was affiliated to Queen Alexandra's Military Hospital. The sister-in-charge was Miss Muriel Wilson, a society beauty and daughter of the wealthy ship owner family Thomas Wilson Sons & Co., whose country house was Tranby Croft near Hull, while Lady Sybil Grey, daughter of the fourth Earl Grey, who served as Governor General of Canada, acted as Commandant of the local Voluntary Aid Detachment. Sir Alfred Fripp, Surgeon in Ordinary to the King, was responsible for the medical care.

With such a high profile hospital it inevitably attracted many high society visitors. Lieutenant Hartman found himself attracted to a young visitor, Lady Hanson, who with others saw it as their duty to visit and comfort the patients. She was in a loveless marriage and had recently lost her only brother Reginald, killed in action during the Gallipoli campaign the previous September.

They immediately struck up a rapport that became more than a friendship. With her efforts he quickly recovered as she was captivated by his charm, as we now see evidence of Willie's persuasive sales pitch, having 'dropped' his family name. To Dorothy Hanson he had become 'Bobbie' and his wife becomes a 'vindictive American', who clearly didn't understand him. They had an affair whilst Lady Hanson's husband was away serving in France with the *Third Battalion Royal Fusiliers*. This affair was to have massive repercussions in the press and the cause two divorces.

★

Lady Hanson was born Dorothy Gwendoline in 1891, the daughter of a successful coal merchant Alfred Peel in Lincoln. She became a trained dancing teacher and moved to London where she met Sir Gerald Stanhope Hanson, recently widowed with a seven-year-old son Richard, known as Dick. They married at St Peters, Cranleigh Gardens in 1912; she was twenty-one, and Gerald was forty-five. Her father had died in 1907 and her brother gave her away – the press announced her mother was unable to attend due to an indisposition. It was not a marriage made in heaven. Gerald had a house in London in New Cavendish Street, and a country residence in Leicestershire at Eye Kettleby Hall near Melton Mowbray in the heart of the Quorn Hunt country.

Bobbie's affair with Dorothy Hanson continued for over a year, variously between New Cavendish Street and Kettleby Hall, and lasted until her untimely death in the great flu epidemic in October 1918.

Dorothy Hartmann became aware of this relationship and with her father's help, took divorce proceedings against her husband through her solicitors Messrs. Cook & Haddock of Horsham, engaging a highly experienced divorce lawyer, Mr W. O. Willis.

The announced proceeding triggered the second divorce – that of Sir Gerald Stanhope and Lady Hanson, as Dorothy Hartmann had cited several acts of cruelty (required under the law of the time) in her petition, such as threatening behaviour, hitting her on the arm, provocatively kissing another woman at a house party, and mental cruelty by coercion to defraud an insurance company as well as the main reason – the affair with Lady Hanson. The press had a field day.

The Times, February 6 1917 announced the details under their heading:

> *"Probate, Divorce and Admiralty Division.*
> *Divorce suit against a Stockbroker*
> *Hartmann v Hartmann*
> *(Before Mr Justice Dow)"*

The comings-and-goings of the affair was observed by Lady Hanson's French cook Elsie Ricau, who had been persuaded to support Dorothy Hartmann's petition. She gave evidence saying that between April and June 1916, at New Cavendish Street, the respondent ('Bobbie' Hartman) used to visit her mistress and occupied her room.

Bobbie didn't contend the divorce and Mr Justice Dow granted Dorothy Rose a decree nisi, awarded costs and the custody of their daughter Betty.

Then eight months later in October the same paper declared '*Divorce suit by Sir Gerald Hanson*' and published the contents of Lady Hanson's private letters:

> *"77 New Cavendish Street,*
>   *February 1917*
>   *… As you know when I married you, I had no love for you. I told you so repeatedly, and without affection naturally our marriage wasn't a happy one. If you issue divorce proceedings, which I think your family will urge you to do, do try and remember I have done my best for Dick* (Hanson's son by first marriage) *who has grown to love me, and with your affairs.*
>   *Bobbie Hartmann hasn't any money at all. Lack of means coupled with his ill-health prevented him fighting the other action. After his active service he is left in a very poor state of health, and his position all given up when he entered the service. I am sorry, Gerald to hurt you; It has all been a great mistake."*

Another letter reflects Dorothy Hanson's view of Bobbie's wife – clearly based on what he had told her – as she was under the impression she was American!

> *"77 New Cavendish Street,*
> *February 9, 1917*
> *… Bobbie's wife was very jealous and vindictive, and she certainly has hit very hard. It has been a dreadful blow to me and I am sure it has to you. This American woman has certainly succeeded in ruining me."*

The provincial press duly reported the edited details under various headings; *"Lieutenant and the Baronet's wife"* and *"Baronet thrashes co-respondent"* – this actually happened to Bobbie Hartman in Albemarle Street.

Stanhope's divorce was undefended too, and he won his case – although perhaps reflecting on the hypocrisy of his own affairs and that it was a loveless marriage, granted her an allowance of £750 a year.

★

By September 1916 Lieutenant Hartman had terminated his commission with the *Royal Naval Air Service* after eighteen months, being declared medically unfit. He had resumed his career as a stockbroker, whilst living with Lady Hanson in her cottage at 2 Jones Street at the top of Berkeley Square. He was now referring to himself as 'Captain' Hartman, late of the *Royal Engineers*.

This was plausible enough as in the early days of the formation of the *Royal Naval Air Service* it had absorbed the Air Battalion of the *Royal Engineers*. His extensive experience of cars in the Transport Division, together with his earlier volunteer experience with the *Royal Engineers* combined to offer him a revised wartime persona. In July 1917 the royal family had renounced their German titles and became the 'House of Windsor', likewise Bobbie had already chosen to anglicise Hartman – without the extra 'n'.

During his time based at HMS *President*, he had struck up a friendship with Henry Berenstein, who had served as driver and air mechanic and would later join him at Lendrum Motors. Born into a pre-war south

London family, he had been employed as a motor fitter with the General Carriage Co. who had revolutionised the taxi trade in London, by introducing a fleet of French-built Unic Renault cabs bought through the Mann and Overton dealership in 1906.

In September 1917, Hartman met Ernest Lendrum at a City function – he had just been made a Freeman of the City of London by the Company of Stationers, in recognition of his achievements in the paper industry. They struck up a friendship realising a mutual interest in motor cars.

Ernest Samuel Lendrum was forty-one, much the same height as Bobbie at five foot ten with a dark complexion, brown hair and eyes. He was already a director of a successful waste paper business, Lendrum Ltd, which he had created in his twenties. They recognised the sales opportunities there would be after the war, particularly for American cars, as the whole of British industry had been devoted to the war effort.

In July 1918, Bobbie learnt the news that his brother Herbert had been killed in France – his parents received the feared telegram – *"Deeply regret to inform you… Lord Kitchener expresses his sympathy…"* It left the Hartmann family devastated – the dull thud of repetitive war casualties – the slaughter of a generation would visit many families throughout the land.

It left Bobbie with a sense of guilt about his own charmed survival, which led perversely to the exaggeration of his wartime status. From being a lieutenant in the *Royal Naval Air Service*, he would emerge as 'captain' in the *Royal Engineers* in the post-war year years.

The same month Dorothy Hanson had rented Gyldercroft House in Marlow, to quietly share with Bobbie for the summer. It was the home of the elderly General Sir George Higginson, who had fought with the *Grenadier Guards* in the Crimean War, having his horse shot from under him at the Battle of Inkerman. He was a close friend of the royal family, and George V and Queen Mary had been regular visitors to the house.

Then within a month of returning to London, as the war was drawing to a close, Dorothy became ill; her mother Amelia Peel was contacted urgently. She travelled from Lincoln staying at the *Hendon Hall* hotel whilst helping to nurse her, but she died of influenza pneumonia on 24 October at her cottage in Berkeley Square. She was twenty-six.

Probate revealed in December that her entire estate of £1,010-4s-9d (£40k today) had been left to *"Frederick William Hartman retired captain of His Majesty's Army"*. Bobbie was named as her sole executor, and his solicitor Charles Culross & Co., of 13 Old Cavendish Street W1, handled the necessary legal papers, publishing the required notice in the *London Gazette* on 17 December.

Charles Culross was a little older than Bobbie, born in London, the son of a successful Scottish printer. He became an articled clerk and eventually set up his own legal practice. He was married and lived in Bickenhall Mansions off Baker Street. Culross and Bobbie Hartman would become life-long friends and Charles would eventually become a business partner in Lendrum & Hartman and very involved in his legal affairs.

-22-

Lendrum and Hartman Ltd

L&H 1939 brochure cover:
Buick, the wonder car of the age

With the war now ended, and unexpected good fortune, the capital left to him by Lady Hanson enabled Bobbie to invest in the motor business. Together with Ernest Lendrum they decided to travel to New York to negotiate a concession from General Motors to sell their cars in England.

There was a great hunger for cars in Britain after the First World War. British factories were not immediately able to get back into car production so many servicemen, who had learned to drive and had money from their demobilisation grants to spend, looked to America.

In 1919, two out of every five cars on British roads were Fords built in England, and anxious to compete General Motors were reviewing their sales and distribution strategy for the UK and Continental Europe. Under the skilled leadership of Alfred P. Sloan, General Motors had taken the automobile lead by the early 1930s, a position it retained for over seventy years. General Motors would become the largest industrial enterprise the world had ever known.

On May 18, 1919 Bobbie Hartman, now thirty-four, still living at Berkeley Cottage and the forty-two-year-old Ernest booked passage with the Cunard line travelling first class from Southampton to New York on the *Aquitania*; both were describing themselves as engineers. They returned to Liverpool on the *Royal George* a little over a month later. Their enterprise and initiative had paid off. General Motors had already established itself in London at Long Acre, but met with variable success over the years. The persuasive 'engineers' had secured a deal as non-franchised importers of top General Motors brands, Buick and Cadillac.

In October, Ernest registered the new company Lendrum Motors Ltd at 26b Albemarle Street, London W1, telephone Gerard 7138, using Bobbie's new apartment address. Share capital of £12,000 was issued in £1 shares mostly held by Ernest Lendrum of Hanover Court, Regents Park and Frederick Hartman, a director of Astoria Ltd., a court dressmaker in Berkeley Street as fellow director. Quite how Bobbie had become involved with a dressmaker is unclear – perhaps a legacy from Lady Hanson.

The following year they acquired the General Motors old premises in Long Acre and a year later moved to a better location in Mayfair, the recently vacated ground floor and basement premises of 26b Albemarle Street. 'Buick House' would be the Lendrum & Hartman Mayfair showrooms for the next thirty years.

The site had been redeveloped in 1905 previously the location of the Episcopal St George's chapel – served in the 1830s by chaplain the Reverend William Webb Ellis, of rugby football fame. It was the start of what would become one of the most prestigious car dealerships in the country.

★

Ernest Samuel Soames Lendrum born in Battersea in 1876 became a self-made man in his twenties. Eldest son of a London civil servant, he became a clerk in a waste paper business and by the time he was twenty-eight had his own company, Lendrum & Co. at Temple Avenue, EC4, with offices in Manchester, Glasgow and the London docks at Millers Wharf.

He had married the twenty-four-year-old Rose Eleanor Wills in Nottingham in 1903 but by the time of his business association with Hartman, the marriage was already in trouble; they had no children and divorced in 1920. Ernest had become involved with Ida Jessett Cracknell, a married red-head and personable barmaid with whom he had become acquainted. She was also in the throes of disengaging from an unsuccessful relationship. Her husband Reginald was an auctioneer and surveyor. Ida had actually been born in a pub as her father John Freeman ran the *Prince of Wales* in St George's Street, St Pancras.

★

By the spring of 1922, Bobbie's ex-wife Dorothy Rose Hartman had married Horace Nettleship Soper in Plymouth. He was a tall man, around six foot four with greying hair, the son of a London surgeon. As a young man he had joined the Eastern Telegraph Co. as a clerk, later becoming an electrician in the company which had laid much of the world's undersea telephone cables. He was posted to the Far East and sailed for Singapore in 1911 on the P&O *India,* and later when war broke out served as a second lieutenant in the *Royal Engineers* in Singapore.

He was particularly creative and inventive during his lifetime and is credited with many company patents related to mechanical and electrical devices.

The Sopers initially settled with ten-year-old daughter Betty Hartman in Callington, a little market town in Cornwall, around fourteen miles from Plymouth along the Tamar Valley.

Two years later they had a daughter Daphne. By the time of Betty's marriage in 1933 they had moved to Nepcroft on Steep Lane, set amongst the Sussex downs at Findon. After the Second World War they retired to London, living at Notting Hill Gate.

★

From the very early days, Lendrum & Hartman had had specialised bodies built on Buick chassis. In the 1920s the most popular were two-seater coupes with dickey seats, built by Page & Hunt of Farnborough, Surrey. It was one of these that the artist Augustus John had acquired in 1920 in exchange for a picture. His biographer records: "... *a powerful two-seater Buick with yellow wheels and a dicky. After enduring half an hour's lesson in London, he filled it with friends and set off for Alderney* (his country house in Dorset)." Despite his erratic driving and endless minor accidents, John would loyally insist his Buick was *"still running very sweet"*. [12]

The limousine version was usually by Vanden Plas of Brussels. The chassis for the latter were shipped from the London docks and they returned finished to Harwich, several at a time, escorted by the Lendrum & Hartman Belgium representative.

In early 1922, Norman Littlejohn joined Lendrum Motors as a new director, and Henry Edward Berenstein had also become part of the sales team, joining after leaving the *Royal Naval Air Service* as one of Bobbie's prodigies.

The same summer, the company took a new lease on the facilities at Old Oak Lane in Willesden, which became the 'Buick Works', as General Motors announced they were looking to appoint another agent in London. Interested parties should attend a series of meetings at the General Motors Building, Fifty-Seventh Street and Broadway to pitch for the business.

On September 6, Hartman sailed to New York on the White Star RMS *Majestic* to attend these meetings. The ship was one of two German-built liners for the Hamburg America line handed over (reluctantly) to the Allies as war reparations. She was the largest ship in the world at the time.

Hartman won the race and after the resulting meetings returned with franchises to sell Buick and Cadillac. Ernest was thrilled with the success of his partner, known as the 'Captain'. Hartman was finding his true vocation – sales and cars, not to mention an eye for the ladies.

Following the success of his New York trip Ernest made the business into a true partnership; on January 13 1923 Lendrum Motors became Lendrum & Hartman Ltd. Bobbie was still living above the car showroom at 26b Albemarle Street, although he also had an alternative flat at 73 St James's Street, away from inquisitive employee eyes.

The same month he was again socially networking and secured an invitation to the prestigious Beaufort Hunt Ball at Neeld Hall, Chippenham, in the presence of the Prince of Wales and Prince Henry – later Duke of Gloucester. The press announced it was a complete success with over 500 attending, including the very cream of society, centred on Badminton House, the home of Duke and Duchess of Beaufort. Whilst the close friends stayed in the house, the others were scattered around the county in various residences.

Captain Hartman as he now presented himself shared the Grey House in Tetbury with around a dozen house guests, hosted by the Cripps family. The house party included a selection of single county girls, including Janice Wykeham- Musgrave of Barnsley Park whose older brother Kit had amazingly survived (although 1,450 sailors were killed) being torpedoed three times on subsequent ships the same day – all within the space of an hour (HMS *Aboukir, Hogue, and Cressy*), whilst serving as a fifteen-year-old midshipman during the early part of the Great War. Janice never did marry.

By May, still maintaining his new ex-military persona, he had met and announced his engagement in *Flight Magazine* to Dorothy Ailsa Discombe, and a month later the wedding was announced in the same magazine:

"Capt. FREDERICK WILLIAM HARTMAN, late R.E., attached R.N.A.S., only surviving son of Mr. and Mrs. Augustus Hartman, of 14, Kensington Square, was married on June 2, in London, to DOROTHY AILSA, only daughter of the late Mr. GEORGE HART DISCOMBE and Mrs. DISCOMBE, of 20, Edith Grove, Chelsea."

On a cloudy, mild and dry London day, they were married at St George's, Hanover Square on 2 June. The witnesses included Charles Culross – Hartman's solicitor and friend. The twenty-five-year-old socially conscious Dorothy had been residing nominally at *Claridge's* before the wedding, so it could be recorded on the certificate.

She was born in Chelsea, a rather tall young woman at five foot nine, with a dark complexion, brown hair and brown eyes. She had been privately educated at *St Stephen's College*, Windsor, run by an Anglican religious order of Augustinian nuns, the Sisters of St John Baptist.

The press announcement of the marriage described Dorothy's father as the 'late' George Hart Discombe. This was incorrect; far from being 'late', he was very much alive. Her parents had been divorced in 1903 and George didn't actually die till 1924. But no doubt it 'saved face' with her socially conscious mother.

Her parents were in trade, Catherine a daughter of a bootmaker in the Kings Road, and George a tailor, when they were married in 1890. Dorothy's older brother Algernon had been sent to a prep school in Horsmonden, Kent, then to *Berkhamsted*, the Anglican independent school in Hertfordshire and became a successful locomotive engineer working for many years in West Africa. On returning to England, rather late in life he married Phyllis Dascombe, daughter of a Bristol police inspector. He died in Swansea in 1950 leaving £1,764-19s-2d to his wife and sister Dorothy.

The newly married Hartmans established a home in London at 58 Brompton Square SW3 close to the Brompton Oratory, with a small Sussex weekend cottage, Ashcroft, in the Kingston Lane, Southwick, not far from Hove.

The remainder of the 1920s was a period of rapid growth for Lendrum & Hartman. In 1924 between April and October the British Empire Exhibition was staged at Wembley Park, which saw the opening of Wembley Stadium. The 219-acre site was the largest exhibition ever staged anywhere in the world, attracting twenty-seven million visitors. It was officially opened by King George V, and General Motors of Canada Limited took the largest space in the Canadian Pavilion, receiving a visit from the Prince of Wales.

James D. Mooney had been made President of General Motors Overseas in 1922, responsible for operations around the world. He spent most of the summer at the exhibition making political contacts with Prime Minister Stanley Baldwin as well as Minister of Transport, Leslie Hore-Belisha. He would later become something of a controversial figure because of his association with Nazi Germany. A year later in November, General Motors acquired Vauxhall Motors in Luton for $2.5 million.

In late August the Hartmans sailed to New York on board the White Star liner *Majestic*, travelling first class with Dorothy's thirty-three-year-old maid Lillian Bailey. Fellow passengers included Constance, the Duchess of Westminster, a socialite and David Oglivy the Earl and his wife the Countess of Airlie – Oglivy's mother the dowager was a courtier and life-long friend of Queen Mary.

They stayed at the *Ritz-Carlton* hotel located at Forty-Sixth Street and Madison Avenue for four weeks. It was here that the hotel's French chef Louis Diat invented the dish known as 'Vichyssoise', served in the hotel's roof garden during the sultry summers. They arrived back in Southampton on 3 October.

Ernest Lendrum, confident that the business was developing well in the capable hands of Hartman, took on the role of silent partner, and early in 1925 married Ida Jessett Cracknell – although Ida had already changed her name to Lendrum by deed poll in 1922. They had been living together at Welbeck House on the corner of Wigmore and Welbeck Street, a purpose-built block of fashionable apartments above shops which included the pharmacist and royal warrant holder John Bell and Croyden. They were married at Marylebone Registry office, and the honeymoon was spent cruising in style.

They left Southampton on the 6 February on the Royal Mail *Almanzora* destined for Madeira, taking their chauffeur Mackay. Amongst other fellow passengers were the Marquess and Marchioness of Bute, travelling as far as Lisbon. The Lendrums stayed at the established and popular *Reid's* hotel, perched majestically on a cliff overlooking the harbour with its sub-tropical garden. After wintering abroad they returned to the Mediterranean and sailed from Monte Carlo to England on Cunard's *Mauretania* in March. Whilst Bobbie Hartman as a driving enthusiast always drove himself, Ernest preferred his chauffeur. The thirty-six-year-old Sidney Mackay and his wife Annie lived above the garage in a mews property at Grosvenor Crescent and remained with the Lendrum family until he retired.

In April 1930 they travelled through France with their indomitable Scottish chauffeur, and their fourteen-year-old daughter Joan Cracknell (from Ida's previous marriage), returning from Marseilles on board the P&O *Ranchi* on her return voyage from India. Ida loved the world of cruising particularly the attention she received, and would spend a great deal of her leisure time at sea. In the coming years this would include a Caribbean cruise with the *Camito*, one of the 'banana boats' as the Elders & Fyfe line ships were known, sailing out of Avonmouth on a round voyage to Jamaica, Colombia and Venezuela.

In 1927 Ernest took Ida on her first visit to New York – a business trip to General Motors on Broadway. Arriving in New York by sea was a spectacular event – like no other city. The ship cruised up the Hudson River past the Statue of Liberty to be manoeuvred into one of the Chelsea piers on Manhattan's West Side or later the much longer piers between West Forty-Fourth and West Fifty-Second Streets.

★

The same year Bobbie's father Augustus, and the remaining family directors of Suter Hartmann, all now retired, decided to sell the company (it had anglicised its name to Red Hand Compositions during the war) to Pinchin Johnson & Associates Ltd., a major supplier of paints at that time. The firm eventually became part of Courtaulds in 1960 and eight years later was merged within their International Paints business. In 1998 it was acquired by the Dutch company AkzoNobel and International Paint is now the leading brand name of the AkzoNobel Marine & Protective Coatings.

The following year, Hartman recruited the thirty-six-year-old Merle Gates Armstrong from Noyes Buick in Boston to run the London servicing operation. Armstrong arrived having travelled first class on the *Aquitania* in September 1924. He initially stayed at 26b Albemarle Street, before obtaining his own flat in Elgin Court, Maida Vale and later Gloucester Terrace in Holland Park. He quickly integrated and became very popular with staff and two years later married a fair-haired Derbyshire girl, Muriel Webster, ten years his junior, at the Paddington Registry Office (in the presence of the American Consul), taking her for a Christmas visit to New York the same year. He remained with Lendrum & Hartman till the outbreak of war.

Hartman recruited well, his choice of manager proved to be most able, assisted by Ted Taylor, his under-manager, who had previously been employed by General Motors, and a very popular Canadian, Bob Berryman, headed the Reception Department. Hartman had initiated a new-car delivery service and Berryman's team was instructed to show anyone interested over the Buick Service Department without prior appointment, all innovative business practices at the time.

Bobbie Hartman went out of his way to cultivate and befriend Alfred P. Sloan, General Motors President since 1923, who would become its chairman in 1937. On his visits to England he and his wife would often stay at *Claridge's* with visits to his country home in Northease.

During the 1920s Sloan also spearheaded the innovative financial and marketing techniques that gave General Motors an advantage over other auto manufacturers. Sloan had an apartment at 820 Fifth Avenue in New York, a company man who ate, slept and lived General Motors. Although he enjoyed high society socialising, he had few other interests, did not smoke, rarely drank, and never engaged in any sport –considering it a waste of time.

He was married to Irene for over fifty years but they had no children. Sloan negotiated what would become GM's largest overseas foreign holding with the purchase of the German family automobile firm Opel between 1929 and 1931 amounting to $33.3 million. This would lead the company inadvertently and controversially to links with Nazi Germany. [13]

In 1927 the Society of Motor Manufacturers and Traders announced that it had achieved 27,949 – the highest number of US imported cars to the UK.

The British car manufacturers like Austin had produced the highly popular Austin Seven at £140 in 1922, and the Morris Minor followed in 1928, then Ford produced its 8hp Model Y for £100 in the early 1930s.

By comparison Lendrum & Hartman were pitching an alternative offer to the affluent, a saloon landaulette with coachwork by Vanden Plas with choice of Buick, La Salle or Cadillac chassis, with silk blinds, dictograph, gentleman's companions (drinks and smoking requisits) and private door locks at £795.

By 1929 on the Old Oak Lane in Willesden, the service depot for the company's Buick, Cadillac and La Salle cars was now covering 114,000 square feet and employing over 200 personnel with a wide range of skills on the premises. These included blacksmiths, welders, trimmers and upholsterers, machine shops, paint shops and a spare-parts department. This coordinated approach was very unusual and advanced for the 1920s.

Lendrum & Hartman then commenced importing Buick cars from the Canadian factory, as these qualified for 'Empire Preference'. This was part of a government scheme for helping the economy and allowed slightly lower import duties on products from the British Empire.

The quality of North American chassis generally made them ideal vehicles for 'bespoke' English bodywork. British car manufacturers were not able to satisfy the demand for comfortable, reliable and well-built touring cars at reasonable prices. Also the import tax on US imported cars was a third of the cost, so it made sense to encourage buyers to choose a Cadillac or Buick 'drop-head coupe' with English bodywork.

★

Bobbie and Dorothy Ailsa now had a country house, Ravenswood on leafy Kingston Hill, in Surrey, curiously just a stroll away from Chintshurst, the house his father bought for his first marriage. They also had a weekend cottage at Little Court in the village of Sonning, close to the river Thames in Berkshire.

In the spring of 1930, we get a glimpse of Bobbie's interest in horses when the March issue of *Polo Monthly* featured the results of the 'Riding Class' of the Arab Horse Society, which included Arab-bred stallions, mares and geldings:

> *"In Reserve: we see Chevalier, a two year old bay gelding, by Rasim (Arab Horse Stud Book) out of Greek Kalends (General Stud Book) by Gorgos. Bred by His Majesty the King George V and exhibited by Capt. F. W. Hartman, of Ravenswood, Kingston Hill, Surrey."*

The interest in polo ponies and links with the City may have been where Bobbie first met Harry Lyons – later Lord Ennisdale, becoming life-long social friends.

Bobbie had already negotiated a lease on Northease Manor, a country house near Lewes in Sussex and was planning to join the Southdown Hunt. The agricultural land surrounding the manor was farmed by the Robinson family, well-known local farmers at Iford since the turn of the century.

-23-

The Gabrielle Brown affair

It couldn't last – Bobbie couldn't resist a pretty girl. Seven years after their marriage, Dorothy Ailsa files for divorce in March 1930 over his affair with Gabrielle Brown. In the petition by her solicitors Messrs Simmons & Simmons, of Threadneedle Street, she states that Bobbie frequently committed adultery and in particular with 'Alice Frederica Brown' on two separate weekends in January and February at the *Cavendish Hotel*, Eastbourne.

Gabrielle was twenty-one, with brown hair and grey eyes and employed as his secretary in Lendrum & Hartman's showrooms at Albemarle Street. There must have been some private understanding between them as the divorce was undefended by Culross & Co., Bobbie's solicitor. (A few years later Sir Percy Simmons, one of the partners in the firm and his wife would be Hartman's guests at a Southdown Hunt Ball at Northease.) There was no mention of Lendrum & Hartman; her petition referred to Bobbie as a motor engineer – not a director, and he had clearly given her dates and the place of adultery, and Gabrielle was referred to by her secondary names Alice Frederica. The decree nisi was granted in May with decree absolute in November, when Dorothy filed a petition for maintenance.

Bobbie had been estranged from her since the previous year. She was now living with her mother at 27 Empire House in Alexander Square. Bobbie, whilst nominally living at Ravenswood, Kingston Hill, was in fact residing at his flat above the showroom in Albemarle Street during the week and motoring down to Northease Manor at weekends. He had taken over the manor house and some outbuildings whilst the farm estate was managed separately by a local farmer.

The same month, Bobbie took Gabrielle on a Mediterranean cruise on board Cunard's RMS *Mauretania*. After the ship's winter overhaul in February she sailed from Southampton visiting various ports including Haifa and Alexandria. Amongst fellow passengers enjoying the sea air away from the chills and depression of England were Thomas, Earl of Litchfield and Evelyn, Countess of Litchfield. Hartman found they had a mutual interest in horses (Litchfield was once Aide-de-Camp to the Acting Master of the Horse to the Lord-Lieutenant of Ireland). This cruise must have paid for itself, as Bobbie sold the Lichfields a Buick. Other passengers included Sybil, Viscountess Powerscourt of Enniskerry, a very tall woman (over six feet) but graceful with a fondness of dogs, especially her Irish wolfhound, and the Marquis of Douro, another title in the Duke of Wellington's family, not to mention two American teenagers who must have crept on board during the voyage and were classified as stowaways.

★

Gabrielle Fredrica Alice Brown was born in London in 1907, to a French mother and English father, and had lived in Ladbroke Road, Notting Hill, with her family, although at the time had a flat at Van Dyck Mansions, 27 Langham Street. After the affair with Bobbie, she had left Lendrum & Hartman's and in the autumn of 1935 married a Canadian surgeon, Charles Jerome Dusseau. He had a practice in Wimpole Street and they lived for a while in Clifton Road, NW1. The marriage did not last however, and they divorced after the war. In 1946 Gabrielle settled in Canada, sailing from London on the Cunard *Condesa* to Montreal.

★

During 1930 Hartman had met Sir Arthur Ernest Guinness of the eponymous brewing family and sold him a custom-built Cadillac V16, a saloon landaulette deluxe with coachwork by Vanden Plas. In true Lendrum & Hartman promotional style it was exhibited at the annual London Motor Show at Olympia in October before delivery to his client. (A good investment, as in 2013 it was sold by Bonhams for £77,918.)

★

Ernest Lendrum was a wealthy man already, he owned a successful wholesale paper business which had become the largest buyer of waste paper in Britain, with offices in London, and overseas in Melbourne and Yokohama. This was together with his interest in Lendrum & Hartman, which was moving from strength to strength – thanks to his partner's energy and salesmanship, not to mention influential contacts.

He was now fifty-five and in November 1931 he resigned as director to spend more time with Ida. Although born and bred in London, he decided to buy a house in the quiet countryside near Maidenhead. He purchased the seventeenth-century Moor Place, at Pinkneys Green, just two miles from Maidenhead but close enough to London, just thirty minutes away by rail from Paddington. It was the perfect country house; exposed beams, with over an acre of garden.

He had dabbled with the idea of the countryside before in the 1920s when he owned Pinkwell Farm at Harlington, West London, but sold it for development to George Wimpey & Co. as the encroaching housing needs of a growing London increased – although its fields still survive and offer a green urban space known as Pinkwell Park.

Ernest and Ida enjoyed just seven years of retirement together. When he died on 27 October 1938 he left her £44,758-18s-5d, something like £2.1 million today. Ida, the forty-seven-year-old grieving widow had within a month set sail from London's King George V dock on the Blue Star *Andalucia Star*, travelling first class of course, bound for Buenos Aires – a journey of eighteen or nineteen days, taking Mary her sister-in-law and Joan Cracknell her twenty-two-year-old daughter from her first marriage, recorded on the ship's manifest as her secretary!

Ida's party arrived in Buenos Aires and stayed at the *Plaza Hotel* over the Christmas period.

Buenos Aires in the 1930s was known as the 'Paris of South America'. The centre of the city had many cafés, restaurants, theatres, movie houses, shops and bustling crowds. In direct contrast these were years of great unemployment, poverty and hunger in the capital, and many new arrivals from the interior were forced to live in tenements and boarding houses.

At this time a struggling actress, María Eva Duarte, was making her way, touring nationally with a theatre company, sometimes working as a model, and had been cast in a few B-grade movie melodramas. She would become better known as the influential Eva Perón, becoming the First Lady of Argentina from 1946 till her death in 1952, after marrying Colonel Juan Perón, elected President of Argentina.

The *Plaza* was built in the European belle époque style in 1909; it was considered at the time the finest hotel in South America, and very modern. The hotel was wholly furnished at its outset by prestigious London interior decorators, such as *Waring & Gillow* and decorated with European marble sculptures and ornate ceilings and friezes.

Argentina was enjoying the golden age of the tango, the dance developed out of the brothels in the 1920s to a sensuous dance form. This was the era of the national icon Carlos Gardel, a French-Argentinian, who was the dulcet voice of tango. Originally considered too risqué for decency, the middle class took to tango in droves, making it popular in the dance halls of Paris, London and New York.

The Lendrum family returned to England, sailing on the *Almeda Star* [14] carrying 180 first-class passengers and refrigerated cargo arriving in February 1939 to a mild, wet but sunny English winter.

It is a testament to Ida's ability with money (she had earlier been made a director of Lendrum Ltd – Ernest's waste paper business) that twenty years later, despite her cruising addiction, and the economic effects of a world war in between, when she died in March 1959 at the King Edward Hospital, Windsor, she left £85,624-10s-2d – nearly twice the amount she inherited, although the intervening years had reduced its buying power to something like £1.3 million today.

★

One of Bobbie's favourite haunts at this time, particularly with Gabrielle, was the *Berkeley Hotel* on the corner of Berkeley Street and Piccadilly, owned by Richard D'Oyly Carte, the theatrical impresario and composer. It was one of those hotels trusted by the parents of debutantes to keep an eye on the reputation of their daughters. Captain Hartman would always oblige. It was also amongst the first London hotels with air conditioning, and later double-glazing. The *maître d'hôtel* Filippo Ferraro, with his wavy black hair and round spectacles, was a fixture of London nightlife in the 1930s. He was one of a group of influential Italian restaurateurs in London at the time – his cousin Arturo Giordano was at the *Savoy,* and he appears in several novels of the period, such as Dennis Wheatley's *Three Inquisitive People* published in 1932. [15]

The steps from Berkeley Street led to the Buttery, a large Art Deco bar in a room set with tables at different levels, patronised almost exclusively by those who considered themselves higher up the social scale. The *Berkeley* was amongst the handful of top hotels to provide a 'Premiere League' dance band. It was where Bobbie noticed the talented trumpeter Jack Jackson playing with the Howard Jacobs band. Jackson went on to become a bandleader himself and would eventually be invited to play at one of his house parties in Sussex.

It was announced in January 1932 that General Motors Ltd. had created Vauxhall and Bedford trucks as a separate organisation from General Motors USA, and that Lendrum & Hartman had become the sole concessionaires of imported (Canadian built) Buick and Cadillac cars.

The affair with Gabrielle continued but after two years had probably run its course, when in the summer they sailed to North America, travelling from Southampton on 11 July on board the *Europa* to New York staying at the *Plaza*. The hotel was located opposite Central Park on Fifth Avenue, built in the French Renaissance château-style some twenty years earlier. The nineteen-story skyscraper hotel had become highly fashionable, in the 1920s the occasional home and social playground of F. Scott and Zelda Fitzgerald and their artistic and literary crowd – he even features the hotel in his 1925 novel *The Great Gatsby*.

Later they travelled by rail on the 'Montreal Unlimited', the overnight sleeper to Montreal leaving Grand Central Station at eleven in the evening arriving next morning at Windsor Street Station at eight. They travelled along the Saint Lawrence River staying at the imposing *Châteaux Frontenac* hotel in Quebec. With its fine public spaces, mahogany panelling, marble staircases and carved stone, it was the epitome of château-style railway hotels; rising over 200 feet, towering above Cap Diamant and the old town, it is the defining symbol of Quebec.

They sailed to England in August on the newly launched Canadian Pacific *Empress of Britain*. It was the end of the affair. It had been fun whilst it lasted.

★

By September 1932 Bobbie had returned to play the Sussex country gentleman, fully immersed in life at Northease attending the local gymkhana where, as 'Captain' Hartman, he presented prizes and started looking around for another wife who could play her part in his business and social life.

Bobbie's ex-wife Dorothy Ailsa in the meantime had also met another suitor, the businessman Cyril Cohen. Their friendship had developed during Bobbie's affair and in the winter of 1930 he had solicitously taken Dorothy and her widowed mother Catherine Discombe on holiday to Madeira, returning to Southampton by the Union Castle line *Kenilworth Castle* in March (the same month Bobbie sailed off with Gabrielle).

A few years later, Dorothy married the thirty-five-year-old Cyril in Kensington during the summer of 1934. They honeymooned in Canada, sailing in September to Quebec on the *Empress of Britain* and holidaying in Banff at the *Mount Royal Hotel* in the heart of the Canadian Rockies.

Cyril was the grandson of the founder of the family business of George Cohen Sons & Co., a highly successful scrap metal merchant in the Commercial Road, East London.

He had been married before to Helene Lebus, and they had a daughter, Angela, born in 1925. Cyril went on to become chairman and managing director of the family firm and by the early 1950s the company was turning over £22 million.

Because of Cyril's generosity, Dorothy's mother Catherine was able to live in some style, moving from Empire House in west London to an apartment in Lowndes Square and later to an even smarter one at Alford House, Park Lane.

When she died in 1959, she left her daughter £6,900 (£112k today). Dorothy and Cyril retired to Hampshire living at Manor House Farm, Alresford where she died three years after Cyril in 1989.

-24-

Northease Manor

After Augustus Hartmann's death in February, Bobbie had with some of his inheritance completely reorganised the share capital of the company and on July 20 Dorothy Cynthia Mirabelle Hartman at the age of thirty-six became a director of Lendrum & Hartman Ltd, and chatelaine of Northease.

Dodo could not believe her good fortune – leaving the aristocratic character of Lady Dalrymple behind, and taking the role of plain Mrs Hartman had been the best part she could have wished for.

From previous marriages, they both carried emotional baggage plus a number of affairs – albeit Bobbie's were by far the most public. They had hit it off – both effective at socialising – Dodo with her theatrical skills and good looks, and Captain Hartman the charmer and the consummate salesman, they formed a partnership that over the coming years proved very successful. They had edited their past lives accordingly and with the wit experience can bring, accepted what each other presented. In Bobbie's case it was 'hook, line and sinker'.

The stage was now set for our two performers to enjoy the fruits of what was going to be the company's golden years. The number of cars sold in 1932 was 150, by 1938 it would reach 2,000; the upper classes were now considering American cars as a credible alternative to Rolls Royce, Bentley and Daimler.

During 1934 a member of the royal family bought a Buick from Lendrum & Hartman – it would be the start of a trend. Lady Patricia Ramsey (1886–1974), who as Princess Patricia of Connaught was a granddaughter of Queen Victoria, but had relinquished her title upon her marriage to a commoner a Royal Navy officer, Alexander Ramsay (although he was the third son of the thirteenth Earl of Dalhousie). She ordered a Freestone & Webb limousine to be built on a Buick chassis. Her request was remembered by company mechanic Russell Johns:

"Her chauffeur, Fred Rix, came to the Willesden works daily to see the building of the chassis, and he went on to do the same at the coachworks. The bodywork had been built especially high, in order that the owner, who was over six foot tall, could enter and alight gracefully. The car was used by its owner until well into the 1960s." [16].

The Hartmans would become very much part of high society in both London and Sussex and their activities would begin to appear in the press.

The thirties would see the obsession with travel, speed and customer competition – shipping lines vied with each other for the 'blue ribbon' to attract first-class passengers on the lucrative Atlantic crossing to New York, whilst rail companies in Britain and on the Continent took passenger comfort and style to a new level, creating a golden age of travel – at least in first class.

Only air travel lagged behind – whilst it had speed it still lacked comfort – cabins were cold and not pressurised and the noise could leave passengers with terrible earache.

In England, the London and North Eastern Railway (LNER), the second-largest of the large railway companies, which connected London with the north east and Scotland, would be described as like having wheels put under a Kensington hotel. On its *Flying Scotsman* route to Scotland, they offered sleeping compartments with proper beds, restaurants, men's and women's hairdressing salons, ladies' retiring rooms, and lavatories which included dressing tables and full-length mirrors. The train had broken a steam speed record in 1934, then in the summer of 1938 their elegant masterpiece *Mallard*, a new streamlined locomotive, achieved 126 miles per hour on its run to Newcastle – a record which still stands today.

Trains, like ocean liners, also had names. Travel to the Continent was provided with the all-Pullman *Golden Arrow*, a daily service departing Victoria at ten-thirty and arriving in Paris in time for cocktails at five-thirty. There were others like *The Blue Train*, the preferred luxury night express train for the rich and famous to the Riviera, and the *Orient Express* taking passengers all the way to Istanbul. These trains would provide inspiration for contemporary novelist Agatha Christie.

For 'Le Weekend' in Paris you could board a train at Victoria on Friday night and wake up for breakfast in the Gare du Nord. The *wagons-lits* were shunted onto tracks built into the decks of special ships at Dover and pulled off at Dunkirk by a French engine.

★

For the Hartmans, the years to the outbreak of war were a round of seasonal country pursuits, hunting, parties, business entertaining, and travel, as Dodo consolidated her position as hostess of Northease.

She was now more than a wife – she had a proper status and purpose in life and she was determined that it would be a success. Bobbie was enchanted by his new partner and basked in the 'head turning' effect she had on entering a room.

Northease, in the little Sussex village of Rodmell, off the Piddinghoe Road lies in the heart of the South Downs near Lewes. The seventeenth-century Queen Anne manor house had passed through many owners arriving at George, the fourth Lord Abergavenny in the eighteenth century, when the estate was eventually broken up in 1919. The memory of his lordship endures through the local pub, known as *The Abergavenny Arms*. The third Marquess of Abergavenny, Henry Nevill had moved to Eridge Castle, and was accidentally killed when thrown from his horse during a fox hunt at the age of eighty-three, a few days before the Hartmans' 1938 hunt ball.

The village was the setting of a satirical comic novel set in the 1920s focusing on English urban and rural society by the Scottish writer A. G. Macdonell, in his affectionate book *England, Their England* published in December 1933. One of a genre at the time, the novel examines the changing nature of English society during the interwar period. Written much in the style of Evelyn Waugh, or perhaps P. G. Wodehouse, it is said to be a *roman à clef*, particularly for its description of traditional village cricket. Rodmell appears as Fordenden in the book.

Bobbie was not a cricketer, but preferred the wealthier country pursuits like hunting and shooting, where socialising could produce more useful business contacts.

Another Rodmell inhabitant at that time who loved the village was Virginia Woolf, the novelist who had acquired Monk's House, a tranquil

[1] Augusta Manchester, née Franklin, (1836-1900) *Dodo's maternal grandmother c.1890s*

[2] 'Maud Coleno' (stage name of Maud Abbott, formerly Wainwright, née Manchester) (1873-1915) *Dodo's mother c.1890s wearing her dancing shoes*

[3] 'Captain' William Vernon Abbott (1857-1923) *Dodo's father, publisher, journalist, 'tall' story telle*r c.1917

[4] *TS Warspite,* c.1910 'Capt Abbotts' ship - he was actually the purser, a Marine Society training ship for boys moored at Greenhithe

[5] Brown's Dairy (Cow's Cathedral) Camden High Road c.1901 Birthplace of Maud Coleno's daughter -Dorothy Maud Abbott in 1898

'Push and Go!' Review ran from 10 May 1915 for 359 performances

[6] Captain Lewis extreme left, with 17 Officers of 2nd Battalion Kings Shropshire Light Infantry, in France, December 1914 (45% would be killed or wounded before the year was out)

(Inset: Capt. Edwin Lewis

[7] [8] Dodo's child Ethel age six months, and nine years later

[9] Sir David Charles Herbert Dalrymple (c.1918) as Lieutenant Commander R.N.

[10] *Royal Albion hotel Brighton* (c.1900) scene of the-tryst with the 'acting' Lady Dalrymple

[11] *Newhailes House*, Musselburgh, Dalrymple's ancestral home

[12] Newhailes library (c.1959) Dr Johnson described it as *'the most learned room in Europe'*

[13] Pair of George II mahogany library armchairs with original Aubusson tapestry, sold (Frank Partridge & Sons) by the Dalrymple Trustees in 1928 to fund Dodo & David's days of 'wine and roses'

[14] Lady Ermine Elibank -Dodo's 'mentor', at the *Empress Club* in Dover Street (Nov 1939)

[15] Gideon Murray 2nd Viscount Elibank (c.1930)

[16] The Hon. Gabrielle Borthwick (c.1921) who taught Dodo to drive

[17] 'Harry' Ennisdale at Baynard's Park, Cranleigh

[18] Helen Ennisdale (left), Sir Thomas Beecham, and actress Peggy Cummins, captain's cocktail party '*RMS Queen Elizabeth*', sailing to New York, Jan 1948

[19] *The Plaza* - hotel of choice in New York

[20] *British Colonial hotel* in Nassau, made fashionable by the 'Windsor's' in the 1940s and by Dodo Hartman, and the Ennisdales post war

[21] *The Palácio hotel Estoril*, where Dodo enjoyed sojourns in the 1930s. Nick stayed in 1941 before flying to New York on the Pan Am Clipper Service, -the hotel was a 'hot bed' of political intrigue in war-time neutral Portugal

[22] Suter Hartmann & Rahtjen's Composition Co. Ltd., - the basis of the Hartmann family wealth

[23] Motor Show catalogue
Oct 1951

[24] Alfred P Sloan [25] James D Mooney
The influential General Motors Executive's during the 1930s

[26] 'Captain' Hartman outside the Lendrum & Hartman showroom in
Albemarle Street, displaying the Royal Buick's for Edward VII and
Mrs Simpson, March 1936

Captain Hartman
(inset)

[27] [28] Northease Manor, Rodmell, Sussex (c.1939) home to the Hartman's 1933-39

[29] Luckington Manor, Wiltshire, Hartman's home 1939-53

[30] Dodo Hartman on her hunter 'Precentor' c.1940s

[31] Dodo and Bobbie Hartman at Luckington Manor (c.1942)

[32] Entrance to Berkeley House Hay Hill, Dodo's Mayfair apartment c1943-57

[33] Dodo and Leonard, Lord Lyle (c.1952) at the opening of her 'basement snack bar' in South Audley Street

[34] Stumblehole Farm, 1953-57 croquet lawn (c.1956)

[35] Dodo's Pekinese dogs Stumblehole (c.1956) l/r: Boo-Boo (favourite), Nina (his wife), Cheesi (son)

[36] Frank Gear Dodo's butler (c.1956)

[37] Valerie Hobson & 'Jack' Profumo (c.1956)
Berkeley House cocktail guests

[38a] Frances Day 1930s heyday

[38b] Frances Day (c 1952)

[39] Charlie & Oona Chaplin (c.1952)
Stumblehole house guests

[40] Dodo at Café de Paris (Dec 1953) *wearing her cyclamen-shaped diamond brooch*

[41] Portrait: Nicky Vansittart
(c.1940 by 'Baron')

[42] Portrait: 'Dodo' Hartman
(kept in Nicky's wallet) (c. 1950s)

[43] A lock of Dodo's hair *(kept in Nicky's wallet)*

[44] Dodo and favourite Hunter (c.1942)

seventeenth-century weather-boarded cottage, which she shared with her husband Leonard and many of her novels were written there. In 1941, concerned she was going mad she committed suicide by drowning herself in the nearby River Ouse.

Whilst Bobbie was cultivating business contacts and General Motors senior executives, like Mooney and Alfred P. Sloan, Dodo focused on family, in particular Edith Hartman. Now in her seventies and recently widowed, she lived alone in Kensington Square, with just her servants Florence and Ellen. Whilst in London her new 'daughter-in-law' would visit her and they would lunch and take shopping trips together. Edith had a small group of friends including the members of the wealthy Greek Ralli family. Dodo adopted them too, and with Countess Gage (known as Mogs) as chairman invited Mrs Stephen Ralli – known as Marietta and in her seventies – to join her on the planning committee of her first Southdown Hunt Ball to be held at Lewes Town Hall. Marietta's mother had died in 1922, and was a great Sussex benefactor, making huge endowments to the Royal Sussex County Hospital.

In March 1935 Captain Hartman achieved one of his social ambitions. The Southdown Hunt held its annual steeplechase event at Plumpton and also hosted a lunch for the local farmers over whose land they hunted in recognition of their cooperation. The hunt had been run by the Dalgety brothers, John and Arthur, for years and as John was retiring, Bobbie had agreed to take his place as joint master. Lord Gage the hunt chairman proposed the health of the masters and Captain Hartman's reply was reported in the *Sussex Express*: "… *that although he was a newcomer to fox-hunting he would do his utmost for the Southdown Hunt, especially the farmers.*"

The same spring, Bobbie's valet Aaron Peters took one of Hartman's Buicks from Northease on an opportunistic but unauthorised motoring trip with Dodo's maid Maria to Lewes. He was spotted driving an expensive American car and the curious policeman enquired to see his licence. He didn't have one and was subsequently prosecuted. They were both dismissed and in May, the same day his case came before the magistrate, the Hartmans were sailing to New York on the *Bremen* with two new servants, George Chapman as valet and Dorothy Wigmore as the new lady's maid.

They stayed at the *Plaza* in New York; it was Dodo's first experience of this highly fashionable hotel facing Central Park – but Bobbie's third visit.

The Palm Court with its stained glass ceiling was the place to lunch or to take tea in the afternoon. It was also the scene of a minor cause célèbre when shortly after the hotel opened in 1907, the British actress Mrs Patrick Campbell did something outrageous: she lit a cigarette in public. The story goes that they put a screen up around her so the other diners wouldn't faint. Whilst in New York they would visit the famed *Stork Club* or *El Morocco* – popular Manhattan nightclubs of the day – full of celebrities and socialites all dressed to impress. They travelled to Canada staying at the *Château Frontenac*, returning from Quebec on the *Empress of Britain*, arriving in England in early July.

★

In the late summer of 1935 the Prince of Wales arrived unannounced at the showrooms of Lendrum & Hartman in Albemarle Street, and asked to see Captain Hartman. At the time Bobbie was at his hairdressers Truefitt & Hill in Old Bond Street, a few minutes' walk away through the connecting Royal Arcade. He was summoned back by a breathless clerk, quickly groomed with his favourite CAR lotion with the delicate scent of lily-of-the-valley, arriving at the showroom only to discover to his delight the Prince wanted to purchase not one but two Buicks.

Hartman immediately arranged for his works manager to attend the Prince at York House to take instructions regarding the details of his special requirements and he was then sent to the Canadian factory to supervise the building of the two cars ordered.

His special requirements were for a car, based on a 5-litre Buick Limited Series 90 Eight Limousine, designed to give two passengers luxury and privacy. Coachwork by McLaughlin with specifications to include drinks cabinets (with six silver topped decanters), vanity mirrors, reading lights, correspondence facilities, radio, smokers' cabinet, jewellery cabinet, compartments for cutlery and luncheon trays, and a drawer to accommodate London telephone directories.

The Prince's specifications were conveyed to Buick's Oshawa plant in Ontario. It was located on the outskirts of Toronto on the shore of Lake Ontario, where Lendrum & Hartman's representative remained until the car was complete.

There was even a holder for 'Swan Vesta' matches as the Prince did not use any other means to light his pipe or cigarettes. A manicure set was fitted in the rear-seat centre folding arm-rest and an interior heater, an unusual fitting in pre-war cars, was fitted into the centre division-panel. Hartman, ever the salesman, added a personal touch by presented the Prince with fitted silver-gilt cigarette boxes. [17]

Captain Hartman had seconded one of his staff to the King to maintain his 'royal' Buicks, as the servicing technician Russell Johns remembers:

> *"I was fortunate in being selected to service both these cars, which were first garaged at Marlborough House and later at Buckingham Palace. My instructions were to spare no expense to maintain them. Once in every four weeks I spent a whole day at the Royal Mews, checking and servicing as was required. Captain Hartman had ordered two duplicate, but different-coloured, cars for use in an emergency but fortunately they were never required."* [18]

In November 1935 Bobbie – now confident of his marriage –contacted his solicitor Charles Culross and revoking all former wills, wrote a new one making Dodo sole executrix.

In the New Year, Dodo's first organised social function took place at Lewes Town Hall, using the Corn Exchange as a lounge and supper room. Nearly 350 people from various hunting groups throughout the county attended on 10 January 1936. The local *Sussex Express* announced:

> *"SOUTHDOWN HUNT BALL*
> *BRILLIANT FUNCTION AT LEWES*
> *Palms, flowering plants and groups of various coloured hyacinths; orange and yellow drapery; mirrors surmounted by masks; brushes reminiscent of many a glorious gallop; and other tasteful decorations in keeping with the function converted Lewes Town Hall into an admirable ballroom for the Southdown Hunt annual ball on Friday Evening."*

Dodo was now established amongst the great and the good of London and Sussex society. It was a mixture of estate owners, aristocracy with interconnected families, business people, politicians, retired and active military men and their wives. They had influence and wealth, such as the hunt chairman, Henry Gage the sixth viscount, who had married Lady

Imogen, daughter of William Grenfell, the first Baron Desborough in 1931. They had two young sons, George and Henry, and lived nearby at Firle Place, an Elizabethan house with Georgian additions on a 5,000-acre estate in the Sussex downs. Henry, educated at *Eton,* had a distinguished war with the *Coldstream Guards* and after went up to *Christ Church* Oxford where he had been a suitor of Lady Elizabeth Bowes-Lyon, later wife of George VI. [19] Hartman had quickly included the Gages within his circle and even sold Henry a Buick.

Other hunt ball guests included Viscount Ratendone, a Liberal politician (later Marquess of Willingdon) who had married Lady Marie Adelaide, the youngest daughter of the first Earl Brassey, and related by marriage to the Earls of Essex (Capells) and De La Warr (Sackvilles). He had recently been Viceroy of India.

A distant relative of the Queen (through the Earls of Strathmore) Jack Leschallas appears amongst the guest list, as does a certain German Princess Löwenstein, and wealthy insurance broker, Sir Henry Lyons and his wife Helen. Another guest, Mollie O'Rorke (who could swear as fluently in Gaelic as in English, calling herself Lady Cusack-Smith, from an ancient Irish family), owned a renowned pack of harriers and farmed and hunted in north Galway. She was a fine horsewoman, and for many years master of the Galway Blazers. As one apocryphal story goes, arriving back from the hunt one day with her horse covered in sweat and obviously exhausted, the reply to her groom has become a classic in hunting circles. He says, *"Jaysus Maam, you have him in a terrible lather."* She replies, *"So would you be my good man if you had been between my thighs for the last four hours."* [20]

After an unsuccessful spell at Sherborne School for girls, she was sent to be finished in Paris, returning to London, establishing herself as a successful couturier specialising in evening dresses. She lived on and off with an Irish baronet Sir Dermot Cusack-Smith, adopting his name although they were only finally married in 1946.

Perhaps one of Dodo's more raffish guests at that gathering was Captain Broughton, as the *Sussex Express* named him, attending with Mrs Broughton. Sir 'Jock' Delves Broughton, the eleventh Baronet, married Vera Griffith-Boscawen in 1913, and they had two children. Broughton's interest in horses was purely financial; he was part of a consortium that owned the Ensbury Park Race Course in Kinson, Dorset.

Vera later deserted him for Walter Guinness, the first Baron Moyne with whom she travelled extensively around south-east Asia and the Pacific Islands. Lord Moyne was a well-connected Anglo-Irish politician, a close confidant of Churchill and cousin-in-law to politician 'Chips' Channon. Moyne was later assassinated by the Jewish terrorist Stern Gang in 1944. Vera never remarried.

Jock was forced to sell off most of the 34,000 acres of the family estate at Doddington Hall [21] in Cheshire to pay his gambling debts.

In 1939 he was suspected of insurance fraud after the theft of his wife's pearls and some paintings, on which he claimed the insurance (à la Bobbie Hartman). They divorced in 1940; he then married Diana Caldwell, moving to Kenya. A year later, as part of the 'Happy Valley set' he was involved in a cause célèbre standing trial for the murder of Josslyn Hay, the twenty-second Earl of Erroll. [22]

Other social contacts included the Wykeham-Musgraves from Barnsley Park (Bobbie had a dalliance with their daughter before Dodo) and the Thesigers who they would visit in Scotland, for the shooting. Another guest, an old Hartman family contact from his father's time, was Sir Stephen Demetriadi, who lived locally at Westmeston in Sussex. He had extensive land at Plumpton and Stanmer, and was a director of Ralli Brothers. He was also President of the London Chamber of Commerce. Later his twenty-one-year-old son Richard, whilst serving with the RAF was shot down into the Channel and killed during the Battle of Britain.

Another young guest at the ball was the teenager Sheila Van Damm, daughter of theatre impresario Vivian. After the war Sheila became a well-known and successful motor rally driver in the 1950s, winning the Monte Carlo team prize with Sterling Moss. She also inherited the *Windmill Theatre* from her father.

★

The Prince's cars were duly delivered early in 1936, by which time His Royal Highness had become His Majesty King Edward VIII, after the sudden death of his father King George V on 20 January.

The two Buicks (unlike cars owned by the monarchy at the time) were officially registered in March as *CUL 421* and the second *CUL 457*, used by Mrs Wallis Simpson, who after the King's abdication became the Duchess of Windsor.

★

In March 1936 the Hartmans and the Gages attended the annual Ditchling Horse Show and Farmers' Ball at the *Downs Hotel* in Keymer Road, Hassocks. Nearly 200 gathered to enjoy dancing to the music of Nat Gilder and his band in the Restorium Annexe of the hotel.

★

The car sale to the Prince of Wales was a marvellous coupe for Captain Hartman, whose prestige within General Motors as their sole concessionaire could not be higher.

In August he rewarded Henry Edward Berenstein, his old (and discreet) friend, the motor mechanic from his *Royal Naval Air Service* days, by sending him and his wife Elsie on a trip to New York, visiting General Motors on Broadway, staying at *Essex House,* set in an Art Deco building overlooking Central Park South, built in the early thirties as a residential hotel. Dorothy recognised his support and loyalty after Bobbie's death by appointing him a director of Lendrum & Hartman after the war.

Under Bobbie's direction, Lendrum & Hartman had become 'the' car dealership in England, boosted enormously by royal association. The sales team were very successful and apart from the King, 'his friend Mrs Simpson' and Lady Patricia Ramsey a few years earlier, they had also sold Buicks to the Duke and Duchess of Kent. Other aristocracy fell under the Hartmans' spell including: Thomas Edward Anson, fourth Earl of Lichfield; Lady Brownlow, wife of the sixth Baron Brownlow, closely linked with Wallis Simpson's circle (out of royal favour after the abdication); the Honourable Mrs Charles Greville, a British society host and philanthropist; the eighteenth Lord Herbert, better known as the tenth Duke of Beaufort and Master of the Beaufort Hunt in Badminton; the Earl of Lincoln; Lord Dalrymple (Dodo's late husband) and of course Lord Gage, chairman of the Southdown Hunt, and friend of the Hartmans.

In the early 1930s a certain young Ian Fleming, described as a rich, aloof old *Etonian* by his Reuters colleagues, had seen the advantage of the Buick sports car, and he is described as a man, *"… who kept himself to himself and whose only obvious extravagance was his dashing Buick motor car."* [23]

Later, to impress his (then) girlfriend Daphne Finch Hatton, the lively young daughter of the Earl of Winchelsea, on one occasion in the summer of 1934 he drove from London to a house party in Anglesey, a distance of 265 miles, in one day. She was impressed – possibly more with the car because she later married Whitney Straight, who also bought a Buick.

Buick cars became the 'must-haves' for leading business people, as well as theatricals and celebrities, including Gracie Fields, actress, singer and comedienne; George Formby, actor, singer-songwriter and comedian; Firth Shepherd, a London theatrical impresario; actress Diana Dors; Raymond Bessone, known as Mr Teasy-Weasy, Britain's first celebrity hairdresser in the post-war years (he trained Vidal Sassoon); leading dance band leaders like Jack Hylton, Jack Payne and Edmundo Ros; John Moore, later 'Sir', businessman and philanthropist who founded Littlewoods retail company; Barbara Hutton, an American socialite, heiress and philanthropist, during her brief stay at the *Savoy* in London; Whitney Straight, a Grand Prix motor racing driver, later a distinguished Air Commodore and deputy chairman of *British Overseas Airways Corporation* (BOAC); Sir Giles Scott, architect of Liverpool Cathedral, Waterloo Bridge and Battersea Power Station – he also designed the iconic red telephone box; Sir Jack Cohen, a grocer who founded the Tesco supermarket chain; the Cartier family of Bond Street, a royal warrant holder since 1921; Sir John Ellerman, English ship-owner and considered one of the wealthiest men in England.

During the thirties Bobbie would enter many of his personal Cadillacs in various *Concours d'Elégance* events at home and abroad where he won many premier awards. The cars were serviced and maintained by his works at Old Oak Lane, in Willesden. These events, essentially 'beauty contests' for automobiles flourished in Europe, particularly France during the interwar period, emerging in 1920s Paris in the Bois de Boulogne and resort cities like Le Touquet in the north and on the Riviera, and continued until the onset of the war. Organised by French newspapers *l'Auto, l'Intransigeant* and the journal *Fémina* (Diana Cooper once briefly edited the English edition in the twenties), the idea in the early days was to mix models in haute couture with a parade of various elegant cars. Later, actresses and celebrities took part.

It allowed Bobbie to 'show off' his two favourite loves – his 'aristocratic' wife and his Cadillacs. Like any beauty contest, the *Concours* emphasised external beauty rather than, in the case of the automobiles, internal workings, although the interiors of coachwork, such as upholstery, amenities and appointments were all on show at the end. These events would often be hosted and judged by André de Fouquières, a witty, cultivated and privileged Frenchman with a natural Gallic eye for attractive things.

★

In the summer of 1936 the Hartmans took a lodge in Scotland near Pitlochry for the shooting in September, before preparing for the annual Motor Show in October. As in previous years James Mooney attended from General Motors, making a speech at the Banquet of the Society of Motor Manufacturers and Traders in London with Bobbie and Dodo hosting a table.

The London Motor Show had been held in Olympia since 1903 – but it would be the last time. From 1937 it was moved to Earls Court. The show traditionally followed on from the *Salon de l'Automobile* – the Paris Motor Show.

Imperial Airways now had a regular daily service that it announced in its advertisements as *"To Paris while you read your newspaper and home again the same day."* The return fare was £7-12s-0d.

★

Mooney had been in the habit of taking on promising young men, and his appointments proved to have been excellent choices in several cases.

In May 1927, Guy Nicholas Vansittart, known as Nick in the company was recruited from a British overseas bank and appointed by General Motors Continental as Sales Manager. His progression was swift; by the summer of 1930 he was promoted Managing Director of General Motors Continental. In 1937, he was appointed Regional Director for Northern Europe with headquarters in Antwerp. He returned to London in November 1938, becoming Regional Director for the British Isles, in charge of the headquarters of General Motors Limited in St James's Square.

★

The social activities of the Prince of Wales were causing concern within government, particularly the security services, with his association with Wallis Simpson. In 1930 Edward's father, George V gave him Fort Belvedere, a house in Windsor Great Park. There, Edward had relationships with a series of married women including textile heiress Freda Dudley Ward, and Thelma Lady Furness, the American wife of a British peer, who unwittingly introduced the prince to her friend and fellow American Wallis Simpson (a few years older than Dodo). They met at a Burrough Court house party, the country house of the Furnesses in Leicestershire, set amongst the Quorn Hunt. Wallis's then husband was Ernest Aldrich Simpson, the heir to an Anglo-American shipping fortune.

Soon afterwards, Special Branch detectives were trailing Mrs Simpson through London high society in an attempt to discover more about the American woman who had captured the Prince of Wales's affections. Diana Cooper, having accompanied them on the yacht *Nahlin* in the Mediterranean, observed in a letter to a friend: *"It is impossible to enjoy antiquities with people who call Delphi – Delhi. Wallis is waring very very badly. Her commonness and Becky Sharpishness irritate."* [24]

Special Branch also noted her affairs, one with a German businessman, Joachim von Ribbentrop, who had been appointed ambassador to Britain in 1936 (encouraged by the Prince of Wales) and also another married man – who it seems, was a motor engineer and car salesman, living in Mayfair. [25]

On the Continent, the rise of Nazism in Germany found admirers in Britain, although relatively small in number. The growth of anti-Semitism and the views of Oswald Mosely and his British Union of Fascists that later developed into the German appeasement movement was polarising society.

Bobbie Hartman although from Anglo-German stock, had been born, educated and integrated into English society from the beginning. He had fought and his brother had died for the country, and the family's wealth was made from maritime England. Dodo and Bobbie although not overtly religious were Anglicans with a small 'a'. They were not markedly political either but had an eclectic mix of wealthy friends and business acquaintances; many were Jewish like Henry Berenstein, Bobbie's friend from the *Royal Naval Air Service* days who became director of Lendrum & Hartman, and they socialised freely with the Simmonds and Kleinworts –often at home.

On Friday 11 December came the broadcast to the nation from Windsor Castle that Edward VIII was to abdicate, and his brother would become King George VI. During the political build-up to the abdication crisis, Wallis Simpson had fled the press, driving to the South of France in her Buick, staying with friends at the Villa Lou Viei near Cannes. After the King's abdication speech, Edward, now Duke of Windsor left Windsor in his Buick for Portsmouth. He was to leave England on board HMS *Fury*, a destroyer, to take him to exile in France. The Buick with registration CUL 421 and driver returned to London.

The Hartmans spent Christmas in Northease and early in the New Year, Bobbie was forced to place an advertisement in the local press over their wire hair terrier *Too-Too,* which had gone missing before Christmas. It was the terrier they had in Scotland, which still carried the Scottish address tag.

Later the same month, they travelled to the South of France and continued from Villefranche to New York on the Italian ocean liner *Conte Di Savoia* taking their new servants, Nora Giles, a twenty-one-year-old local girl from Newhaven, as Dodo's maid and another Welsh valet, Richard Rees. The party stayed at the *Plaza* and returned at the end of February on the Norddeutscher Lloyd *Bremen* to Southampton.

★

The last hunt ball at Lewes was generally agreed to be the best yet, thanks to Dodo's contribution to the organisation – her theatrical creativity had been a large factor in transforming the town hall into a magical venue. Buoyed with this event and the success of the Lendrum & Hartman business, Bobbie encouraged her to plan an even greater ball utilising their home at Northease Manor.

A few days before the event, the Hartmans laid on a lavish tea party and entertainment for around eighty children from the estate, using Northease's supper room. It was followed by a Punch and Judy show, and the arrival of Father Christmas (aka Bobbie Hartman) appearing to come down the chimney to distribute gifts from a huge Christmas tree. During the evening they played games and competitions. The Hartmans were good employers, and their generosity to staff set a pattern that would continue.

During the Christmas period Bobbie had been unwell and had just returned from a London nursing home in time to host the event as joint master of the Southdown Hunt. The local paper the *Sussex Express* announced on January 1938 that she had exceeded all expectations.

The novelty of supper in converted cow stalls, and dancing beneath oak beams, once part of a barn, was too unconventional not to be appreciated by the young people at the Southdown Hunt Ball at Northease Manor, near Lewes on Friday.

The unusual surroundings caused a gaiety that was infectious, and did a lot to make the event one of the most successful ever organised… Illuminated by clusters of orange lights, the ballroom was a perfect setting for the 250 guests. Along walls were oak seats relieved at intervals by shining suits of armour, and a large log fire blazed in the open fireplace. The conversion from an old barn was carried out with marvellous effect… a striking addition was a cocktail bar in dark oak in the form of a country tavern… if the ballroom was perfect, the supper and sitting-out rooms were masterpieces of invention… tables set between the partitions of the stalls, enhanced by the light natural colour of the walls, the high interwoven beams and the square stone doorway, through which could be seen the lounge. From the loft of the sitting-out room, floated music from the recently installed organ. The sides of the 'barn' were hidden by huge draping in yellow and orange and the alcoves, were enclosed by 'jumps' cleverly made from laurels and other bushes."

The guests danced to the music of the fashionable Jack Jackson's band – the Hartmans' favourite from the *Dorchester Hotel.*

Northease's hostess appeared wearing a pearl-coloured silk marocain gown cut low at the back, ornamented by a single row of buttons.

Many of the guests were quite naturally the same as previous hunt balls, including the hunt chairman Lord Gage together with Lady Gage, who wore lavender lace with a wide flounced skirt of lavender net.

Dorothy's mentor Lady Elibank and her husband Gideon would be house guests, as well as Nick Vansittart from General Motors Antwerp, and his wife Marguerite. Nick was soon to be transferred to London to take up a new position.

Other guests included the politician, Douglas Hogg, Viscount Hailsham and his wife Elizabeth, friends of the Elibanks (and now Dodo); the Earl of Chichester; Captain 'Jock' Delves Broughton and his wife Vera; Sir Percy and his wife Barbara Simmonds, who lived close by at Chelwood Corner, Nutley. Percy Coleman Simmons, a wealthy Jewish solicitor, had served as a pilot during the Great War. He was a founding partner of Simmonds & Simmonds with his brother Edward, an established City law firm (they handled Bobbie's divorce to Dorothy Ailsa).

Other influential guests were the Kleinwort brothers, Cyril and his wife Elizabeth and Ernest and Joan – they were partners in Kleinwort, Sons & Co., merchant bankers of Fenchurch Street and Brigadier-General the Honourable Alexander Russell and his wife. There were local Sussex landowners like Lady Rosabelle Brand who ran Littledene duck farm near Lewes; she was the daughter of the fifth Earl of Rosslyn. Her only daughter Rose – a society beauty and an unconventional girl –a 'modern woman' as she was described, liked a drink, smoked and could swear like a sailor. At nineteen she married Charles Greville, the seventh Earl of Warwick – the first British aristocrat to be offered a Hollywood contract by Metro-Goldwyn-Mayer Studios. The marriage like his film career did not prosper. Rose then married an American, William 'Billy' Fiske, a banker and Olympic bobsled champion. Whilst serving with the *RAF* during the Battle of Britain, his squadron intercepted some German aircraft, Fiske found his fuel tank badly damaged and on fire. Although badly burnt he nursed his aircraft safely down, but died of surgical shock two days later. [26]

After the ball, one can almost hear the congratulatory conversation between Bobbie and Dodo after the event: *"Darling, you were marvellous."* *"Yes, wasn't I though?"*

The exhausting round of business entertaining –Lendrum & Hartman sales had increased twelve-fold – the Hartmans and two servants set out once again for New York to renew their relationships with General Motors, no doubt to bask in the company's successful sales performance, and at the same time extend the trip by taking a cruise to South America.

At the end of January 1938 they sailed from Southampton on the magnificent French Line's *Normandie* to New York, at the time the largest and fastest passenger ship afloat, and by common consent the most luxurious. The luxurious interiors were designed in Art Deco style, the main 300-foot dining room, three decks deep, sparkled with illuminated fountains and was decorated with Lalique glass chandeliers, compared by many observers to the Hall of Mirrors at Versailles.

On arrival in New York they again stayed at the *Plaza*.

The following day they re-embarked *Normandie* from the French line pier 88 for a three-week cruise to the Bahamas, Trinidad and Rio de Janeiro, where they stayed for four days, returning via Martinique, to New York. It would be the first of two such cruises the ship would make before the war.

The cruise fares started at $395 and continued upwards; all passengers would receive a 'Rio Cruise medal' as a souvenir, although rather parsimoniously, deck chairs, steamer rugs and chair cushions were available for rental at $3 dollars and $1.50 respectively.

They returned to the *Plaza* for a few days in New York, enjoying the music of Pancho's Orchestra whilst sipping cocktails and enjoying supper in the hotel's exclusive 'Persian Room'. After mixing business with pleasure and socialising with General Motor's directors, they returned again on *Normandie* to England, arriving in Southampton on 7 March.

★

In June, the annual carnival queen was crowned at Lewes amongst great excitement as a film celebrity was chosen to crown Mrs Esther Parsons as carnival queen for 1938 at Lewes Town Hall.

The minor stage and film actress Marjorie Sandford had agreed to crown the queen. The organising committee, headed by Mrs Dorothy Hartman, declared *"that it had been a difficult task to make a choice among so many beautiful Lewes girls, and she asked the mayor to give each a kiss on her behalf."*

Marjorie Sandford, the twenty-eight-year-old actress was a guest of the Hartmans whilst on a publicity tour to promote the film *"Lassie from Lancashire"*, due to be released in the August.

In the October there was a widely publicised burglary at Northease Manor – hard to believe it wasn't an inside job.

The press headlines ran:

"Safe Thrown From An Upper Window

    Country House Burglary

    Burglars entered the house of Captain and Mrs F W Hartman at Northease, near Lewes early yesterday morning and stole jewellery belonging to Mrs Hartman who was in London at the time. The intruders took a ladder which was standing against a neighbouring haystack and entered Mrs Hartman's bedroom which they ransacked.

    Finding a large heavy 6½ cwt safe, (330 kilos) they wrapped bedclothes round it and pushed it through the window, from where it fell, smashing the paving below. They then carried the safe into a field 30 yards away, where they blew open the door with an explosive and took the jewellery. They made their escape in a car. Although six servants slept in the house they were not disturbed, and the theft was not discovered until a maid found the room ransacked at 7am."

It seems extraordinary that the staff heard nothing at all, smashing paving and an explosion in the quiet countryside, and the dogs quiet? Mrs Hartman told an *Express & Herald* reporter: *"I always keep my jewels in London, and I never leave anything of value here whilst we are not in residence."* The article explained there was little in the safe except a few bracelets, which were gifts to Mrs Hartman as a girl; they were of small intrinsic value although of considerable sentimental value to the owner.

The paper went on to report that: *"Captain and Mrs Hartman had gone to London on the previous Wednesday morning to attend the opening of the new Warner Theatre, where they welcomed the Duke and Duchess of Kent at a performance in aid of the British Empire Cancer Campaign. Mrs Hartman is chairman of the Ladies Committee of the campaign. Scotland Yard are assisting the Lewes police in their investigations and photographs were taken by officers who visited the house."*

★

The same month Bobbie heard the news that his retired partner Ernest Lendrum had died in Maidenhead. He was sixty-one, and Ida his widow was off to South America.

In the meantime, Hartman had for some time been pursuing the idea of a new country life away from Sussex and considering the Cotswolds, particularly close to the Beaufort Hunt, the grandest of all hunts at Badminton.

Immensely proud of his wife, he suggested 'his Dorothea' should have her portrait painted. Rather than look to de Lazlo – which perhaps would draw comparisons with Ermine Elibank – he suggested instead the Scottish portrait painter James Gunn.

The same year Gunn had worked on portraits of the actress Gracie Fields, who was the same age as Dodo, and the Prime Minister Neville Chamberlain.

For her sitting, Dodo had chosen a black velvet gown with ermine edged décolletage, displaying her green emerald and diamond necklace together with matching ring.

Gunn had gained a national reputation as a society portrait painter of the rich and famous during the 1920s. The portraits he painted of his female sitters particularly are very evocative of the time and period – like the Countess of Sefton, (lifelong friend of the Duchess of Windsor), American-born Josephine Armstrong, who was a Patou model in Paris during the 1920s, known as 'Foxy' because of her abundance of auburn hair.

Gunn had studied at the Glasgow School of Art before attending the Academie Julian in Paris, and had served with *The Artists Rifles* in the Great War.

He married the beautiful Gwendoline Hillman, widow of Guy Thorne, in 1919 and they had three daughters. However, in 1926, Gwen ran off with one of Gunn's sitters, the wealthy chartered accountant Sir Arthur Whinney [27] taking the children with her. The subsequent divorce was very acrimonious and Gwen denied Gunn access to the children and even obliged them to change their name to Whinney.

In the summer of 1929 by chance he saw his daughters in Regent's Park with their nanny – who recognised him, but sympathetically kept quiet and carried on knitting. At subsequent 'chance' meetings he secretly managed to paint a group portrait of his children [28] and poignantly it was the only means of preserving their memories and spending time with them. They were moved to America and allowed to believe that they had been abandoned and neglected by their father. Gunn did not meet them again until they were fully grown.

His paintings are on show in a number of galleries and his 1953 portrait of Queen Elizabeth II is in the Royal Collection. He is considered one of Scotland's greatest painters, on an equal footing as such luminaries as Sir John Lavery, Sergeant and Orpen.

★

In the New Year of 1939, the annual Southdown Hunt Ball, the second to be held at Rodmell, had quickly become 'the' ball to attend. With 400 guests, and a further eighty-five on the waiting list for tickets, it was a brilliant success thanks to Dodo's creativity and attention to detail, with help of course from the organising committee, as the local press duly reported:

> "*RECORD ATTENDANCE*
> *AT SOUTHDOWN HUNT BALL*
> *Brilliant function at Northease*
> *There was a record attendance of guests on Friday at the Southdown Hunt Ball, at Northease, Rodmell, the country residence of Captain F W Hartman the joint master and Mrs Hartman. Nearly 400 members and friends of the Hunt were present, and festivities continued until the early hours of the following morning.*"

Dodo had built on the 'cow stall' theme again and this time created a fairlyland effect with clever lighting. She had commissioned a local company, Newhaven and Seaford Electricity Ltd., to install the electric lights, floodlighting the house, giving the exterior of the house a fairyland effect with coloured lights along the pathways and garden. To add to the drama guests arriving by car were directed by Lewes 'Bonfire Boys', [29] who lined the roadway holding flaming torches.

Dodo had used the same soft lighting inside, again using the oak-rafted ballroom, with its huge log fire, this time they had introduced a thatched-roof bar complete with an old inn sign, supported with flowers and palms. The live music was supplied by Jack Harris and his *Ciro's Club* Orchestra. In the supper room with its cow stalls and alcoves Dodo had contracted Frederic Bayco, the organist from the *Dominion Theatre* in London's Tottenham Court Road, to play for guests. One of the big attractions was the 'Oyster and Stout' bar.

Dodo revelled in the 'theatre' of this social event and greeted guests wearing a strapless gown of white slipper satin, designed with a ruched hem and neckline and trimmed with golden-bead bows, and carried a Victorian bouquet.

Other lady guests were suitably reported: (Mogs) Viscountess Gage chose a two-piece ensemble of deep purple velvet. Cut along military lines, the jacket coat had long sleeves and golden braid trimmings at the back, with small pink and white tassels of silk cord around the back of the collar. The frock was fashioned simply with a tight-fitting skirt.

The wife of the joint master, Mrs Dalgety, wore a shell-pink silk marocain gown and deep purple feather bolero, whilst Mrs Gerald Donner wore a blue and silver dress with a silver fox cape, Mrs Churchill Hale was gowned in dove grey chiffon, and so on. The men of course all wore the same evening dress.

Those familiar names from previous events who took part included Viscount and Viscountess Elibank; Viscount and Viscountess Gage; Viscount and Viscountess Hailsham (a Conservative politician, Lord Chancellor in Stanley Baldwin's government); Brigadier-General the Honourable Alexander Russell and his wife Marjorie (née Guinness, descendent of the famous Irish brewing family), he had been the Military Attaché to Berne after the war and was now a director of Sun Insurance. Local Balsdean farmer Arthur Dalgety, joint master of the hunt (with Bobbie Hartman) and his wife; Nick and Marguerite Vansittart – the Hartmans' friends from General Motors; Vice-Admiral Fisher who had retired in the late 1920s; the Kleinwort merchant banking brothers Ernest and Cyril with their wives; Rear Admiral and Mrs Tufton Beamish, who was Conservative MP for Lewes; Mrs Esther Burdett-Coutts, a local classically trained musician who lived at Marks Cross with her husband, a local councillor. She played the violin and was leader of the Tunbridge Wells Symphony Orchestra, a descendent of the wider Coutts banking clan. She was frequently involved with local charity events – and had supported the fundraising for the Southdown Hunt kennels. There were many more from the county set, including the Hartman's influential business contacts and friends. It would be the last hunt ball before war was declared.

★

In February Bobbie was pursuing suitable property and stables for his hunter *Viking II*, around the villages within a few miles from Badminton. He was hard at work networking by attending the Assembly Rooms in Bath, once the hub of fashionable Georgian society, now recently restored by interior designer Oliver Messel, to host the Beaufort Hunt –the most important assembly of its kind in the city since the reopening ball a year previous with the Duchess of Kent in attendance.

The press declared: *"It brought to Bath many well-known County people from Somerset, Wiltshire, Gloucestershire and Dorset… and the blue and buff of the Beaufort Hunt mingling with the scarlets and greens of neighbouring packs… music supplied by Jack Jackson's Orchestra and catering by Fortt's of Bath."* (They bake the famous 'Bath Oliver' biscuits.)

Bobbie Hartman was already socially connected with the aristocracy (Lord Gage, his chairman at the Southdown Hunt was a close friend of Queen Elizabeth) but clearly eager to be part of a 'premier' hunting society such as the Beaufort, with its political and influential members. The Beaufort guest list contained 'top draw' aristocratic names such as the Duke and Duchess of Beaufort; the Countess of Westmoreland; Lieutenant-Colonel Edgar Hugh Brassey (*Life Guards*); Lord Apsley, eldest son of the seventh Earl Bathurst, a Defence Minister in Government; Queen Elizabeth's close friend Lady Avice Spicer [30] and others who were politically influential such as Colonel Stewart Menzies. Educated at *Eton* like Nick Vansittart although a few years older, he was deputy director-general of MI6 – Britain's Secret Intelligence Service (SIS inside the organisation, MI6 outside it) as an inter-service organisation responsible to the Foreign Office. The organisation came to be called 'The Firm'.

The Chief of the Intelligence Service was known as 'C', after its first head Sir Mansfield Cumming. It was a government post that did not exist, either in the statute book or in common law, by tradition and usage – since Tudor times the service, too, was as secret as its chief was anonymous. The service believed in one cardinal rule; to be effective a secret service must remain secret.

That spring Bobbie heard from Menzies, a long-time village resident, that Luckington Manor was available as the current occupant Captain Robert Treeck had relinquished the lease at the end of the hunt season. He began negotiations and also set about getting planning permission for stabling at the manor.

As the summer drifted to a close, the enevitable war clouds were looming. Neville Chamberlain, the British Prime Minster made a radio broadcast on the BBC Home Service.

On Sunday morning, 3 September at quarter past eleven he announced:

"I am speaking to you from the Cabinet Room at Ten Downing Street. This morning the British Ambassador in Berlin handed the German Government a final note stating that, unless we hear from them by eleven o'clock that they were prepared at once to withdraw their troops from Poland, a state of war would exist between us. I have to tell you now that no such undertaking has been received, and that consequently this country is at war with Germany."

Bobbie was again out with the Beaufort Hunt in November, rubbing shoulders with the Duchess of Beaufort and Captain Spicer, and by December, Hartman had officially retired as joint master of the Southdown.

At his last meeting at Firle Place he was presented with a silver fox mounted on an ebony plinth. The local *Sussex Express* was on hand to report the proceedings; Lord Gage was on active service with his regiment, so it was left to his wife to make the presentation. Lady Gage said: *"I am happy to present to you this small token of gratitude and affection from the members of the Southdown Hunt."* Hartman replied: *"It was during the last war that I really got the 'hunting bug'. However downhearted you may be, you can get up on a horse and find a wonderful remedy."*

The *Sussex Express* reporter also commented: *"I noticed that Mrs Hartman who was wearing an attractive tweed hooded coat was filming the proceedings."*

In July, their Northease gardener Mr Low entered flowers in the annual summer flower show held at the Dome and Corn Exchange, arranged by the Brighton, Hove and Sussex Horticultural Society. The entry on behalf of Captain Hartman was awarded second place in the 'twelve vases distinct varieties' section.

There was a small footnote in the *Yorkshire Post* confirming that Captain Hartman had put Northease up for sale with Knight, Frank and Rutley together with its 120-acre estate. However, in September Bobbie Hartman must have had plans for using Northease as a naval hospital, as he placed an advertisement in the local *Sussex Agricultural Express* for a part-time lady secretary for work in connection with a naval emergency hospital: *"… must be a good shorthand-typist… it would be an advantage to be able to drive a car."*

★

The summer turned to autumn, and before Christmas, Bobbie and Dodo had moved from Sussex to Luckington Manor in Wiltshire and could be telephoned on Sherston 236.

The years that followed from that summer of 1939, for Britain, was a 'total war'; the government coalition became the National Government, and introduced the 'Emergency Powers Act' with sweeping powers; a National Register was created, everyone received a buff-coloured identity card with a personal number; gas masks were introduced and made compulsory; overseas mail was censored and rationing was introduced which lasted well beyond the end of the war.

It applied to food, petrol and clothing, although never to beer, cigarettes and potatoes.

No section of society remained untouched by military conscription, air raids, the shipping crisis and the war economy. It was to last for six long years – British casualties would be nearly three times that of the USA. Britain would spend more than a quarter of its national wealth waging war against the Axis powers, and by 1945 the country was exhausted and nearly bankrupt.

The returning servicemen and women wanted change and voted in a new Labour government, which swept to power with a landslide majority under Clement Atlee. Churchill the war leader was now in opposition. Industries like coal and railways were nationalised and the Welfare State and National Health Service was born. Society had changed forever, and so had the world order.

-25-

The Beaufortshire spies

Luckington Manor is a typical Cotswold stone country house built of distinctive local yellow limestone, dating to the late seventeenth century with later additions. It is located in the village of Luckington, on The Street, part of the B4040 road that runs through the village, close to the Wiltshire–Gloucestershire border. The old house with its rabbit warren rooms and alcoves spread over two floors, with numerous outbuildings was to be the Hartmans' new country home. Bobbie had first glimpsed it in the spring of 1939 with its garden full of yellow crocuses and forsythia, when Stewart Menzies advised it was vacant. It was ideal for hunting close to the Badminton estate which also had its own railway station with direct connections to Paddington via the *Spa Express* with their cream and brown livery (which would stop at the station on request). The small village had all the classic English ingredients; the twelfth-century parish church of St Mary and St Ethelbert, a post office and pub, the *Old Royal Ship Inn*, which sold local Ushers and Wadworth ales and where the Beaufort Hunt would occasionally meet.

The previous tenant, a certain Captain Treeck from Germany had arrived in London in 1934 initially staying at the *Park Lane Hotel*, later renting a house at 12 Cheyne Place in Chelsea. In 1935 he leased Luckington Manor from Captain Hodgkinson, who had been joint master of the Mendip at one time.

It was ideal for the Beaufort Hunt – which he joined, full of political aristocracy with its influential members. He paid a handsome £150 contribution towards the hunt's funds for the season 1937–38 and mixed freely with its members. He competed in a polo tournament as part of the Beaufort team at Ranelagh in 1937 and also rode in steeplechase events on his hunter *Remus II*. Locals were impressed. If perhaps they did not like the cut of his jib, they liked the size of his wallet.

Robert Treeck lived a parallel life, as his main country residence was Guilsborough House in Northamptonshire –which he rented for £500 pa. Equipped with twenty-one rooms and a staff of eleven, he entertained lavishly. He rode with the local Pytchley Hunt – almost as grand as the Beaufort, and quickly become popular, particularly with Colonel Lowther, the hunt's master. He had acquired an 'English manner' and rarely talked politics, but when he did, like von Ribbentrop he insisted that there would be no war between Britain and Germany. He spent his summers in Germany, ostensibly to hunt on an estate he rented in Bavaria.

Treeck is described as six foot tall, with fair hair and broad shoulders, an ex-cavalry officer who had fought against the Allies in the Great War.

He had plenty of money it seems, was a good all-round athlete, excellent horseman, polo player and moved in influential social circles, keeping in touch with von Ribbentrop at the German embassy when staying at his London home.

In the spring of 1938 he married a Chilean divorcee, Violeta the Baroness de Schroeder in London (her former husband was a polo player and they had a son, Arturo), and together they mixed and rode with English hunting society. He was in fact a German spy, and reported directly to Hitler.

★

Stewart Menzies had moved to Luckington in the 1920s. He had fought with distinction as an officer with the *Life Guards* in the Great War, was awarded the DSO, badly wounded and honourably discharged – joining the counterintelligence section of Field Marshal Douglas Haig.

It was said that he was the natural son of the prince, (traces of red hair and those 'Windsor' blue eyes) who in 1901 became King Edward VII. Menzies' mother Susannah West, née Wilson, was the rich heiress of a shipping magnate. She was known as 'the pocket Venus'; small, very fair with forget-me-not blue eyes and fluffy golden hair. A great beauty, vivacious with great poise, and it was said not without foundation, the Prince's paramour – and as such his career enjoyed the royal favour. He was around five foot ten, slim, at *Eton* he had excelled in sports and cross country running, and won prizes for his studies of languages.

In 1918 he married Lady Avice *(Avie)* Ela Muriel Sackville, the youngest daughter of Gilbert Sackville, the eighth Earl De La Warr and Lady Muriel Agnes Brassey, (daughter of Thomas Brassey, the first Earl Brassey) in St Martins-in-the-Fields, one of the bridesmaids being Lady Diana Somerset from the Duke of Beaufort's family, and they honeymooned in the sixteenth-century Walmer Castle near Dover.

Avice's older sister Idina was once married to the twenty-second Earl of Erroll, who was later murdered in East Africa in 1941 allegedly by 'Jock' Broughton – but he was acquitted. Broughton was a Hartman guest at Northease in the late thirties.

In 1923 they bought the eighteenth-century Bridges Court, a Cotswold stone farmhouse, set in thirty acres adjoining the Badminton estate, adjacent to Luckington Manor. They had fully renovated it by the following year. However, their relationship did not prosper; after Avice's adulterous liaison in Paris they were divorced in 1931, when she left him for a certain Captain Frank Fitzroy Spicer, who had served in the twelfth *Lancers* in the Great War and was joint master of the Beaufort Hunt, living at Spye Park in Chippenham. [30]

Stewart then married the attractive Pamela Thetis Garton the following year. She had been married briefly in 1929, but was now living with her parents in London at 34 Grosvenor Street. She was the youngest daughter of the Honourable Rupert Evelyn Beckett, a partner in the private Yorkshire bank of Beckett & Co., that later merged with Westminster Bank. He was also proprietor of the *Yorkshire Post*. They honeymooned at the Villa La Mauresque, owned by novelist and ex-spy Somerset Maugham in the south of France.

Early in 1934 they had a daughter, Fiona Daphne, born in London – becoming the apple of her father's eye. However, soon afterwards Pamela began suffering from clinical depression including anorexia nervosa for most of their marriage and became a semi-invalid for many years.

In November 1939, on the death of Admiral Sinclair, Stewart Graham Menzies, now forty-nine was appointed Chief of Secret Intelligence Service, and took on the mantle of 'C'. At the same time he appointed two assistants, one from a Belgian banking family, Peter Koch de Gooreynd, a music-publisher and song writer, and the other his close friend David Boyle, a cousin of the Earl of Glasgow and Dodo's ex-husband Lord Dalrymple. Boyle had been in SIS since the Great War and amongst other things had been involved in the aborted attempt to kidnap Eamon de Valera, president of Sinn Fein in New York, causing uproar in America. He was quickly sent to Canada to be Aide-de-Camp to the Prince of Wales on his tour in 1919.

The Prince of Wales had taken a house in Sherston Magna to be nearer the Beaufort Hunt, a good reason for Captain Treeck to be close by. It was said during a social hunt gathering that he had sidled up to Menzies and asked if he was interested in forming closer links with the Nazi leadership in Berlin. Treeck knew Menzies was a close friend of Hugh Grosvenor, second Duke of Westminster (who had a long affair with Coco Chanel), one of the leading appeasers in the British establishment at the time, and about to become a prominent member of the 'Right Club'. [31] However, Menzies, aware of Treeck's motives, rejected the offer out of hand. [32]

Treeck spent some six weeks in Germany during the Munich Crisis of September 1938 eventually realising his efforts to influence appeasers within the British establishment, a key part of German strategy, had failed.

The following year knowing war was inevitable Robert Treeck and the Baroness left Guilsborough House rather hurriedly – taking only a few suitcases with them. The couple had their English chauffeur drive them to Croydon Airport and on 2 July 1939 they flew to Germany, and disappeared.

★

In November 1939, on the border of Holland and Germany, in what became known as 'the Venlo incident', an abduction took place of two British MI6 officers by a covert operation run by the 'Sicherheitsdienst', the German intelligence agency who lured the men into a trap. The result was devastating as much of the European spy network fed through The Hague was blown after their interrogation. It was fortuitous that Claude Dansey's alternative Z network was unknown and left intact.

By 1940 Guilsborough had been placed under the control of the 'Custodian of Enemy Property', [33] which had ordered a sale of the furnishings and personal effects as the *Daily Express* reported on 27 November:

An auction was organised on their behalf by Robinson & Hall in Bedford in December. The auctioneers had an expectation that the sale would realise something like £1,200. It achieved £2,000, largely because the wealthy tobacco manufacturer Captain Wills from nearby Thornby Hall had bid heavily. [34]

In the meantime Menzies had expanded wartime intelligence and counterintelligence departments and supervised codebreaking efforts at Bletchley Park with its 'Ultra Secrets', reporting directly to Churchill. He coordinated his operations with other clandestine organisations such as Special Operations Executive (SOE), British Security Coordination (BSC) – a covert organisation set up in New York, Office of Strategic Services (OSS) – a wartime intelligence agency of the United States, the predecessor of the Central Intelligence Agency (CIA) and the Free French Intelligence Agency (BCRA).

After the Great War, intelligence offices had been based at 24 Queen Anne's Gate, but with increased funds Menzies had in the 1920s leased the third and fourth floors of 54 Broadway off Victoria Street to house the expanding service, under the guise of the 'Minimax Fire Extinguisher Company'.

★

In the spring of 1939, Nick and Marguerite Vansittart were living in London at 8 Stanhope Terrace, a few doors away from the old family home.

James Mooney, the General Motors director, had arrived in England on 27 March 1939 on board the SS *Europa*.

In earlier years he would be accompanied by his wife Ida and sometimes children – preferring to stay in the countryside at *Aldenhall House Club* or *Bushey Hall Hotel* near Elstree. On this occasion, travelling alone he stayed at the *Berkeley Hotel*, on the corner of Piccadilly and Berkeley Street.

He did not meet with the Hartmans but more urgently with Nick Vansittart, the Regional Director for General Motors and Geheimrat Wilhelm von Opel, chairman of the board of Adam Opel A.G., recently arrived in England.

Vansittart and von Opel had disturbing news about several engineering executives who had been taken into German police custody on a charge of alleged activities inimical to Germany's national economy in general, and its automotive industry in particular. It was agreed that Mooney would proceed to Berlin to investigate.

He spent a week strenuously negotiating with the help of Raymond H. Geist, the American Chargé d'Affaires in Berlin and Joachim von Ribbentrop, the Reich Foreign Minister. By early April the men were released. Mooney, who had been joined by his second wife Ida (twenty years his junior), sailed from Cannes on the SS *Conte Di Savoia* and were back in New York by May, reuniting with their four sons at their home in Oyster Bay.

Nick Vansittart followed soon after to New York on the RMS *Queen Mary* in May to meet up with James Mooney at the Export Company of General Motors on Broadway.

It has been suggested that Mooney had links with British Intelligence – his contacts with the Nazis at the highest level would have been of great interest. Before America came into the war – officially – he was briefing President Franklin D. Roosevelt in 1940 after his meetings with Adolf Hitler and Göring. The American press were critical of his negative views of England and relations with Nazi Germany. All this could have course been deliberately placed by British Intelligence (BSC) working from the International Building at the Rockefeller Center in New York, as a useful smokescreen. In any case he resigned as President of General Motors Overseas in 1940 to concentrate on gearing up GM for wartime production.

By 1945 Mooney, now a captain in the *United States Naval Reserve* retired from his intelligence work on the staff of the Chief of Naval Operations and rejoined General Motors.

★

In June 1940 the newspapers were full of the miraculous evacuation by the Royal Navy assisted by a fleet of civilian 'little ships' rescuing over 300,000 British and French soldiers trapped on the beaches of Dunkirk, as a headline in the *Daily Sketch* declared: *"Four-Fifths of B.E.F. saved"*.

This was followed quickly by the arrival in England of General de

Gaulle on 9 June. Captain Hartman had seized the publicity opportunity of presenting him with a Buick limousine. Madame de Gaulle and her three children had managed to get out of France with hastily arranged passports aboard the last ferry out of Brest, arriving in Falmouth on 18 June.

His headquarters at 3–4 Carlton Gardens, overlooking St James's Park, nearby his intelligence offices (BCRA) at 10 Duke Street, conveniently next door to one of London's gentleman's hairdressers, 'Geo. Thomas' – purveyor of the ubiquitous green 'Royal Yacht' hair lotion. It had a branch at *Eton,* and had been a favourite among senior Royal Navy officers from the early 1900s. De Gaulle, physically impressive at six foot four was meticulous in appearance with his black hair, slicked down with Brilliantine. Hartman as a member may have introduced him to the *Royal Automobile Club*, where he would lunch whilst in London. His family eventually settled in Hampstead.

Another wartime Buick owner was Admiral Sir Max Horton, a Great War submariner, who was Commander-in-Chief, Western Approaches, who had his headquarters in a large block of flats, Northways, in north London. He is remembered by a Lendrum & Hartman mechanic Russell Johns who describes him thus: *"He was a character and capable of giving us and his naval-rating chauffeur a broadside, using nautical terms if all was not well with his car."* [35]

With the arrival of European exiles during the war years, a small service department was required in addition to the war work being carried out at Willesden. As Johns explained:

"I was instructed to deliver King Peter of Yugoslavia's Buick to a small isolated country house near Huntingdon and had some difficulty in locating the place as all direction signs had been removed for the duration. Soldiers in Yugoslav uniforms stopped the car when some distance from the house and escorted me the last few hundred yards. King Peter came out to inspect the car. We then went into the kitchen and, after asking questions about the car, he said 'I must get the garage key,' took it from a hook on the dresser, and put the car away personally. His mother Queen Maria then purchased a Buick which I demonstrated for her in Chelsea." [36]

Other Buicks serviced by Lendrum & Hartman at Willesden included those of Queen Wilhelmina of the Netherlands, Władysław Sikorski,

Prime Minister of the Polish Government in Exile, and the Russian Ambassador, Ivan Maisky.

★

In the Spitfire summer that followed the skies above London were criss-crossed with white vapour trails from the fighter aircraft of the *Royal Air Force*, the 'few' doggedly defending the island against the onslaught waves of Luftwaffe bombers.

The Vansittarts had moved to 42 Upper Brook Street. Nick was asked to get some photographs made and took the opportunity to have a portrait of himself by Baron, a society and court photographer at his studios in Park Lane.

After what became known as the 'Battle of Britain', the Blitz followed from September through the autumn and winter months to the spring, the following May, as London and many provincial cities suffered bombing raids night after night. In September an incendiary raid completely burnt out the Oxford Street store of John Lewis. Although Albemarle Street was hit several times by bombs there was no damage to Lendrum & Hartman showrooms (they had in fact been closed during the war – only operating servicing and repairs from Old Oak Lane in Willesden). Pelham Place had been hit by high explosives too – but the Elibanks had moved earlier to Cadogan Gardens.

In April 1941, Nick again travelled to New York – this time by the longer and more circuitous wartime route via Lisbon.

At a cost of £35-15s-6d, he flew out from England with the KLM service from Whitchurch (Bristol) to Lisbon's Sintra airport staying at the *Palácio* hotel at Estoril on the mouth of the Tagus. The hotel (which Dodo knew well) in neutral Portugal was already a hotbed of intrigue with spies and the flotsam and jetsam of European aristocracy and people seeking refuge from war or passage to the Americas.

Two months before, the double-cross spy Arthur Owen [37] had travelled the same routes from England staying at the Art Deco *Metropole Hotel* facing Pedro IV Square. A month later, a certain Lieutenant Commander Ian Fleming also arrived in Lisbon – he too stayed at the *Palácio* hotel. It is said he based his future James Bond book *Casino Royale* around his experience of Estoril. He, like Nick Vansittart, took the Pan

American Airways Clipper Service to New York on intelligence work, staying at the *St Regis* – a hotel built by John Jacob Astor IV (who died on RMS *Titanic*) – a Beaux-Arts masterpiece on New York's Fifth Avenue. It was here in 1934 that its bartender Fernand Petiot is credited with inventing the *Bloody Mary* cocktail. They say he spiced up a basic tomato juice and vodka mix that had been served at *Harry's Bar* in Paris with added ingredients, which is often suggested as the 'hair of the dog' cure for hangovers.

Although the flights to Lisbon were designated *British Overseas Airways Corporation (BOAC)* 777 the aircraft were flown entirely by Dutch *KLM* aircrew, and not without their dangers. In 1943 one of its civilian aircraft was deliberately targeted by German fighters over the Bay of Biscay and shot down, killing all on board including the actor Leslie Howard. It had been rumoured that Winston Churchill was travelling on that flight.

Nick boarded the *Pan Am Clipper* at the Cabo Ruivo Seaplane Base in Lisbon. The flying boat was the only regular civilian air route to the USA at that time. It carried about twenty-two passengers in relative comfort on a flight that took twenty-three hours from Lisbon, via Horta in the Azores, Bermuda to New York arriving at the Marine Air Terminal, at what is now LaGuardia International Airport, on 17 April. The pre-war fare one-way would be US$375.

We now get a glimpse of Nick's appearance from the US arrival records; he is forty-seven, height five foot eleven with a fair complexion, red hair and blue eyes, and his US address was listed as c/o General Motors, 1875 Broadway and he was staying at the *Hampshire House*.

British Security Co-ordination (BSC) was a covert organisation established in New York at the Rockefeller Center. They had offices on the thirty-fifth and thirty-sixth floors of the International Building, as well as apartments at the *Hampshire House*. BSC was run by the immensely able Canadian William Stevenson who had won the Military Cross and Distinguished Flying Cross in the Great War, and is largely credited with changing American public opinion from an isolationist stance to a supportive tendency regarding America's entry into the Second World War.

A year earlier, Noël Coward saw Stephenson, known colloquially as 'Wild Bill', at the end of July 1940 when on a world entertainment and propaganda tour. He wrote that the *"… suite in the Hampshire House with the outsize chintz flowers crawling over the walls became pleasantly familiar to me..."* and that Stephenson *"had a considerable influence on the next few years of my life."* Stephenson offered him a job, but this was vetoed by London. [38]

★

During the summer of 1941, Bobbie was increasingly unwell. The hectic demands of his thriving business in the pre-war years and social entertaining, the move to Luckington, the effects of war on the business had taken their toll. The Hartmans still had the flat in Albemarle Street (although the showroom had been closed for the war) and during the Blitz they had spent more time at Luckington than London.

The war had left Lendrum & Hartman sales at a standstill, and many of his staff had been conscripted into the forces. Henry Berenstein was able to oversee the reduced office, and the Willesden works had been put on a war footing, largely occupied with repairing vehicles for the military. Bobbie had diversified, and was now concentrating on horse-breeding and livestock farming.

The same summer an advertisement appeared in the *Western Gazette* for a *"GARDENER (head, working); very good place vacant; have knowledge and be hard working, Two assistants. Good wages and excellent cottage. Electric light and bath. On bus route. Apply Captain Hartman, Luckington Manor, Chippenham, Wilts."*

With the arrival of the first American Forces in January 1942 the L&H works were instructed to prepare a bullet-proof car for the use of General Eisenhower. This was done, using armour plate inside the doors, flooring, roof, as well as special Triplex glass and Dunlop tyres. By now petrol rationing for civilian motorists was practically extinguished.

The same month, whilst convalescing at the *Imperial* on the fashionable English Riviera in Torquay (local author Agatha Christie often featured the hotel in her crime novels), Bobbie put an advertisement in *The Western Morning News*: *"BUTLER wanted, for country house, Wiltshire; two in family; some staff; must be a gentleman's servant, with good references; over age or exempt; good wages; comfortable post. – Apply Capt. Hartman, Imperial Hotel, Torquay."*

The applicants were interviewed and a suitable candidate selected.

In the spring of 1942 there followed a series of heavy bombing attacks on cathedral cities, which became known as the 'Baedeker' raids because the Germans were using the ubiquitous travel guide book as a reference in response to the *Royal Air Force*'s attack on the historic Baltic town of Lübeck.

The *Luftwaffe* deliberately targeted Exeter, Bath, Norwich, York, Canterbury, with the heaviest casualties in Bath, only sixteen miles from Luckington, causing 400 deaths alone in two nights of raids in April. The Assembly Rooms –the scene of the pre-war Beaufort Hunt Ball was completely burnt out. [39]

The Hartmans' new butler, Frank Bernard Gear, had been invalided out of the Royal Marines because of a leg injury after serving as a steward on HMS *Renown*, a battlecruiser which had frequently conveyed royalty on their foreign tours in the 1920s. He was thirty-four, born in East Grinstead into a large working-class family. His father, mother and eldest brother Fred were all house painters. He had barely been with the household six months before Captain Hartman died.

On Saturday 5 September 1942, at Luckington Manor Bobbie fell into a coma and died of cancer of the rectum and a secondary carcinoma – liver cancer. He was fifty-seven.

It was recorded he was a retired captain in the Royal Navy by his forty-year-old local general practitioner Eric William Winch MRCS – one time House Physician at St George's hospital, but no one sort to correct him, and the informant was a certain Mr E. Morris of 135 Old Brompton Road, SW5, whose role and presence was uncertain.

Bobbie had been unwell for some time, and perhaps knowing his illness was terminal had chosen Gear to be 'on hand' for Dodo. Like many of his decisions, it would prove to be a good choice.

Gear would be the one consistency in the Hartmans' household for the next fifteen years.

Ironically, a few days later, in the September 9 issue of the *Tatler & Bystander* magazine there appeared a double page photo feature article under the title: *"At Luckington Manor The Wiltshire home of Captain and Mrs F.W. Hartman."*

The interview had been given early the same year, and describes their chief occupations as farming and breeding horses. One of Dodo's mares, *Beaufortshire Beauty* had a foal sired by the 1936 Grand National runner *Davy Jones*.

There was no mention of Lendrum & Hartman, only to say that their previous home Northease had been given as a naval convalescent home, although it appears to have been used by the Canadian Forces during the war as a recuperation base. In 1963 it became *Northease Manor School,* for boys.

Mrs Hartman, the article went on to say, runs Cowage Farm, a recent acquisition adjoining Luckington.

The reporter was accompanied by Albert Swaebe [40] a Jewish press photographer, now well into his seventies. He had previously been a gold miner in South Africa an actor/comedian performing under the name of Bert Edwards, and since 1927 was enjoying a new career as a top society photographer, including the royal family and Wallis Simpson. One of his numerous images included Dodo and Bobbie together in the garden sitting on cushioned recliners each with their dogs. It was almost certainly their last photograph together.

A memorial service was arranged in London, on September 15 at St George's, Hanover Square (scene of his first two marriages), and reported in *The Times* the following day.

The service was taken by the Honourable Stephen Phillimore, Archdeacon of Middlesex, who had won the Military Cross in the Great War. He was the son of Lord Phillimore, an eminent ecclesiastical lawyer.

Many of their close friends and business acquaintances were present including Viscount and Viscountess Elibank; Lord and Lady Ennisdale (the former Henry Lyons, a wealth insurance broker raised to the peerage in 1939); Brigadier-General the Honourable Alexander Russell and his wife; Bobbie's eighty-one-year-old mother Edith Hartmann was too distressed to attend – she was represented by her London solicitor David Grimes of Kerly, Sons & Karuth, of Great Winchester Street. Nick Vansittart attended alone and there was a large turnout from Lendrum & Hartman staff, including Henry Berenstein and his wife, Charles Culross was there as were trade connections, like Bennett from the Importers Association, Connolly from the Society of Motor Manufacturers and Traders, and Ward from the Canadian Chamber of Commerce.

The Hartmans' company and personal bankers Lloyds were represented by Blencowe from the Cox & Kings branch and Rowley-Morris from the Strand (he would later become a director of Lendrum & Hartman), together with a smattering of military wives and some politicians.

Charles Culross, their solicitor, read Bobbie's will to Dodo. She knew of course she was sole executrix but his words were rather poignant:

"I Frederick William Hartman of Northease, Rodmell near Lewes in the county of Sussex, late Captain R.E. …devise and bequeath all my real and personal estate…to my dearly beloved wife Dorothea Mirabelle Cynthia Hartman as a token of my deepest love for her and of appreciation for the happiness she has brought me and of her sacrifice in giving up her title and income on marrying me…"

Dated 27 November 1935, witnessed by Charles Culross and Lendrum & Hartman's company secretary, I. M. Cecil.

★

In the middle of October, Dodo's friend Frances Day opened on the London stage playing the role of May Daly in Cole Porter's musical *Du Barry Was a Lady*, at *His Majesty's Theatre*. It ran for 178 performances. Less than a month later on November 15 the church bells of the parish church of St Mary and St Ethelbert in Luckington and throughout England rang out to celebrate the great victory at El Alamein and as Churchill explained at his most buoyant, addressing a meeting in the City of London: *"Now is not the End. It is not even the beginning of the end. But it is, perhaps, the end of the beginning."* [41]

Probate was complete by the end of December and in January 1943, the contents of Bobbie's will was announced to the press who published the details as:

"£311,473 LOVE TOKEN
Captain Frederick William Hartman, former joint master of the Southdown Hunt (Sussex), of Luckington Manor, near Chippenham, Wilts. has left £311,473-6s-10d gross, to his wife 'as a token of my deepest love for her and of appreciation for the happiness she has brought me."

They had been married for nearly nine years and during that short time had learnt to complement each other's strengths. She had been the perfect hostess and taken an interest in the business; their partnership had been very successful.

Dodo, perhaps for the first time, felt her confidence ebb. It was the beginning of a period of inner loneliness only a close bereavement brings, for Bobbie did love his Dorothea to the end and believed in her completely.

Act V
Nicky Vansittart – 'at last'
(1938–57)

"At last my love has come along
My lonely days are over
And life is like a song…"

Song featured in musical film Orchestra Wives (1942) with Glen Miller

-26-

Luckington

After the Hartmans moved to Luckington Manor, and joined the Beaufort, they became immersed in local life, made repairs to the outbuildings for the horses and were close neighbours of the Menzies at Bridges Court. Other hunt neighbours in the village of Badminton included Lord Edgar and Lady Margaret Brassey who lived at the Old Vicarage – a Cotswold stone house facing the end of the high street. Margaret Brassey (neé Trefusis) kept Pekinese dogs, a black one called *Souki,* and a white one, *Tang.* She was related by marriage to the Queen Mother through the Earl of Strathmore. Edgar had been a lieutenant-colonel in the *Life Guards* and High Sheriff of Wiltshire in the late twenties. They had two children, Marjorie and Hugh – who after *Eton* and *Sandhurst* married Joyce Kingscote in 1939. During the war he would serve with distinction with the *Royal Scots Greys*, famous for their charge at Waterloo. The regiment was soon to be mechanised as part of an armoured division.

Another wartime neighbour Queen Mary had been evacuated from London at the request of King George VI for safety during the Blitz. She arrived at Badminton House, to stay with her niece, Mary Somerset, Duchess of Beaufort. Her household, which comprised seventy pieces of luggage and fifty-five servants, occupied most of the house until after the war. Her visitors during the war included Eleanor Roosevelt and Haile Selassie, who was in exile at Fairfield House near Bath.

Badminton House, described as a large seventeenth-century country house, with its surrounding gardens and deer park, lies in Gloucestershire. It was in the winter of 1863 that the game known as 'Badminton' was invented by the children of the eighth Duke in the Great Hall, where the featherweight shuttlecock would not mar the life-size portraits of horses.

Its association with hunting and horses naturally led to hosting the annual Badminton Horse Trials, held since 1949.

★

The Menzies pronounced their name 'Mingiss' – as did the family clan in Hallyburton, their estate near Balmoral in Scotland. Their wealth was founded through distilling Scotch whisky, in one of the largest distilleries in Europe in the Haymarket Edinburgh.

During the Great War, Stewart Menzies serving with the *Second Life Guards* was seriously wounded and retired from active combat to join the counterintelligence section.

He was a member of the British delegation to the 1919 Versailles Peace Conference. Whilst mingling with fellow French and American intelligence officers of the *Bureau Interallie* in the *Travellers Club* in the Champs-Elysées he was known as 'Le Kernel Ming-*eez*'.

It was one of his team (a contempory at *Eton*) Rex Benson – of the banking family Robert Benson & Co, whose firm would eventually merge with Kleinwort in the post-war years – who was responsible for apprehending the spy Mata Hari.

Benson, Stewart Menzies and Nicky's brother Robert Vansittart would remain friends and politically connected throughout their lives. Benson had hosted a New Year's dinner in his Belgravia house in 1936, with the Prince of Wales, Mrs Simpson, and the Duff Coopers, together with 'Van' and Sarita Vansittart days before George V died.

★

Pamela, Stewart's second wife, came from a rich family from the North Country. Although she brought no money to the marriage, she did however have style and dress sense, and she was a darkly beautiful woman with an intense air. They seemed happy enough, but it soon became evident that Pamela was suffering from some sort of mental illness that defied diagnosis. Most of the time she appeared lucid, calm and enchanting, but occasionally and with increasing frequency she would become despondent and take to her bed. Her illness appears to have been complicated by Stewart's work.

She was totally excluded, and she did not know he was a high officer of the British secret service. In fact she believed he was engaged on routine confidential work at the War Office that required considerable liaison with the Foreign Office. The mystery troubled her – as it had his first wife Avice – and Pamela became to fear that Menzies had a mistress, a suspicion that seemed to be unfounded at the time but was actually correct. [1] Menzies' secretarial team included the formidable Miss Kathleen Pettigrew, the senior secretary, originally inherited from 'C's predecessor Admiral Hugh Sinclair and the other two were Miss Evelyn Jones and Miss Elaine Miller.

This situation continued through 1941, with Pamela remaining at their Luckington home whilst her husband was fully occupied in 54 Broadway (SIS Headquarters) in London until a scrambler telephone was installed in the house. This was eventually achieved at Bridges Court, and situated in a boot and shoe cupboard. In the meantime, it did however have a 'pigeon loft' – to communicate with Broadway if need be. Menzies, because of pressure of work, could make only fortnightly trips to Luckington, using his 'service' chauffeur Cyril Lovelace, often allowed to bring his family with him, staying in a flat over the stables.

As Nick recalled of that time in a rare interview:

"His wife's illness was very distressing to him, both because she was ill and, on occasions, she seemed like a wraith. We thought he might have been wiser to place her in custodial care, for the burdens in London were very great, much greater than almost any other man's, and he badly needed contentment when he came home. But that he did not find and he used to come regularly to our house seeking, we thought, respite. But even so Stewart would not hear of committing her, and remained terribly loyal to her." [2]

The Hartmans had been friendly and close neighbours, and the same year after his return from America Nick Vansittart, also a friend of the Menzies, was established nearby in Luckington Court, a short distance away in Church Street. Nick had use of this property from Colonel Edward Johnson-Ferguson, a director of the Tredegar Iron & Coal Co. Ltd. Although this seems to be contradicted by the address quoted by SOE files in 1943 – it was of course all part of the clandestine world of 'smoke and mirrors' which Vansittart and Menzies inhabited.

To add more confusion both Bridges Court and Luckington Court appear in the 1941 and 1942 telephone directories as being occupied by Lt Colonel J. C. Brinton CVO, DSO. John Brinton was possibly a convenient cover. He was a fellow officer in the *Second Life Guards* and at one time attached to George V's household, regimental friend of Menzies and also had property in Spain near Gibraltar.

Nick's weekend retreat, at Luckington, (although he is listed in telephone directories as being at Cholsey Grange at Ibstone) suited Dodo. With his useful contacts in General Motors and wider interest in farming he became an invaluable friend after Bobbie's death, as their relationship progressed.

During 1941 some Italian prisoners of war, captured in North Africa, were brought to work in the fields at Luckington to help with farming alongside the Land Army girls and they seemed to be well received locally.

During the late 1930s farmers had been going through difficult times, but on the outbreak of war, with the nation's need to feed itself, demand increased producing much better financial returns for all farmers, particularly milk production, which could also be turned into butter, cheese and even dried milk. Consequently those astute people with capital bought farms.

Nick had bought Cholsey Grange at Ibstone near High Wycombe with its herd of seventy-eight pedigree Ayrshire milk cattle. This was his 'published' address during the war years. Later he invested in Broadcommon Farm at Hurst near Tyford in Berkshire, with its herd of fifty-six British Friesans.

Essentially these were investments, managed on his behalf whilst he was in London. At that time Nick shared a flat at 55 Park Lane with Marguerite.

After the war during 1946 Nick sold Broadcommon through Thimbleby & Shorland, the land and estate agents in Reading. Although he continued with his interest in Pankridge Farm, Bledlow Ridge, near High Wycombe (once the home of opera singer Betty Bannerman, a classically trained mezzo-soprano), he finally gave up milk production and the farm with its Chiltern herd when it was sold again through Thimbleby's in 1953.

In an interview with the author Anthony Cave Brown, [3] Nick stated that around 1941 Menzies asked him to come into the billiard room at

White's Club in St James's and asked him what he knew about explosives and Romania. Nick said that he knew nothing about either, but later learned that a group had gone out to the Baku oil fields to blow up the powerhouses to stop the pumping of oil to Germany.

The same year the General Motors historian records that an American employee, a certain Miss Brook (later Mrs Dorothy Rylands), who was at the time secretary to the company treasurer, at the St James's Square headquarters remembered Nick Vansittart as being *"in a world of his own"*. She continued, saying that on one occasion a gentleman arrived and asked to speak to him. After an hour or so, he left. Subsequently, Nick approached her asking if she would like to work in the War Office, vaguely talking about work in a typing pool, but Miss Brooks was not interested so the job was not pursued. Her American citizenship, sex and age would presumably have been of interest in the intelligence spheres. [4]

Then in March 1943, Sir Charles Hambro who was the then Chief of SOE approached and recruited him as an adviser on France and the Low Countries. He was still of course on the General Motors payroll. Hambro was a little younger that Nick, he too had been educated at *Eton,* later the *Royal Military College* at *Sandhurst* and served with the *Coldstream Guards* in the Great War, winning the Military Cross. After a spell in North America with J. P. Morgan he returned to join the family bank J. C. Hambro & Sons, later Hambros Bank. His first wife Pamela Cobbold (youngest daughter of a Suffolk brewing dynasty) had died in a hunting accident in 1932, and he married again in 1936. At the start of the Second World War he was asked to join the Ministry of Economic Warfare, by another old *Etonian*; it was the cover organisation for the Special Operations Executive.

In June 1940 Winston Churchill held a meeting at *St. Ermin's Hotel* in Caxton Street, just a stroll from Dodo's old flat in Chandos Court, and close to where she married Bobbie at the Caxton Hall. The hotel entrance is set back from the street, designed originally as a residential red-brick mansion block converted to a hotel in 1899. It was close enough to the Houses of Parliament to have a 'Division Bell' installed, and with its *Caxton Bar* was a natural meeting point for many of the nearby intelligence services at Broadway.

Churchill had asked a group of remarkable people to join him in 'Setting Europe Ablaze' – under Hugh Dalton (the then) Minister of Economic Warfare, he was to head an elite team, known as the SOE –

Special Operations Executive. The unit was to carry out covert operations during the war, based initially in the hotel, where they took over an entire floor. The senior staff were invariably ex-public school and Oxbridge, but the agents came from all walks and included a former chef, an electrician, several journalists and the daughter of a Brixton motor-dealer. A few months later they moved into 64 Baker Street where they remained for the rest of the war. This earnt them the nickname the 'Baker Street Irregulars', after the fictional street urchins who appear in various Sherlock Holmes stories, employed by Holmes as intelligence agents.

★

In May Dodo heard her mother-in-law Edith Hartman had died in London. She was eighty-one. With her husband Augustus and both sons now dead, a granddaughter Betty she never saw, her solicitor David Grimes from Kerly, Sons & Karuth advised Dodo she was the sole beneficiary.

When the will's probate had been completed in the July it was revealed she had left £208,823.

Within a space of seven months Dodo had inherited something like £16.5 million in today's money from the Hartman family. At the age of forty-five Dodo was now the owner of a major London car dealership, a country manor and farms, and was a very wealthy woman.

Dodo decided to move from the London flat above the showrooms in Albemarle Street with its memories and found a new apartment at 2 Berkeley House, a Victorian red-brick mansion block taking up the whole of one side of Hay Hill just a short distance away. She had decided to continue as director of Lendrum & Hartman but manage its affairs from her own office. Around the same time she employed a London housekeeper, Winifred Stroude. Like Gear she was brought up in the country, the eldest daughter of a coal merchant from Charing in Kent. Winifred Harrison Stroude was the same age as Dodo – in fact born the same month – and proved to be very capable managing the London apartment and office. She remained with the household until her death.

In Luckington she had a small staff; apart from Gear her butler who also acted as estate manager, she kept a house-keeper Olive Allen, a local woman in her early forties, a gardener and other 'help' came from the village.

Dodo's life alone was moving forward slowly. Since moving to Wiltshire, the Hartmans had acquired in addition to their main home at Luckington Manor, the Cowage Farm at Foxley, which came with the fifteenth-century Bremilham church, claiming to be the smallest still in use in England. It measures just thirteen foot by eleven foot. In Dodo's time it was used for storage and only reconsecrated in the 1980s – the deeds of the farm specify the upkeep of the church. A service is held here once a year on Rogation Sunday, the sixth Sunday of Easter.

Dodo also had Pump House farm and some staff cottages, including the Old Police cottage in Luckington, and a cottage at Idover Farm, in Dauntsey.

In August 1944 Dorothy won a prize at the Beaufort Hunt Pony Club Gymkhana. Albeit first prize in the 'Family turn-out' section – after all it was still wartime. It had been organised by Cannon J. S. Gibbs. The judges included the Duke of Beaufort; his sister Lady Blanche Douglas, a keen aviator; Colonel the Honourable Algernon Stanley who had won the DSO in the Great War with the first *Life Guards*, he was retired but serving with the *Wiltshire Home Guard*, together with Major Arthur Poynter who had also fought in the Great War with the *Scots Guards*. He had married Lady Agnes Isabel Howard, third daughter of the eighteenth Earl of Suffolk; they lived at West End House in Didmarton.

It was the beginning of a revived interest in horses, recalling what Bobbie had said to Lady Gage on receiving his farewell gift from the Southdown; *"However downhearted you may be, you can get up on a horse and find a wonderful remedy."* [5] It proved to be true.

In the September Nick was again travelling to America – bound for the General Motors office on Broadway, this time via *American Export Airlines* flying the twenty-five hour and forty minute direct flight from Foynes flying boat base in Southern Ireland. The base was located on the southern bank of the Shannon estuary near Limerick (eventually superseded by Shannon Airport), where it is said *Irish Coffee* was invented to warm up a group of American passengers disembarked from a *Pan Am* flying boat on a miserable winter evening one night in 1942. The Foynes chef, Joe Sheridan, simply added a liberal measure of Jameson's Irish whiskey to their coffee, the Americans liked it – and a new coffee cocktail had been born.

-27-

The Vansittarts'

The wider Vansittart family has been established in England since the late seventeenth century, becoming notable merchant adventurers, who produced many military men, politicians, and the occasional ecclesiastic son.

Peter van Sittart (1651–1705) was a wealthy merchant adventurer and director of the Russia (Muscovy) Company, the first joint stock company in England. He had emigrated to England in 1670, and became a director of the East India Company. The family name was taken from the ancient market town of Sittard on the German border, in the Limburg province of the Netherlands. The family settled at Shottesbrooke Park near Maidenhead, a Tudor brick mansion built in the sixteenth century, which over the years they re-developed.

The direct family descendants include Nicholas Vansittart (1766–1851) born in Bloomsbury and raised in Foxley's Manor in Bray, Berkshire, the youngest son of Henry Vansittart, one time Governor of Bengal, and member of the notorious 'Hellfire Club' at Medmenham. [6]

Nicholas studied at Oxford, was called to the bar at Lincoln's Inn and entered the political world as a young pamphleteer supporter of William Pitt. He became a Member of Parliament, and was sent on a diplomatic errand to Copenhagen in February 1801 – in which presumably diplomacy failed as in April a British fleet under the command of Admiral Sir Hyde Parker engaged a huge Danish fleet anchored just off Copenhagen, with Vice Admiral Horatio Nelson leading the main attack.

He became Chancellor of the Exchequer in 1812 and bought Foots Cray Place in 1821, a Palladian mansion that had been built the previous century in Kent. He was ennobled a few years later becoming first and last

Baron Bexley. He married the twenty-eight-year-old Catherine Isabella, daughter of William Eden, the first Baron Auckland, in 1806. She became ill and despite taking the cures in Malvern and Torquay, died four years later. The marriage was childless and Nicholas never married again, dying at Foots Cray in February 1851.

The Vansittart family retained the house and estate until the late nineteenth century, when it was sold to Samuel Waring (1860–1940), chairman of *Waring & Gillow*, a noted firm of English furniture manufacturers.

During the Second World War, Foots Cray Place was requisitioned by the Royal Navy as Thames Nautical Training College. Dilapidated after its wartime use, Waring's widow sold the house and grounds to Kent County Council in 1946 for use as a museum. A fire in October 1949 caused extensive damage, and the house was demolished in 1950. The stable block remains, but the grounds known as Foots Cray Meadow are now a public park.

Robert Arnold Vansittart, the eldest son of Colonel Robert Vansittart of Shottesbrooke, was born on 21 October 1851 in London. He became a career soldier, marrying Alice Blane in the summer of 1878 in Easthampstead. She was born in Bombay, the daughter of James Blane [7] from an old Scottish family and East Indian Civil Servant, who had returned to England to retire at Foliejon Park in Berkshire. [8]

They had seven children – three boys, Robert Gilbert, born 1881, Arnold Bexley in 1889 and Guy Nicholas in 1893 and four girls, Sibell Alice the eldest born in 1879, Honoria Edith in 1883, Majorie Marie in 1888 and Audrey Bexley in 1896 – who died in infancy.

Robert was a captain in the *Seventh Dragoon Guards* and served in the Anglo-Boer War of 1900–1. He was invested by the Royal College of Surgeons (FRCS) and as a Member of the Order of the British Empire (MBE). The family lived in Farnham, Surrey. As a military man, he was a member of the *Junior United Services Club* in Charles II Street, and after retiring from the army became a Justice of the Peace.

The family moved to Kensington in London, variously to Ennismore and later Ovington Gardens, where his wife Alice died, and to 41, Stanhope Gardens where he died.

Foots Cray Place, an estate of some 2,000 acres, had been unexpectedly inherited in 1886 and was used as their country retreat. The children's mother Alice died in February 1919 and their father Robert in January 1938, leaving a fortune of £80,648. He, his wife and daughter Honoria are all buried in the graveyard of St James's church, North Cray, situated in the meadows beside the River Cray – once the private chapel to the estate.

The three older sisters never married and continued to live at home with the parents at Stanhope Gardens. Arnold after attending *Eton* and Oxford was also living at the family home, whilst working for Parker & Son, chartered accountants. At the outbreak of war he joined the army, and whilst serving as a second lieutenant with the *Eleventh (Prince Albert's Own) Hussars,* died of wounds received in action at Ypres, May 1915. He was twenty-five. His older brother Robert reflected in his autobiography: *"The telephone rang with my sister's broken voice: 'He's dead.' Lord Kitchener regrets… I locked up my papers, lurched across Horse Guards Parade, plunged into the mutilated plane-trees of the Mall, as far as possible from light or sight, and sobbed my heart out."* [9]

His death would later add significantly to Robert's views on the Germans.

Robert Gilbert Vansittart, born at Wilton House in Farnham, was thirteen years older than Nick; both attended *Eton,* and although chose different careers, their lives became intertwined in pre-war politics and intelligence.

After *Eton,* he had planned on a diplomatic career, so travelled the Continent for over two years improving his proficiency in French and German. In March 1903 he sat for the diplomatic examination and passed out top of the list.

Later that year he was appointed to the Paris embassy, where he was promoted third secretary in March 1905, passing an examination in public law in the December. He was appointed Member of the Royal Victorian Order (MVO) in April the following year. In April 1907 he was transferred to Tehran. He was promoted to second secretary in December 1908, and transferred to Cairo in January 1909. In August 1911 he was sent to the Foreign Office, where he was to spend the remainder of his career.

In the Foreign Office and elsewhere Robert Vansittart was known as 'Van', and has been described as tall, broad-shouldered, ruggedly athletic, exuding decency and warm common sense.

Robert became Principal Private Secretary to the Prime Minister (firstly Stanley Baldwin and then Ramsay MacDonald) from 1928–1930 and Permanent Under-Secretary at the Foreign Office from 1930–1938. He is best remembered for his opposition to appeasement and his hard-line stance towards Germany during and after the Second World War. He was also a published poet, novelist and playwright. As a young attaché, he had written a play *Les Parias* in French which had been performed at *Théâtre Molière* with great success.

Whilst working in Paris on the endless round of meetings as first secretary, part of the British delegation to the Versailles Peace Conference, he met the beautiful French speaking and cosmopolitan Gladys Robinson-Duff and they became engaged, although she was still going through a prolonged divorce. She was the daughter of the influential American banker 'General' William Heppenheimer, [10] a graduate of Harvard Law School, who had earlier brought his wife Blanche and teenage children Gladys and William to Europe for a prolonged holiday staying in Paris. The following year in 1911 he gave his debutante daughter a lavish reception and dance in the ballroom of the *Plaza* in New York. She then married a Wall Street banker, Jay Robinson-Duff, ten years her senior the following year and they had two children, as Robert observed: *"… two little boys, the younger (Robert) – particularly handsome – as delicate as his brother (Jay) was robust."* [11]

Robert and Gladys were eventually married in London at St George's, Hanover Square in the summer of 1921. The same summer, her father hosted Jack Dempsey the heavyweight boxer at his New York home before the fight with Frenchman Georges Carpentier – the first to take a million dollars at the gate before a 90,000 crowd.

Their daughter Cynthia was born two years later. But then their idyll changed when Gladys tragically died at 103 Park Street, London, during the summer of 1928 at the age of thirty-seven, leaving him £23,447. She was buried at North Cray. The following year Robert sailed with his six-year-old daughter on the Cunard RMS *Mauritania* to meet her Heppenheimer grandparents in New York.

Robert's friend Sir Colville Barclay had died the same summer, and after a period of what he describes as 'solitude', he married Barclay's widow in 1931, the forty-year-old Sarita Enriqueta Ward in 1931. Barclay had been the British Ambassador to Portugal; they had three sons, Colville, Cecil and Robert, all now teenagers. In his will, Barclay left Sarita £48,760.

After their marriage they were able to acquire Denham Place, a magnificent seventeenth-century manor house in Buckinghamshire, standing in almost 100 acres of gardens, designed by 'Capability' Brown beside the River Misbourne on the edge of the village of Denham, where they employed a staff of twelve servants and five gardeners.

There is a popular flowering shrub, Camellia japonica named *Lady Vansittart*, with large, semi-double blooms, which are white with dark rose pink streaks and blotches. The flowers appear in mid-season, winter to spring. It was introduced in 1887 from Japan.

Denham Place was where in the 1930s they would entertain King Boris of Romania and his Italian wife during their visits to England, and occasionally the Soviet Ambassador Ivan Maisky and his wife. When in London, they entertained at 44 Park Street, Grosvenor Square.

Sarita was the eldest daughter of the celebrated African explorer (he had joined Stanley's expedition to the Congo in 1884) and sculptor Herbert Ward (1863–1919) who had moved from London to establish his family in Paris. Through the Ward family, Robert became brother-in-law to Sir Eric Phipps (1875–1945), British Ambassador to Berlin and Paris in the 1930s during the rise of Nazism.

Phipps second marriage was to the youngest daughter, Frances Ward in 1911. Charles, the sisters' younger brother had been killed on the Western Front in 1916 at Neuve Chapelle whilst serving as a lieutenant with the *Royal Warwickshire Regiment*.

Amongst visitors to Denham Place was the tall Lady Ottoline Morrell, an artistic social hostess with flaming red hair, closely linked to the Bloomsbury group, including Virginia Woolf. Her circle of friends included many authors (some of them loosely portrayed her in their novels), artists, sculptors and poets. She also had an enduring friendship with Welsh painter Augustus John. On one of the visits to Denham Place in 1935 she took a photograph of Sarita outside the front entrance – a rare family photo which has found its way into the collection at the National Portrait Gallery.

★

The increasing violence towards Jews particularly in Germany in the mid-thirties and in the run-up to the war was a major concern for their representative leaders and as a result of lobbying, Britain took in nearly

10,000 predominantly Jewish children from Europe in what became known as the 'Kindertransport'.

After the Dunkirk evacuation in 1940 and likely imminent invasion there was an increasing mood in the country to evacuate children to the safety of Canada or America. An evacuation scheme [12] had been quickly set up using the offices of Thos. Cook & Sons in Berkeley Street.

Cynthia, Robert's daughter from his first marriage, now a tall seventeen year old – standing at five foot ten, with brown hair was evacuated to the USA with her forty-six-year-old travelling companion Ivy Westmorland. It was believed that the names of the Vansittart family were on a Nazi 'black list'. [13] They sailed from Liverpool bound for New York on the Cunard RMS *Scythia* in June 1940, to stay with her uncle in Easthampton, Long Island. Despite wartime rationing, the ship's catering didn't have those restrictions as a dinner menu of the voyage shows:

Hors d'Oeuvre Varies
Consomme Rossini Cream Marie Louise
Poached Fillets of Halibut – Royale
Calf's Head – Financiere
Roast Quarters of Lamb – Mint Sauce
Brussel Sprouts Vegetable Marrow Bechamel
Boiled and Browned Potatoes
Medallions of Turkey, Piemontaise
Regency Pudding
Ice Cream and Wafers
Fruit Coffee

There was also general controversy over the evacuation of children – Churchill was against it, and in a letter to the Foreign Office on Windsor Castle notepaper Queen Elizabeth expressed her views: *"The children will not leave unless I do. I shall not leave unless their father does, and the King will not leave the country in any circumstances whatever."* [14]

After the death of her husband, Sarita's American mother Sarita Ward published a volume of *Poems and Sketches* in conjunction with her son Rodney in 1925, and two years later a book about her husband titled *A Valiant Gentleman: Being the Biography of Herbert Ward, Artist and Man of Action*. It was published by Charles Dickens' old publisher, Chapman & Hall.

During the twenties she moved to Lower Berkeley Street in Mayfair. At the outbreak of war she moved closer to Denham Place, residing in the village at Dickfield House, where she died in her early eighties in November 1944. Other village residents at this time included the actress Merle Oberon and her husband Sir Alexander Korda (knighted for his contribution to the war effort – the first film director to receive the honour). They lived in the Tudor seventeenth-century Hill's House until their divorce. It was later bought by actor John Mills and his wife Hayley in the 1970s.

Robert's marriage was clearly a happy one, as he describes falling in love: [15] *"I do not like that expression about falling in love – it betokens decent – but one can certainly slide with velocity… Anyhow it is time that we stopped trying to say something new about marriage; there is nothing original about the Bois by moonlight or picnics at Fontainbleau, but they are sufficient."* In his autobiography which was published after his death, he penned a dedication, *"To SARITA in gratitude for unblemished bliss."*

In 1941 he became the first Baron Vansittart of Denham. He died in 1957 aged seventy-five, and with no children the barony became extinct. Sarita continued to live at Denham Place and she died in June 1985 aged 94.

Guy Nicholas Vansittart was his younger brother – although Robert and the family referred to him as 'Guy', General Motors always called him 'Nick' or 'Nicky'. As he explained many years later in a letter to Ethel Salmon: *"I answer mostly to Nicky, Nick or Nicholas! Dodo called me the first. So take your pick!"*

He was the only family child born at Foots Cray Place, delivered on 8 September and baptised on 18 October 1893 in the chapelry of St James's church by the Reverend A. W. Baldwin, the chaplain of HM Prison Wormwood Scrubs.

His eldest sister Sibell had been born in the village of Fulford a few miles from York – but baptised in London some weeks later by her uncle, the Rector of Fulford, the Reverend Henry Blane M.A., who later became Bishop of Wearmouth.

Honoria was born in Glasgow at one of the homes of the Blane family, and Marjorie at Norfolk Gardens in London. By the turn of the century the family with their retinue of servants were living in Chelsea at Cadogan Gardens, with the children's Swedish governess Sophie Muntzing.

Nick's great aunt, Martha Louisa Vansittart (1812–1889) had married a William Chapman (1811–1889) in 1841, and they had four children: William Eden, Thomas Robert, Francis Vansittart and Caroline Margaret.

Thomas Robert became the seventh and last Chapman baronet, enjoying the life as an Anglo-Irish landowner of South Hill near the village of Devlin and Killua Castle estate in Westmeath, Ireland. He married Edith Sarah Hamilton Boyd, daughter of George Rochfort-Boyd of Middleton Park, in 1873, another Irish landowning family, and they had four children.

Then in the 1870s the Chapmans took on a governess, a capable and cheerful young Scotswoman who was known as Sarah Lawrence. By this time, Edith Chapman had become zealously religious, subjecting members of her household to frequent prayer meetings and disapproving of many of their pleasures, while Chapman himself had become a heavy drinker. He fell in love with Sarah Lawrence, who was some fifteen years younger. They had an affair, and after their 'secret' son was discovered by chance in Dublin and reported by the Chapmans' butler, Thomas left his wife and set up home with Sarah, under the name of Mr and Mrs Lawrence. They moved to north Wales, and at Tremadog their second child was born in the summer of 1888. He was named Thomas Edward, who would become known as 'Lawrence of Arabia'.

Nick and Thomas Lawrence, who was five years older, were second cousins. Although they had followed similar but independent paths, it seems unlikely they ever met, although his brother Robert did in Paris during the negotiations at the Treaty of Versailles. As he describes in his autobiography, *"Lawrence was one of the people whom I was glad to have known and not to have known better. He was an acquaintance not a friend, a relative so distant that we never mentioned the subject."* [16]

They both attended Oxford University to read History, Guy at *Trinity* (1911–13) and Thomas at *Jesus* (1907–10). They became linguists, were commissioned in the army and worked in different spheres for British intelligence. Lawrence had studied archaeology in the Middle East and spoke Arabic. He was posted to the intelligence staff in Cairo and led the 'Arab Revolt' in the First World War.

Nick served in the Indian Army during the Great War, as a captain in a cavalry regiment the *thirty-ninth King George's Own Central India Horse*, and after a brief spell in Mesopotamia in 1917 returned to England, leaving the army after the war. His grandson Jonathan Mennell would later recall being regaled by his adventures as he was Aide-de-Camp to the Governor of India. He spent his time playing polo, procuring young ladies for the Governor and having affairs with the wives of his senior officers. When asked why with the wives of senior officers, his reply was *"Well the risk made it very exciting!"*

At the age of twenty-nine in the spring of 1922, he married Margaret Procter known as 'Madi', eldest daughter of Sir Henry Procter, an East Indian merchant. They had two children, Prudence (Prudie) Helen in March 1924, and Arnold (Mark) three years later. After leaving the army he had taken up a position with a banking joint venture between Lloyds Bank and the National Provincial Bank. Fluent in French, they sent him and family to the Continent to live in Antwerp spending three years in various banking departments, in France and Belgium. In 1925 he resigned and joined the sales department of General Motors International in Antwerp to capitalise on his financial experience – later the same year he moved to General Motors Acceptance Corporation.

His progress within the company was swift. In May 1927, Nick moved to General Motors Continental as Sales Manager, promoted to Assistant Managing Director two years later. In July of the following year, he was promoted again, Managing Director of General Motors Continental.

During this time, the young Vansittart family was living in a large house at 186, Chaussée de Malines; however, his marriage to Madi had faltered and she and the children returned to England, as Nick had found a new interest. They were divorced – amicably it seems – around 1932.

Dodo met the second Mrs Vansittart – albeit briefly in New York in January 1933 – Marguerite Emily Grisar (née Good), a Belgian divorcee with two children of her own, Denise and Jean-Louis.

In the spring of 1936, Madi Vansittart married Geoffrey Dearmer in Chelsea and two years later they had a daughter, Juliet. Perhaps influenced by her grandfather, Juliet became a Deaconess in 1977, and married Kenneth Woollcombe, the recently retired Bishop of Oxford in the spring of 1980 who had taken the post of Assistant Bishop of London. They had a daughter Catherine the following year. Woollcombe retired to Worcestershire in 1991, taking over four parishes with his wife, who became ordained as a priest in 1994.

Dearmer was the son of a celebrated cleric and author of numerous works on ecclesiastic themes, his mother too was a well-known author of children's books. He served in the Great War at Gallipoli. He was a poet and his verse was highly praised during and just after the Great War, but soon forgotten, although he saw at least as much action as Owen or Sassoon. His verse contains none of the inspired bitterness of other notable contempories, perhaps best illustrated in his intensely moving poem *The Turkish Trench Dog* which continues to appear in anthologies.

He was described as kind, with an unfailing good humour and hospitality, with an utter lack of cynicism. Perhaps this is what drew Madi to him, although the children from her first marriage Prudie and Mark felt differently. The wider Dearmer family settled in Clifton Hill, north London and he became editor of BBC Children's Hour from 1939 until the late fifties. He outlived all his contempories, dying in Kent in 1996 at the age of 103.

In March 1937, Nick was appointed Regional Director for Northern Europe, responsible for General Motors Continental, General Motors (France), General Motors Suisse and General Motors Limited and their territories, with headquarters in Antwerp. The responsibility also included General Motors G.m.b.H., Wiesbaden; Adam Opel A.G.; General Motors International, Copenhagen; General Motors Nørdiska, Stockholm, and the Balkan countries.

In January 1938 Nick attended his father's funeral in London, and in November the same year the family returned to England when he was appointed Regional Director for the British Isles, based at offices at 3 St James's Square. The original house on the site was once the home of General Augustus Pitt-Rivers, the renowned army officer and archaeologist, who lived there as a child during the 1830s and 1840s. By the 1930s it had been redeveloped into an office block. It was next door to the grand London residence of Nancy Astor, the American-born English socialite and politician until 1942.

Nick and Marguerite found a home at 8 Stanhope Gardens, a few doors away from his father's old residence.

The Vansittarts also retained a substantial house near Antwerp until May 1940, where it seems just before the invading Germans arrived, Jan Engles, the General Motors Continental Plant chauffeur was sent to his home to rescue some family possessions before escaping through France to Bordeaux and evacuation to England. [17]

-28-

Smoke & mirrors

Nick Vansittart's older brother Robert has had his life and political career widely publicised; he wrote an autobiography in 1943 *Lessons in my Life* and again *The Mist Procession* in 1958, published after his death. Whilst he reminisces in a fluent literary style about the people of his time and some historic events, he rarely lets slip any personal feelings or writes about his involvement with Malcolm Christie, for example. This is perhaps the result of his late Victorian and Edwardian upbringing, and the secretive environment of the Foreign Office in which he spent his working life. Paradoxically, he was a maverick at a time when England needed one.

Within government, as Permanent Under-Secretary 'Van' was party to official intelligence; in fact diplomacy is hand-in-glove with intelligence. He however, seems to have a particular interest in intelligence, and one of his main private sources of information was through his relationship with Group Captain Malcolm Christie.

They came to know each other in the 1920s whilst Christie was Air Attaché in Washington, and Vansittart was Head of the American Department at the Foreign Office (1924–8); it would lead to a meeting of minds and develop into an informal private detective agency. The virtue of their network was its broad base, ranging from the Catholic Church to an agent close to Hitler – all still remain anonymous.

Christie had gained a first-class Chemistry degree at Aachen University and joined the *Royal Flying Corps* in 1914, continuing when it became the *Royal Air Force*, as Air Attaché in Washington, and then Air Attaché in Berlin, 1927–1930. The same year he retired from active employment due to ill health. From 1934 until the outbreak of war he investigated the political situation in Germany and Central Europe on behalf of Vansittart. He had valuable contacts in aviation in Germany, Austria and the Sudetenland. He would spend a number of months of the year travelling in Germany.

As the situation in Europe became more precarious Christie gathered more of his information from anti-Nazi informants and dissidents within the German government. It was one of the sources that surreptitiously supplied (with Vansittart's knowledge) Winston Churchill whilst he was out of office, through a Foreign Office official Ralph Wigram, which helped raise the alarm about German rearmament under Hitler and was used by Churchill in Parliament. [18] More than any other Whitehall mandarin, Vansittart stood for rearmament and opposition to appeasement.

Another of Vansittart's 'collection of assets' was a press officer working for the German Embassy, Jona von Ustinov. He had become concerned about the developments in Nazi Germany and in 1935 he resigned from his job at the German Embassy in London. He agreed to work for the secret service. His case officer, Dick White (then in MI5, later Head of MI6) described Ustinov as the *"best and most ingenious operator I had the honour to work with."* Their son Peter Ustinov was born in London and went on to become an internationally acclaimed actor, writer and dramatist.

Even the brave aviator Amy Johnson approached Vansittart in the Foreign Office looking for some dangerous mission in the secret service. [19]

Vansittart's advice to ministers frequently went unheeded, and all too often irritated his political masters. In January 1938 Vansittart was 'kicked upstairs' by the new Prime Minister Neville Chamberlain, assuming the high-sounding, but politically meaningless, title of chief diplomatic adviser to the government. The same year it was said that Noël Coward was also recruited by Vansittart at the Foreign Office, although his brief intelligence career came to an end, it was suggested, because of his ongoing affair with the Duke of Kent – who died in an air crash in the summer of 1942.

However, Coward's intelligence experience was put to good use later, as he appears as a spy in the film *Our Man in Havana* released in 1959.

★

Far less is known about the clandestine activities of his younger brother Nick, his life is only rarely mentioned – perhaps a glimpse in the newspapers attending this or that. Late in life he agreed to be interviewed at his home in Mayfair by Anthony Cave Brown for his book, and only on specific points, to which the General Motors historian David Hayward would years later add some company details to flesh out his career. Even to his family, he remained an enigma. As his daughter Prudie later commented: *"My father kept his life in compartments."* [20]

In the late 1960s, Nick relates that around 1925, he was in *White's* billiard room when Menzies came in. Nick asked him if he could have a word, and advised him that he wanted a job in the secret service.

Menzies said that he would see what he could do for him, and was told to be there at the club the next day at five o'clock. When Nick turned up at the appointed time, he was collected by a car with blinds drawn and was taken from 37 St James's Street, travelling for about an hour or so to a large Victorian house in an area that he did not know. Two men interviewed him about his politics, money, whether he was 'queer' (gay) etc., and then said that they would be in touch with him.

He was then taken back to *White's* in the same car. Menzies told Nick the following day that everyone was impressed, but they were tight for money and it might be some time before they could take him on.

He then states: *"So I went off and got a job as European representative of General Motors."* [21]

He did join General Motors, and as his promotion progressed rapidly he became of interest to another section of British Intelligence headed by Claude Edward Marjoribanks Dansey, Menzies' deputy. He was described as a rugged, bear-like man with a bitter tongue, but a successful and even brilliant intelligence officer, although he was an unpopular figure within the SIS. One officer who worked with him described him as a troublemaker, dishonest and a man of irrational dislikes. Another however, later the Regius Professor of Modern History at Oxford University, Hugh Trevor-Roper, considered him quite simply as *"an utter shit"*.

Dansey had spent three years in New York State spying on wealthy Irish-Americans during the Great War and would have known about David Boyle's operation to kidnap Eamon de Valera. In the late 1920s he was employed as 'passport control officer' in Rome – the cover name for intelligence officers. Dismayed at the poor infrastructure of the service, in the mid-1930s Dansey returned to England and with the approval of Admiral Hugh Sinclair set up a parallel MI6 structure, a hidden shadow and deniable network that could take over when the inevitable happened.

The Z network had its headquarters in Switzerland in 1939; in London it operated a so-called export-import office in Bush House in the Strand, under the codename Z. They used a variety of business and journalistic covers, some authentic, others to accommodate Z agents. Dansey's small staff included Jewish émigrés and other exiles. Eventually he had something like 200 personnel across Europe. His network was prohibited the use of radio, and most of his agents were businessmen doing work for the thrill of it. They used their own credentials as cover.

Among them were Frederick Voigt, formerly the Berlin correspondent of the *Manchester Guardian*, Eric Gedye and John Evans of *The Times* and the *Daily Express* correspondent in Vienna, Geoffrey Cox.

Bush House was also where Menzies' friend David Boyle was based with his section N, whose skilled team at 'Lammin Enterprises' were involved in the ancient skill of intercepting diplomatic mail.

Business covers were managed by Dansey's deputy Commander Kenneth Cohen, son of a barrister of Inner Temple and supplied through various sources like Alex Korda's London Films, a Highgate travel firm Lammin Tours, Sir Geoffrey Duveen's art gallery, wine shippers H. Sichel & Co., (who created the success of the Blue Nun Liebfraumilch brand) and Ian Hooper's General Steamship Trading Company. Nick Vansittart with his European role in General Motors located in Antwerp was ideal Z material, fluent in French with a legitimate reason to visit car and industrial plants in Germany and elsewhere.

His brother Robert had become a friend of producer Alexander Korda, a Hungarian Jew who had left Hollywood for England. He had helped Korda with the financing of London Films, and their film studio in Denham. Under the pseudonym 'Robert Denham' he even provided song lyrics for Korda's *The Thief of Bagdad* (1940) and *The Jungle Book* (1942).

Whilst in different spheres, Nick was in constant touch with his brother, as intelligence gathering increased towards the outbreak of war in 1939. America would 'officially' join in later in 1941; in the meantime Nick and his immediate American boss James Mooney would be concerned with General Motors' business interests and its considerable multi-million dollar assets in Germany.

Mooney was involved in a series of meetings between October and

December 1939, acting as a go-between on peace overtures between the German and British governments, whilst keeping in touch with the American ambassadors in London and Paris. Mooney was acting in an 'unofficial role', involving the contacts of both Nick and Robert Vansittart.

He arrived back in America – gaining the confidence of President Roosevelt before returning again to Europe in February 1940 on a similar mission. He arrived in Berlin in February staying at the long-established *Adlon Hotel* directly opposite the Brandenburg Gate, at 1 Unter den Linden. He wrote the following request on hotel notepaper:

> *"February 16,*
> *To The Fuehrer and Reich Chancellor,*
> *I have just arrived in Germany from the United States and should welcome*
> *an opportunity to call and pay my respects to you."*

At the time the hotel was host to the author P.G. Wodehouse who occupied a fourth-floor suite – until the later Allied bombing became too much.

These meetings with Hitler and Göring came to nothing, and by early May he returned, taking the night train to Rome and a passage on the Italian Art Deco liner SS *Rex* from Naples to New York, as events were overtaking any peace talks. After Pearl Harbour, Mooney resigned from General Motors, joining the intelligence staff of the Chief of Naval Operations.

★

In the summer of 1940 the new Minister of Economic Warfare in charge of Special Operations Executive (SOE) Hugh Dalton, asked Robert Vansittart to offer political advice to the new organisation, as head of the Foreign (Overseas) Resistance Committee. It was a natural choice.

In 1939, after an introduction by Freddy Voigt of the *Manchester Guardian*, he had already introduced Christine Granville to SOE, [22] the brilliant and brave Polish compatriot who became an outstanding agent. Later in the war she would use the names of Field-Marshall Montgomery and Lord Vansittart to assist an audacious escape from the Nazis. [23]

'Van' continued his campaign against Nazi Germany by publishing a slim volume *Black Record: Germans Past and Present*, (price sixpence) in

January 1941, which caused considerable controversy when published, with hostile questions raised in Parliament. His critics suggested that a civil servant should not be allowed to air such controversial issues in public. He retired from government in July 1941, and was raised to the peerage, becoming the first Baron Vansittart of Denham, in the House of Lords.

He wrote his autobiography *Lessons of my Life* in 1943, worked on film song lyrics with Alex Korda, and published *Green and Grey: Collected Poems* in 1944.

★

Nick's surviving wartime SOE personal file is very thin, no doubt carefully 'weeded' out, so we only learn of the essentials, that he was 'an adviser on France and the Low Countries' and it seems he ceased to work for them in March 1945 when he is recorded as having 'proceeded overseas'. This was the same month that Captain James D. Mooney, *United States Naval Reserve*, retired from his intelligence work and joined General Motors again. Although not for long; he resigned in 1946 and became chairman and president of Willys-Overland Motors, Inc.

After the war, Nick continued his career with General Motors in the United Kingdom. Vauxhall Motors became a major government contractor post-war for the supply of Bedford trucks to Ministry specifications. He was elected chairman of Vauxhall Motors in July 1948, and of General Motors Ltd. in London in 1953, finally retiring at sixty-five. As David Hayward, the General Motor historian wrote:

> *"By the time of his retirement, Nick had had a life every bit as remarkable as his elder brother's, and for a time their professional careers touched each other for the betterment of the country."* [24]

After the war a number of German intelligence officers were captured and debriefed; one of those was the high-ranking Walter Schellenberg, head of the SS counter espionage section of the *Sicherheitsdienst*.

He had played a major part in the Venlo Incident, and in 1940 was sent to Portugal to intercept the Duke and Duchess of Windsor and try to persuade them to work for Germany, although this ended in failure. Later in the war his lover, French couturier Gabrielle 'Coco' Chanel, whilst living in the *Ritz*, Paris, was involved in yet another espionage operation conceived to capitalise on Chanel's long-standing associations with British aristocracy, and specifically her pre-war friendship with Winston Churchill. She was to act as an intermediary in a plan appropriately named 'Operation Model Hat', a covert separate peace between Nazi Germany and Great Britain independent of other Allied powers. It too ended in failure.

During his debriefing, Schellenberg claimed knowledge of suspected companies or individuals that worked in the British interest in Berlin. Opel Limited, an automobile manufacturer which had close connections with General Motors whose 'European representative, a certain Hartmann' was Menzies' neighbour at Luckington Manor.

He also stated that another representative of General Motors, 'an American called Mooney', alias 'Stallforth', was found to have had secret connections with dissidents within the German General Staff. This latter reference appears to be in connection with an alleged visit by Mooney to Germany on official business as a director of Opel in the spring of 1941. However, all this was conjecture, and in any case he was confusing people. James Mooney was not Federico Stallforth, who was in fact a New York banker with a contact Ulrich von Hassell in the German Foreign Office, who had approached him in 1941 about maintaining the peace between the US and Germany.

The other mistake was confusing the General Motors European representative Nick Vansittart with Captain Hartman, who had taken over Luckington Manor from Robert Treeck, the spy who fled from England just before the war.

Schellenberg gave evidence at the Nuremberg trials, and was subsequently sentenced to six years' imprisonment, during which time he wrote his memoirs. He was released in 1951 on the grounds of ill health, and died the following year.

★

The Ministry of Economic Warfare was wound up in May 1945, and its functions, including responsibility for SOE, passed to the Economic Warfare Department of the Foreign Office.

All these wartime interwoven events, intrigues, meetings, with many international players would of course have been totally unknown outside that secret circle. Dorothy Hartman's husband had been mistaken for a spy; Pamela Menzies, Marguerite Vansittart, and probably Sarita Vansittart all knew nothing one suspects of their husbands' real working life – other than that they were all busy in the War or Foreign Office.

They would not know the parts their partners played in the momentous events in Britain's history; that would be left for future generations to discover.

As for the participants themselves, all had signed the Official Secrets Act, which meant they could not talk about their activities in government or of the secrets they knew on pain of a fine, imprisonment or worse – their lips were sealed. And for Nick this was a 'compartment' in his life that was forever closed.

The activities of SOE only came to light many years later, when the military historian M. R. D. Foot's book emerged in the 1960s – he had been an intelligence officer in the Second World War. Others followed. However, personal details only appeared under the Waldegrave Initiative on Open Government; the first batch of SOE files, were released to the Public Records Office and National Archives in the autumn of 1993.

As Prudie reflected on her father's relationship with Dodo and his pre-war involvement with the secret world:

> "I don't remember when (Bobbie) Hartman died or exactly when Nicky went to live with her – probably during the war. I know my father was tied up with SOE and as PUS (Permanent Under Secretary) my uncle was well involved with intelligence services – my father having lived in Belgium for so many years was very useful to SOE, but having signed the Official Secrets Act we didn't talk about what we were doing, though he got me my job in MI6 so I knew he had intelligence connections." [25]

-29-

Post-war years

Britain and Lendrum & Hartman emerged from the war in a similar condition – battered, intact, but virtually bankrupt. Dodo had inherited two fortunes, and this sizable capital helped keep the business going during the immediate post-war years. Since the beginning of the war, she had diversified into farming which sustained her image amongst the county set in Wiltshire and Gloucestershire.

In 1941 after Britain had exhausted her gold and cash reserves in the United States, Franklin Roosevelt introduced a Lend-Lease scheme to continue supplying war essentials and other commodities like food and oil. However after his death in April 1945, he was superseded by Harry Truman who delivered a surprise economic bombshell, announcing in August that the US would suddenly and unexpectedly end the Lend-Lease programme immediately.

It was a surprise too for many Allied countries to see the triumphant wartime leader Churchill defeated inexplicably (to them at least) in a landslide election that put Clement Atlee and the Labour government in power.

To fund their welfare aspirations, the following year Britain had to negotiate a crippling $3.75 billion post-war loan from the US, causing the country amongst other things to introduce bread rationing for three years – ironically something it never had to do during the six long years of war. Rationing only finally ended in 1954, and the loan was finally repaid in 2006.

★

In 1946, Dodo had started to review her portfolio of businesses and property assets, intending to release some funds. She started with an auction of surplus antique furniture, largely from Northease Manor and Edith Hartman's London house. They had been stored at Idover Demesne Farm in Dauntsey. The local auctioneers R. J. Tuckett & Son of Tetbury (and members of the Beaufort Hunt) arranged the sale over two days in May. The items for auction included a Sheraton and Chippendale secretaire and bureau bookcases, Sheraton, Georgian and Queen Anne tables and writing-tables, antique tall case clocks, seventeenth-century oak chairs, refectory tables, settles, coffers etc., oil paintings and water colours, Persian and other carpets and rugs, etc., also a 1935 Chevrolet with 'van body', and an excellent rubber-tyre trap. The sale was 'admission by catalogue only', obtainable at one shilling.

In London she had already changed the registed office of Lendrum & Hartman Ltd to her new Hay Hill flat at 2 Berkeley House. Dorothy had also acquired a new lady's maid, the forty-year-old Somerset-born Elsie Bates (her fifth since the Chandos Court days), who together with her butler Frank Gear and London housekeeper Winifred Stroude formed the core of her post-war household servants. Gear would often refer to Stroude as 'Stroudie', or out of hearing the 'sergeant major', in an affectionate way, on account of her 'no- nonsense' attitude.

Gear had been invaluable to her after Bobbie died, and her close friendship with Nick Vansittart with their shared interest in farming and General Motors began to refocus her life.

She had found a new expression in riding her two five-year-old hunters *Sir Melville* and *Precentor* at steeplechase events and during the hunt season with the Beaufort. During the next two years she regularly attended National Hunt meetings, perfecting her riding as her confidence grew as an amateur, throughout the West Country at meetings from Cheltenham, Taunton, Exeter and Newton Abbot to Buckfastleigh. Dorothy's riding weight recorded at this time varied between eleven and twelve stone. Nick Vansittart was often a riding companion during hunt meetings, his daughter Prudie recalls.

The sign of post-war normality began with the revival of the social gathering around the Beaufort Hunt held in January 1947, which was duly reported by The *Western Daily Press* as a great success.

It was held in Badminton House, the seat of the Duke and Duchess of Beaufort with over 700 attending, dancing to Geoffrey Howard's Band, a well-known society band-leader, last heard socially by many at Lady Baillie's dance for her debutante daughter's coming-out party in Bryanston Square in 1939. (She was an Anglo-American heiress and owner of Leeds Castle.)

The press duly reports the important guests, starting with the hunt committee, including the Duchess of Beaufort and Lady Avice Spicer, Mr R. J. Tuckett, the Tetbury auctioneer as honorary secretary, and went on to announce those taking part including Diana Fane, Countess of Westmorland, now on her third marriage. She was the youngest daughter of Thomas Lister, fourth Baron Ribblesdale (who spent his later years as resident guest of Rosa Lewis's at *The Cavendish* until his death).

She had firstly married Captain Wyndham who was later killed in action in 1914, and secondly 'Boy Capel' in 1917, a successful businessman and keen polo player living in Paris. Captain Arthur Capel had previously had an affair with Coco Chanel and financed her first fashion boutique in 1910. Capel died in a road accident in 1919 and Diana married Vere Fane, fourteenth Earl of Westmorland, four years later.

Other guests included Violet, Lady Apsley, who had succeeded her husband as Member of Parliament for Bristol Central in 1943, holding the seat until 1945 when it was taken by a Labour candidate, Major Hugh Brassey, who lived in Tetbury, having had a distinguished war, awarded the Military Cross in 1945 while serving in the *Royal Scots Greys*; the Countess of Londesborough, widow of the fourth Earl; Dodo Hartman – of course – and her Luckington neighbour Major-General Sir Stewart Menzies, and his older brother Keith who had won the Military Cross in the *Welsh Guards* in the Great War.

There were hundreds of other guests including the fourth Baron Brougham and Vaux, a career politician but soon to succumb to gambling debts and Sir Duff Cooper, the diplomat and ambassador to France since 1944, who had married Lady Diana Manners, a famously glamorous social figure who had helped make the ambassador's role in Paris a great success. Like Nick Vansittart, Duff was also a member of *White's Club* and shared his pre-war views on Germany. It was London's most exclusive club, established in the reign of James II in 1693, where being a member one entered the inner circle of a ruling generation, although it did not serve as the secret service club – that was *Boodles* further down St James's Street.

On 29 January a few days after the ball, Dorothy was sailing to New York on the refurbished Cunard RMS *Queen Elizabeth* from Southampton after her wartime service, accompanied by her lady's maid Elsie Bates.

It was the first visit since before the war and after the death of Bobbie Hartman, it would be essential to re-introduce herself to General Motors on Broadway as the sole Managing Director of Lendrum & Hartman, their pre-war premier British distributor, and to assure the men in suits it would be business as usual.

Arriving at the Cunard pier in the brightly lit and buzzing city of New York on 4 February, after enjoying five nights of unrationed dining, dancing and socialising on board the premier transatlantic liner, was an intoxicating revelation to many. Leaving drab and tired post-war England – still with food and clothing rationing – was an eye-opener for the servants, and Dorothy planned to stay a few months.

The ship had brought many fellow passengers, including directors of manufacturing and importing companies, all eager to start commercial relations and develop new business with the USA. Among them were George Bulmer from the ubiquitous cider family of Hereford, which had held a royal warrant since 1911, and the young Ian Whigham, author of *Sites of Antiquity*, a friend of author Patrick Leigh Fermor and historical consultant to the famous *Blue Guides*.

Dodo curiously still considered the Hartman family as her next of kin, even with her husband and mother-in-law now dead; she recorded Betty Gwinner, her stepdaughter from Bobbie's first marriage. She notes her address as Luckington Manor – even though Betty was at the time living in Milford on Sea. Her brother Jack, her real next of kin and very much alive, had it seems been out of favour at this time.

She stayed as before at the *Plaza*. Nick Vansittart was scheduled to travel with her but for some reason his name had been crossed off the shipping manifest. It may have been a visa problem, because when he arrived later, on 5 March, his visa was dated only ten days before departure. He was also staying at the *Plaza* – unusual as he generally resided at *Essex House*, immediately recognisable at night by its red neon rooftop sign. Perhaps he had a reason.

After business meetings, and a round of socialising, there was shopping at stores on Fifth Avenue like *Bergdorf Goodman*, the Beaux-Arts building in Midtown Manhattan, *Bonwit Teller & Co.* or perhaps *Saks Fifth Avenue*, across from the Rockefeller Center, with ten floors of luxury merchandise. Not to mention *Macy's* in Herald Square, the largest departmental store in the world at the time, already an 'institution' when Dodo first arrived in New York in the 1930s. They had created a carnival-like atmosphere with the traditional novelty balloons in their Thanksgiving Day Parade, a prelude to the Christmas shopping period, supported with their elaborate animated holiday window displays on Broadway.

To recover from all that activity, a holiday in the Bahamas was needed. Dodo loved the sun, and travelled south to Miami and on to the Bahamas by *Pan Am*, who had introduced their first nonstop seaplane service between Florida and Nassau in the 1940s.

The Hartman party stayed at the *British Colonial Hotel*, 'the' place in the Bahamas at the time. It had been rebuilt during the 1920s after the original had been destroyed by fire. In 1939, the hotel had been purchased by Sir Harry Oakes, a flamboyant American entrepreneur, who had taken British citizenship and for tax reasons lived in the Bahamas. He was knighted for his philanthropy on the island. He had made his fortune from a gold mine in Canada, and when the Duke and Duchess of Windsor arrived in 1940 to take up the post of Governor-General, Harry Oakes became a friend. He had also developed Oakes Field into Nassau's airport, and he owned the golf course and clubhouse.

The *British Colonial* overlooks Nassau Harbour and the tip of Paradise Island. With its eight acres of gardens along the beach, shaded by coconut palms, it was the centre of social life.

The Windsors gave numerous soirées at the hotel, which became more numerous as the pair grew more bored. The Duchess of Windsor likened Nassau as their version of Napoleon's Elba – imposed exile. The cosmopolitan Duchess sometimes found life in the Bahamas somewhat parochial.

They stayed at Cable Bay at Westbourne, the pink, two-storey home of Sir Harry Oakes overlooking the bay, while Government House was being refurbished.

Then in 1943 Harry Oakes was murdered in his mansion under mysterious circumstances, which have never been fully explained.

The Windsors left the Bahamas in 1945, but the *British Colonial* would continue to entertain the rich and famous during the post-war years. Years later the hotel would be the filming location for the 1965 James Bond film *Thunderball*.

Returning to New York, Dorothy and Nick travelled together on RMS *Queen Elizabeth* arriving at Southampton on the first of May. Travelling with the party were Nick's business acquaintances, the forty-five-year-old Canadian born James Gault, a member of Lloyds and a certain Kathleen Simpson, all giving their address as 55 Park Lane. This was a luxury residential block of service flats, developed in the 1930s next door to the *Dorchester Hotel*, opposite Hyde Park on the corner of South Street. The site had once been home to Florence Nightingale, where she died in 1910.

Amongst the first-class passengers on this voyage were the celebrated British comedian and actor Arthur Askey and his wife Elizabeth. Another was the prolific English bi-sexual novelist Pamela Frankau, who pre-war had a stormy friendship with the author and journalist Rebecca West. In 1945 she had married an American naval intelligence officer, Marshall Dill. She was travelling alone under the name of Dill, having recently suffered the death of her infant child – they later divorced.

This trip would set the pattern for the coming years 1948 to 1955; winter trips to New York on Lendrum & Hartman business, then a few weeks in the Bahamas, sometimes with business friends like the Ennisdales (whose images at the captain's table featured in *Life* magazine during one of their crossings), before the return to England via New York. They always travelled on the Cunard *Queens*.

This was the second golden age of the ocean liners, only to be replaced in the 1960s by air travel.

After their wartime service, the 80,000 ton *Queen Mary* and *Queen Elizabeth*, now completely refurbished, dominated the transatlantic market between England and New York and the journey of five days travelling in first class created a club atmosphere for privileged well-heeled travellers (over 700 of them), many familiar to each other socially, or through business, although others would soon get to know one another. The passenger lists were sprinkled with the names of famous actors and celebrities. Actor Cary Grant preferred the *Queen Mary*, calling her the 'Eighth Wonder of the World' – she was Dodo's favourite too.

The *Queen*'s typical weekly schedule ran like clockwork, departing on a Thursday for the westbound journey from Southampton, and a Wednesday for the eastbound trip from New York.

Victualing a ship of this size was astonishing; carrying 2,000 passengers with a crew of 1,000; typically the *Queen Mary* would require the following for just one voyage: 20 tons of beef, 20 tons of potatoes, 4,000 lbs of tea and coffee, 70,000 eggs, 1,000 jars of jam, 5 tons of bacon and ham, 160 gallons of salad oil, 9 tons of fish, ½ ton bananas, 500 lbs of smoked salmon, 4½ tons of lamb. The bars on the same trip would carry 5,000 bottles of spirits, 40,000 bottles of beer, 10,000 bottles of table wine, 60,000 bottles of mineral water, 6,000 gallons of draught beer, 5,000 cigars and 20,000 packets of cigarettes. And of course in international waters the drinks were duty-free!

Among the facilities available on board were two indoor swimming pools, beauty salons, libraries, a music studio and lecture hall, telephone connectivity to anywhere in the world, outdoor paddle tennis courts, and dog kennels. The largest room on board was the first-class main dining room, spanning three stories in height.

For five days at sea, with stewards and attendants, not to mention any personal servants, first-class passengers were cocooned a world apart in an atmosphere of privilege, taking leisurely meals, promenades around the deck, discussions, meetings and entertainment with other guests. A list of passengers was always slipped under individual cabin doors on departure, so plans could be made. Table settings could be rearranged and the very important could always expect an invitation to the captain's table.

During the 1920s and 1930s – and this continued to some extent after the war years – much of the typical socialite's time was taken up with changing clothes, something like five times a day. Of course everyone 'dressed' for dinner in first class – but never on the last night, and travelled with vast amounts of luggage. Dodo for example took twelve pieces with her to New York in 1952 and eighteen pieces by 1955; however this was nothing like the Duke and Duchess of Windsor who always travelled with at least ninety pieces. The ship provided fine laundering, and accommodation for servants next door to the best suites was 'de rigueur', so madam was kept looking her best.

In September 1947, Henry Berenstein sailed to New York to represent Lendrum & Hartman (he would be appointed director the following year), taking his wife Elsie and staying at *Essex House*.

The following month, the October 16 issue of the *Gloucestershire Echo* announced the card for the first day of the National Hunt race meeting at Cheltenham. Listed in the 2.30 Nailsworth Handicap Hurdle Race was a Mrs D. M. C. Hartman, entered to ride *Precentor*, her five-year-old hunter, at a riding weight of ten stone one pound (63.5 kilos).

★

The following year on the traditional winter trip to America, Dorothy would take Frank Gear her butler, who is described in the manifests as her estate manager; he seemed to be managing both duties, together with her lady's maid Elsie Bates. They would all ensconce at the *Plaza* until, business concluded, they would make their way to Miami and on to the Bahamas for a month or so, staying at the *British Colonial Hotel*, warmly welcomed as a returning guest by Reginald G. Nefzger, the hotel's influential general manager.

As the hotel advertisements of the time explained:

> *"If you are seeking an exotic holiday, then select the British Colonial, in Nassau, the 'New World's' most fascinating 'Old World' town. The British Colonial is one of the world's most distinguished hotels, with an internationally known cuisine… two private bathing beaches… magnificent salt water swimming pool… championship tennis courts… putting greens… golf… colorful natives… quaint markets."*

The Hartman party had sailed to New York on the *Queen Mary* in January, and returned on the *Queen Elizabeth* in April, sharing the first-class social environment with Arthur John Gielgud, the forty-four-year-old actor, who was basking in the attention of winning an award for the Outstanding Foreign Company in the touring play, *The Importance of Being Earnest*. He acted in and directed the production throughout the USA and Canada.

On the 31 October, the *Commercial Motor* magazine announced that, *"Mr. Guy N. Vansittart has been elected chairman of the board of Vauxhall Motors, Ltd., of which he has been a director since 1938. A brother of Lord Vansittart, he has been in the motor industry for 20 years and has extensive knowledge of export markets and overseas conditions."*

The first post-war International Motor Exhibition was held at Earls

Court between October and November 1948. Because of the aftermath of war it combined a Motor and Commercial Vehicle Exhibition. It was an event that attracted royalty and senior politicians; it was announced that over 1,100 persons had passed through the turnstiles on the first day. By the time the event closed it had attracted something like 275,000 people.

It was the show in which a number of cars made their debuts, like the new Morris Minor, designed by Greek-born Alec Issigonis and the Jaguar XK120, which had the press and public drooling over its curvaceous shape and with a top speed of 120 miles an hour, all despite an era of general austerity.

For Lendrum & Hartman it was a showcase for the new American Buicks and Cadillacs that couldn't be easily purchased at the time – but became aspirational to many eager buyers attending those early exhibitions. Other exhibitors included the General Motors stand, and several American rivals like Lincoln, Chrysler, Oldsmobile, Pontiac and Studebaker.

It was going to be the autumn of those nostalgic English car manufacturers that have long since ceased production, names like Alvis, Armstrong-Siddeley, Bristol, Singer, Jowett, Lea-Francis, and Lanchester. During the 1950s, the car industry continued its recovery from the immediate post-war period. By around 1956 something like over half a million people were directly employed in motor vehicle and parts production.

Communications had become easier too with the General Post Office's (GPO, now British Telecom) programme of automating telephone exchanges gradually through the country since the late twenties – particularly in major cities like London. They created easy to recall local names using the first three letters of the exchange combined with a four-digit number, which had become part of society and business culture. Dodo's flat in Berkeley House originally had a telephone number REGent 0470, later it was changed to a 'more fashionable' HYDe Park 0470. Everyone knew the names like MAYfair, ABBey, VICtoria – which conjured up a mental image of where the person was living, and of course the widely publicised WHItehall 1212 – the number of Scotland Yard.

Paris too had equally memorable exchange names like ÉLYsées, POMadour, LOUvre, and PIGalle. By the late 1960s technology had changed to a completely digital and a less memorable system.

In October 1949 Henry Berenstein – now a Lendrum & Hartman director – travelled to New York, this time first class on the *Queen Mary*.

After Christmas, as was becoming the tradition, the 'Hartman set' started to migrate to New York and further south to Florida for some winter sunshine. As Nicky Vansittart would inquire years later to Dodo's newly 'discovered' daughter, *"Are you like your mother in needing the sun? She loved it and at one time could spend hours sun bathing. I never could, get burnt to a cinder."* [26]

The Ennisdales sailed early from Southampton arriving in New York on 10 January, and heading for the *Breakers* on Palm Beach, accompanied by their fourteen pieces of luggage, and a medley of celebrities. These including Alec Guinness as guest of Miller Productions, based at Rockefeller Plaza; Cecil Beaton staying at the *Sherry-Netherland* on Fifth Avenue; Nadia, the Marchioness of Milford Haven, who was entertained privately at 30 Beekman Place as guest of forty-eight-year-old *Eton*-educated William Bateman Leeds, the wealthy son of Princess Anastasia; Henry Carnarvon, the son of the fifth Earl, whose seat was at Highclere Castle in Hampshire and who was linked by marriage to Mark (third Bt.) Dalrymple's wife. Carnarvon was recently divorced from his second wife, Austrian dancer Tilly Losch who had appeared in Noël Cowards' *This Year of Grace* on the London stage in the twenties. He was staying at the *St Regis Hotel,* before transit to Bermuda.

A couple of weeks later, on 20 January 1950, another exodus led by Dodo Hartman (now described as chairwoman of Lendrum & Hartman), together with her twenty-nine-year-old maid Doris White, and fellow director Henry Berenstein, again sailed on Cunard's *Queen Mary* for New York, on their annual pilgrimage to New York and the General Motors offices on Broadway. Business dealings over, they would shop and then make their way south to Florida and the Bahamas.

Berenstein stayed at the *Wellington Hotel* on Seventh Avenue, whilst Dodo mysteriously stayed at 7 Beekman Place – not the usual *Plaza*.

Beekman Place is a small street located on Turtle Bay, the east side of Manhattan, associated with 'old money', home variously to the Rockefeller family and Huntington Hartford, heir to the A&P fortune. Theatrical personalities also lived here, among them Ethel Barrymore and Irving Berlin. In the 1950s, and perhaps some time before, 1 Beekman Place was the residence of the British Consul General in New York.

On the same voyage, travelling alone was Beatrice, Countess of Granard, now in her late sixties, an American heiress from Rhode Island who had married Anglo-Irish soldier and Liberal politician the Earl of Granard. He had been Master of the Horse to King George V. She inherited a stable of thoroughbreds from her father, and her interest in horseracing continued throughout her life. The Granards had houses in London and Paris, and it was her money that largely helped to restore Castle Forbes in County Longford. She was travelling to Palm Beach in Florida to meet her socialite twin married sister Gladys Phipps for a holiday. She also ran a thoroughbred stable in the USA.

Another solo passenger was the English stage and film actor, Charles Hawtrey, staying at the *Waldorf Astoria* – with just four pieces of luggage. He had just completed filming the Ealing comedy *Passport to Pimlico* the previous year, which was screened at the Cannes Film Festival in the September. He would go on to achieve popular success in the 'Carry On' films of the late 1950s onwards.

Others like James Horlick, chairman of the ubiquitous malted drink firm, made their way to the *St Regis*, a companion hotel to the *Waldorf Astoria* located between Madison and Fifth Avenue, an eighteen-story hotel in French Beaux-Arts style, the tallest in the city when built, opened in 1904. It ushered in a new era of lavish soirées and notable names, making it a very fashionable place to stay. In 1932, the now iconic 'Old King Cole' painting was installed in the hotel's new bar, and has remained a New York institution ever since.

On the return journey in March, again on the *Queen Mary*, Dorothy was accompanied by her friends the Ennisdales (Harry having recently recovered from a car accident which happened whilst being driven to the airport in Palm Beach in February), together with Harry Shurey, her tall, well-tanned stockbroker neighbour from Berkeley House.

Another passenger travelling alone, Major General Francis Rodd had become the second Baron Rennell in 1941 on the death of his father, one-time British Ambassador to Italy. He spoke four languages fluently and had served in intelligence in the Great War. In the 1920s he had made two great expeditions into the central Sahara, which provided him with material for his book about the 'Tuareg'. He later joined the Bank of England before becoming managing director of merchant bank Morgan Grenfell. At the outbreak of the Second World War, he was recommissioned as a staff officer, Chief of Civil Affairs. After the war he had helped to re-establish the Royal Geographic Society, and was now in the civil service.

Another solo passenger was the wealthy Nina Ogilvy Grant, twelfth Countess of Seafield, returning from the Bahamas. As a young woman she was known as the richest heiress in Europe, extremely eligible for those mothers with sons to marry off. She was described as a lovely child with masses of auburn hair and big, solemn blue eyes. Now in her mid-forties, she had married in 1930, had two children, but was soon to divorce her husband. When she died in 1969, she was the second richest woman in Britain after the Queen.

★

By the 1950s, despite London's soot-blackened buildings and tired and shabby looking infrastructure and the occasional bomb site, the economy was slowly recovering and changing. It was women who benefited most from these new service jobs, outnumbering men in London's offices for the first time ever, accounting for just over fifty per cent. In the manufacturing sector they accounted for around forty-two per cent.

As winter approached, the weather in November and early December 1952 had been very cold, with heavy snowfalls across the region. To keep warm, Londoners were burning large quantities of coal in their homes. Smoke was pouring from the chimneys of thousands of houses throughout the capital.

Then for around a week in early December, the windless weather conditions proved ideal for the 'London particular' as the smog had been known since Victorian times, causing severe air pollution and creating breathing problems, particularly for vulnerable people like the elderly and children. Visibility was reduced to a few yards creating travel disruption that lasted for days. What was different this time was that it was denser and longer-lasting than anything previously experienced, becoming known as the 'Great Smog'. Traffic police wore face-masks and carried flaming torches, and women used their headscarves to wrap around their mouths to walk to work.

It even seeped indoors, resulting in the cancellation or abandonment of concerts and film screenings as visibility decreased, making it harder to see from the seats. By the middle of December, the skies had cleared but the pollution had left in its wake over 4,000 Londoners killed from respiratory diseases.

–30–

Mayfair hostess

…who had become six years younger?

Dodo was now entertaining on a frequent basis. She had become the centre of attention – in control of her businesses, wealthy and with a different set of friends, some remained from when Bobbie was alive and others she acquired through her love of theatre and entertainment.

Dodo for all her aspirations was only ever a minor actress and dancer – her mother had received better press reviews. Whilst her mother 'played' aristocracy on the stage, Dodo had actually married in to it. Inevitably her best roles had been reserved for real-life marriages, partnering older men.

She had now become independent, more assertive and something of a celebrity. Mayfair was her playground and the press would describe her entertaining as legendary – even by Mayfair standards. *"At six o'clock she likes to entertain both business and personal friends to cocktails. Her one rule is that no one shall talk business… a rule which English guests, she finds, keep easily and Americans rarely."*

To amuse her guests, these events would often include David Nixon, one of the most popular stage magicians in the country. He appeared on television with Dodo's friend Frances Day as panellists on *What's my Line?* Edmundo Ros, whose seductively-orchestrated Latin American songs set British feet tapping in the 1940s and 50s, would also be hired to play at parties. His band performed regularly at the *Coconut Grove Club* in Regent Street, attracting members of high society and royalty. [27]

Flowers were always an important part of Dodo's life and she used them effectively in her entertaining, with clever floral decorations – supplied in London by the established Berkeley Square florist Moyses

Stevens. She also cultivated her own flowers, particularly 'Christmas carnations', in the hothouses at Stumblehole.

In the press interviews she gave in the early 1950s she was described as one of a *"New type of executive appearing on the financial scene – a woman on her own."* She had subtly introduced a new, refreshed Dodo, six years younger that the 'old' Dorothy.

She would essentially be described as in her late forties forever. As the biographer Michael Holroyd wrote, *"It is understandable and right that people should seek to protect themselves... during their lives. We all need our prevarications, evasions, our sentimentalities and silences."* [28]

Dodo *"the Queen Bee"* as Prudie Mennell saw her, professed to be childless as many in her social and business circles were, with the exception of Nick.

Ermine and Gideon Elibank, Harry and Helen Ennisdale, Henry and Elsie Berenstein, Charles and Bessie Culross were all without children, so too was Rowley-Morris, although he was a confirmed bachelor, and her actress friend Frances Day was childless as far as is known.

★

Nick Vansittart as chairman of Vauxhall Motors was taking a more strategic role after a distinguished pre-war career with General Motors on the Continent and in the UK.

In addition he had been elected chairman of General Motors Ltd., London in 1953 with an office in Buckingham Gate. Vauxhall Motors had built the Churchill tanks during the war and with Nick's influence, became a major government contractor post-war for the supply of Bedford trucks to Ministry specifications. Car models like the famous Wyvern and Velox were also introduced, strongly influenced by contemporary American styling.

He continued to live at 55 Park Lane, although becoming increasingly estranged from Marguerite. By this time Denise, her daughter from her first marriage now in her thirties, had married a Belgian, Baron Jacques van den Branden de Reeth; her son Jean-Louis married a girl called Claudine and they departed to Australia in 1951.

Nick still had farming interests at Cholsey Grange and Marguerite was listed at Luxters Farm, near Henley.

Madi Dearmer's children from her first marriage to Nick had grown up. After boarding school, Prudie had joined MI6 in 1941 and later transferred to SOE in Delhi. After the fall of Japan, she was posted to Cairo where she met Peter Mennell, an army major. Peter was the son of a distinguished physiotherapeutic doctor, at St Thomas's Hospital, and after *Oundle School* and *King's College*, Cambridge, joined the army. He had been mentioned in despatches whilst serving with the *sixty-seventh Field Regiment of the Royal Artillery*, and awarded the OBE for service in the field.

After the war, Peter had sat Foreign Office exams, and prior to a posting to America they married in the autumn of 1946, and departed for New York on Cunard's RMS *Franconia* [29] which was still in government service. They sailed from Liverpool to take up the post as Vice Consul in charge of commercial affairs in New York, both now employed in the Foreign Service. Nick had helped with introductions.

Prudie's younger brother Mark, now living in Peel Street, off Kensington Church Street, had become an investment banker by the early 1950s with Lazard in London and later Wall Street in New York. During his time in North America, he had met a Canadian divorcee Shelagh Gilmour and they were married in Toronto in 1954. Mark moved into stockbroking and they settled in Rosedale.

Madi and Geoffrey Dearmer, together with their teenage daughter Julie, were well established in Clifton Hill in north London, Geoffrey continuing his work for the BBC.

Prudie and Peter had returned from New York after their tour of duty and settled into north London with their young daughter Lindsay. Dodo would take an interest and Prudie remembers her buying baby clothes, for her youngest child:

"I remember being surprised when we invited them to our flat in Swiss Cottage for lunch soon after Jonathan was born (1954) and she brought some lovely clothes for him but such elegant ones that needed ironing each time that I wondered when I would use them! I was surprised that she would be so out of touch." [30]

Nick was increasingly becoming Dodo's social companion and friend. They had first met – albeit briefly – in New York at the General Motors 'Motorama' event in January 1933.

As Nick was based in Antwerp, he did not feature in the Hartman social scene until his return to England just before the war. He had been a frequent visitor to Luckington during the war and later they rode together with the Beaufort.

As Prudie remembers:

"I don't remember my father ever mentioning his first meeting with Dodo and her then husband – as I said he kept his life carefully in compartments!

We lived in Antwerp until I was six and my brother three when obviously my mother felt she had had enough and took us back to England. I was too young to have any notion of acrimony but I think it was a fairly amicable divorce. Until I was nearly grown up I hardly saw my father – he wasn't good at family responsibility!

He was splendid with my children and grandchildren and they adored him; by the time I was married he realised that we really did want him around for his company and not for financial support! Nicky behaved just as badly with Marguerite as he had with my mother!" [31]

With his knowledge of the motor industry, Nick had been able to give her business advice, particularly after the death of Bobbie Hartman. They had a mutual interest in farming, a friendship grew and they eventually became occasional lovers; *"And life is like a song..."*

Again Prudie reflects:

"I think she really was the only woman my father really did love – he was devastated by her death and wrote me – I was in Africa (Kinshasa) at the time – the only letter I ever had from him which seemed to give his true feelings.

Dodo was always perfectly dressed – I used to think of her as the Ice Woman although she was always very pleasant and kind to us and when we were in London she would ask us to a party at the flat in Hay Hill at which we felt very out of it – all very well-heeled and social!" [32]

Jonathan Mennell, Prudie's son recalls his grandfather's relationship with Dodo:

"Strangely, given Nicky's escapades, he never took Dodo to Denham Place to his brother 'Van'. Sarita his wife said that Nicky would not take Dodo

to Denham Place simply because they only 'lived together' and that seemed the reason.

Actually it may be that they were both beautiful women who had fascinating lives and several amorous stories and they might just have hated each other!

Sarita had dined with 'Van' and Hitler in Berlin in 1933 and her sister was Lady Phipps whose husband was ambassador in Berlin during the 1930s, so a lot going on.

Nicky never divorced Marguerite and indeed kept her apartment in Park Lane until she died – I suppose mid-1970s. I knew Marguerite and thought she was a very gentle and kind person. She was an exceptional step mother and my mother (Prudie) had very good relations with Marguerite's children." [33]

In August 1950, the Scottish newspapers announced that *"The 'Twelfth' Has Good Prospects"* and that Mrs Dorothy M. C. Hartman (reporters often misplaced her initials) had taken Invermark Lodge, a classic mid-Victorian shooting lodge built of Aberdeenshire granite overlooking Loch Lee and to the cliffs and corries of Invermark estate, from the Earl of Dalhousie for a private shooting party of six guns. It went on to say that the Duke of Marlborough and Mr Herbert Pulitzer of New York were shooting over at Cannochy.

It explained that proprietors of the Perthshire moors were reaping the benefits of not over-shooting in the difficult post-war years. Later the papers were detailing the first grouse fetching twenty shillings a brace rushed to the London train, to appear on hotel and club menus.

In September, Dorothy's old friend Ermine Elibank and her husband Gideon finally moved to South Africa. They had left their Pelham Place house – the scene of Dodo's flirtation with Bobbie, and settled in Sloane Gardens, before finally moving after the war to an apartment in Arlington Street, just a stroll away from the *Ritz*.

They had been planning the move for some years; there was nothing to keep them in England, they were now in their early seventies and wanted to enjoy a milder climate after the long war years and with post-war rationing, the country had lost its charm. They planned to move to Cape Town, and after farewell parties, sailed from Southampton on the Shaw Savill & Albion ship QSMV *Dominion Monarch*. The ship was bound for New Zealand, but out of the 508 first-class passenger berths, 100 were set aside for passengers between Britain and Cape Town, at a competitive fare of £150-8s-0d.

Barely six months has passed when Dodo received news in the New Year that Gideon had died at the *Mount Nelson Hotel* in March the following year. He was succeeded by his younger brother, Arthur Cecil Murray, a politician once married to the actress Faith Celli Standing, who died in 1942.

It was sad news and Dodo wrote to Ermine suggesting she should return to England, where she would be amongst her old friends.

The same month the reclusive Pamela Menzies had died at Bridges Court in Luckington; she was forty-eight. It came at a difficult time for 'C', as Stewart was known. He was deeply attached to her, and her tragic illness had manifested itself during the years he was heavily preoccupied with intelligence matters, and more recently during the time the great deceiver 'Kim' Philby was under scrutiny by both the American Federal Bureau of Investigation (FBI) and MI5. It was a mercy really – she had been suffering considerably for many months.

★

In 1950 Lendrum & Hartman Limited, declared its annual return, showed a capital of £48,000, made up of 36,000 ordinary £1 shares, and 1,200 6 per cent preferential £1 shares.

Dorothy held both ordinary and preferential shares with the exception of nominal £1 shares held by other directors Charles Culross, Henry Berenstein and Rowley-Morris. In other words, Dorothy had total control of the company.

The company's secretary was John Sheehan, and the solicitors Culross & Trelawny. The registered office was Dorothy's London apartment at Berkeley House in Hay Hill.

Typically, business relations pre- and post-war were based on people 'you know' and it is not surprising that the board of Lendrum & Hartman was based on this. All members had been known to Bobbie and Dodo for many years and were therefore trusted; some of them like Charles and Henry also probably knew where any metaphoric 'bodies might be buried'.

Henry Edward Berenstein, born in South London in 1895, the youngest son of Henry senior, a rent collector who later became a herbalist. Like his brother, on leaving school Henry became a motor fitter with Miller's Trade Cabs, one of London's taxi companies. When war was declared he joined the *Royal Naval Air Service* in 1915 as a driver-motor mechanic. It was whilst serving at HMS *President* he met Bobbie Hartman and they struck up a friendship. Henry had become fully aware of Bobbie's extra-curricular activities, particularly with Lady Hanson.

It was because of his skill with cars and his discretion that Bobbie offered him a job with Lendrum & Hartman after the war. Henry married Elsie Underwood in Hendon during the spring of 1927. Possibly with the prospect of children, they chose to live in leafy Buckinghamshire at a house they named Brooklyn in Woodside Road, Amersham.

By the 1930s he had been appointed sales manager, and undertook his first trip to New York as the company representative, travelling tourist class on the SS *Pennland*, of the American-Belgian Red Star Line, along with two minor film actors seeking their fortune in the USA. He would be dealing with General Motors Export Office on Broadway, whilst staying at the residential hotel *Essex House*.

He managed the business on a day-to-day basis and after Bobbie died, helped navigate the company safely through the war years. At six foot, he was tall with brown eyes and hair, and after the war Dodo made him a company director in 1948 for his loyalty and service.

He would accompany Dodo on further trips to New York – this time travelling first-class with his wife on the *Queen Mary*. Elsie died in March 1970 and Henry, grief-stricken, followed three months later.

Another of Bobbie's old trusted business associates was Charles Hill Culross, born in London into a comfortable middle-class family in 1881, the younger son of Alan and Arabella Culross. His father was a Scot and a partner in a successful printing business in the city, Culross & Sproston Ltd, which still flourishes today as Radclyffe, Culross and Sproston. The 'Hill' name came from his mother's family. His older brother followed into the family printing firm, but Charles studied to become a solicitor and was admitted to the Law Society in 1905, going into partnership forming Warner Bromley and Culross, at Finsbury House in Blomfield Street.

He married Bessie Grindley in 1910, and they initially lived in Marsh Lane, Stanmore.

On the outbreak of the Great War, although in his mid-thirties, he volunteered for the *Royal Naval Volunteer Reserve* at HMS *President* in February 1915 – the same month as Bobbie Hartman, but resigned a month later. In June he joined the army, was appointed a lieutenant railway transport officer and immediately embarked for France. He was invalided from service the following March and resumed his career, branching out and forming his own company Culross & Co at 13 Old Cavendish Street.

This was how he met Bobbie Hartman, who had sought his advice on the Lady Hanson affair. Finding they had HMS *President* in common, they became friends and Charles remained Hartman's solicitor for the rest of his life.

Charles's father died in 1930 and he inherited some of the fortune of £10,685. He was also a witness to Bobbie and Dorothy's wedding in 1932.

The same month in a separate case, Charles acted for Sub-Lieutenant Guy Camille Myler Falla of HMS *Renown*, a well-known services rugby player who had been charged with forgery by a Naval Court Martial in Chatham. Culross had been appointed by Falla's mother to represent him. He had been charged with altering a gunroom mess account, with intent to defraud. He was found not guilty on a charge of forgery, but guilty of altering an entry in the mess account with intent to defraud and of fraudulent conversion, and ordered to be dismissed from the service.

Charles and his wife Bessie had become childless, so decided to move into central London taking a flat at 88 Bickenhall Mansions off Baker Street, near neighbours to Vivian Van Damm, the London impresario of the *Windmill Theatre*. This red-brick mansion block would also be home to certain clandestine departments of the Special Operations Executive during the war.

He was a successful solicitor, acting for a wide range of clients including *The Times* newspaper. On one occasion he acted for them in the aftermath of the Spanish Civil War concerning a journalist George Steer's report on the bombing of Guernica. [34] Culross was invited to be a director of Lendrum & Hartman – taking a nominal share-holding.

He briefly and it seems unwisely had taken a younger business partner after the war, the *Westminster*-educated, splendidly named James Reginald Dorrington Salusbury-Trelawny. He was tall – over six foot – with blue eyes and came from an old Cornish family, forming Culross & Trelawny, at 65 Duke Street. That partnership was subsequently dissolved after he may have been 'led astray' by James over an embarrassing legal case concerning the £170,000 probate of a contested will to which they were executors. Although Culross was cleared, after the dust had settled he continued as Culross & Co.

Over the years he had become a close friend of the Hartmans. Taking Dodo's advice to take time to relax on sea voyages, in the post-war years he made his first trip to South America, and then Madeira just before Elsie died in 1951. He continued to travel in later years.

He undertook a long cruising holiday to South Africa in the summer of 1957, sailing from Southampton on a forty-two day round trip voyage to Durban on the Union Castle Line *Stirling Castle*. Unknown to him at the time, it was where the Salmon family were now living. By now Culross was in his seventies, and made one last voyage to Madeira the following year.

The remaining director, Rowley Morris, or to give him his full title Rowley Millichamp Rowley-Morris, was the son of a Welsh wool merchant from Montgomery, born in the Welsh Marches in 1875 and educated in Hooton, Chester.

At the turn of the century, he and his widowed mother moved to London. He firstly became a bank cashier, then tried his hand at being a solicitor before finally joining Lloyds Bank in the Strand where one of his banking clients was Winston Churchill. [35] He moved to their Cox & Kings branch at 6 Pall Mall and was designated at the time one of three official ships' banking agents, featured in the navy list.

He was a confirmed bachelor, lived in Cranley Gardens, Kensington, and had retired from banking by the late 1930s, describing himself as a 'gentleman'. He had a passion for cars and travel and through his membership of the *Royal Automobile Club* in Pall Mall, had social and business links with the Hartmans, and with their accounts at Lloyds Bank.

He was invited to join Lendrum & Hartman as a director, taking a nominal share interest. After the war he moved to Lower Bourne, Farnham in Surrey, but kept an apartment in London. He continued to travel, particularly to South Africa.

He died at the *Alexandra Hotel* in St Leonards on Sea in November 1954, leaving his two close friends Wing Commander Herbert Orr, and Captain Charles Farquharson, a share of £30,273. They were officials in the *Royal Automobile Club*. Farquharson, late of the Indian Army, had married a Margaret Limpenny in India in 1932, whilst his friend Herbert Orr married her younger sister in London four years later.

★

Berkeley House stands on one side of Hay Hill, a thoroughfare which links Berkeley Square with Dover and Grafton Streets. It is a handsome purpose-built red-brick mansion block dating back to the late 1890s. The building takes up the entire block from the corner with Berkeley Street up to Dover Street; at the time it had something like forty-five private apartments ranged over six floors. At its centre is an imposing two-storey archway entrance, mid-way along Hay Hill. The street level exterior was taken up with a few high class retail or antique shops.

Other residents at that time included Sir James Horace Barnes, Permanent Under-Secretary of State for Air at number 25, film producer Michael Baleon – knighted after the war, and his wife Aileen at 29. He had helped launch the pre-war career of Alfred Hitchcock, working with Gainsborough Pictures, Gaumont British and MGM-British, but he was possibly best known for his work with Ealing Studios, such as *Whisky Galore!* and *Kind Hearts and Coronets*, both in 1949 with Valerie Hobson playing Edith in the latter, and *The Ladykillers* in 1953. His daughter Jill Balcon became an actress and married the poet laureate Cecil Day-Lewis.

At number 40 was Lady Veronica Hussey, daughter of the third Marquess of Dufferin and Ava, at the time on her third (and soon to be divorced) husband, a retired West Country sailor, Captain Thomas Andrew Hussey of the Royal Navy. At number 42 were Harry Nathan and his wife Eleanor, a Labour politician who became Lord Nathan of Churt in 1940, stepping down to make way for Ernest Bevin. He served as Minister for Civil Aviation in the post-war government.

Another business acquaintance was Harry Shurey, much the same age as Dodo when he moved into number 5 after the war, with his daughter Sonia. He was in his late fifties, over six foot with brown hair and grey eyes and a stockbroker. He was the son of a prosperous London publisher, which had produced a range of popular magazines in the early part of the century. He was educated at *Westminster School*, and initially joined his father at Shurey Publications in Fleet Street. His older brother had been killed on the Somme in 1916. He married Dorothea Foster in 1927 they had two children, Dorothea Sonia in 1929 and Michael John in 1932. Both children were evacuated to the USA at the outbreak of war.

Shurey had been a one-time neighbour of Dodo's friends the Elibanks in Buckingham Gate in the early 1930s and they are likely to have met socially around that time. He was a member of the *Portland Club* (reputedly the oldest card club in the world) and may have given her advice on various investments. He became a social acquaintance and they travelled together as part of a wider group on post-war trips to New York.

★

In January 1952 the winter pilgrimage to New York was undertaken – for the first time with a new private secretary Enid Fischer – sailing on the *Queen Mary*, with only twelve pieces of luggage. Amongst the other passengers was HM the Queen's successful thoroughbred Newmarket racehorse trainer, Cecil Boyd-Rochfort. *Eton* educated, he fought with the *Scots Guards* during the Great War and had enjoyed major racing successes in the *Oaks* and *Derby* at Epsom and the *St Ledger* at Doncaster.

As usual, the Hartman party stayed at the *Plaza*, with Dodo making an entrance wearing her Russian sable coat, to be greeted by genial Canadian Alphonse W. Salomone [36] – the manager at the time.

Once General Motor's meetings and business were completed, Dodo's party travelled on the new flight service introduced by *BOAC* from New York to Nassau, staying at the *British Colonial* as before.

Whilst they were away news came through from England that George VI had died in early February and his eldest daughter was now HM Queen Elizabeth II.

★

In the summer of 1952, Dodo read in the press that Gertrude Lawrence had died in New York; she was the same age, and had apparently fainted backstage immediately after finishing a Saturday matinee of *The King and I* on Broadway and died in September a few weeks later. They had both been chorus girls and their paths had crossed in the 1920s when 'the acting' Lady Dalrymple was performing in *Murray's Club* and both lacked the 'maternal touch'. Gertie had many affairs, including the Prince of Wales – which had infuriated his mother Queen Mary.

On the day she died, they dimmed the lights along Broadway and London's Shaftesbury Avenue.

★

The same summer Stewart Menzies decided to retire and leave Broadway for Luckington. Shortly after his retirement, his long-standing second secretary Miss Evelyn Jones, a beautiful brunette, was found near death in her flat through an overdose. Fortunately she was found in time and through extensive medical attention in hospital nursed back to life. She had been 'C''s mistress for many years, possibly going back as far as 1941, and had sought death rather than face the future alone.

★

When Ermine Elibank returned to London from Cape Town, the *Empress Club* in Dover Street was long past it heyday and in its latter days before closure. So she duly took up residence at the *Landsdowne*, a private members' club which had been established in 1935, at 9 Fitzmaurice Place, near Berkeley Square, just a stroll from Dodo's flat at Berkeley House in Hay Hill.

It was quite different to other London clubs as it was open to men and women from its very inception, as a 'social, residential and athletic club for members of social standing'.

The house was originally built as a residential home for Lord Bute, the Prime Minister in 1761, with Robert Adam the principal architect. In the 1920s Gordon Selfridge, the American founder of the eponymous department store, leased the house and entertained guests at many raucous and vivacious parties. A road-widening scheme effectively cut the house in two in 1930. After structural alterations and a new frontage, White Allom, the firm who were responsible for the fitting out of the great Cunard liners *Queen Mary* and *Queen Elizabeth*, were commissioned to decorate the club in the 'Art Moderne' style.

Its eclectic membership had included actress Frances Day before she moved to her own place at 15 Three Kings Yard, Richard Dimbleby the

BBC broadcaster, and Joachim von Ribbentrop, German Ambassador in the late 1930s.

★

Dodo was effectively running her businesses from her flat at 2 Berkeley House with Enid Fischer, a married woman in her mid-forties, as a private secretary who managed her social and business life. Enid lived with her husband Henry in Gloucester Square, Paddington.

With socialising increasing, Dodo had also leased another flat at number 44 Berkeley House to house the servants, whilst using number 2 for business and entertaining. Number 2 was lavishly decorated with Persian carpets, Chippendale furniture, and some inherited pieces from her mother-in-law.

To amuse her business guests – particularly the Americans – she had a designated lavatory, a 'gentleman's cloakroom' in the Berkeley House flat painted in black and red, with a series of Boris O'Klein prints decorating the wall, which she had picked up in Paris on her various trips.

O'Klein was a Russian anthropomorphic artist, known for his numerous prints and watercolours of dogs getting up to mischief. The prints are generally called *The Dirty Dogs of Paris*. Many of his prints appealed to tourists, particularly from the 1930s to the 1950s. One of the prints titled *Comme nos maîtres* (Like our masters) shows a range of seven different breeds of dogs urinating against a wall – a copy of which adorned the lavatory.

Another painting, Dodo's portrait by Gunn with its special lighting would be another talking point, situated as it was in the entrance hall of the London flat. Any new guest being escorted through the hall after a cocktail party or dinner would inevitably receive her reflective casual comment, *"Rather a nice painting, that one of Gunn's. It is a portrait of a fish wife!"*

It was a reference to her purchase of a fishmonger's shop in New Quebec Street at that time.

★

Dodo's brother Jack had married Mary Driscoll in 1930, and they had a daughter Patricia born in 1942, the same year Bobbie died. The family were living in Totteridge and later moved to Hendon in north London. Jack had been in the fire service during the London Blitz and had been invalided out. They had an on-off sibling relationship over the years and were not that close.

However just after the war, when Dodo learnt that Pat had taken up dancing, she started to take more interest. She would bring gifts back from her trips abroad, and Pat recalls little dolls dressed as a 'Can-Can' dancer from Paris, or wearing a kilt from Scotland. When she was five she remembers receiving a Cocker Spaniel puppy, which had been bred on one of Dodo's farms in Luckington.

By the early fifties, Pat Abbott, now a young girl, who had been a keen dancer since about the age of three, was attending *Manor House School*, a convent run by the Sisters of Marie Auxiliatrice in Finchley.

Dodo had always declared she would have loved to become a trained ballet dancer, something Prudie, Nick's daughter, remembers her father recalling [37] rather than acting in musical comedies as she had done in her younger years. Although it is unlikely she ever confided the fact to her social friends.

Pat would be 'sent for' and collected by Cadillac to have tea at Berkeley House.

> *"She used to send Paul, her chauffeur to pick me up. It was all quite formal. He would take me to the Hay Hill flat and leave me in the sitting room where Dorothy would join me. Dance was always the main topic of conversation and on one of her trips when she was in Paris she brought me back a doll dressed as a Can-Can dancer. There were some occasions when my mother came with me but the visits always seemed to be much shorter."*
> [38]

Pat remembers various visitors coming and going, and always being introduced as *"my niece"*. There was an undercurrent of friction between her parents and Dodo, because it seemed she wanted to get more involved with her upbringing.

Pat recalls: *"I remember my dad telling me that she wanted to take me and bring me into the world of society but, naturally, he would not agree with that."* This in turn led to a cooling of their sibling relations, which lasted until her death.

★

In the autumn of 1952, Dorothy was courting the press. She was still something of a 'novelty' being a woman in a man's business world, and her interviews reflected that. Headlines in various newspapers at that time would declare:

"60 MEN WILL TAKE A BLOND BOSS OUT"

It was a reference to the mechanics and staff of Lendrum & Hartman who she was hosting at their annual works event that year, a Saturday coach trip to St Leonards on Sea with lunch.

"MRS HARTMAN RUNS THEM ALL,
FOUR FIRMS, TWO FARMS"

Another wrote:

"From Monday to Friday she is a smart, neatly-tailored Mayfair businesswoman. At weekends she tends her two farms near Chippenham, in Wiltshire and the 250 head of pedigree cattle which are her pride. Mrs Hartman, the only woman to exhibit at the Motor Show, has just driven back from Rome to prepare for it."

"SIX IRONS IN FIRE FOR HER!"

Another headline article in the (far left) *Daily Herald* under the theme *"Living and Learning"* by Amy Landreth, [39] posing the question about:

"A new type of executive is appearing on the financial scene – the Woman On Her Own.

Take Dorothy Hartman one of the new faces on the scene. Forty-eight year old, Mrs Hartman until ten years ago was the wife of prosperous businessman, living in Wiltshire, hunting, working for her pet charities and going to America with her husband on his business trips. Today you will find her behind an executive-size desk in a suite of Mayfair offices…"

Valerie Hobson (she only drank champagne) and her husband were frequent guests at Dodo's six o'clock cocktails, recalls Prudie Mennell, Nick's married daughter. *"Valerie Hobson and her husband were the two we liked most I seem to remember – she was ways friendly to us."*

Hobson was born in Northern Ireland, and had appeared in a number of British films during the 1930s through to the 1950s. Her two most memorable roles, playing Estella in David Lean's 1946 adaptation of *Great Expectations*, and as the refined and virtuous Edith D'Ascoyne in the 1949 black comedy *Kind Hearts and Coronets*. Hobson's last starring role was in the original London production of Rodgers and Hammerstein's musical play *The King and I* which opened at the *Theatre Royal, Drury Lane* in October 1953 – which ran for 926 performances.

She had divorced her first husband in 1952, the film producer Sir Anthony Havelock-Allan and had married John 'Jack' Profumo in December 1954. They lived in the rather grand neo-classical Chester Terrace at Regent's Park. At the time John was Joint Parliamentary Secretary to the Ministry of Transport and Civil Aviation in the Conservative government. [40]

There was a social connection too, as Harold, the first Baron Balfour of Inchrye, was the nephew of Dodo's close friend Ermine Elibank, who had married Profumo's younger sister Mary Ainslie (known as Maina) in 1946.

Dodo had known Viscount Westbourne, the industrialist and Conservative Party politician (ennobled in October 1945 in Churchill's resignation honours list), through her connections with the Tate family – she had cruised in the Caribbean with the late Sir Ernest Tate and his travelling party just before she met Bobbie Hartman.

As Leonard Lyle, he came from a family of major ship-owners who had diversified into sugar refining, as Abram Lyle & Sons, who merged with Henry Tate & Sons in 1921 to form Tate & Lyle. He had been educated at *Harrow* and *Trinity Hall* Cambridge. He was a notable athlete who represented Great Britain at lawn tennis and competed in the Men's Singles at the Wimbledon Championships in the 1920s. He had married Edith Levy in 1904 but she died a few months after Bobbie Hartman in 1942. He lived in the *Dorchester* when in London but also had a house at Canford Cliffs in Bournemouth.

He responded to Dodo's charm and provided her with a press photo opportunity when she invited him as guest at the opening cocktail party of her new self-service snack bar, *"by a clever conversion of a basement"*, in Mayfair's South Audley Street.

Another female journalist wrote a less flattering piece about the snack bar and posed the question "Why are things modern so very uncomfortable?"

> *"I popped into a West End café run by Dorothy Hartman. It was so original that I have seldom spent such a miserable twenty minutes. May I have a spoon? I asked. And they gave me a dead-straight thin, three-inch strip of wood. I sat on a chilly-wooden-topped stool, in a long row, with my nose almost on the wall... Picasso may adore this sort of thing. But for my morning coffee I like comfort – and a spoon."*

In another social piece around the time of Chaplin's film premiere under the title *"Beef à la Mayfair"*, a female journalist wrote:

> *"In Mayfair a girl could get around nicely on three conversation gambits, clothes, men and other women. Now to be in the swim you've got to talk about farming. I met three smart women this week and they all swopped stories about their herds the way they used to swop hairdressers.*
>
> *Mrs Dorothy Hartman, this year's hostess with the moistest, talked about her Aberdeens bred for beef, there was Greer Garson cooing about Shorthorns and Florence Desmond, swears nothing could touch Redpolls."*

Florence Desmond, a few years younger than Dodo, born in Islington, was the sister of Fred Desmond, part of a comedy acrobat act. She and her second husband Charles Hughesdon were amongst the social set Dodo entertained, with farming interests in common as they bred Redpolls at Dunsborough Park, their home after the war in Ripley near Guildford. She had essentially retired by 1953, but attended Dodo's charity ball in December.

Desmond had recently appeared in a Royal Variety Night performance and been invited to appear on Roy Plomley's *Desert Island Discs*, which had been broadcast on the BBC Home Service in October 1952.

Dodo had known her since the thirties when she appeared with

Naughton Wayne in cabaret, and during 1928 she was in Cochran's *This Year of Grace*, as Coward's partner in *Dance, Little Lady*. Both in its London and New York Broadway productions, she understudied and played for Beatrice Lilley.

She was an entertaining comedian and a born mimic; she could impersonate many stars, but was especially good at Greta Garbo and Mae West.

During the war she had a long run in the Palladium revue *Apple Sauce* with Max Miller and Vera Lynn, and also toured the Mediterranean entertaining the troops with ENSA (The Entertainments National Service Association). In the 1930s she had appeared with Gracie Fields (she could impersonate her too) in *Sally in Our Alley*. She was a good dancer and cabaret star, but a truly gifted impersonator –considered the best of her generation. It was in that role that she took New York by storm at *The Blue Angel* nightclub in 1946.

The Ennisdales were friends of both Bobbie and Dodo Hartman since the thirties. He was one of the friends Bobbie didn't sell a Buick to; instead Harry drove a cream and black Rolls Royce saloon – and had the 'Flying Lady', the usual mascot on the front of the chassis changed to his own personal winged horse 'Pegasus'. They regularly socialised both in England and on holidays in the Bahamas.

Harry Lyons – he later became Lord Ennisdale – was a self-made man, born in Wandsworth, London. He had started work at fourteen as a post-boy at Lloyds, where his father worked as a musician (he had previously served in the army as a trumpeter with the *Ninth Lancers*) and later became a liveried waiter – where one of his jobs would be to ring the Lutine Bell traditionally rung to herald important announcements – one stroke for bad news and two for good.

In the 1890s Harry made a name for himself in Lloyds by targeting the US market. Together with Thomas Frost and Charles Gould, they would change the face of broking from a pedestrian profession to a dynamic role; this is where he made his fortune. He had managed to impress banker J. P. Morgan to persuade American insurance companies to reinsure their risks at Lloyds through his company. [41]

He had fought in the Second Boer War, married Helen Bishop, daughter of a middle-class photographic manufacturer in Kensington in the spring of 1905 and gained the rank of Major-General during the First

World War. He had retired by the age of thirty to play polo, a member of the Ranelagh Club (largest in the world), often lending ponies to the Prince of Wales.

Harry's younger married sister 'Ruby', Rubena Lakeman lived in Beaconsfield, she and her husband Wilson were concert singers, and without any other relatives both he and Helen recorded her as next of kin on their travels to the USA.

Harry became a Liberal politician, and was knighted in 1933. The Ennisdales bought the 2,000 acre estate Baynard's Park with its classical Georgian style manor house, sunken rose garden together with home farm in Surrey and kept a London apartment at 29 St James's Street, above the established chemist D. R. Harris & Co. By 1937 he was raised to the peerage as first Baron Ennisdale.

During the early part of the war Harry Ennisdale was still travelling to America and had sailed with Helen on the SS *Rex* from Genoa in March 1940, staying at the *Waldorf-Astoria* in New York before enjoying the Florida sunshine as guests of honour at a dinner given by Isabel Van Wie Willys. She was the widow of John North Willys, one of the US automotive pioneers and one-time ambassador to Poland in the 1930s. She had a considerable art collection including works by Rembrandt, Hals and Velasquez at her home Casa Virginia, in Palm Beach. Amongst others the guests included the Prince and Princess Balthasar Odescalchi from a minor noble Italian banking dynasty – apparently in the late eighteenth century Beethoven had dedicated his Piano Concerto No.1 to one of the family, Princess Babette Odescalchi (herself an accomplished pianist).

The Ennisdales were amongst the first to return to the USA after the war, sailing with fellow passengers Winston and Clementine Churchill on the *Queen Elizabeth* in January 1946.

Harry, son of an Irishman, loved horses. He bred race horses that had been trained pre-war by Harry Cottrill of Lambourn, with racing colours mauve with black sleeves and a black and red quartered cap. After the war he used trainer Frederick Sneyd and one of his horses, four-year-old *Foxy*, ran at *Royal Ascot* in June 1947, and later in the *Irish Derby*.

Harry died at Beaumont House nursing home in Marylebone in August 1963, days before his colt *Christmas Island* won the *Irish St Leger* in September by a length and a half. He left Helen £249,867. She sold Baynard's Park in 1965 to helicopter entrepreneur Alan Bristow, and died in London five years later at the age of eighty-five. As they had no children, his title became extinct.

Dodo had known 'Frankie' Day since they met in New York in 1929, and they had struck up an unlikely friendship that lasted over the years. Day had a flat in Mayfair, and enjoyed a successful London musical stage career in the 1930s, appearing in many films as well. She had entertained during the war with ENSA and performed in a musical *Night and Day* written and produced by Jack Profumo, then serving in the army.

Frances was flagrantly bisexual, attracting men and women equally. It was said she had been the mistress of four royal princes, and also of a future British Prime Minister Anthony Eden. She also inspired the passionate admiration of America's bisexual First Lady, Eleanor Roosevelt, as well as that of the world's most famous dramatist, George Bernard Shaw, who wrote one of his last plays for her.

She was one of the first truly liberated show business lesbians – although there is no evidence that she had an affair with Dodo, she was a frequent house guest. However, although Tallulah Bankhead and Marlene Dietrich were involved in sexual interludes with her, Day's primary reputation it seems was as a 'man-eater'.

Frank Muir, the English comedy writer recalls an encounter with Frances Day, around 1952. He was appearing in a radio performance of *The Name's the Game*, a panel game where a contestant presented as say 'Julius Caesar' was asked questions by the panellists to ascertain if it really was their name – or were they bluffing? It was broadcast from the BBC Aeolian Hall studio in New Bond Street.

On that occasion the guest member for the show's panel was Frances Day, as he recalls *"then mature and all the more attractive for it."* The panellists were gathered together in the ante-room, chatting, sipping wine, and waiting for their guest –none of whom had met her before. Muir describes the scene, with his back to the door, one foot up on a chair expounding away to his fellow writer Denis Norden, *"when, from behind me, a hand came between my legs and grabbed my vitals. I turned around, considerably shocked, to find Frances Day looking up at me with her cute little pixie smile. Still holding on, Hello she said."* [42]

In September 1952 Charlie Chaplin had arrived in London from the Southampton boat train at Waterloo to a rapturous welcome. He had come to promote and attend the world premier of his film *Limelight*.

Although some nine years older, Chaplin's early life had many similarities to that of Dodo's. Both born in London, to music hall parents, their mothers were daughters of shoemakers, both had fathers who drank, and both had experienced some poverty and periods away from a disfunctional family at an early age, both enjoyed comedy, and shared a rags to riches story. Dodo's mother Maud had played in many of the same English provincial theatres around the same time that Chaplin was touring in his early days during the 1880s and 90s.

Now at the height of his success, Chaplin was under increasing pressure in America – like many Hollywood stars such as Orson Welles and Paul Robeson who were on the 'black list' for what were considered Un-American Activities.

The House Un-American Activities Committee (HUAC) did more harm than good. It was created in 1938 to investigate alleged disloyalty and subversive activities on the part of private citizens, public employees, and those organisations suspected of having Communist ties. In the late 1940s, America's Cold War paranoia reached its peak, and Chaplin, as a foreigner with liberal and humanist sympathies, was a prime target for political witch-hunters, particularly Senator Joseph McCarthy.

Chaplin blissfully sailed to England on board the *Queen Elizabeth* with his wife and four children, and whilst on board he learnt with dismay his US visa had been revoked.

After arriving in England and following his promotional tour around the country before the premier of *Limelight*, it became apparent that he would not be able to return to America.

On October 16, 1952 it was screened at the *Odeon Leicester Square*, in the presence of Princess Margaret, and a host of actors and celebrities cheered on by the crowd of 20,000 fans outside. The *Odeon* dominates the square with its huge black polished granite façade, built in 1937 on the site of the old *Alhambra Theatre*. It could seat 2,000 with its Art Deco auditorium, and complete with a royal retiring room, it became popular for film premiers. He appeared with Claire Bloom; it was her film debut and it made her into an international film star.

Later the same month he was the actor that drew most attention, amongst the host of other stars like Yvonne de Carlo, Petula Clark, Gene Kelly, Douglas Fairbanks Junior, Rock Hudson, the Mills and Oliviers who all featured in the post-film line up. That year HM the Queen and the Duke of Edinburgh together with Princess Margaret all attended the Royal Film Performance at the *Odeon Cinema* to see a musical comedy film *Because You're Mine* starring Mario Lanza.

After the highly successful premiere, Chaplin, his third wife Oona (daughter of American playwright Eugene O'Neill) and children settled in Switzerland, at the Manoir de Ban, a thirty-five acre estate on the banks of Lake Geneva at Vevey where he lived until his death in 1977.

★

That year at the annual London Motor Show, to promote its design leadership, General Motors introduced a fiftieth anniversary special-bodied, low-production convertible (only 532 units were produced). It was the production version of the 1952 El Dorado 'Golden Anniversary' concept car, just over eighteen feet in length. The press announced:

> *"Another woman in the motoring news is Mrs Dorothy Hartman, head of a firm which distributes some leading American cars in Britain, who will be the only woman exhibitor at the Motor Show. To-night she gives a party to introduce a 'Golden Anniversary' Cadillac."*

This car had been shipped from the US to General Motors, Antwerp, converted to right-hand drive and prepared for the London Motor Show at Olympia where it was on display with two other Cadillac models. From London it was shipped to Australia for the Melbourne show; after that it was sold.

★

Another actress Dodo had known since the thirties was Greer Garson when she was living in Conduit Street in a flat above Redfern's, the high-quality ladies' tailors, who had made tailored clothing chic for women. They had been appointed to nearly every European royal family since late Victorian times. They had created a simple jersey travelling dress for Lillie Langtry, the noted beauty and actress, which was widely copied and remained a favourite in the Redfern line for many years.

Greer had been born in Essex, and was well educated, finding her way via advertising into theatre repertory in the 1930s. Spotted by a casting director, she was signed by MGM becoming one of the most popular actresses during the war appearing in *Goodbye, Mr Chips* in 1939, and *Mrs Miniver* in 1942 – winning the Best Actress award. She had been married three times – now Greer Fogelson, wife of a millionaire Texas oilman and horse breeder, 'Buddy' Fogelson, living on a ranch in Dallas where they also raised Shorthorn cattle.

She had flown from New York on *Trans World Airlines* in late November to attend Dodo's charity ball in London in December 1953 with Charlie Chaplin.

★

Earlier in May the same year Dodo took on a new London cook at Berkeley House in the form of Ivy Hinton, who had recently been in the household of the late George Blades, the first Lord Ebbisham and his wife Margaret at their house in Upper Brook Street. He had been a Conservative politician, one-time Lord Mayor of London, and chairman of the family printing firm of Blades, East & Blades Ltd.

The great social event of the year was the Coronation of Queen Elizabeth II on June 2. London was bursting with visitors from all over the world.

The famous travel firm of Thos. Cook & Sons –experienced in large-scale events (they had handled accommodation for the Great Exhibition of 1851), had commissioned a VIP stand outside Apsley House for distinguished guests to view the Coronation procession. They built a giant 5,500 seater stand on the Coronation route and entertained a party of 500 American visitors who had arrived in Southampton on Cunard's RMS *Caronia*, which had been christened by the Queen on her launch six years earlier. Travelling to London by specially chartered train, each guest received an elaborate 'Pullman style' meal box. The ship was used as a hotel, as most of the accommodation in London and the surrounding countryside was fully booked.

There were altogether three liners in Southampton at the time and *The Times* announced on 31 May: *"THE WORLD THRONGS INTO LONDON"* and reported that something like 4,000 visitors would disembark.

An enterprising BBC executive Peter Dimmock, who was the head of outside broadcasts, was responsible for persuading the people who mattered that the Coronation of the Queen should be televised. He succeeded and it became a seminal moment – watched by more than twenty million people throughout the country.

London was full of parties and Dodo took the opportunity to entertain senior US General Motors executives and their wives, in London and Luckington.

In October Nick Vansittart put an advertisement in the local county papers to sell his interest in Cholsey Grange and the farm, with its herd of seventy-eight Chiltern cattle.

In November Dorothy succeeded in enticing Charlie Chaplin from his home in Switzerland, to be guest of honour at a charity ball to be held on the 13 December, a Sunday evening, at the *Café de Paris* in Leicester Square, in aid of the British and Empire Cancer Research Campaign, and afterwards for he and Oona to be guests at Luckington Manor.

The press reported under the title:

"CHARITY COUP

A woman has pulled off the greatest charity coup of the year. She asked Charlie Chaplin to make a personal appearance at a Christmas party to help raise money for medical research. It will be at the Café de Paris, London, next month. He has accepted. His reply by cable said 'Delighted'. She is Mrs Dorothy Hartman, a widow who has a cool business brain."

Monday's press coverage was overshadowed by the loss of her brooch, variously reported as:

"£1000 BROOCH VANISHES AT CHARITY BALL"
"£800 BROOCH LOST AT CAFÉ DE PARIS"

Typically the press reported the value as anything from £800 to £3,500, describing Dorothy Hartman variously as a London businesswoman, or a forty-nine-year-old widow who runs a motor firm, or chairman of the organising committee in aid of Cancer Research.

Hart & Co, the city assessors, had offered a reward of £350 for the cyclamen-shaped diamond brooch. With that incentive it was found later – by a waiter, who presumably received his reward.

The following day Dodo signed a new will prepared by Charles Culross, which was witnessed by Enid Fischer, her private secretary, and Winifred Stroude her London housekeeper. It made Nicky sole executor.

-31-

Dodo's child

"Oh, what a tangled web we weave,
When first we practise to deceive!"

The baby put up for adoption at Falkland Lodge in 1916 had long been erased from Dodo's conscious memory – so had the father Captain (later Major) Lewis, except of course for his pension, as the War Office records show.

Any feeling of angst Dodo may have had had long since evaporated as it had happened a long time ago. Did it in fact happen? Her life had been carefully edited and as the press reported as far back as 1932, she was the daughter of the late Captain Abbott RN and the late Countess of Granarni. [43]

After Dalrymple's death she became Dorothea Cynthia Mirabelle Hartman, she was now widowed again and known socially as 'Dodo' with a new interest in the form of the suave, well-groomed and connected Nicky Vansittart, chairman of Vauxhall Motors. As his daughter would comment later, *"My father would always go to Trumpers in Curzon Street for his hair-dressing and smells."* (Amber Floreaka.) [44]

She had inherited fortunes from her late husband and mother-in-law and was now wealthy – and unusually at the time a businesswoman in a man's world, with farming interests in Wiltshire, a London apartment and a wide social network of influential friends.

The press always reported that she was childless. It was a status she would insist on maintaining until her death.

Ethel Florence grew up unaware that Frances and Titus Goaman were not her biological parents. The Lewis and Abbott names on her birth certificate were perhaps a clue, but she knew nothing of that document, why would she? Her memories of early childhood are that of an only child, periods of loneliness, and particularly those Welsh Sundays when it seemed everything was closed or banned by her strictly religious parents. She was not even allowed to 'bounce a ball or read', as she recalls.

Not to mention the interminable rain. In the Welsh language there are over a dozen different descriptions for rain, from drizzle (*glaw mân*) to downpours (*bwrw glaw*). The English phrase 'raining cats and dogs' becomes '*Mae hi'n brwr hen wragedd a ffyn*' in Welsh – 'it's raining old women and sticks'.

All this weather set amongst austere rows of Welsh stone terraced streets, which darken over time, leaves an indelible impression for any child who lived there.

One can imagine the young Ethel, lost in thoughts, gazing out watching the rain trickle down the window panes, perhaps catching a glimpse of her own reflection as dusk approached. In complete oblivion of her 'real' mother, – by now Lady Dalrymple – was wearing pretty dresses, partying in London nightclubs, without a care in the world.

Everything had been planned. Around the time the Goamans returned from Torquay, an advertisement had appeared in the local *Western Mail* newspaper about the adoption which would confirm to any inquisitive neighbours some public documentary evidence that the arrangement had been properly conducted. It had of course been all arranged privately before between the wider Goaman and Abbott families who were well known to each other in north Devon.

Ethel grew up in south Wales from the spring of 1916 to about the age of ten with her mother Frances and father Titus Goaman. Titus, the youngest of seven children was born in Welcome, a small village by the sea on the Cornish border of north Devon, where on a clear day you can see Lundy Island some twelve miles off the coast.

He moved to south Wales as a teenager to seek work as a carpenter, living initially as a lodger at 26 MacIntosh Place in the Roath Park district of Cardiff. Later he had moved to Pontypridd, where he met and married Frances Ethel Cook in 1908; he was twenty-six and Frances a year younger. She was the youngest daughter of George Cook, a grocer, and his second wife Frances Mills.

It had become a childless marriage and they had decided to adopt. They had been living at 19 Brook Street, Treforest, but before the baby arrived they moved away to Church Village, Llantwit Fardre, about ten miles north of the Welsh capital Cardiff. Close enough to Pontypridd where Frances's elderly mother and father lived, and where the road and river divides towards the mining valleys of Rhonda and Merthyr.

Work was difficult to find; the general economic depression had set in, particularly in heavy industrial areas such as south Wales, so Titus moved the family to Wimbledon in south London renting a semi-detached house at 101 Clarence Road, where business opportunities were plentiful.

After Ethel had left school she met Eric Salmon and at the age of twenty-two on Saturday 15 October 1938, they married at Holy Trinity Church, Wimbledon and initially went to live with her husband's family at 51 Trinity Road, close to South Park Gardens.

At the time Eric was working as a municipal electrical engineer at the Fulham power station.

When war was declared he joined the *Royal Air Force*, but because of his skills he was transferred to a civilian 'reserved occupation' to work on classified radio and radar development for the service. Some of these vital components had been smuggled out of Holland from the Philips factory at Eindhoven at the outbreak of war, and brought to England. Their radio tubes formed the basis of that research and development – much of it 'secret' at the time. Philips more or less owned Mullard in England, who opened their first research laboratory in Bournemouth with a technical department at Mitcham, not far from Wimbledon.

The Salmons moved further out to the Surrey countryside during the London Blitz of 1940–41 and found a bungalow in Meadow Walk, Ewell, to avoid the high explosive bombs which had begun to fall on nearby streets in Wimbledon.

In the spring of 1943, Eric and Ethel had a baby girl they called Veronica, a year later followed by twins Erika and Norma. After the war they relocated to a larger semi-detached house in the tree-lined Marchmont Road, Wallington, Surrey.

In February 1948 Ethel's mother Frances died and it was whilst sifting through some family papers some time after, Ethel made a devastating discovery, as Veronica explains:

"… My grandfather lived with us for a while in Marchmont Road. After he had left to go and live in Hartland, (Devon) *my mother tells me that*

she found some papers in a drawer which he left behind and that is how she discovered that she was fostered. It was some time later that she approached him about her parentage." [45]

She had found her birth certificate stating that her mother was actually Dorothy Maud Lewis, formerly Abbott and her father an army captain, and she had been born in Torquay, not Wales as she believed. She had been adopted.

On confronting her father Titus, he could offer no proper explanation as to why they hadn't told her before, perhaps 'parents' put off difficult things, and it may explain why Titus left these papers behind 'to be discovered'. In any case they were her parents for all intents and purposes. They thought it best, they brought her up, she had been fed, clothed and schooled, and he had given her away at her wedding to Eric like any other father.

Titus had moved back to Hartland, to live with his niece, and in those post-war years Ethel's oldest daughter Veronica remembers being taken there on visits during childhood.

The effect of the revelation on Ethel was profound, and it triggered a search for her 'real' mother and father.

For Titus and Frances, telling Ethel that she was adopted became a formidable, anxiety-provoking task, and thus they put it off or avoided it. The received wisdom today is to tell a child as soon as possible – however this was an informal adoption and ten years before any legal framework and any social support was in place.

The concealment caused a family rift – inevitably, as deceit does, creating a sense of aggrievement with her late mother and a loss of trust with her adopted father that would never be completely reconciled. Titus it seems could add little to the search as he really knew nothing of Captain Lewis. Any surviving links with the Abbotts in Devon had long since disappeared.

Ethel had been searching records on and off until the early summer of 1950, when she had a stroke of luck. She had been in contact with the War Office trying to trace Lewis, and her enquiry arrived on the desk of a very sympathetic clerical officer, a certain Mr C. S. Stevens.

Quite by chance Stevens had been responding to yet another enquiry about the same Captain Lewis – this time from his sister-in-law Lily Lewis (née Jeffries), who was living in Cholderton village some ten miles from Salisbury. She had married 'Harry' Lewis, his younger brother, who had died at the end of the war in 1945.

On this occasion she was trying to trace Edwin Lewis, the family's eldest son, as they hadn't heard of him for years, and to inform him about the recent death of his youngest sister Eliza Lewis (who had married John Finney in 1916 but had no children). She had been the last to see him alive when they met at Brynllwydwyn House in Wales in 1915, where she was working as a maid to the Campbell family. He had arrived unexpectedly as a house guest.

Stevens was able to help them both. In his letter of June 1950 he explains:

"Dear Mrs Salmon,

Appropos our several recent conversations on the subject of your parentage I enclose for your confidential information a copy of an official letter just despatched to a lady who is seeking to trace the next-of-kin of her brother, the late Major E Lewis. … If at any time you feel that I can be of further assistance please do not hesitate to call on my services. With best wishes,

Yours sincerely,
C S Stevens."

The information given to Lily Lewis was very clear and succinct. It revealed Ethel's biological father had been dead for over twenty years and it was likely from the nature of their enquiry his family knew no more than she did. Ethel did not consider pursuing any contact with Lily.

The story of Edwin's meeting his sister at Brynllwydwyn House would in typical Welsh oral tradition be remembered and passed down the generations and talked about within the wider family social gatherings. The copy letter read:

"Madam,

I am directed to refer to your recent enquiry regarding the late Captain Edwin Lewis, King's Shropshire Light Infantry, and to furnish from the records of the Department the following information with regard to this officer.

Recorded as having married Elizabeth Agness Elliott in Poona on 12th December 1900.

He is reported as having died on 23rd April 1923 and after his death a lady, Dorothy Maud Lewis formerly Abbott (born 4th January 1898) who stated she married Captain Lewis on 23rd December 1915, applied for a pension as his widow.

This lady subsequently married Sir Charles H. Dalrymple, Bart. On 31st August 1923, who died in 1932, and she afterwards became the wife of a Captain F. W. Hartman; there is no information as to whether she is still living.

We have previously had an enquiry from a Mrs. Ethel F Salmon of 34 Marchmont Road, Wallington, Surrey, who was born at Torquay on 24th March, 1916 and whose Birth Certificate records her parents as Captain Edwin Lewis, K.S.L.I. and Mrs. Dorothy Maud Lewis formerly Abbott.

I am, Madam,
Your obedient Servant,
C. S. Stevens"

Stevens had taken a personal interest in Ethel's search, so much so that he visited the family one Sunday afternoon in Wallington to offer advice. One of his suggestions was to search through *Who's Who*, a standard library reference book giving autobiographical entries of the great and the good throughout the country, as it had been doing since its inception in 1849. It was invaluable because the name Dorothy Hartman duly appeared amongst its list, and gave details of her addresses.

She then wrote to her London address at Berkeley House, Hay Hill and some weeks later Dorothy telephoned saying she wanted nothing to do with her – remarking it was history – and commenting about her father saying *"you know as much about him as I do."* That was a little disingenuous as she was nominally married to him for over seven years, had an allowance from Lloyds Bank and even applied for his widow's pension from the War Office.

As her eldest granddaughter, Veronica recalls years later, *"My mother said she will never forget that comment."*

Dodo the 'ice woman' not only refused to meet her but wouldn't entertain the idea of meeting her three young granddaughters either.

Ethel was dumfounded; not only had she been rejected as a baby – it was happening all over again. Why?

Dodo provided no answer, but perhaps not meeting her daughter face to face she could still maintain the illusion it hadn't happened. If she had met her who knows if some little maternal spark might have changed her attitude?

She too had experienced the loss of a mother being 'farmed out' to strangers miles away from the age of two to six – surely she would have some empathy with Ethel?

To the outside world and indeed her close social circle Dodo had created a persona that started two weddings ago –not three. She was the former Lady Dalrymple, now describing herself as in her late forties, six years younger than the date on her birth certificate – that would mean she had a baby at twelve, below the age of consent!

Of course there was a stepdaughter, Betty Gwinner, from her late husband, but she – Dodo – was childless.

She simply couldn't articulate the truth; she was in denial because she had by this time come to believe her own propaganda.

It was said that, *"The English follow the principle that when one lies, one should lie big, and stick to it,"* often attributed to Joseph Goebbels, Hitler's Propaganda Minister or as Oscar Wilde once observed with his usual wit, *"If one tells the truth, one is sure, sooner or later, to be found out."*

Without a reason for her rejection, Ethel continued a quest to learn more about her mother, to search for clues as to why she had been dismissed out of hand. She started to collect newspaper and magazine cuttings about her activities, creating a portfolio about Luckington Manor, its farms, the Beaufort Hunt, society and charity events. Slowly, Ethel was able to form an image of her later life. The press revealed she was considered a good employer to her immediate business and household staff, and a compassionate employer when needed, so why the rejection of her own daughter?

Ethel was still nonplussed; surely she deserved an explanation, at the very least? The question 'why' lingers in the mind, so she sought the pastoral help of the Rector's wife, Mrs Farr from Dodo's local village parish church in Luckington, in the hope she might provide a clue, or perhaps be able to broker a meeting.

She was very sympathetic of course and over time became Ethel's confidant, all the time giving her some hope she might be able to arrange some sort of reconciliation – she was always waiting for the right opportunity, but this never happened.

However, Jean Farr was just the Rector's wife in Luckington. Whilst she may have had influence in its social scene she had little with wealthy landowners outside church matters. She clearly was not really going to jeopardise her status, such as it was, in that tight-knit rural community.

If she had confronted Dorothy Hartman (as her husband had reminded her) she certainly would have received short shrift for interfering, and Hartman would deny any connection. As a result she would almost certainly be cast as an interfering busy-body, and upset a well-connected and influential village resident.

Her husband was right; best leave well alone. Herbert Foulkes Farr, the rector, had entered the clergy late in life after gaining wide social experience. He was the son of a Lancashire bank manager, studied at *St Catherine's College* Cambridge, and after taking his degree he became a schoolmaster. He served in the Great War in the Royal Navy as a lieutenant instructor before transferring to the *Royal Flying Corps*, and was sent as naval assistant on an Admiralty mission to Washington in 1918.

Herbert had met and married the twenty-nine-year-old widow Jean Swinscoe in Suffolk in the summer of 1930, before they moved to Luckington, and later had a son, Charles.

Jean Mary Savage was one of twin girls born in Derbyshire, just before Christmas 1900, the daughter of Walter Savage born in the USA to English parents who had returned to England to work in the steel industry, where he met and married Louisa Cooper.

When Jean was twenty-two she married Henry Swinscoe, the eldest son of a confectionery dealer in Sheffield in 1923. Within a few years Jean was to suffer a series of personal tragedies when her first son Francis died in infancy in 1924. Two years later her mother died and a year after that, the death of her second son Anthony together with husband Henry occurred within days of each other.

The revelation that Ethel was Hartman's daughter still intrigued however, but in truth Jean Farr new nothing of substance about any child of Dodo or in fact anything about her childhood, and unkindly perhaps, she seems to have given Ethel a lot of misinformation. At one stage in the correspondence she talks of the name Wainwright – her mother's first married name after Manchester, but largely irrelevant to the story. As she writes "… *there is no doubt I knew your mother – even probably in my childhood.*"

One gets a sense of Mrs Farr's personality – a tendency to fantasy with *asking Nicky for your address – a few moments conversation – my mind switched on to Luckington, so much changed and built up."* She reminisces and says, *"Like you I just live for the grandchildren – like yours mine are little charmers. With all the very best wishes… and I can say not only have you between you enriched Nicky's life – but mine as well."* [47] Jean Farr died in Fareham, Hampshire in 1992 aged ninety-one.

★

The Salmon family had moved several times in the immediate post-war years; after leaving Marchmont Road in Wallington they moved to Lancashire, before settling in Exeter by the mid-1950s where Eric had secured a new managerial position with a laundry company. Eric Salmon had become increasingly interested in the science of time-motion study, which had developed out of pioneering research in America and was now increasingly being used in Britain in a wide range of companies in the early 1950s.

It was developed from the combined business efficiency technique of Time Study and Motion Study based on the pioneers Taylor and Gilbreth's earlier research. The two techniques became integrated and refined into a widely accepted method applicable to the improvement and upgrading of work systems, in industrial as well as service organisations. Although the attitude of some workers to the 'Time and Motion' process became synonymous with the 1959 British comedy film *I'm All Right Jack* – in which they treated the process with deep suspicion, and went on strike.

In 1955 Eric had responded to an advertisement for a position in South Africa, and the family became excited about the prospect of a new life overseas. He was successful and the international company Frasers invited him to join them in Durban.

As Ethel's daughter Veronica remembers, *"There was a lot of deliberation about us moving to Africa – lions in the streets etc.!"* [48] There was a flurry of activity, with the prospect of moving to another country, and arrangements to be made. Eric flew out of Heathrow with *BOAC* on their newly introduced Britannia turbo-prop airliner – the largest in the world at the time, flying to Johannesburg, then on to Durban in February 1956, avelling alone with the family to follow two months later.

Ethel had the task of finalising the house sale in England, packing, nging travel documents, and deciding what to leave and what to take, for their life-changing adventure to Africa. They would be able to stay with Eric's brother Norman in Ruislip for the remaining weeks before their departure. A passage had been booked for Ethel, her daughters Veronica, twins Norma and Erika and their pet dog with Union Castle's chief passenger office at Rotherwick House, in Old Bond Street, to travel on one of their regular voyages to Durban.

On 12 April 1956, Ethel and her girls and the family French poodle, *Suzette* emigrated to a new life, sailing from London on the SS *Rhodesia Castle*, with her distinctive red funnel set against her lavender and white superstructure.

She was a new ship for the 'round Africa service' built five years earlier, the first of three sister ships, by the famous Harland and Wolff yard of Belfast. She was 17,041 tons capable of seventeen and a half knots carrying just over 500 passengers. The three and a half week outward voyage would be filled with games on deck, 'crossing-of-the-line' ceremony, indoor games, cards, dancing – usually to records, fancy dress, a ship's concert (usually a passenger talent show), all arranged through the purser's office.

The *Rhodesia Castle* eased her way out of the King George V Dock in London, sailed down towards the Thames estuary and on to Rotterdam, then through the English Channel into the Atlantic to Las Palmas, with alternative stops at Ascension and St Helena islands, Cape Town, Port Elizabeth, East London, and finally Durban.

As Veronica remembers:

"… in those days the dogs were placed in kennels, and we had the duty of walking her on the deck (amongst all the other dog owners) and the deck hands ran around cleaning up after us! I even had my thirteenth birthday on board and my father arranged with the Union Castle for me to be presented with a birthday cake, full of candles, to be brought in to the dining room at dinner time!" [49]

Ethel left England with some of Dodo's and Maud Coleno's artistic talent, as Veronica explains:

"My mother actually trained as a music teacher in England and passed her exams through the Royal Academy of Music. She taught music at Durban Girls' College … as well as playing at some productions and operas." [50]

She was none the wiser about her biological mother. Dorothy had continued to refuse a meeting, and was it seems unaware that her only daughter had now decided to leave the country. No one in the Hartman's social circle knew of her existence or where she had gone, except of course Mrs Farr, the wife of the Rector of Luckington.

-32-

Stumblehole

Pen and ink drawing used on DCMH's Christmas cards
(Courtesy of Audrey Cook)

Charlie Chaplin's visit to Luckington Manor had been one of the last by a house guest before it was sold. A brief footnote announcement appeared in the local press: *"A visit by Mr Charles Chaplin to the Manor, Luckington, near Malmesbury, Wilts, as guest of Mrs Dorothy Hartman was revealed yesterday. The Manor is up for sale."*

Dorothy had been concerned with her health and sought advice from an experienced physician and surgeon Henry Rowan MRCS at his private practice in Knightsbridge, discreetly away from Mayfair and her social contacts. Rowan, a married man, was a little older than her, but with years of experience having served as a surgeon in the Royal Navy in the First World War. His eldest son Michael had followed in his footsteps and served as an RNVR surgeon in the Second.

His practice was in an imposing red-brick and terracotta built house at 65 Sloane Street, a few steps from the *Cadogan Hotel* opposite Cadogan Gardens.

His advice was blunt. He strongly advised that the exertion of steeplechasing or even a boisterous hunt meet with the Beaufort during the season could kill her. She had been diagnosed with a heart murmur. She was fifty-five, and it was time to withdraw from hectic physical activity.

The journey from London to Wiltshire was also tedious and she decided to purchase a country property nearer London. She chose Stumblehole.

Stumblehole Farm situated near the small village of Leigh, (pronounced 'Lye') some three miles south-east of Reigate in Surrey, less than an hour away from London.

The farmhouse has been inhabited since the fourteenth century at least, owned by the de Bures. Stumblehole and adjoining Dean Farm came into the possession of the Charrington family in the seventeenth century and had remained with the family until one John Charrington sold it to Dodo in 1953.

He was a descendant of the brewing family, established in the eighteenth century and he was president of the merged brewers, Bass Charrington, now in his fifties had married to Barbara Cunard, a daughter from the eponymous shipping family. Their children had grown up and they had decided to retire to Netherton in Hampshire.

The mixed arable estate and farm came with around 274 acres stretching from the village of Leigh to the banks of the River Mole, merely a stream at Stumblehole as it meanders its way northwards towards the Thames.

Dodo moved her household in early 1954, and was planning to continue rearing beef cattle with a herd of Aberdeens, and it also had a pig unit. She would take on the farm staff – the estate manager, a Scot called Mr Craig, together with his wife and two children, Johnnie and Cynthia who lived in Dean Farm. (He was later replaced by Mr Allison after some costly farming error – Dodo was out of pocket – and not amused.) Some of Charrington's other staff were employed, particularly the Cooper family, who had a cottage on the estate.

Walter Cooper, a cheerful and unflappable man had served in the *Royal Armoured Corps* during the war as a sergeant with a Reconnaissance Regiment in the Normandy invasion and beyond. Like most that had experienced war, he never talked about it.

Walter would act as general handyman, looking after the house boilers and as under-butler at weekend house parties and his genial wife Mildred would help in the kitchen as well as with cleaning. They had four children; two boys and two girls, Audrey and Sheila, the oldest son David away in the Merchant Navy, the youngest Roger was severely physically disabled and Dodo helped with his special needs at Chailey Heritage School in Sussex. Once she had learnt of the difficult journey his parents had to visit Roger, she immediately told Cooper that she had a garage full of cars and he was to use one whenever he wanted. This was a great blessing for the family as their daughters had been unable to visit Roger at school as it had previously been too difficult and expensive. [51]

Stumblehole had been enlarged and redeveloped in the earlier part of the century with a servant and kitchen wing, linked to the central house through a green baize door. The old part retained much of its medieval beamed timber frames, with nooks and crannies and galleried hall and staircase, presenting to the world a typically home-counties tile hung property, surrounded by a mature garden of about seven acres.

It had various outbuildings, a swimming pool, croquet lawn, sunken rose garden and kitchen garden, surrounded by farmland and various staff flats and tenant cottages.

The farm would be nearer Dodo's friends, the Ennisdales who lived at Baynard's Park with its farm near Cranleigh, and another social friend the actress Florence Desmond who bred Red Poll cattle, at Dunsborough Park in Ripley, living with her second husband, the aviator and insurance broker Charles Hughesdon. He was a bit of a philanderer, having affairs with her numerous theatrical friends, including the teenage singer Shirley Bassey.

Nick Vansittart was still farming at Pankridge Farm, near High Wycombe, but had sold it by the time he retired in 1958.

★

The friendship with Charlie Chaplin and his wife Oona continued and they were Dodo's guests at a Stumblehole weekend, as one of the estate children recalls: *"I remember Dad coming home one day and saying he was never going to wash his right hand again as Charlie Chaplin had just shaken his hand."*

One thing that can be said about Dodo from her clothes, homes, and taste in furnishings is that she had style: *"She loved to spend her money."* [52].

One of the features at Stumblehole was the dining room – which was completely lit by candles in the evening. No electric lights whatsoever. The society hostess believed she would always look at her best by candlelight, particularly wearing the diamond and emerald necklace she wore for the Gunn portrait. These were antique 'old' cut gems from before the turn of the century. These diamonds were cut to look their best by candlelight as they created the soft reflection and romantic glow for which they are known.

Both she and Nick preferred light entertainment rather than classical music although they both loved ballet: *"... only the top flight ballet – Nicky was always slightly ashamed to admit he enjoyed it!"* [53]

The Grand Ballet du Marquis de Cuevasis, formed in 1944 was the creation of George de Cuevas, a friend of Dodo. He was a Chilean-born ballet impresario and choreographer. The ballet came to London and performed at the *Stoll Theatre* on Kingsway in 1950. As Nicky explained in a letter to Ethel:

> *"... he is getting great write ups. The old boy was a pal of your mother's and we used to go and see his ballet when it came here. His wife is fortunately a Rockefeller so he can afford the large fortune he spends on it!"*

★

Dodo's taste in paintings and etchings was eclectic; one, which was hung in the sitting room, always caught the eye. It was by Victorian artist Atkinson Grimshaw – one of many 'moonlight' dock scenes he painted, possibly Glasgow or Liverpool. He was an imaginative painter, much influenced by the Pre-Raphaelites. His paintings could be bought for a few hundred in the 1950s but now they feature in a number of galleries, and today occasionally come to auction fetching six-figure sums.

Dodo had brought her Luckington cook Mrs Gilbey to Stumblehole, but now in her sixties she was finding the demands of entertaining exhausting, not to mention any new kitchen gadget brought back from Dodo's trips to America. Set in her ways, she retired in the early summer of 1956 and returned to Wiltshire.

A new Welsh cook joined Stumblehole in the form of Mrs Dann and her young son. Dodo had learnt during the interview that she had been cook to Edward Ford, Queen Elizabeth's private secretary. However she was more impressed when she learnt she had also cooked for Lady Brassey in Badminton – where she had dined many times in her Luckington days, and employed her on the spot. Dodo was always one for 'first impressions'. Her maxim was *"I provide the best and expect the best."*

The kitchen on the ground floor facing the farm buildings was at weekends a hive of activity. The Cadillac bringing Dodo and servants would arrive from London on Friday afternoon, and leave on Monday morning. Mansell and later Brady and finally Edmonds, the last chauffeur, would drop off Dodo, Gear and her lady's maid Dupont at the front door, before sweeping around to the rear of the house and kitchen entrance. The chauffeur would appear bringing any additional produce sourced in London for the weekend's menus, and Cooper would be on hand to manage the luggage. The kitchen garden would provide everything else in season, and the hothouses would provide some fruit, and cut flowers – particularly chrysanthemums at Christmas time.

Essentially Dodo had two residences, London and Surrey, and the only servants to shuttle between both were Gear the butler and Dupont the lady's maid, where they had their own rooms.

There had been dogs in Dodo's life since the early days of marriage to Bobbie Hartman. At this time she had acquired three Pekinese dogs, *Boo-boo* her favourite, *Nina* (a keen rabbiter) and *Cheesi* – they were related as father, mother and son.

Boo-boo would often travel to London but the other two would stay on the farm. *Boo-boo* was spoilt, and would be brushed to perfection smelling of expensive scent – sometimes Balenciaga's new 'Quadrille', supplied in its squat fluted glass bottle with dome stopper, but usually Chanel 'No 5' – a Hartman perennial favourite. Dodo would inevitably walk around the estate at weekends but *Boo-boo* would refuse to go anywhere near the piggery and its smells. There was a farm cat, *Ginger*, who slept in his own basket in the kitchen, close to the Aga. Adjacent to the kitchen and the servants' hall was a boot-room that also housed the farm's small telephone switchboard (Norwood Hill 123) and the dog baskets at night.

Menus for the weekend were often discussed from London by telephone and could include fruit or vegetables that were out of season in England. These would be sourced from the Continent through Dodo's own London shops. Food was prepared to impress guests – and with Dodo's extensive travel experience and knowledge of dining on the

'*Queens*' and in New York restaurants, she knew what she wanted and demanded the best.

Several old recipes and menu notes survive from the collection of Mrs Dann giving an indication of how rich the food and sauces were served at that time. Cream and alcohol would it seems appear in many dishes.

For example, 'Crayfish in a Brandy Mornay Sauce', Method: take ten boxes of frozen Danish crayfish… simmered in a court-bouillon – which in itself included two cupfuls of white wine, then there was a 'Lemon Syllabub', containing half a pint of cream, adding a small glass of sherry or brandy, or perhaps 'Filets of Sole Baumaniere' – poach six fillets of sole in dry vermouth – and so on. Sometimes 'Crêpe Suzettes' with the intoxicating sauce aroma, served hot from a chafing dish with Gear performing his *maître d'* role, pouring Grand Marnier over the crêpes, served flambéed – all very theatrical.

All dishes cooked using the 'country-house standard' Aga cooker, introduced in England in the 1930s. The secret to its success is its heavy iron castings, which absorb and retain heat – meaning the food is cooked by radiant heat, not heated air as in most ovens; consequently the food retains more moisture and flavour.

One of Dodo's amusing maxims when asked how she liked coffee prepared was simply *"Coffee should be black as night, hot as hell, and strong as love."* She had an ear for a phrase she liked, and the actress's ability to use them effectively in her vocabulary. Like many of her remarks they were probably influenced by her visits to America; inevitably they would cause amusement 'below stairs'.

In contrast to the rich food, 'Summer Pudding' was a Hartman favourite, the classic English pudding since the late nineteenth century. Prepared by lining (stale) sliced bread, layered in a deep bowl with fruit and fruit juice, such as raspberries, strawberries, blackcurrants, blackberries and redcurrants, left to soak overnight, served cold (with the inevitable double cream). For tea, as an alternative to afternoon scones, 'Welsh cakes' (unheard of then outside rural Welsh home kitchens) made an appearance on the menu. They too were a big success. With the amount of alcohol being used in cooking, it was easy for Gear to 'manage' the wine cellar. Dodo exercised a certain 'blind eye' tolerance to his 'weakness for drink', probably because of his consistent loyalty.

One of the wines drunk at Stumblehole, particularly in the summer, was the Portuguese Mateus rosé that had been developed by the Sogrape family at the end of the war. It was exported in quantities to England, with its distinctive narrow-necked, flask-shaped bottle, featuring its baroque historic mansion label. These empty green bottles were prized as they could be converted to table lamps.

★

In May 1954 the newspapers and BBC announced, *"Bannister breaks four-minute mile. Roger Bannister, a 25-year-old British medical student, has become the first man to run a mile in less than four minutes."* He had carefully planned the race, aided by two friends Chris Brasher and Chris Chataway who acted as pacemakers. His achievement of 3 minutes 59.4 seconds, elusive until then, was watched by about 3,000 spectators at the Iffley Road track in Oxford.

The same month the *Hastings and St Leonard's Observer* reported (complete with photo) that Dodo was the opening speaker at a new branch of the National Children's Home, named Malmesbury House in St Leonards. It was a substantial building dating from the 1850s on West Hill, in a prominent position overlooking the West Marina. It could cater for up to thirty-eight children. Crowds of well-wishers including the great and the good, Aldermen and Councillors of the borough attended including the Mayors of Malmesbury (near Luckington) where the children's home had been located since the late thirties (known as Stainsbridge House) and throughout the war years.

With a certain amount of irony, Dodo was a patron of the Sussex branch of the National Children's Homes.

In July it was announced that all food rationing would end. Housewives celebrated the end of fourteen years of food rationing in Britain, since the beginning of the war. It had been the last phase of a series of commodities, when restrictions on the sale and purchase of meat and bacon were lifted. Petrol rationing had ended in May 1950, followed by soap in the September. Three years later sales of sugar were off ration and in July 1954, the rationing of all other foods ended.

In the summer of 1954 Dodo exhibited her prize heifer *Handcross Belle* at the Royal Show at Windsor Great Park in July, winning second place in the class awards for cattle.

During the latter part of 1954 another distinguished Stumblehole guest was the Home Secretary Sir David Maxwell Fyfe and his wife Sylvia, who was the sister of actor Rex Harrison, and Vice Chairman of the Conservative Party. They had driven over from their home in Withyham, near Tunbridge Wells, about twenty miles away. *"He* (the Home Secretary) *arrived in an Austin Seven with his detectives following in the posh limo – to the great amusement of the staff."* [54] The Scots-born politician was soon to become Viscount Kilmuir, an influential Conservative lawyer and one of the prosecutors at the Nuremberg Trials. He was also instrumental in drafting the European Convention on Human Rights.

Entertaining estate children had become something of a January birthday event for Dodo, before her business trip to America.

> *"I know Mrs Hartman supported an orphanage at St. Leonard's as all the children and us (from the estate) went to London for ringside seats at the Circus or an ice show followed by tea at her London flat in Berkeley House usually in January which I think celebrated her birthday."* [55]

In the last week of January 1955 the Hartman entourage again departed on its annual winter visit to New York and the Bahamas. It would be her last.

Sailing on the *Queen Mary* – this time with eighteen pieces of luggage, an all-time record – she arrived at the *Plaza* with her fifty-one-year-old lady's maid Nellie Sadler. She would have left her employment within a year, and been replaced by Helene Dupont.

Fellow passengers inevitably included her close friends the Ennisdales, and on this trip Lord Trafgarne and his wife, who as George Garro-Jones was a Welsh barrister and politician until he was raised to the peerage after the war, together with fellow traveller the Earl of Carnarvon. The Hartman party returned again on the *Queen Mary*, with Harry and Helen Ennisdale, arriving in Southampton on March 21.

The following day she learnt the sad news that her old friend and mentor Ermine Elibank had died at the *Landsdowne Club* at the age of seventy-six, four years to the month after her husband Gideon's death in South Africa.

When probate was announced in June it was revealed Ermine had left her fortune to her nephew, Harold Harington Balfour, first Baron Balfour of Inchrye.

The results of the May General Election gave victory to the Conservative Party, with Anthony Eden as Prime Minister, beating Clement Atlee with a substantially increased majority in government. It was a country where nearly sixty per cent of men still smoked, and a pint of beer cost 1s-3d.

In July the newspapers were full of a controversial case concerning Ruth Ellis – a twenty-eight-year-old nightclub hostess and mother of two children who was to be executed for murdering her lover, shot outside the *Magdala* public house in Hampstead. Sentenced at the Old Bailey before Mr Justice Havers (grandfather of actor Nigel Havers) to be hanged at Holloway prison. There were protests outside the prison, and a last minute plea by her counsel on the grounds it was a 'crime of passion' recognised on the Continent – but not under English law. It was quickly dismissed by Havers. She would be the last woman to suffer the death penalty in Britain.

Following the Paris Motor Show, the annual London Motor Show took place at Earls Court in October. This year General Motors announced from its Lendrum & Hartman stand that it had been the best year for Buick sales ever, with over 738,800 sold. One of the star exhibits was a display model of the Cadillac 'La Espada' – the only one built for exhibition purposes, there was no price tag but it was insured for $35,000.

At the end of the month Dodo's old friend Frances Day had been invited to appear as a 'castaway' on Roy Plomley's *Desert Island Discs*, the long-running BBC radio programme, in a broadcast on 31 October. Her choice of records ranged from some of her own songs and orchestral pieces, to Frank Sinatra's *My Funny Valentine*, an unknown recording of a Rhodesian Lion Dog, and Tchaikovsky's *Romeo and Juliet Fantasy Overture*.

In the November Dodo gave a twenty-first birthday party for Betty Gwinner's eldest son, Martin, now serving as an officer in the Royal Navy. It was a lavish event including a spectacular firework display. The estate children would be able to see the event from the farm road: *"… it was a huge firework display featuring a chicken walking across where the Ha-ha was located* (a walled recessed landscape device to stop cattle entering the garden) *when it stopped and laid a golden egg."* [56]

The same autumn Frances Day came to visit; a frequent guest, she was the bane of the kitchen staff as she like to 'hang around' getting under their feet. She was often confusingly thought (wrongly) by the staff to be linked to the music publishers Francis, Day, and Hunter.

Day was to star in a forthcoming film, a comedy crime drama *There's Always a Thursday,* directed by Charles Saunders, a low-budget production shot at Southall Studios.

It was due for release the following year. She appeared along with Charles Victor, Jill Ireland and Bruce Seton, a career soldier turned actor. Seton had been playing the police inspector in the popular BBC television series *Fabian of the Yard,* being screened at the same time. He later inherited the title Sir Bruce Lovat Seton of Abercorn, becoming the eleventh Baronet.

After the film release in March 1956, she elected to make a number of rock records, under the pseudonym 'Gale Warning'. One of them, a version of Elvis Presley's *Heartbreak Hotel*, proved to be a disastrous error of judgment. It was slated in the music press.

Her popularity had taken a dramatic downturn after the war, since her heydays in the 1930s. After a number of poor West End stage performances, she began showing signs of increasingly erratic behaviour, causing rows with theatre management with her prima donna-like antics. In the 1950s she had turned to television appearing as a panellist on the BBC game show *What's My Line?* -irritating the chairman Eamonn Andrews by her insistence on 'special lighting'.

In April, with buoyant sales Lendrum & Hartman received a timely piece of additional publicity in the form of the voluptuous twenty-five-year-old blonde actress Diana Dors, arriving in her light-blue Cadillac convertible at the Cannes Film Festival. It was to promote her new film *Yield to the Night,* a crime drama which was nominated for the Palme d'Or.

Traffic in London was increasing and now getting very congested. There were over three million cars in Britain. The government introduced new parking restrictions, and the first yellow 'no parking' lines started to appear on London streets, followed soon afterwards by the ubiquitous Venner parking machines dotted along the pavements of Mayfair and elsewhere. This also ushered in a new official 'hate' figure – the Parking Warden.

In the summer, the first Premium Bonds went on sale. These were lottery bonds issued by the government through their National Savings and Investments agency. They were introduced in the spring budget to encourage people to save after the war. The bonds are entered in a regular prize draw and the government promised to buy them back, on request, for their original price, and became very popular. The bond numbers were randomly selected by 'ERNIE', the acronym created by their 'Electronic Random Number Indicator Equipment', invented by one of the original Bletchley Park code breakers. The same summer British Railways abolished its anachronistic 'third-class' carriages, and redesignated them 'second class'.

That summer Frances Day was again one of the house guests at Stumblehole for the weekend. As usual the house party would arrive on Friday and leave on Monday. On this occasion Dodo Hartman left with her servants Gear and Dupont in the Cadillac on Monday morning for London –leaving only Day behind. This was unusual, so later the same morning Mrs Dann the cook who was busy in the kitchen sent her teenage son (it was school holidays) through the green baize door with a message to enquire what Day would like for lunch. On arriving at the garden sitting room, he found the amply-upholstered blonde actress completely naked lying on the rug in front of the log fireplace. Unable to remember the request or articulate any words coherently, he fled and reported the incident to his mother. The cook returned finding Day – now sitting with a kimono wrapped around her shoulders nonchalantly smoking one of Dodo's complimentary Philip Morris cigarettes – no, she didn't want any lunch and could someone take her to the station. That someone was Walter Cooper who was summoned on his day off, taking the estate shooting-brake, driving her the five miles to Redhill station. [57]

Frank Gear, Hartman's butler had been with the household for over ten years – Dodo's longest serving employee. As Prudie Mennell recalled,

"Yes we certainly knew Gear and of course I remember staying at Stumblehole and buying new pyjamas because I knew our suitcase would be unpacked!" [58]

Gear also enjoyed a drink, and on one occasion was slightly, as the nautical saying goes, 'three sheets to the wind'. It was a sunny summer day and guests were scattered relaxing around the garden swimming pool.

He had been serving drinks, when some of them noticed a distinct sway in his walk around the pool with his tray. Unkindly perhaps, they started to bet amongst themselves as to when he might fall in the pool. Later that afternoon, he duly returned with another full tray, swaying as he manoeuvred around the guests, all pent with excitement, waiting in anticipation. He faltered at one point but always managed to continue with the tray upright – he never fell 'overboard'.

What guests didn't know is that Gear had served as a steward in the Royal Navy before the war and had learnt the art of walking around a swaying deck with ease.

On another occasion:

"… he once walked from the Butler's pantry through the green baize door with a tray of drinks, instead of turning left into the dining room, walked straight past through the garden door and was found wandering in the rose garden with his tray – probably with the mystified guests watching from the windows." [59]

In October, David Lean's Academy Award-winning film *The Bridge on the River Kwai* was released, and the film chosen for the Royal Film Performance was *The Battle of the River Plate* – the epic story of the wartime engagement between a British cruiser squadron and the mighty German pocket battleship *Admiral Graf Spee*.

Ever since the Egyptian Gamal Abdel Nasser had led the overthrow of King Faruq in 1952, the revolutionary government adopted a staunchly nationalist, anti-imperialist agenda, and wanted the end of British occupation of the country, particularly the Suez Canal, as approximately two-thirds of Europe's oil passed through the canal at that time. This political unrest resulted in the Cairo riots, when many British institutions were set on fire, like the *Turf Club*, *Shepheard's Hotel*, and Thomas Cook's office; this ultimately led to the Suez War between October and November 1956.

It was a partial military success – it featured the first helicopter-borne amphibious assault in history, using troops on a large scale from HMS *Ocean* at Port – the technique that impressed and was later copied by the US military in Vietnam. However, it was described as a fiasco by many and a political disaster resulting in Prime Minister Anthony Eden's resignation.

The Hartman household, wary that these events would affect food prices or limit supply, particularly Far East imports via Suez, stocked up on various commodities, particularly rice – despite government warnings on food-hoarding. Certain Stumblehole cupboards were stockpiled and staff sworn to secrecy. The canal remained closed until March the following year, with inevitable effects on prices.

Christmas was always a special time and Dodo would arrange parties for her employees and estate staff. In January 1957, she had arranged for the children to be driven from the estate in Stumblehole in the Cadillac to an afternoon matinee performance of *Peter Pan* at the *Scala Theatre*. That year the actress Margaret Lockwood played the main role with her daughter Julia as Wendy. Afterwards, the children were taken to tea at Berkeley House before being driven home in the evening.

The same month Harold MacMillan, then Chancellor of the Exchequer succeeded the ailing Anthony Eden as Prime Minister. This year was destined to be a series of endings.

In February Nick's brother Robert died in Denham. He was seventy-five. In retirement, he had started his reminiscences five years earlier, writing slowly and meticulously as his wife Sarita would explain in a prefatory note to his autobiography *The Mist Procession*, published posthumously the following year. In the autumn probate was published through Rowe & Maw, solicitors of Stafford House, Norfolk Street in the Strand. He had left a share of his £59,262 estate to his wife Sarita, his stepson Colville and to Nick.

The popular music known as 'rock and roll' was in its early days, and in the spring a couple of songs had been released with similar lyrical themes of departures and loneliness. Played repeatedly on the radio they became amongst that year's most popular songs. The Everly Brothers with their 'Bye Bye Love', and a few months later Buddy Holly launched his 'That'll Be the Day'.

In April the *Royal Court Theatre* in London premiered John Osborne's *The Entertainer* with Laurence Olivier playing Archie Rice in the title role. It transferred to the West End in September. The plot revolves around a failing third-rate music-hall performer, who tries to keep his career going even as the music-hall tradition fades into history and his personal life falls apart, told against the shadow of the recent Suez War. The original music included a music hall song, once sung fifty years earlier by Dodo's mother 'Maud Coleno' – "The Boy I Love is Up in the Gallery". The play ends with Archie at the music hall, this time though not with his usual slick patter, but rambling philosophically, after a reprise of "Why Should I Care?" he leaves the stage in darkness. *"Archie Rice has gone. There is only the music,"* reads the stage direction. [60] It could have been a metaphor for Dodo's life – beginning now to turn full circle.

★

Nick's old pre-war boss from General Motors, James Mooney, now in his early seventies, had set up his own consultancy becoming President of J. D. Mooney Associates based in New York. He still maintained a punishing schedule and in the spring and summer of 1957 had crossed the Atlantic four times, flying with *Trans World Airlines*. Dodo and Nick had met him in London in June, only to receive news in September he had died in Tucson, Arizona. After his death, his business and private papers were deposited with Georgetown University.

In October after a particularly bad outbreak of Asian flu which had killed thousands in Britain – more than previous outbreaks – the government successfully introduced a vaccine which was distributed free on the National Health Service. The same month, news appeared in the press that Jack Buchanan, the theatre and film actor had died in London. He was known for three decades as the embodiment of the debonair man-about-town. He had appeared in a stage review with Dodo's fellow artiste, Gertrude Lawrence in the 1920s. In the same show he sang Ivor Novello's "And Her Mother Came Too", making it his signature song.

This year's annual Royal Film Performance was *Les Girls* with Gene Kelly and Kay Kendall, a musical comedy film with music and lyrics by Cole Porter. It was screened at the *Odeon Cinema* in Leicester Square on Monday 4 November, always a society royal occasion adored by film and stage celebrities, but on this occasion without the Mayfair hostess.

When Dodo had been diagnosed with a heart murmur she had been given a few years to live; it was something she kept to herself. Although she had partially shared the secret with Nicky and he was aware he was executor to her will, she had largely persuaded close friends – and Nicky in particular – that she had been working too hard, and the doctors had told her she needed to take things easier, All true to a point.

In the early days there were no obvious signs – only her physician's stethoscope and perhaps some subtle symptoms indicated anything was wrong. Henry Rowan had been treating her for some time. Now, there were chest pains, shortness of breath and in the last few weeks she had taken to bed, with only her close household staff Miss Jordan her private secretary, Gear and Dupont in attendance.

The usual Mayfair apartment activity at Berkeley House slowed as she found her energy and appetite slipping away – but as always, Nicky Vansittart kept a vigil at her bedside.

Then on Guy Fawkes Night, Tuesday 5 November 1957 at around eight o'clock in the evening, the curtain closed for the last time. She died quietly two months before her sixtieth birthday.

One of the estate children wrote in his diary, *"Mrs Hartman died at eight o'clock. We had a nice bonfire."* [61]

-33-

Dodo's bequest

The old established Marylebone funeral directors W. Garstin & Sons had been appointed to handle the arrangements (they had assisted in embalming HM George V in 1936), taking the coffin direct to St Bartholomew's church in the little village of Leigh. The first few days of November 1957 had remained mild and sunny, but the following were changeable with some strong winds and heavy rain at times. It became colder around mid-month, but still remained mainly dry with sunny periods.

The details had been arranged swiftly and efficiently by Miss Jordan, Dodo's private secretary, who released the information to the press:

"HARTMAN – On November 5th 1957, at Berkeley House, Hay Hill, W.1. Dorothy, widow of Captain F. W. Hartman of Stumblehole Leigh. Funeral service, Monday, November 11th at 12-noon, St Bartholomew's Church Leigh, near Reigate. One-o'clock Surrey and Sussex Crematorium, Forge Wood, Balcombe Road, Crawley. Flowers to W. Garstin & Sons, 5 Baker Street, W.1."

Leigh church was originally fifteenth century but much restored and enlarged in Victorian times, paid for largely by the Charrington family – previous owners of Stumblehole as the estate farm land boarders the village.

All household and estate staff attended the funeral service – but only a few close servants attended the newly-built crematorium in its thirteen-acre garden, before returning to Stumblehole. The young Audrey Cooper recalls: *"I remember Dad saying the* (Hartmans') *three Pekingese's* (sic) *howled on the lawn bordering the driveway and facing Leigh Church at the hour the service was held."* [62].

Afterwards, events happened quickly; the will was announced and the press informed, probate officials visited Stumblehole and the estate put up for sale early in the New Year.

Miss Jordan had been working through Dodo's contacts and had informed relevant business employees, friends and acquaintances within days of her death. Included in that list was the Rector of Luckington's wife, Jean Farr, who would in turn pass the news to her friends in the village and within the Beaufort Hunt.

One of those Farr would inform was unknown to anyone else, a certain Ethel Salmon in South Africa. She immediately sent a telegram informing her of the situation: *"Mother died 5th, cremation Monday + Farr."* [63] Ethel acted promptly and wrote an air mail letter to Dodo's solicitors Culross & Co., in Duke Street.

In the meantime the press had discovered the outline contents of the will and with journalists raiding their cuttings archives, they started to write articles about Dodo's death, inevitably using the Gunn portrait to illustrate their pieces.

The Daily Express ran an article by Keith Morfett on page seven of their November 22 issue headed:

"ONE MAN ALONE INHERITS THE ENTIRE FORTUNE OF RICH MAYFAIR HOSTESS
One of Mayfair's most lavish hostesses has left her entire six-figure fortune to one of the highest paid men in Britain's motor industry."

The article went on to say that not one of her servants, nor one of the hundreds of employees or charities are mentioned in the will, and that there was no mention either of Captain Hartman's daughter by his first marriage. This presumably inspired Betty Gwinner – the stepdaughter – to start her legal challenge.

John Womersley of *The Daily Sketch* wrote in their 23 November issue:

"HEIR TO SHARE OUT WIDOW'S FORTUNE
She left the lot to him."

In his piece he quotes friends who knew her: *"It's so unlike her,"* for generosity was second nature to twice-married Mrs Hartman. (Twice married – she was in fact married three times – but as we know Major Lewis had been written out of her revised script.) The article goes on to quote an official from Lendrum & Hartman saying, *"She (Dodo) used to give wonderful Christmas parties for the staff. And if anyone fell by the wayside they were not neglected."*

Culross & Co. gave a press statement to the *Daily Sketch* on behalf of Nick:

> *"Though from the legal point of view he is sole beneficiary, he would like it to be known Mrs Hartman has expressed to him certain wishes in regards to her estate. These are not legally binding, but when the value of the estate is known, which will not be for some time – he wishes, if possible to implement these wishes."* [64]

Another *Daily News* headline appeared the same day:

"Most Extraordinary will
Heiress Leaves Her Fortune To One Man*"

There was curiously no mention of Stumblehole in the papers – there were references to the Southdown Hunt, and Luckington – which she had sold and left in early 1954. It may have been because of the unexpected contact she had with her daughter Ethel that she instinctively withdrew from 'courting' the press around that time.

Jack Abbott, Dodo's brother was shocked to learn about her death from the newspapers; no one had thought to tell him, presumably he was not even listed in Miss Jordan's contact book. Consequently he was denied the opportunity of attending his sister's funeral. His daughter Pat Abbott, now Woor recalls what really upset her parents, was reading in the press that she had no living relatives.

★

The following month in December the London fog had returned with a devastating effect; a commuter train crashed at Lewisham in the evening of 4 December killing ninety-two.

Later the same month, Dodo's theatrical friend Frances Day's last lesbian lover, Moie Charles, the forty-six-year-old author of the 1943 film *The Gentle Sex*, was found gassed in her Chelsea flat. Death was judged accidental, but it provided the final tipping point to Day's stability.

She gave up her Mayfair home, in the quiet mews cul-de-sac Three Kings Yard, off Davies Street (Mayfair 6670 –long since ex-directory) and retreated to Maidenhead, changed her name by deed poll to Samta Young Johnson and became a recluse.

When she died from leukaemia at the age of seventy-five in 1984, she too left everything to one 'bewildered' man, in her surprisingly poignant will.

It directed him:

"... there be no notice or information of any kind of my death, except for and if a death certificate is obligatory. Any persons, private or Press, you shall simply say that I am no longer at this address. 'Gone away. Destination unknown', and that is the truth." [65]

It was shortly after Dodo's death, and probably after reading the press reports, there was an incident observed by the Stumblehole staff when the forty-five-year-old Betty Gwinner drove from her home in New Milton and arrived unannounced at the house demanding entrance, for what reason isn't clear. Betty Hartman had married Clive Gwinner, the younger son of a London stockbroker, the same year Dodo married Bobbie Hartman. Clive had a distinguished war serving as a lieutenant-commander in the Royal Navy earning the DSO and DSC. Their sons were now in their early twenties; Martin the eldest had followed his father into the navy. Dodo had hosted his lavish twenty-first birthday party at Stumblehole, and the younger Christopher after *Charterhouse* was taking his degree at Oxford. He would later have a successful career with Courtaulds. [66]

Despite Betty's insistence – 'and of course Madam was recognised', she was still refused entrance and asked to make contact with Miss Jordan, Dodo's private secretary in London. Those were the instructions. She flew into a rage and drove off in high dudgeon, scattering gravel in the driveway and disappeared with a clatter as her car sped over the metal cattle grid at the farm road entrance. Shortly afterwards she began her legal action.

Betty may have had a point perhaps, as all the money inherited by Dodo came from her father and grandparents.

Her father left Dodo £311,473 in 1942 and a year later her grandmother Edith Hartman left her £208,823, altogether £523,295 – something like £16.6 million today.

She may have had 'expectations' as his only child, but in reality she was just five when her parents divorced and ten when her mother married Horace Soper – the stepfather she would have known most of her childhood and adolescence.

It was Horace, not Bobbie that gave her away at her marriage to Clive Gwinner over twenty years ago. Soper had died a year earlier in April 1956 at the King Edward VII hospital in London. Probate revealed he left £2,658 – possibly a disappointment, and she may not have been a beneficiary.

Her father Bobbie Hartman had not been part of her life since she was a young child; she hardly knew him. He was now married to his third Dorothy. The will he wrote two years after her marriage was unambiguous too – Dodo was sole executrix.

Six months later, in the High Court of Justice, the Principal Probate Registry announced the finding of the action brought by Betty Gwinner challenging the validity of Dorothy Hartman's will. It concluded:

> "… the Honourable Sir Arthian Davies Knight one of the Justices of the said High Court… by his final decree in the action entitled Vansittart against Gwinner pronounced for the force and validity of the said Will."

Betty lost her action – perhaps she was wrongly advised, perhaps she ignored any advice. Dodo's will had been legally unambiguous and drawn up by her Mayfair solicitor, the experienced Charles Culross.

-34-

End of the tour

"Wish me luck as you wave me goodbye.
Cheerio, here I go, on my way."
Sung by Gracie Fields in the musical comedy film Shipyard Sally (1939)

Like any stage production at the end of a tour, everyone departs searching for new opportunities using their agent, or scanning the 'small ads'; some friendships remain, others fade away. The Hartman servants behind the green baize door with their employer, the star of the show, now dead, were themselves effectively jobless and homeless too, unless of course any new buyer of the estate decides to take them on?

This was an unsettling time. Working in domestic service is unlike any other job – essentially living-in, and on call twenty-four hours a day, with limited time off, your life is not your own but it can create its own wider family. The Hartman household had been a happy community whilst it lasted.

Nick Vansittart as sole executor of his beloved Dodo had to unravel the administration of her estate. Dodo had expressed certain oral wishes; not legally binding as Culross reminded him, which were that essentially her faithful staff should be 'looked after' appropriately. There may have been other wishes too – but they remain undiscovered. Nick fulfilled these obligations but he had the unenviable task of informing some of them what was going to happen – naturally with his own apartment in South Street there was no use for the Berkeley House flat or Stumblehole Farm.

In order to realise the major assets, which were largely in property and businesses, they would have to be sold.

There was Dodo's Lloyds bank accounts, shares and personal jewellery such as the diamond and emerald necklace she wore for the Gunn portrait, and the cyclamen brooch she wore at the *Café de Paris* charity event, not to mention two Russian sable coats and a selection of stoles. There were extensive pieces of antique furniture, and original paintings, Purdey sporting guns (kept in a secret room), and a miscellany of personal papers including an 8 mm film camera.

Lendrum & Hartman was a limited company, and a separate entity. Dodo had owned most shares and these now passed to Nick. The company could continue trading with its existing management team and staff. The same applied to the little shops Dodo had bought and traded under her own name – 'Dorothy Hartman'. These included a grocer and cheese purveyor at 65 South Audley Street (with snack bar underneath), a short distance from the showrooms of James Purdey & Sons – Hartman's shotgun maker, and next door to the Constance Spry Flower School. Her other shops included a fishmonger at 12 New Quebec Street, and another grocer, wine and spirit merchant at number fifteen.

The probate men arrived in Stumblehole quickly in December 1957 to assess the contents value. It was put on sale by Knight, Frank & Rutley, the leading estate agents in London, and the property details feature in the January 23 edition of *Country Life* a month later.

It became clear that all household and some estate staff would now be dismissed with the exception of Miss Stroude, the London housekeeper and Miss Dupont, Dodo's lady's maid who would be re-employed within the Vansittart household.

He would also retain Dodo's favourite dog *Boo Boo*; the other two were adopted by Stumblehole staff.

Frank Gear, who had been Dodo's butler for sixteen years, now forty-nine would have to find another appointment. Early in 1958, with the help of Nick's influence he was found a position as valet to Bertram Francis Currie, a partner of Glyn, Mills, Currie & Co., a banker now in his fifties who had a London apartment at Orchard Court, in Portman Square, and a country house, Dingley Hall, set in 180 acres of parkland near Market Harborough.

The Currie's family life had been abruptly pruned when news arrived that their only son John, just nineteen, had been killed a few days before the end of the war, fighting with the *Scots Guards* in Germany, the regiment his father had served in the Great War.

The same year Gear accompanied him on a visit to New York sailing on the *Queen Mary* but unfortunately Currie was to die in March 1959. Gear was on the move again.

This time he found employment with the sixth Marquess and Marchioness of Bristol, who had a London house in Chapel Street whilst retaining the family seat at Ickworth House in Suffolk. Although it had been given to the National Trust in 1954 in lieu of death duties, they retained an apartment within the house.

Bristol was a member of the House of Lords, Chancellor of the International Monarchist League, and an active businessman who later became a tax exile in Monaco. He was a colourful and flamboyant personality, who in his youth ran guns during the Spanish Civil War – to both sides – was jailed for a Cartier jewel robbery and had been a ringleader of a gang of former public school boys known as the 'Mayfair Playboys'.

Gear decided at his age, he'd had enough of the 'colourful life' and retired around 1963 at the time of his Lordship's second marriage, and went to live in Trinity Road, Wandsworth later moving to Loxley Road where he died in December 1980, aged seventy-two.

Marjorie Daisy Jordan, Dodo's quiet personal secretary who had joined the staff after the death of Enid Fischer in September 1955, stayed on to help Nick with the business administration. A single lady in her early forties, living with her elderly parents in Oldham Terrace, Acton, she had inexplicably fallen for Dodo's last chauffeur, a lively cockney called George Edmonds. Much to everyone's surprise she went to live with him in Thetford, Norfolk. She died in September 1993.

Mrs Gwen Dann, the Stumblehole cook secured a new position through the ubiquitous Massey's Agency in Baker Street with Charles and Celine Armytage-Moore at Winterfold House, [67] a 200-acre estate in the Surrey hills, near Cranleigh. Charles, then an invalid was from an old Irish aristocratic family, his sister was the Countess of Annesley. He was a founding partner in stockbrokers Buckmaster & Moore. In contrast, they did little entertaining.

Gwen kept in touch with both Winifred Stroude and Helene Dupont with whom she had developed a friendship, and they would often meet on visits to London.

After a number of years with the Vansittart household, Stroude developed diabetes, and complications set in; she died in hospital in December 1977, aged seventy-nine.

Helene Cecile Dupont, Dodo's eighth and probably her most experienced lady's maid, about two years younger than her, would eventually retire to her family home in Ruffec in the Poitou-Charentes region of south-west France. Nick and Marguerite were able to converse easily in her native language.

Helene had previously been lady's maid to Mrs Edith Strachan, of Heacham Hall, Norfolk and Lowndes Square London, before she died. Strachan had been left a sizable fortune by her husband Charles, a chartered accountant, and had travelled the world with Dupont.

Her friend Gwen the cook from Stumblehole, now retired, enjoyed several visits to Helene's home in Ruffec, which had played a significant role in the Second World War –it had been the centre of the Marie-Claire Escape Line [68] based at *L'Hôtel de France*, later *L'Angle d'Or Hotel*, since closed. As a war widow she would always be welcomed by *'Monsieur le Maire'*, enjoying the last *'Repas des Aines'* in Ruffec Ville December 1988. They both died within months of each other in the autumn of 1994.

Walter Cooper returned to his previous employers, the retired Charrington family who had moved to Netherton near Andover. The family took one of Dodo's dogs, *Cheesi*, who lived to a ripe old age enjoying a happy life. Walter had been born on the Beaurepaire Park estate in Hampshire, once owned by Sir Strati Ralli, a friend of Bobbie Hartman's parents. He died in the spring of 1984 at the age of seventy-eight and his wife Mildred three years later.

Another Stumblehole servant, Mrs Summerfield, adopted *Nina* the remaining Pekinese. She too had a long life.

After the Curtain

-35-

Rapprochement

Out of the blue, a few days after the funeral an air mail letter arrived at the offices of Charles Culross & Co. in Duke Street, from Ethel Salmon in South Africa. Its revelation came as a shock. Their formal reply dated 14 November 1957 was cautious.

> "Dear Madam,
>
> We are very much obliged to you for your letter of the 11th instant, and confirm that we act for the Executor of the late Mrs Hartman, Mr G N Vansittart.
>
> We note that you are the daughter of Mrs Hartman by her first marriage. We regret however that there is no mention in Mrs Hartman's Will of yourself or your three daughters.
>
> We have informed the Executor…
>
> Yours faithfully,
> Charles Culross"

The second letter Ethel received at the end of November was more conciliatory:

> "Further to our correspondence with you we have now had an opportunity of talking to our late client's Executor and he assures us that in due course any photographs and other items of personal interest will be sent to you.
>
> Although the Executor and our Mr C H Culross and the writer had known Mrs Hartman for many years we were quite ignorant of the existence of any daughter or grand-children of Mrs Hartman.

We may say that the Executor is most sympathetic and later on will consider what, if anything, can be done to show his sympathy...

Yours faithfully

Charles Culross"

Nick was bewildered by the sudden appearance of Dodo's 'lost' daughter, ruminating that in all the years he had known her she had never hinted her existence; not to mention three grandchildren. Culross was at a loss too.

He wanted to know more about her, and so started a correspondence with Ethel which over the years brought her and her family into the wider Vansittart social relationship. This was acknowledged by his daughter Prudie in her recollections: *"I remember my father's astonishment when he discovered Ethel's existence after Dodo died – he was her executor – a secret that she can't have divulged to anyone."*

Dodo's will, prepared a few years earlier by Charles Culross, was simplicity itself, and read:

"I Dorothy Cynthia Mirabelle Hartman, sometimes known as Dorothy Mirabelle Cynthia Hartman of Berkeley House Hay Hill London W.1. hereby revoke all former Wills and Testamentary dispositions made by me and declare this to be my last Will which I make this Fifteenth day of December One thousand nine hundred and fifty three.

1. I give devise and bequeath to my friend Guy Nicholas Vansittart for his own use and benefit absolutely all my real and personal estate of whatever kind and wherever situate including property of which I have general power of appointment or disposition by Will and I appoint him sole Executor of this my Will.

2. I desire that my body may be cremated." [1]

It had been witnessed by Enid Fischer, her private secretary and Winifred Stroude, her London housekeeper.

The probate of Dodo's estate had been delayed into the summer the following year because of Betty Gwinner's challenge to the will in the High Court.

It was finally announced on 18 July 1958 in favour of 'Guy Nicholas Vansittart' and after estate duty of £45,547-14s-3d it left a net amount of

£108,831-18s-0d, something like £1.7 million today. However he indicates his frustration in a letter: *"… made a settlement with the odious step daughter which was duly registered with the court, and I am very relieved to be able to tell you that the inevitable publicity was quite small and entirely amiable."* [2]

The combined fortunes Dodo inherited in the 1940s from her husband and mother-in-law, something like £16.6 million today, had been drastically reduced to a fraction of this amount fourteen years later. Estate duties, the economic effect of the war and keeping Lendrum & Hartman afloat, had all no doubt taken their toll, not to mention the expensive lifestyle and travel.

In May, under Nick's chairmanship, Vauxhall Motors achieved an impressive milestone in their history with the millionth Bedford truck driven off the assembly line by the Parliamentary Secretary, at the Ministry of Supply with a fanfare of publicity. Nick finally retired as director and chairman of the boards of General Motors Limited and Vauxhall Motors in September, at the age of sixty-five. He was succeeded by the managing director, Philip Copelin.

The same year he had negotiated the sale of Lendrum & Hartman to the Lex Group. The remaining directors resigned and retired; it was the end of the Hartman era.

A year earlier Lex had bought the US franchise for Chevrolet and Oldsmobile by the acquisition of British and Colonial Motors in St Martins Lane, and the Lendrum & Hartman concessions of Buick and Cadillac fitted into their strategic plans.

The 1960s saw new opportunities for American cars and under new ownership, Lendrum & Hartman went about achieving a high profile selling cars to the newly-emerging celebrity market – film and television personalities and pop stars preferred to be seen in an American car over any other type – it was the sign of success. Cars like Rovers or Armstrong Siddeleys were just not hip in sixties Britain.

In 1961, they supplied a Cadillac Fleetwood Sedan to singer Cliff Richards, whilst comic actor Sid James, Tommy Trinder and fellow comic Bob Monkhouse all had Buicks, as did the singer Dusty Springfield.

By the end of the 1960s, the showroom in Albemarle Street had been closed and Lendrum & Hartman moved to Flood Street in Chelsea, just off the Kings Road. In the 1970s the name changed to Lex (L&H) Ltd., and then to Lex Transportation Ltd.

A Lendrum & Hartman-imported Cadillac appears in the 1971 film *Get Carter*, a British crime thriller starring Michael Caine (as Jack Carter), Ian Hendry (as Eric the chauffeur) and Britt Ekland (as Anna).

The 1980s were not so kind and unfavourable legislation introduced earlier finally led to the company being dissolved and put into receivership in September 1990. The Lex Group was acquired by Aviva, a British multinational insurance company in 2005.

★

Dodo's solicitor and business friend Charles Culross died in August 1960 at the age of seventy-eight at St Mary's Hospital, Paddington. His wife Bessie had died nine years earlier and he had lived alone. There were no children and when probate was announced in October, he left £26,303 to old business friends John Jassman Dykes, a solicitor and William Emms, a chartered accountant.

Nick's love for Dodo had extended to her 'lost' daughter and grandchildren; he drew them instinctively into his circle. As Veronica, Ethel's eldest daughter recalls:

> *"I do believe Nicky had a great fondness for all of us and it was reciprocated, he was a very special person. I do not believe that my Grandmother ever shared with Nicky any hint of my mother's existence and that is why she wanted nothing to do with any of us. If Nicky had known before Dorothy had died, I like to think that he would have communicated with us!"* [3]

In the early 1960s, Veronica Salmon, Ethel's oldest daughter left South Africa to spend a year working in England, as she remembers:

> *"I first met Nicky when I travelled to England in 1963. He met me at Southampton as he had offered me accommodation at his flat in South Street with Miss Stroude his housekeeper, until my friend and I had found our own digs in Kensington. I stayed with him for about three weeks. He was such a gentleman, so kind to me and spoilt me rotten! He even took my friend and I to the Savoy Grill for dinner on my twenty first birthday – such a treat for us. I came home for my sister's wedding in August 1964."* [4]

Ethel's adopted father, Titus Goaman, had by this time reluctantly left England for Australia with his niece (she didn't want him to be alone in Devon) and they settled in Croydon, a suburb of Melbourne. He managed to travel to South Africa to attend the wedding of his granddaughter Veronica in 1963; it was the last time the Salmon family saw him. He died six years later at the age of eighty-seven.

In the 1970s Nicky had moved to flat number 7, in a substantial Mayfair Georgian house at 20 Charles Street, with his housekeeper Winifred Stroude. It was the same house in which Archibald Philip Primrose, fifth Earl of Rosebery, a Liberal statesman and Prime Minister was born in 1847. By coincidence a few doors away at number 22, once the home of the Duke of Clarence in 1826, who later became King William IV, was the London home of Dodo's brother and sister-in-law (when she was Lady Dalrymple), the Earl and Countess of Cassillis.

After Miss Stroude had died and Helene Dupont retired to France, Nick essentially looked after himself, supplemented with occasional visits to his club for dinner or lunch keeping in touch with old friends – who were it seemed getting fewer. He would occasionally walk from his flat to Oxford Street to travel by bus to Richmond, where his daughter Prudie was living at the time. During the last few years of his life his social companion was yet another 'Mayfair lady' who would fuss and look after him. [5]

Nick's first wife 'Madi', now Margaret Dearmer, died in London during September 1980 at the age eighty-two. Her husband the poet Geoffrey outlived all contempories, dying at the age of 103 in a Birchington-on-Sea nursing home in Kent.

The following year, Prudie also lost her husband Peter in April at the age of sixty-three. They had travelled the world; after the war, he had a distinguished career in the Foreign Service, was made a Companion of the Order of St Michael and St George (CMG), and a Member of the Most Excellent Order of the British Empire (MBE). He had served in New York, then as First Secretary in Moscow and Head of Chancery in Madrid. Later he was appointed Counsellor in Kinshasa, culminating as Ambassador to Ecuador, and High Commissioner for the Bahamas during the 1970s. In a confidential US State Department telegram (now declassified) from Ecuador to their Bahamas station, their confidential briefing explained: *"Both very gregarious, maintaining an unusually large*

range of professional and social contacts, aside from being an avid tennis player;
Mrs Mennell was very prominent and active in various charitable activities." [6]

Nicky kept up correspondence with Ethel and in one letter described to her how Stroude his housekeeper disapproved of dogs in general – but made an exception for *Boo-Boo*, who she adored. As Nicky explained, *"Once in a while you get a super dog and he was one, and your mother loved him best of all the dogs she ever had, and she was a great dog-lover."* [7]

Nicky had visited the Salmons in South Africa and reciprocal visits to London had been arranged.

On their first visit, Prudie explains that her father seemed reluctant to share his new-found South African family, and out of curiosity she became very insistent on joining him to meet them at some point during the visit. She asked Nicky if she could join them for lunch at his flat – 'no' was his evasive reply – come for tea instead.

Knowing her father 'rather well' she resorted to subterfuge, as almost certainly they would have left by then and there may be no other opportunity, so she ignored the 'put-off'. She turned up at the end of lunch as coffee was being served, and did get the opportunity to meet the Salmons. Reflecting years later, Prudie said it was so like her father – putting his life into compartments, and being instinctively evasive. [8]

These visits culminated in the celebration of Nicky's ninetieth birthday, at a dinner party in September 1983.

This milestone birthday was held at his sister-in-law Lady Sarita Vansittart's London house at Hyde Park Gardens. She was ninety-four.

Dodo's three grandchildren – Veronica, Erika and Norma – flew from South Africa to join in the celebration. Other guests included Prudie Mennell and her eldest daughter Lindsay.

The dinner table was set for twelve. *"Gerard, my brother in law came to London at the last minute and because he was the 13th, was not included in the dinner, but did come for a pre-dinner drink."* [9] Gerard and Norma kept a London flat in Chelsea, close to the Kings Road shops and walking distance to *Peter Jones*, the department store in Sloane Square, soon to earn its royal warrant (in 1987).

In a letter written the same month as his birthday Nicky writes to Ethel:

"19th September 1983

I can honestly say that never have I seen three more enchanting girls, so natural and unspoilt and here enjoying everything with unforced gaiety that was a joy to see. Their shopping expeditions were fabulous! The Twins both have a great resemblance to their grandmother and all three have inherited her brains. You and Eric can be justly proud of them, and so would she be if I could tell her about them. We had a good birthday dinner and my sister in law (Sarita, Lady Vansittart) was enchanted with all of them." [10]

The following year in South Africa, Ethel's husband Eric died at the age of seventy-two, and a year later Sarita Lady Vansittart died at the age of ninety-six. She had moved to a smaller property, Dickfield House in Denham village, once owned by her mother.

Much of Lady Vansittart's Denham Place estate was dispersed; many of the family possessions were sold or bequeathed. A canvass oil painting for example of Martha Stonehouse, Mrs Arthur Vansittart by Jonathan Richardson the Elder (1665–1745), considered to be amongst the foremost English painters of his time, became the property of the National Trust at Lyme Park House, Cheshire. Many of the Vansittart manuscripts were taken by the Cambridge University Library. A rare family snapshot of around 1935, taken of Lady Vansittart, Sarita Enriqueta by Lady Ottoline Morrell, outside the front doorway of Denham Place is now in the collection of the National Portrait Gallery.

★

It comes to everyone that inevitable sound of distant *"thunder at a picnic"*, as it rolled in four years later. At the age of ninety-five, Nicky Vansittart died in February 1989. He had outlived all his contempories. He was cremated and his ashes scattered in the little garden behind 20 Charles Street. [11]

He had long since disposed of all the Hartman assets. Few personal items remained; the Gunn portrait of Dodo that hung in his flat in Charles Street, together with some memorabilia was sent to Ethel, as Prudie reflected: *"She* (Dodo) *was very attractive and elegant – I sent her (Gunn's) portrait to Ethel after my father died…"* – together with a particular photograph and poignantly, a lock of Dodo's hair, both kept in Nicky's wallet until his death.

In one undated letter to Mrs Farr, Nicky describes the Salmon family thus:

"The family in South Africa are all well and very happy. The girls all married very nice husbands who have done exceedingly well. …They are as nice a family as you can imagine, and I have had much pleasure from them, and my only real regret is that I didn't know about them long before I did!" [12]

Ethel's three daughters have collectively produced eight grandchildren. In turn some of those children have married too, giving her over a dozen great-grandchildren, a truly large family of her own. They all flourish and live happily in South Africa.

★

One of the results of researching this book was the discovery of an ivory-covered Church of England *Book of Common Prayer* that Dodo Dalrymple carried at her wedding at Caxton Hall to Bobbie Hartman in 1933, and the following blessing at Christ Church, Broadway. Inside a simple inscription had been written in pencil stating, *"Dodo Dalrymple 1933 married Bobbie Hartman"*. After her death Helene Dupont, Dodo's lady's maid passed it to Audrey Cooper, one of the children on the Stumblehole estate. It has since been returned to Ethel.

Ethel achieved her 100th birthday in March 2016, and received the traditional birthday card from HM Queen Elizabeth II. At the party, surrounded by her family, the great grandchildren sang "Happy Birthday" to their 'Gigi'.

-36-

Envoi

'Chance favours the prepared mind.'
Louis Pasteur

This story was probably destined never to be written –certainly not by me – had it not been for a chance discovery during unrelated research.

Dorothy Hartman and her close friend Nicky Vansittart, had, it seemed, been socially linked to the murky world of pre-war political espionage. This was interesting enough to pursue. However, with other projects at the time I put my notes aside. Then a year or two afterwards I discovered that the glamorous society hostess and successful businesswoman I had known briefly as an adolescent, had a hidden past.

Her 'missing' earlier life and first marriage had been shrouded in mystery, a deceit she deliberately cultivated spanning those momentous years from the turn of the century until after the First World War. Uncovering the details revealed a rags-to-riches story, one I felt worth telling, and had she been alive would most certainly not have authorised.

She was born a 'Tuesday's child' – one which is full of grace, they say, another way of saying 'very lucky'. She had all the disadvantages of birth: a disfunctional childhood; little formal education; her mother an illiterate music hall artiste died whilst she was a teenage chorus girl, and with little guidance from a restless father who had a partiality for the tavern. So she had to make use of her ingénue good looks to make a living.

Dodo was no 'femme fatale' unlike her close friend Frankie Day, but had set out to use her theatrical charm to captivate older men and she really revelled in being spoilt. Sharing any of this attention with a child would have been an anathema to her. She manipulated an inconvenient pregnancy with the hapless Captain Lewis into a stepping stone quest for social status.

She had much in common with the fictional Becky Sharp in Trollope's *Vanity Fair*, neglecting her child – she was almost entirely non-maternal – but succeeded in charming and manipulating older men through a series of marriages.

The actress pitted her wits against convention, climbing the social ladder. She was a product of her time – a 'new woman' born in the Victorian *fin de siècle*, an era of social change. She was adaptable; wanting more out of life, reinventing herself – adopting new names and mannerisms, discarding people who were no longer useful. Adept at social networking in a man's world, *"she knew how to make men feel comfortable"* as Rosa Lewis, the *Cavendish* hostess would have said, moving through every level of high society – the ideal hostess, in fact.

She had dismissed her only daughter out of hand, yet in contrast was generous to other peoples' children; she was a dog and horse lover, charity fundraiser, even a benefactor of a children's home. She was opportunistic and pitiless, courted attention, but with a self-deprecating sense of humour as we've seen. *"Rather a nice painting, that one of Gunn's. It is a portrait of a fish wife!"* [13]

Petite, a little over five foot two, she was a cold coiffured blonde with blue eyes – the 'ice woman' as Prudie Mennell would think of her, always appearing immaculately dressed, but with little maternal instinct. Reticence to talk about her earlier life developed over the years, inevitably leaving some questions unanswered, so for the moment Maud Coleno's daughter remains an enigma but had been endlessly seductive to the end, casting her charm way beyond her last performance. So much so that Nicky Vansittart was to keep a lock of her hair in his wallet for the rest of his life.

Notes

Before the Curtain

[1] W. H. Auden, *Marginalia* (1965–68)

[2] Audrey Cook correspondence

[3] Salmon papers

ACT I: A Child of the Fin de Siècle (1898–1915)

[1] *The Fields Beneath*: *The History of One London Village*, Gillian Tindall, 2005, chapter seven, page 130

[2] *The Cardiff Rugby Football Club, History and Statistics, 1876–1906*, compiled by C. S. Arthur, Club Secretary, 1906

[3] Griffin family published research (*Ancestry.com*)

[4] (*www.oldbaileyonline.org*) The proceedings of the Old Bailey, London's Central Criminal Court (1674–1913); case of Henry Ebsworth, Alexander Donaldson, George Edward Griffin, Deception & Fraud, 2 July 1888 (Ref. No. t18880702-703)

[5] Woor family papers include a manuscript of Charlotte Abbott's unpublished (?) work

[6] Griffin family published research (*Ancestry.com*)

[7] In an unrelated case, Judge (Edward Abbott) Parry had awarded suffragette Emily Davidson damages in 1910 because of her inhuman forced feeding whilst on hunger-strike in prison. She was killed in June 1913 after throwing herself under the King's horse at the Epsom Derby. Parry was also a writer of children's books – some of which were performed on the stage

[8] *History of the First World War*, Liddell Hart, 1976, chapter four, scene four, pages 130–131

[9] Originally built as HMS *Waterloo*, a 120-gun first-rate ship of the line launched in 1833. She was reduced to two decks and converted to steam in 1859 and later renamed *Conqueror*, serving on the China station. Paid off in 1866, and in 1877 renamed *Warspite* as a training ship

[10] Pat Woor correspondence

ACT II: Captain Lewis Takes Leave (1915–1923)

[1] *History of the First World War*, Liddell Hart, 1976, chapter five, scene three, page 183

[2] *Black Heart: Gore Browne and the Politics of Multiracial Zambia (Perspectives on Southern Africa)*, Robert I. Rotberg, 1992, chapter two, page 53, based on correspondence between Ethel Locke-King and Gore-Browne. Ethel was a paternal aunt of Lieutenant-Colonel Sir Stewart Gore-Browne. Her wealthy husband Hugh built Brooklands – the world's first purpose-built motor racing circuit. Ethel also turned her house near Cairo into a luxury hotel – the *Mena House* still flourishes today

[3] *Diana Cooper*, Philip Ziegler, 1981, chapter three, pages 55–6

[4] *British Theatre in the Great War*, Gordon Williams, 2003, chapter five, pages 49–51

[5] Daisy Goodwin's book review in *The Sunday Times Culture magazine*, Jan 2015, *In the family Way: Illegitimacy Between the Great War and the Swinging Sixties,* Jane Robinson, 2015

[6] Salmon papers

[7] Pat Woor correspondence

[8] *The Yorkshire Post,* Friday Sept 19, 1919, page 5

Act III: Lord Dalrymple entertains (1919–1932)

[1] Lt-Cmdr. Dalrymple naval records, National Archives ADM 196/45/31

[2] Henry Allingham (1896–2009), a First World War veteran, emerged from obscurity to become a 'press celebrity' being the last survivor of

the Battle of Jutland, and the oldest surviving British man ever. Obit, Max Arthur, article *Independent*, Sunday 19 July 2009 (see bibliography: Allingham, Henry, *Kitchener's Last Volunteer*)

[3] Sir Charles Dalrymple (1839–1916) Will, Vol.589, p.15, (161) 18 Dec 1916

[4] Ibid (170) 18 Dec 1916

[5] William Burke and William Hare, both Irish immigrants, committed a series of sixteen murders in Edinburgh, over a period of about ten months in 1828. Until that time, there were insufficient bodies (cadavers) legitimately available for the study and teaching of anatomy in medical schools. Edinburgh Medical School relied increasingly on body-snatchers for a steady supply of 'anatomical subjects'. With financial inducements, the illegal trade continued to grow. It was a short step from grave-robbing to murder. Burke and Hare then sold their murdered corpses for sums £8–£10. However, suspicions led to their detection and eventual trial. Burke was hanged in January 1829, but Hare escaped the gallows by 'turning King's evidence'

[6] Lt-Cmdr. Dalrymple naval records, National Archives ADM 196/45/31

[7] Reproduced courtesy of Don Gillan © *www.Stagebeauty.net*, article from *The Throne*, c.February 1913

[8] *Augustus John*, Michael Holroyd, 2011, part two, chapter four, page 444

[9] Gabrielle Borthwick's biographer, Sally Davis ©, 3 February 2012, *www.wrightanddavis.co.uk/gd/BorthwickGMA.htm*

[10] Actually another Dorothy. It was Mary Duff Stirling, Lady Twysden (1893–1938), a British socialite and model for Hemingway's character 'Brett Ashley' in his novel *Fiesta: The Sun Also Rises*. Curiously, her given name was Dorothy, but after her parents divorced she changed it to Mary Duff and kept her mother's maiden name of Stirling as her own

[11] *Still Memories,* John Mills, 2000, 'The 1930s', page 38

[12] That residential building is now *St James' Court Hotel*, a Taj property

[13] 'Cottie' (Mary Ann Dolling O'Malley, née Sanders), would become a popular novelist from the 1930s onwards under the pseudonym Ann Bridge (1889–1974)

[14] *Gibraltar: Hands off the Rock* (reference to Philby and Burgess), *Daily Telegraph*, travel article, Jim Keeble, 19 Oct 2002

[15] Margaretha MacLeod, née Zelle (1876–1917), better known by her stage name 'Mata Hari', was a Dutch exotic dancer and courtesan who

was convicted of spying and executed by firing squad in France under charges of espionage for Germany during the First World War

[16] In January 1910 Dr Crippen made a request with chemist Lewis & Burrows at 108 New Oxford Street, for five grams of hyoscine hydrobromide which came in the form of small soluble crystals. The chemist had to order it from their wholesaler BDH, who in turn got it from Merck & Co., Darmstadt in Germany. 'Alex' Hill made a statement at Crippen's trial. (Erik Larson, *Thunderstruck,* 2006, page 211)

[17] Angels (the world's longest-established costumier) supplies the film, theatre and television industries, as well as the general public (including the royal family). Founded in 1840 by Morris Angel and later with his son Daniel, he ran the business from a shop in Shaftesbury Avenue

[18] *Shake the Bottle*, W. Buchanan-Taylor, 1942, chapter 15, page 93

[19] A memorial service was held for Winifred four days later at St Peter's in Eaton Square, London. Many who had been at the lunch attended, including Viscountess Elibank; Lt.-Col. Shelmerdine, Director of Civil Aviation; Lady Acton and Kathleen, Countess of Drogheda representing the Women's Committee, Air League

[20] (Amy Johnson) *Daily Mail*, Thursday 5 January, 1933, page 8

[21] Dalrymple Testate papers: Sir DCH's Will, record of Deeds, and Inventory, 20 Feb 1933

Act IV: Captain Hartman's Business (1933–1942)

[1] Lendrum & Hartman advertising stunts of the 1920s included a couple dancing on the roof of a Buick saloon while it was being driven in London's West End. An original film clip of this event was used to introduce the P. G. Wodehouse BBC TV series, *The World of Wooster* (1965–67). Another Buick was driven up a long flight of stairs in the grounds of the Crystal Palace. Russell Johns' article about his life with Lendrum & Hartman in *Motor Sport Magazine*, October 1980 (pages 1560–62, 1580)

[2] Ivory-bound *Book of Common Prayer* (Church of England) Eyre & Spottiswoode edition, with sterling silver cross on cover hallmarked (1929) by William Spurrier Ltd., London

[3] *Rosa Lewis: An Exceptional Edwardian*, Anthony Masters, 1977, chapter six, pages 159–60

[4] Augustus Hartmann, *Waterloo Archive Vol II: German Sources*, Ed., Gareth Glover, 2010; also a portrait painted by Paul Dumortier, 1815, oil on panel, National Army Museum

[5] Suter Hartmann advertising panels are on display at the Beamish Museum, in County Durham. The original painting by Bernard Finegan Gribble (1873–1962) of a Dreadnought Class Battleship in a floating dry dock, Portsmouth, oil on canvas sold for £16,250 at Bonhams, New Bond Street, 2011

[6] Arthur James Balfour, Conservative politician, first Earl of Balfour KG OM PC DL (1848–1930), Lord Esher, (1852–1930) Liberal politician

[7] *Geographies of Nineteenth Century Science*, David N. Livingstone and Charles W. J. Withers, 2011

[8] *Public Schools and the Great War*, Anthony Seldon & David Walsh, 2013

[9] *The History of a History Man or, the Twentieth Century Viewed from a Safe Distance*, Patrick Collinson, 2011, chapter twelve, (Regius Professor of Modern History Cambridge 1988–1996 and Fellow of *Trinity College*)

[10] Ibid

[11] During the 1928 'Calcutta Cup' England v Scotland International Rugby Football match at Twickenham in front of King George V, the monarch is said to have asked former president of the Scottish Football Union, James Aikman Smith, why Scotland were not wearing numbers on their jerseys that day. The arch Conservative Aikman Smith replied tersely, *"This sir is a rugby match not a cattle sale."* RugbyFootballHistory.com

[12] *Augustus John*, Michael Holroyd, 2011, part two, chapter nine, pages 447–8

[13] *General Motors and the Nazis: The Struggle for Control of Opel, Europe's Biggest Carmaker*, Henry Ashby Turner, 2005

[14] SS *Almeda Star* was sunk in 1941 off Rockall by *U-96* with devastating savagery and a loss of all 360 hands. Despite sending a radio distress call and launching four lifeboats, a search by seven destroyers revealed nothing – not even wreckage

[15] *From Candlelight to Flashlight*, Filippo Ferraro, 1952

[16] Russell Johns' article on Lendrum & Hartman in *Motor Sport* magazine, October 1980 (pages 1560–62, 1580)

[17] The Buick Limited Series 90 Eight Limousine – owned by King Edward VIII – sold for £100,500 at Bonham's in their London auction in December 2007

[18] Russell Johns' article on Lendrum & Hartman in *Motor Sport* magazine, October 1980 (pages 1560–62, 1580)

[19] *Elizabeth: The Queen Mother*, Hugo Vickers, 2006, chapter four, pages 52–3

[20] Doddington Hall, Cheshire still belongs to the Delves Broughton family, but during the Second World War it was requisitioned for Home Guard training. In 1944 it became the HQ for the American 15th Army; post-war it housed the evacuated *Goudhurst Ladies College* until the 1980s

[21] Anecdotal reminiscing from the past chef of *Snaffles* restaurant in Leeson Street, Dublin frequented by Molly O'Rourke during the1960s. See November 2005 archive: *"A Little Light Name Dropping" www. martindwyer.com*

[22] 'Jock' Broughton is today chiefly known for standing trial for the murder of Josslyn Hay, 22nd Earl of Erroll, part of the so-called Happy Valley set living in Kenya in 1941. His wife had been having an open affair with Erroll at the time. He was found shot in his Buick car –*"The question of the scent in the Buick was made much of, (in the trial) when it was probably no mystery at all. Joss reeked of the Truefitt & Hill scent CAR, as all his close friends knew,"* – excerpt from *The Life and Death of Lord Erroll*, Errol Trzebinski, 2000. The event was the basis of the 1987 film *White Mischief* with Joss Ackland playing 'Jock'

[23] *Ian Fleming*, Andrew Lycett, 1995, chapter two, page 51

[24] *Diana Cooper*, Philip Zeigler, 1981, chapter eight, pages 177–8

[25] It was not 'Bobbie' Hartman but in fact Guy Marcus Trundle (1899–1958), son of a Yorkshire clergyman, a charmer, married man and excellent dancer. He was a 'motor engineer' with the Ford Motor Co., who later had an affair with the sister of the Duchess of Sutherland. *Elizabeth: The Queen Mother*, Hugo Vickers, 2006, chapter 12, page 163

[26] *Speed Kings*, Andy Bull, 2015, page 298

[27] Sir Arthur Whinney (1865–1927), was a partner in accountancy firm Whinney, Smith & Whinney (1894), then later through a series of mergers became Ernst & Whinney (1979), then Arthur Young combined with Ernst & Whinney to create Ernst & Young (1989), and today (branded EY) one of the largest professional services firms in the world

[28] Gunn's portrait of his children was sold at Bonhams New Bond Street for £26,400 in June 2010

[29] The Sussex market town of Lewes is home to the 'Bonfire Boys'.

They reintroduced an old tradition in the 1820s that celebrates the foiling of the gunpowder plot of November 1605, an attempt to blow up Parliament by Catholic conspirators. It also remembers the demise of the seventeen Protestant martyrs, burnt at the stake in Lewes, fifty years earlier. Members of six main bonfire societies celebrate with fireworks in a procession through the high street carrying flaming torches and crosses. Today it is the largest and most celebrated bonfire tradition in England

[30] During the 1950s and 60s Queen Elizabeth (then the Queen Mother) would stay at Spye Park in Chippenham, the home of the Spicers to attend the three-day 'Cheltenham Festival' in March. *Elizabeth: The Queen Mother*, Hugo Vickers, 2006, chapter 29, page 371, chapter 35, page 459

[31] In May 1939 Archibald Ramsay, a Tory MP, formed an anti-Semitic secret society he called *The Right Club*. Many of its members were Nazi sympathisers and an inner core were politicians, peers of the realm, prominent socialites and officers in the armed forces. They would meet at the *Russian Tea Room* in South Kensington. Ramsay recorded their names in a red leather-bound ledger that was seized by Special Branch in May 1940 (their organisation had been infiltrated by MI5). Membership apart from the Duke of Westminster included William Joyce, remembered as 'Lord Haw-Haw' for his wartime propaganda broadcasts from Germany (he was later caught and hanged for treason); Anna Wolkoff (a close friend of Wallis Simpson) the daughter of Admiral Nikolai Wolkoff, who had been Aide-de-Camp to Nicholas II in London during the First World War; the 5th Duke of Wellington; the 12th Earl of Galloway (father of Antonia, wife of Dodo's stepson the 3rd Bt. Dalrymple) and Lord Redesdale (father of the Mitford sisters) amongst others. Some were imprisoned at Brixton gaol for the duration of the war

[32] *'C', The Secret Life of Sir Stewart Menzies*, Anthony Cave Brown, 1987, chapter three, pages 177–8

[33] 'Trading with the Enemy Act 1939' makes it a criminal offence to conduct trade with the enemy in wartime, with a penalty of up to seven years' imprisonment. The bill passed rapidly through Parliament in just two days, in September 1939 as war was declared on Germany. It is still in force today

[34] Robert Treeck, National Archives ref: KV2/2743

[35] Russell Johns' article on Lendrum & Hartman in *Motor Sport* magazine October 1980 (pages 1560–62, 1580)

[36] Ibid (pages 1560–62, 1580)

[37] *Hitler's Spy: The True story of Arthur Owens, Double Agent Snow*, James Hayward, Simon and Schuster, 2014, chapter eleven, pages 205–6

[38] *Future Indefinite*, Noël Coward, 1954, pages 159, 194

[39] *The Baedeker Blitz: Hitler's Attack on Britain's Historic Cities*, Naill Rothnie, 1992, pages 49–73

[40] *The Palgrave Dictionary of Anglo Jewish History*, (Ed.) William D Rubenstein, 2011, page 972

[41] *The People's War: Britain 1939–45*, Angus Calder, 1969, chapter five, page 305

Act V: Nicky Vansittart – 'at last' (1938–57)

[1] Menzies did indeed have a mistress – his second secretary Miss Evelyn Jones. (*'C', The Secret Life of Sir Stewart Menzies*, Anthony Cave Brown, 1987, chapter ten, page 716.) It was said he had others such as Winnie, the Australian wife of the 6th Earl of Portarlington, a renowned London hostess with a house in Belgrave Square and close royal connections. (*The A-Z of British Intelligence*, Nigel West, 2005, page 353)

[2] *'C' The Secret Life of Sir Stewart Menzies*, Anthony Cave Brown, 1987, chapter five, page 314

[3] Ibid (chapter two, page 141)

[4] The Vansittart Brothers, *www.gmhistory.chevytalk.org* David Hayward, General Motors historian

[5] *Sussex Express & County Herald*, Friday Dec 1, 1939, page 5

[6] The notorious 'Hellfire Club' was established by Sir Francis Dashwood, a rake and politician (Chancellor of the Exchequer 1762–1763). Members met during the 1750s at his estate in West Wycombe and nearby Medmenham. It was a club for 'persons of quality' who wished to take part in acts socially perceived to be immoral. Many members were involved in politics. It had close associations with Brooks's Club in London

[7] Dr Sir Gilbert Blane (1749–1834), a Scottish physician brought out a small book in 1780, *On the most effectual means for preserving the Health of Seamen, particularly in the Royal Navy*. By 1793 the Lords of the Admiralty had accepted his recommendations of the use of lemon juice as a

preventative against scurvy and by 1795 regulations were issued for its universal use in the navy

[8] During the German occupation of Norway in World War Two, King Haakon VII and his son Olaf (previously evacuated by the cruiser HMS *Devonshire* together with the country's gold reserves), resided at Foliejon Park from March 1942 to June 1945. During this period, the property became the seat of the Norwegian government in exile

[9] *The Mist Procession*, Robert Vansittart, 1957, chapter nine, page 146

[10] 'General' Heppenheimer's (1860–1933) title came from service in the old *Seventh Regiment* of the New York National Guard and then in the New Jersey National Guard as Inspector General and as Aide-de-Camp of the Governor of New Jersey. He rose to the rank of Brigadier General when he retired in 1895

[11] *The Mist Procession*, Robert Vansittart, 1957, chapter thirteen, page 251

[12] Children's Overseas Reception Board (CORB) was set up quickly by the government in 1940 to evacuate British children at a critical time in England, with the imminent risk of a German invasion and enemy bombing. The scheme was never popular with Churchill or the royal family, but managed to evacuate over 2,600 children by sea, mainly to Canada. It wasn't until the sinking of the SS *City of Benares* by a U-boat in mid-Atlantic in September, with a loss of 77 of the 90 children on board that the evacuation programme was brought to a halt

[13] Special Search List G.B *(Sonderfahndungsliste G.B.)* – known as *The Black Book* was compiled by SS-Oberführer Walter Schellenberg. It contained the names of 2,820 people ranging from Winston Churchill to Jewish refugees living in Britain. They were to be immediately arrested upon the success of *Operation Sea Lion* in 1940, the invasion, occupation, and annexation of Great Britain to the Third Reich. Robert Vansittart's name appears on the list

[14] *Queen Elizabeth: The Queen Mother,* official biography, William Shawcross, 2009

[15] *The Mist Procession,* Robert Vansittart, 1957, chapter thirteen, page 251

[16] Ibid (page 205)

[17] The Vansittart Brothers, *www.gmhistory.chevytalk.org* David Hayward, General Motors historian

[18] The BBC (2002) film, *The Gathering Storm*, featuring Albert Finney as Churchill, depicts the characters and events at this time

[19] Robert Vansittart, *The Mist Procession*, 1957, chapter twenty-two, page 453

[20] Prudie Mennell, correspondence

[21] *'C' The Secret Life of Sir Stewart Menzies*, Anthony Cave Brown, 1987, chapter two, pages 140–41

[22] (Christine Granville) *The Women Who Lived for Danger*, Marcus Binney, 2002, chapter three, page 53

[23] (Christine Granville) *The Spy Who Loved*, Clare Mulley, 2012, chapter thirteen, pages 245–6

[24] The Vansittart Brothers, *www.gmhistory.chevytalk.org* David Hayward, General Motors historian

[25] Prudie Mennell, correspondence

[26] Salmon papers

[27] Audrey Cook correspondence

[28] *Basil Street Blues,* Michael Holroyd, 2002, part two, chapter eleven, page 143

[29] In February 1945 RMS *Franconia* was used as a headquarters ship for Winston Churchill and the British delegation at the Yalta Conference

[30] Prudie Mennell, correspondence

[31] Ibid

[32] Ibid

[33] Jonathan Mennell correspondence

[34] *Telegram from Guernica: The Extraordinary Life of George Steer, War Correspondent,* Nicholas Rankin, 2003

[35] Churchill Archives, CHAR 1/249/27 Letter from W. H. Bernau, Lloyds Bank, to WSC, on his illness, asking WSC to contact R. M. Rowley Morris at the bank if he had any problems, 28 Jan 1933

[36] Alphonse Salomone (1919–1993) the hotel's Canadian General Manager was immortalised in the first and last 'Eloise' books. These were a series of children's books written in the 1950s by Kay Thompson (1909–1998), a long-time resident of the *Plaza*

[37] Prudie Mennell correspondence

[38] Pat Woor correspondence

[39] Amy Landreth became the *Sun*'s women's editor in the 1960s

[40] 'Jack' Profumo would resign in disgrace from politics because of a scandal in 1963, involving his affair with model Christine Keeler. The political repercussions brought the Conservative government down a year later

[41] *The Kick: A Life Among Writers*, Richard Murphy, 2002, pages 114 & 120

[42] *A Kentish Lad*, autobiography of Frank Muir, 1997, chapter 4, page 83 and 85

[43] *Sussex Express* Friday Nov 24, 1933, 'County Notes', page 10

[44] Prudie Mennell correspondence

[45] Veronica Lavoipierre correspondence

[46] Salmon papers

[47] Ibid

[48] Veronica Lavoipierre correspondence

[49] Ibid

[50] Ibid

[51] Audrey Cook correspondence

[52] Ibid

[53] Prudie Mennell correspondence

[54] Audrey Cook correspondence

[55] Ibid

[56] Audrey Cook correspondence

[57] Author's experience

[58] Prudie Mennell correspondence

[59] Audrey Cook correspondence

[60] *The Entertainer, (play)* John Osborne, 1957, pages 86–89

[61] Entry in author's 1957 *Lett's* schoolboy diary

[62] Audrey Cook correspondence

[63] Salmon papers

[64] Ibid

[65] *The Siren who Disappeared: Uncovering the mystery of Britain's first sex symbol,* Michael Thornton, *Mail Online*, March 2008

[66] Rosemary Fitch conversations

[67] Winterfold House in the Surrey Hills was requisitioned during the Second World War for use as a SOE training school. Designated STS 4, later STS 7 as the location of the Student Assessment Board, the many female recruits that passed through included Muriel Byck, Denise Bloch, Noor Inyat Khan (Nora Baker) and Violette Szabo

[68] Marie Claire was the cover name of an Allied escape line in the Second World War run by an exceptional English woman, Mary Lindell (1895–1986) also known as Comtesse de Milleville. After the war, she became the Royal Air Forces Escaping Society's representative in France

After the Curtain

[1] Salmon papers

[2] Ibid

[3] Veronica Lavoipierre correspondences

[4] Ibid

[5] Prudie Mennell conversations

[6] *A Directory of British Diplomats: The Diplomatic Service List*, Colin Mackie, © 2013, update January 2016, and US State Dept. a declassified 1975 telegram Ecuador-Bahamas, Public Library of US Diplomacy, 2006

[7] Veronica Lavoipierre correspondence

[8] Prudie Mennell conversations

[9] Veronica Lavoipierre correspondence

[10] Salmon papers

[11] Prudie Mennell conversations

[12] Salmon papers

[13] Dodo's Obit. November 22 1957, *Daily Express*, Keith Morfett article

Bibliography

ALDRICH, R. J. & CORMAC, R., *The Black Door: Spies, Secret Intelligence, and British Prime Ministers*, William Collins, 2016

ALLINGHAM, Henry, *Kitchener's Last Volunteer: The Life of Henry Allingham, the Oldest Surviving Veteran of the Great War*, Mainstream Publishing, Edinburgh 2009

ARTHUR, C. S., (Club Secretary) *The Cardiff Rugby Football Club, History and Statistics, 1876–1906,* compiled and published by Cardiff RFC, first edition 1906

BINNEY, Marcus, *The Women Who Lived for Danger*, Hodder & Stoughton, 2002

BUCHANAN-TAYLOR, W., *Shake the Bottle*, Heath Cranton Ltd., London 1942

BULL, Andy, *Speed Kings*, Bantam Press, 2015

CALDER, Angus, *The People's War: Britain 1939–45*, Jonathan Cape 1969

CARDER, Timothy, (Ed.) *The Encyclopaedia of Brighton,* Lewes, 1990

CAVE BROWN, Anthony, *'C': The Secret Life of Sir Stewart Menzies, Spymaster to Winston Churchill,* Macmillan 1987

CHANEY, Lisa, *Chanel: An Intimate Life*, Penguin, 2011

COLLINSON, Patrick, *The History of a History Man or, the Twentieth Century Viewed from a Safe Distance*, Boydell Press, Suffolk, 2011

COWARD, Noël, *Future Indefinite,* William Heinemann, London, 1954

EDINGTON, Sarah, *The Captain's Table*, The National Maritime Museum Publishing, 2005

FERRARO, Filippo, *From Candlelight to Flashlight*, The Falcon Press Ltd., London, 1952

GLOVER, Gareth, (Ed.) *Waterloo Archive Vol II: German Sources*, Pen & Sword, 2010

GOODMAN, Bryan, *American Cars in Europe, 1900–1940: A Pictorial Survey,* McFarland & Co. Inc., 2005

GRAHAM, John Parkhurst, (Ed.) *Uppingham School Roll, 1824–1905* (third issue), Edward Stanford, (O.U.) London, 1906

HAYWARD, James, *Hitler's Spy: The True story of Arthur Owens, Double agent Snow*, Simon and Schuster, 2014

HELM, Sarah, *A Life in Secrets: The Story of Vera Atkins and the Lost Agents of SOE,* Abacas, London, 2006

HEMINGWAY, Ernest, *Fiesta: The Sun Also Rises,* Arrow Books, 2004

HOLROYD, Michael, *Augustus John,* Pimlico, London, 2011

KEATING, Jenny, *A Child for Keeps: the History of Adoption in England, 1918–45,* Palgrave Macmillan, 2009

LARSEN, Erik, *Thunderstruck*, Bantam, 2006

LESUEUR, Patrick, *Concours D' Elegance: Dream Cars and Lovely Ladies*, Dalton Watson Fine Books, Illinois, USA 2011

LIDDELL HART, B. H., *History of the First World War*, Pan Books, London, 1976

LIVINGSTONE, David N. & WITHERS, Charles W. J., *Geographies of Nineteenth Century Science*, University of Chicago Press, 2011

LYCETT, Andrew, *Ian Fleming*, Weidenfeld & Nicolson, London, 1995

MacDONELL, A. G., *England, Their England*, Picador, 1983

MacELHONE, Harry, *Harry's ABC of Mixing Cocktails*, 1919, (still in print today)

MASTERS, Anthony, *Rosa Lewis: An Exceptional Edwardian*, Weidenfeld and Nicolson, London, 1977

MILLS, John, *Still Memories: An Autobiography in Photography,* Hutchinson London, 2000

MOORE, James Ross, *Andre Charlot: The Genius of Intimate Musical Revue*, McFarland & Co. Inc. USA, 2005

MUIR, Frank, *A Kentish Lad*, Autobiography, Bantam Press, London 1997

MULLEY, Clare, *The Spy Who Loved*, MacMillan, London 2012

MURPHY, Richard, *The Kick: A Life Among Writers*, Granta, 2002

NORMAN, F. M. Commander, (Ed.) *Memoirs of the Life of the Right Hon. David, seventh Earl of Glasgow, G.C.M.G., R.N., 1833–1915;* W. Brown, Edinburgh, 1918

PLATT, Len (Ed.) *Popular Musical Theatre in London & Berlin 1890–1939*, Cambridge Univ. Press, 2014

POCOCK, Tom, *1945: The Dawn Came Up Like Thunder*, Tom Pocock, Collins, London, 1983

RANKIN, Nicholas, *Churchill's Wizards: The British Genius for Deception, 1914–1945*, Faber & Faber, 2008

RANKIN, Nicholas, *Telegram from Guernica: The Extraordinary Life of George Steer, War Correspondent*, Faber & Faber Ltd., London, 2003

RICHARDSON, Angelique, (Ed.) *Women Who Did: Stories by Men and Women, 1890–1914*, Penguin Classics, 2005

ROBINSON, Jane, *In The Family Way: Illegitimacy Between the Great War and the Swinging Sixties*, Viking, 2015

ROTBERG, Robert I., *Black Heart: Gore Browne and the Politics of Multiracial Zambia (Perspectives on Southern Africa)* University of California Press, 1992

ROTHNIE, Niall, *The Baedeker Blitz: Hitler's Attack on Britain's Historic Cities*, Ian Allen Publishing, 1992

RUBENSTEIN, William D., (Ed.) *The Palgrave Dictionary of Anglo Jewish History*, Palgrave Macmillan, 2011

SELDON, Anthony & WALSH, David, *Public Schools and the Great War*, Pen & Sword Books, 2013

SHAWCROSS, William, *Queen Elizabeth: The Queen Mother, Official Biography,* Pan Macmillan, 2009

SLOAN, Alfred P. Jr., *My Years with General Motors*, Doubleday & Co., New York, 1964

TINDALL, Gillian, *The Fields Beneath: The History of One London Village,* Phoenix Press, paperback edition, London, 2005

TRZEBINSKI, Errol, *The Life and Death of Lord Erroll*, Fourth Estate, London, 2000

TURNER, Henry Ashby, *General Motors and the Nazis: The Struggle for Control of Opel, Europe's Biggest Carmaker,* Yale University Press, 2005

VANSITTART, Lord, *The Mist Procession: The Autobiography of Lord Vansittart*, Hutchinson & Co., London, 1957

VANSITTART, Rt. Hon. Sir Robert, *Black Record: Germans Past and Present,* Hamish Hamilton, London, 1941

VICKERS, Hugo, *Elizabeth, The Queen Mother*, Arrow Books, London, 2006

WALLER, John D., *The Unseen War in Europe: Espionage and Conspiracy in the Second World War,* I. B. Tauris & Co., London, 1996

WEST, Nigel, *The A-Z of British Intelligence,* Scarecrow Press, USA, 2005

WILLIAMS, Gordon, *British Theatre in the Great War*, Continuum, London, 2003

WOJTCZAK, Helena, *Notable Sussex Women,* Hastings Press, 2008

ZIEGLER, Philip, *Diana Cooper*, Hamish Hamilton, London, 1981

Index

This index is not comprehensive, not every person, place or event has been included, just the ones perhaps relevant to the story narrative. Inevitably in a lifetime there are numerous incidental people, events, places that drift past but they essentially remain 'walk-on parts'.

I have not included Dorothy Maud Abbott, who reluctantly became Mrs Dorothy Lewis then willingly Lady Cynthia Mirabelle Dalrymple and finally Mrs Dorothy Cynthia Mirabelle Hartman –sometime Dorothea or in the second half of her life Dodo, since the whole book is about her.

Blake, Lady Margaret (*formerly Dalrymple*) 106, 112

Blake, Sir Patrick (*5th Bt. Langham*) 112

Blane, Alice 243

Boo-boo 313

Boris, King of Romania 246

Borthwick, the Hon. Gabrielle 85, 120, 132, 152

Borthwick, Wark & Co. 85, 120

Bowes-Lyon, Elizabeth (*later wife George VI*) 202

Boyle, Captain David (*later 7th Earl of Glasgow*) 103-104

Boyle, David (*Dalrymple cousin*) 221, 254-255

Brace, Rose (*Chandos Court*) 133, 157

Brand, Lady Rosabelle 210

Brassey, Lady Margaret, (*née Trefusis*) 313

Brassey, Lt. Col. Lord Edgar 216

Bremilham church 241

Bridges Court, Luckington 221, 235, 237-238, 277

Bristol Hotel, Gibraltar 131

British Colonial Hotel, Nassua 264, 267

British Drug Houses (BDH) 139

British Empire Exhibition 185

British Overseas Airways Corporation (BOAC) 205, 227, 282, 306

Broadway, *London SIS HQ* 237, 239

Broadway, *New York General Motors* 183, 186, 204, 224, 227, 241, 263, 269, 278

Broadway, *New York Theatreland* 41, 61, 116, 124-126, 264, 282-283, 289

Broughton, Sir 'Jock' *11th Bt.* 202, 210, 221, 350

Brown, Gabrielle 153, 190-191

Brown's Dairy 8, 10

Buick House (*L&H showrooms Albemarle St.*) 151, 156, 181, 183, 187, 190, 200, 226, 228, 240, 337

Bute, *4th Marquis*, John Crichton-Stuart 102, 131, 154, 186, 283

C

Café de Paris, London 113, 295, 330

Caffé Roma, Alassio 145

Campbell, Sir Malcolm 143, 172

Campbell family (*Brynllwydwyn House*) 59-60, 301

Capell, Lady Iris 132, 135, 137-138, 144, 152

Cassillis, Countess (*later Marchioness of Ailsa*) 85, 99, 103, 112, 117, 119, 126, 339

Castlerosse, Viscountess Doris 161

Cavendish Hotel, London 56-57, 59-60, 62-64, 67, 72, 262, 344

Caxton Hall Registry Office 160, 239, 342

Cecil hotel, London 118

Chandos Court 127, 130, 132, 136-137, 139, 145, 147, 157, 239, 261

Chanel, 'Coco' (Gabrielle) 123, 222, 258, 262

Channon, 'Chips' (Henry) 161, 203

Chaplin, Charlie 8, 12, 160, 288, 291-295, 309, 311

Chapman, George (*Northease*) 199, 247, 249

Chapman, William 199

Charrington family 310, 324, 332

Charterhouse School 166-167, 171, 327

Châteaux Frontenac hotel, Quebec 194

Cheesi 313, 332

Chester, Renee (*cousin*) 69

Cholsey Grange 238, 273, 295

Christ Church, Broadway (*London*) 160, 342

Christie, Malcolm, Group Capt. 252-253

Churchill, Rt. Hon. Winston 88, 132, 203, 218, 223, 227, 231, 239, 247, 253, 258, 260, 273, 280, 287, 290

Ciro's Club, London 97, 214

Cohen, Cyril 195

Coleno, Maud *stage name* (see Abbott) 1, 3, 10, 11, 19, 20, 33, 36, 37, 38, 49, 159, 307, 322, 344

Concours D' Elegance 136, 205

Cook, Thos. & Sons Ltd 247, 294, 320

Cooper, Diana (*née Manners*) 58, 115, 205, 207, 236

Cooper, Sir Duff 58, 115, 158, 205, 207, 236, 262

Cooper family (*Stumblehole*) 310-311, 313, 319, 324, 332, 342

Cowage Farm 230, 241

Cowans, Maj-Gen. Sir John 58, 65

Coward, Noël 96-97, 111, 115, 131, 227, 253, 269, 289

Cows' Cathedral (See Brown's Dairy)

Cox & Kings, *bankers* 109, 230, 280

Crackers 72-74, 76, 93, 108

Cracknell, Joan 181, 186, 192

Crawford, Lady Gertrude 120

Crippen, Doctor 45, 140, 348

Cukor, George 116, 125

Culross, Charles 160, 179, 184, 201, 230-231, 273, 277-280, 296, 328-329, 335-336, 338

Culross & Co 190, 279-280, 325-326, 335

ROYAL HIPPODROME

W. Buchanan Taylor Submits
A Roaring Farce

SNOOKUMS,

Being the Adventures of
NEWLYWEDS AND THEIR

Music by Nat. D. Ayer.

Cast includes RHODA GORDON
Y ABBOTT, ALBERT DARN
LI' WHEELER, RAY HOLGA
Gorgeous Dresses and Scenes
N & LESLIE, CLIFF BERZAC
WHIDDEN AND B
field, City Office, Woolworth's

ROYAL HIPPODROME.

Royal Hippodrome, this week,
the ubiquitous revue. Mr
Taylor, in a production which
writ large across every page
troduces the Newlyweds and
The farce, entitled "Snookums,"
upon the ideas embodied in the
of Mr. George M'Manus. Last
audiences found much enjoyment in
the adventures of Mr. and Mrs.
Newlywed. There is some pleasing
Nat D. Ayer, and the dresses and
are big factors in the spectacular
A capable cast includes Miss Rhoda
Miss Dorothy Abbott, Mr. Albert
jun., Dolf Wheeler, and Ray
In the general numbers of the pro-
are Cliff Berzac and his Jackass
prove a source of great amuse-
Billy Kuming, who
mental

ALHAMBRA THEATRE

ARCADE, STIRLING.
PHONE 401 STIRLING.

6.50 —— TWICE NIGHTLY —— 8.5
EARLY DOORS, 6.30   EARLY DOORS, 8

MONDAY, DECEMBER 30th, 1918.

New Year's Day   Thursday, 2nd January   Friday, 3rd January
SPECIAL HOLIDAY MATINEES
Saturday, 4th January   At 2.30.
Full Programme guaranteed at Each Performance.   Doors open at 2.
Colossal Attraction.   Direct from London Success.
MESSRS UGAR AND LANGLEY present the GRAND MUSICAL REVUE

CRACKERS

A Rattling of Delight in Two Pulls and a Bang
Strong London Cast includes:

Mr HARRY UGAR   Mr CHAS. H. PHYDORA.
Miss LILY DUVAL   Miss LILIAN ROSEBERY.
Miss WINIFRED MACK   Miss BLANCHE MERRYWEATHER.
Miss FLORRIE PRENTON   Miss DOROTHY LEWIS.

Miss ELLA LANGLEY

POPULAR PRICES (including Tax):— Pit, 9d.   Upper Circle, 1/   Side Circle, 1/6
Stalls, 1/6 (Booked), 2/0   Front Circle, 1/6   Side Circle, 1/6
Orchestra Stalls, 2/ (Booked) 2/4   Upper Circle Centre Seats, 2/ (Booked), 2/4.
Seats can be booked at the Theatre or by Phone 401 Stirling
Children Half-Price in all Parts.

6.45—TWICE

Mr. HARRY DAY Presents
(By Arrangement with the MOSS EMPIRES, LTD.
THE SENSATIONAL REVUE SUCCESS,
Already seen by 1,000,000 People.
NOW PLAYING AT THE LONDON HIPPODROME

"PUSH & GO!"

GRAND COMPANY OF 50

PALACE
BURNLEY   TEL. 3726.
— TWICE NIGHTLY. — 8-45
onday, Week Commencing January 2nd.
MR. ARCHIE PITT PRESENTS

DERS IS ORDERS"

NEW REVUE WITH A STORY.
CAST INCLUDES
ne and Freddie Hackin, Fai Robina
Dare, Dorothy Lewis, The Pitt Girls
and the Pitt Boys Chorus.

1/10; CIRCLE, 2/- (Booked, 1/2); PIT, 6d. (Saturdays & Holidays, 9d)
GALLERY, 4d. (Saturdays and Holidays, 5d.)

TO THE ENORMOUS SUCCESS
HE SENSATIONAL REVUE,
SH & GO

HIPPODROME.
6.40   TWICE NIGHTLY.   9.0
Telephone 2368.
THIS WEEK:
W. BUCHANAN TAYLOR submits a
Roaring Farce
"SNOOKUMS."
Cast includes RHODA GORDON,
DOROTHY ABBOTT, ALBERT BARNSLEY,
Jun., DOLF WHEELER, PAUL RELPH,
C. WENTSS, LILY GRIFFIN, H. DANBY,
and RAY HOLGATE.

GRAND THEATRE.

musical revue "Crackers," is a good attr
t the Grand Theatre this week, and it deser
well supported. It is spoken of as a bon
of delight in two pulls and a bang—a succinct
scription. It is full of laughter, capital so
some good dancing, and speciality turns.